HOLOCAUST PUBLIC MEMORY IN POSTCOMMUNIST ROMANIA

STUDIES IN ANTISEMITISM
Alvin H. Rosenfeld, editor

HOLOCAUST
Public Memory in Postcommunist
ROMANIA

Edited by
Alexandru Florian

Indiana University Press

This book is a publication of

Indiana University Press
Office of Scholarly Publishing
Herman B Wells Library 350
1320 East 10th Street
Bloomington, Indiana 47405 USA

iupress.indiana.edu

© 2018 by Indiana University Press

All rights reserved

No part of this book may be reproduced or utilized in any form or by any means, electronic or mechanical, including photocopying and recording, or by any information storage and retrieval system, without permission in writing from the publisher. The Association of American University Presses' Resolution on Permissions constitutes the only exception to this prohibition.

The paper used in this publication meets the minimum requirements of the American National Standard for Information Sciences—Permanence of Paper for Printed Library Materials, ANSI Z39.48-1992.

Manufactured in the United States of America

Library of Congress Cataloging-in-Publication Data

Names: Florian, Alexandru, editor.
Title: Holocaust public memory in postcommunist Romania / edited by Alexandru Florian.
Description: Bloomington, Indiana : Indiana University Press, [2018] | Series: Studies in antisemitism | Includes bibliographical references and index.
Identifiers: LCCN 2017041142 (print) | LCCN 2017040235 (ebook) | ISBN 9780253032744 (e-book) | ISBN 9780253032706 (hardback : alk. paper) | ISBN 9780253032713 (pbk. : alk. paper)
Subjects: LCSH: Holocaust, Jewish (1939–1945)—Romania—Historiography. | Romania—Ethnic relations.
Classification: LCC DS135.R7 (print) | LCC DS135.R7 H645 2018 (ebook) | DDC 940.53/180720498—dc23
LC record available at https://lccn.loc.gov/2017041142

1 2 3 4 5 23 22 21 20 19 18

Contents

List of Abbreviations	vii
Memory under Construction: *Introductory Remarks* / ALEXANDRU FLORIAN	xi

Part I. Competing Memories and Historical Obfuscation — 1

1. Ethnocentric Mindscapes and Mnemonic Myopia / ANA BĂRBULESCU — 3

2. Postcommunist Romania's Leading Public Intellectuals and the Holocaust / GEORGE VOICU — 41

3. Law, Justice, and Holocaust Memory in Romania / ALEXANDRU CLIMESCU — 72

4. Romania: *Neither "Fleishig" nor "Milchig": A Comparative Study* / MICHAEL SHAFIR — 96

5. "Wanting-Not-to-Know" about the Holocaust in Romania: *A Wind of Change?* / SIMON GEISSBÜHLER — 151

Part II. National Heroes, Outstanding Intellectuals, or Holocaust Perpetrators? — 173

6. Mircea Vulcănescu, a Controversial Case: *Outstanding Intellectual or War Criminal?* / ALEXANDRU FLORIAN — 175

7. Ion Antonescu's Image in Postcommunist Historiography / MARIUS CAZAN — 208

8 Rethinking Perpetrators, Bystanders, Helpers/Rescuers,
   and Victims: *A Case Study of Students' Perceptions* / ADINA BABEŞ   242

   Index   283

List of Abbreviations

AFDPR	Asociația Foștilor Deținuți Politici din România (Association of Former Political Prisoners in Romania)
ALDE	Alianța Liberalilor și Democraților (Alliance of Liberals and Democrats)
ANR	Alianța Noastră România (Our Alliance Romania)
BIRN	Balkan Investigative Reporting Network
BPN	Biroul Politic Național (National Political Office)
CA	Consiliul de Administrație (Administrative Council)
FCER	Federația Comunităților Evreiești din România (Federation of Jewish Communities in Romania)
FIDESZ	Fiatal Demokraták Szövetsége Magyar Polgári Szövetség (Federation of Young Democrats–Hungarian Civic Alliance)
GpR	Grupul pentru România (Group for Romania)
HČSP	Hrvatska Čista Stranka Prava (Croatian Pure Party of Rights)
HDZ	Hrvatska demokratska zajednica (Croatian Democratic Union)
HOP	Hrvatski oslobodilački pokret (Croatian Liberation Movement)
HRT	Hrvatska radiotelevizija (Croatian Radio–Television)

IHRA	International Holocaust Remembrance Alliance
IICCMER	Institutul de Investigare a Crimelor Comunismului şi Memoria Exilului Românesc (Institute for the Investigation of Communist Regime Crimes and the Memory of the Romanian Exile)
INSHR-EW	Institutul Naţional pentru Studierea Holocaustului din România "Elie Wiesel" (Elie Wiesel National Institute for the Study of the Holocaust in Romania)
JTA	Jewish Telegraphic Agency
KGB	Komitet Gosudarstvennoy Bezopasnosti (Committee for State Security)
LPR	Liga Polskich Rodzin (League of Polish Families)
ĽSNS	Ľudová strana–Naše Slovensko (People's Party–Our Slovakia)
MCA	Asociaţia pentru Monitorizarea şi Combaterea Antisemitismului din România (Center for Monitoring and Combating Antisemitism in Romania)
MpR	Mişcarea pentru România (Movement for Romania)
NATO	North Atlantic Treaty Organization
NCHA	National Central Historical Archives
NCSSA	National Council for the Study of the Securitate Archives
ND	Noua Dreaptă (The New Right)
NDH	Nezavisna Država Hrvatska (Independent State of Croatia)
PiS	Prawo i Sprawiedliwosc (Law and Justice)
PNL	Partidul Naţional Liberal (National Liberal Party)
PNŢCD	Partidul Naţional Ţărănesc Creştin Democrat (Christian Democratic National Peasants' Party)
PRM	Partidul România Mare (Greater Romania Party)

PRON	Patriotyczny Ruch Odrodzenia Narodowego (Patriotic Movement for National Rebirth)
PSM	Partidul Socialist al Muncii (Socialist Labor Party)
PUNR	Partidul Unității Națiunii Române (Party of Romanian Unity)
SC	State Council
Smer–SD	Smer–Sociálna Demokracia (Direction–Social Democracy)
SNS	Slovenská národná strana (Slovak National Party)
SNSPA	Școala Națională de Studii Politice și Administrative (National School of Political Studies and Public Administration)
SRI	Serviciul Român de Informații (Romanian Intelligence Service)
SS	Schutzstaffel
TpȚ	Partidul Totul pentru Țară (Everything for the Country Party)
TVR	Televiziunea Română (Romanian Television)
UEFA	Union of European Football Associations

Memory under Construction
Introductory Remarks

This volume concludes a research project on Holocaust memory in post-communist Romania, supported by the Romanian Ministry of National Education, CNCS–UEFISCDI, under grant number PN-II-ID-PCE-2012-2-4-0620.

The project was prompted by what seemed to be a very simple question: how do we explain that seventy years after the end of the Second World War, in Romania the public memory of the Holocaust is still disputed, and approaches that minimize or even deny it have become more dominant in the public sphere?

To answer this question we should first examine the clear differences between the prevailing practices in public memory in countries with long-established memorial institutions and those in postcommunist countries.

East versus West

According to Jacques le Goff, the victim became a subject of public memory after the First World War.[1] The subject was more fully developed at the end of the Second World War, when two types of victims were distinguished: on the one hand is the soldier and on the other hand is the civilian, who appears for the first time as the victim of a conflict that reached the limits of dehumanization. The history of the development of these two memorial subjects—soldiers and civilians—is different in the West and the East.

In Western Europe, memorials, plaques, busts, and street names remind the public of crucial moments of the Second World War, of military men and politicians who heroically dedicated their lives to fighting fascism or Nazism. Public spaces also memorialize those who opposed Hitler's Germany or his allied regimes by taking up arms against them (the Resistance Movement), as well as civilians who were exterminated because of their ethnicity or race. Moreover, the memory of the Holocaust as such was institutionalized in the 1970s by public commemoration policies in Western states.

Jean-Michel Chaumont, a scholar who analyzed the gradual steps by which Holocaust victims were publicly recognized and commemorated, noted competing public memories of the French and Belgian Resistance movements and the exterminated Jews. In *The Competition of Victims* (1997) he points out that "until recently, there were no public monuments or textbooks to specifically evoke the fate of the Jews."[2] He reminds us that it was several decades before there were effective public reactions to concealment of the facts of the Holocaust. It was only in 1995 that the word *Jew* was engraved on the monument erected in memory of the victims of Auschwitz in the Père Lachaise cemetery in Paris, and "in 1968, at the inauguration of the monument in Birkenau, Professor Waitz resigned from the chairmanship of the International Auschwitz Committee as a protest against the fact that Jews were not nominated as a group on commemorative plaques. It was a futile gesture, because the text was corrected only in 1994."[3]

The situation was quite similar in Romania, where until two decades ago, the only victims commemorated on public monuments were antifascists who, following the ideology of class struggle, were sometimes described as "representatives of the working class." However, there is an important difference between Romania and France: in Romania, until the International Commission on the Holocaust in Romania issued its *Final Report* in 2004, the perpetrators of the Holocaust had always been cast as members of the "fascist dictatorship." This was a strategy to deny the Holocaust in Romania by pointing toward another perpetrator rather than the real, historical one: the Romanian government led by Ion Antonescu between 1940 and 1944.

In Western Europe today, public monuments or memorials of the Holocaust have become commonplace. They are institutionalized by the state and constitute a public space that is not disputed or countered by revisionist memories of groups that engage in reinterpretation of recent history. In Romania, Hungary, the Baltic states, and Poland, these processes are ongoing. To understand how these processes develop, one must consider that the public sphere is receptive to any memory that represents the organized expression of an associative group. Thus, different associative groups project their own memory into the public domain in order to legitimize and establish themselves as credible social or political actors. However, their memory is not always the same as historical memory, and it sometimes conflicts with state institutionalized memory, when, for example, those responsible for genocide or the Holocaust are promoted as respectable symbols of acceptable values. In this case, we are dealing with partisan memories that reinterpret political or cultural history through a filter that replaces the legal or ethical criteria of democratic society with an intellectual value promoted by a group—often, absolute religiosity or anticommunist militancy to the point of death.

The disparity between what is acceptable and unacceptable to display in the public sphere, between what is "good" and "bad" memory of the Holocaust as a public message,[4] is undoubtedly due to the gap that exists between the two regions of Europe with regard to the development of Holocaust memory. Whereas in Western Europe this memory takes the form of a place of remembrance for the victims, the situation is different in Eastern Europe. After the fall of communism, the opening of the public sphere during the formation of a civil society entailed the development of a memorial space with a very different agenda. As a result, it was only in the late twentieth century that the academic world began to grasp the distinction between collective memory and historical memory that Jacques le Goff talked about. Following in the footsteps of Pierre Nora,[5] le Goff noticed the diversification of memories and the loss of a unique and statal historical memory that would inspire collective memories. Thus,

collective memory, defined as "what remains of the past in the existence of groups or what groups do with the past" might, at first glance, seem to oppose *historical memory*, just as I once referred to *affective and intellectual memory* as being opposed. So far, "history and memory" were the same, and history seems to have developed "according to a model of remembrance, of anamnesis and memorization." Historians provided the formula of "great collective mythologies," "as they went from history to collective memory." But this evolution of the contemporary world, under the pressure of *immediate history*, which is mostly made on the spot by the media, tends to develop several collective memories, and history is written, more than ever, under pressure of these collective memories.[6]

Today, more than ever, the historiographic discourse is influenced by the memorialistic narrative, and "history on the spot" often replaces an objective approach to the research.

To make this approach more clear and to better illustrate the differences between West and East, it is instructive to examine the memorial experiences of Spain after Franco and Germany after reunification. Even if these countries did not have a special debate on the memory of the Holocaust, they both demonstrate a means of reconciling the memory of social groups and historical memory, as well as developing public memory, that has two channels: the state's role in representing official memory and the public use of memory in convergence with democratic values.

In both Spain and Germany, the state played an active role throughout the reconfiguration of the state public memory, and also in the promotion of collective memories that are reasonable for the public sphere. In Germany during the 1980s there were two projects, one in the West and the other in the East, to establish national history museums. These projects of memory aimed at producing narratives from the public debate between historians and politicians. Michael Werner examined the way in which the federal executive participated in the development of subjects and historical sequences for display in the museums. The reunification of Germany in 1990 radically changed the plans for the two museums, but the projects continued, albeit with changed goals. The messages of the two museums were compliant with the standards of public memorial communication: "The organization and activity of the two museums are part of a new policy on memory which is trying to develop a connection of the present to history. The political constraints that led to the establishment of the two projects continue to determine various effects, although the situation is different today. Meanwhile, officials associated with the two projects successively integrated the constraints and reacted more or less subtly, being concerned with having a relative autonomy."[7]

In terms of reconciliation with its history through historiography and memory, Spain is different from Germany and almost the opposite of Romania. After the death of Franco in 1975, during the nation's transition to democracy there was a process of a voluntary, assumed "forgetfulness" of the civic and political sensitivities created by the repressive dictatorship. As Pedro Ruiz Torres writes, the political elites were interested in providing a balanced, reformist, nonviolent path for the development of a democratic state;[8] history would be revisited only in the late 1990s. This policy was enacted by the ruling Spanish socialists. A relevant factor in this context was the debate about national unity and the specific identity of political actors during the Franco regime, which was started by historians and fueled by political leaders. Torres discusses the debate among traditionalist and progressive historians who sought to impose a new vision and mentality upon history, and he describes the role of the state and political actors in remaking the representative matrix of the nation-state as an agent of modernization.

During the period of transition, the Spanish state did not convey a memorial message in compliance with the new civic standards, but its role changed during the socialist government. After decades of being kept out of the public sphere, the victims of Franco's terror and the republicans who were killed during the civil war claimed a right to identity and expression, and the government decided that it was time to begin a process of reconciliation with recent history, with a view to upholding democratic values. Although the Law of Amnesty in 1977 had effectively eliminated any chance of punishing perpetrators or compensating victims of the Franco regime, in 2007 the Law of Historical Memory opened the way to commemorate victims of the dictatorial regime and to remove from the public sphere instruments of memory or culture intended to pay homage to Franco or his allies. In this context, the historians' debate was meant to enhance reactive memories that support the reconstruction of civic mentality:

> The political role played by history in Spain today is nevertheless not comparable to the one it had under Franco's dictatorship, and is in sharp contrast with the silence and oblivion maintained, during the period of transition to democracy, by political representatives (the party, the government) for political purposes (the successful transition from dictatorship to democracy after Franco's death, in 1975).... In the late 1990s, the individual and collective need to recover the past, in a different way, was increasingly clear, far from the sites of memory created by old ideologies, of the silence and oblivion which, during the period of transition, falsely helped close the wounds of Spain's recent history.[9]

In Romania, the memorial experiences of Germany and Spain have not prompted a similar approach to the public memory of the past. Indeed, the specific circumstances of Romania's break with the communist regime resulted in a completely different course for the institutionalization of memory of the recent past, including the Holocaust. In the first decade of transition, the Romanian state was extremely permissive and left the public space open to all manifestations of divergent memories. At the time, the main objective of the authorities was the development of state policy and governance aimed at managing the transition. Those in power did not understand the usefulness of historical memory, and consequently, it became the focus of civic and political actors who used excerpts of recent history in developing a collective memory to strengthen their public, social, or political statuses. Of course, each of these actors promoted the memory they argued represented historical truth.

In the late 1990s, however, the state's decision to join NATO and the European Union (EU) prompted it to oppose certain memorial sites, public speeches, symbols, and so on that were inconsistent with the values of the new democratic society. Many of the landmarks that directly glorified Romania's fascist past, for example Antonescu's statues, were banned only by diplomatic interventions from Western countries. As a precondition for joining NATO and the EU, Romania was required to establish special criminal laws to punish those who promoted Holocaust denial or the cult of persons convicted of war crimes. In 2002 the Romanian government issued an emergency ordinance that banned fascist, racist, and xenophobic organizations, as well as promotion of the cult of persons found guilty of crimes against peace and humanity. In 2015, following legislative amendments to the ordinance that explicitly criminalized public promotion of the cult of the Legionary Movement, Romanian far-right organizations, representatives of the media, and prominent Romanian intellectuals referred to it as the "anti–Iron Guard law." Although before its promulgation there was no significant opposition to its adoption, and it was unanimously approved in the parliament (with three abstentions), once it came into force, public intellectuals, pro-legionary associations, and the media joined forces to press for the law's withdrawal.[10] Some suggested it was unconstitutional, or that it restricted democratic freedoms.

Romania is not the only European nation that has such a law. France, Germany, Austria, the Czech Republic, and Belgium have similar regulations that prohibit references to the memory of the fascist past for propaganda purposes. Fundamentally, these are laws that aim to prevent a recurrence of tragic and dehumanizing experiences. Today, more than twenty-five years after the implosion of communism in Romania, there is no peace or balance in matters of reconciliation with its traumatic history.

Given that Romania's transitional state was weak and did not make memorial policies one of its priorities, in the 1990s virtually any collective memory could find its way into public venues. In this context, Tzvetan Todorov's essay about public memory clarifies some issues that with the use of Holocaust memory by various groups, rather than drawing distinctions between "good" and "bad" memories, he refers to "literal" and "exemplary" memories.

Todorov contends that the modern world "demoted memory in favor of other faculties"[11] such as those based on knowledge, according to a formula that holds that rationality equals modernity and tradition seems to be replaced by contract, that is defined as having no historical or anthropological reality. He concludes that recent decades have brought public memory into the spotlight: "Retrieving the past is indispensable; this does not mean that the past has to dominate the present. On the contrary, the present should use the past as desired. It would be infinitely cruel for someone to be always reminded about the most painful events of their past; people are entitled to forget too."[12] Despite these fluctuations, Todorov points out that memory as public expression is the source of legitimation, identification, and promotion for social and political actors. Even contracts, because they are made voluntarily, need an ethical, legal, or memorial element in order to be stable. In this case, memory acts as a common denominator of adherence to certain symbols and values. However, not every memory is worthy to be advertised. Drawing on the theory of the contract as a cohesive factor in contemporary society and the common good as an objective of democratic governance, Todorov proposes a criterion of memorial selectivity for public use. Tradition as a source of legitimacy becomes acceptable in a democracy only if it satisfies the criteria of the common good. The "use of memory and of the past is replaced by resorting to the option and agreement of the majority.... [Thus] all traces of legitimacy by tradition are not eliminated, far from it; but, and this is essential, tradition is allowed to be challenged in the name of the general will or common good."[13] It is within this algorithm of older or newer traditions and the common good that one can find the key for an answer to the rhetorical question of the philosopher: "in the sphere of public life, not all memories of the past are admirable; the one who harbors a wish for revenge or payback will be met with a certain reserve, in all cases.... Now, the question is: are there ways to distinguish a priori between the good and bad uses of the past?"[14] In other words, memories that promote the values of political extremism or incitement to discrimination represent bad public uses of memory. The state, as a representative of the common good, disavows them. This perspective on memory could also be applied to laws concerning hate speech and hate crimes.

Todorov proposes two other ways to identify collective memories that cannot be aired in public. One way is to assess the effects of the particular public memorial message; the obvious limitation of this is that its post-factum evaluation may come too late to prevent a move from symbolic to physical aggression. Germany under Hitler and Romania during the Ion Antonescu regime provide clear examples of escalation from hate speech to hate crimes, genocide, and the Holocaust. Todorov's second method, entailing prevention, seems more effective, socially speaking. He proposes a criterion based on the exercise of distinguishing the content of the memorial message; he calls this the functionalist method: "One way—that we practice every day—to distinguish the good uses from abuses [of memory] consists of asking ourselves what their results are and to assess, depending on what's good and bad, those that claim to be based on the memory of the past: those that, for example, prefer peace instead of war. But it is possible, and this is the hypothesis that I would like to analyze here, that criticism of the use of memory be based on the distinction between several *forms* of memory. The remembered event can be interpreted either *literally* or *exemplary*."[15] Literal memory is an actualization of the past for individual or group purposes; exemplary memory is an amplification of literal memory and is symbolically positive, generating a model worthy of being followed. It is about the extension of content from the personal or private sphere to the public one. As such, Todorov considers that "the literal use makes the old event insurmountable, and it ends up subjecting the present to the past. Instead, the exemplary use allows a view of the past for the benefit of the present, so that the lessons of injustice suffered in the past may combat those of today. It allows the departure from the ego so as to become the other."[16] Finally, he considers that literal memory is simply what we call memory, whereas exemplary memory is justice.

These two categories are used by Todorov to assess the memories of two competing traumatic experiences of the twentieth century: the Holocaust and the Gulag. He notes that, depending on whether one accepts the similarity of these two events, there are four groups that appeal to different memories. Thus, literal memory corresponds to two groups: 1) the Holocaust victims, who object to an assertion of similarity because they see it as a minimization factor, and 2) the Stalinist executioners, who oppose similarity because they see it as a factor assimilating them with the Nazis. Exemplary memory also corresponds to two groups : 1) the Nazi executioners, because they are in favor of a kind of similarity that could serve as an excuse for their actions; and 2) the victims of the Stalinists, who are in favor of similarity because it serves to put the Holocaust on a par with the Gulag.[17] Essentially, the difference between the memories depends on the acceptance or nonacceptance of the comparative approach with regard to the extermination camps of the Holocaust and the Stalinist concentration camp system. For Todorov, merely accepting the comparison is sufficient to make a delimitation of memories, as this process actually generates the possibility of generalization.

However, from the perspective of the public utility of the four memories, the conclusion drawn from this typology is not very productive. It is unlikely that the memory adopted by Hitler's executioners, for example, could be an exemplary public memory just because its promoters accept the comparison (and thus mitigation of responsibility for their actions!). The same interpretation applies to victims of Stalin's labor camps. Respectively, this mix of the memories of the victims and of the executioners generates memorial patterns that could not become public without causing serious distortions to the balance of democratic values. The exemplarity of a memory and its promotion as a symbol of the past for the present and future is achieved to the extent that its message is in line with the values of a democratic society: solidarity, equality, freedom, tolerance, dialogue, and so on. In other words, memory or memorialization of the perpetrators, whichever regime they belonged to, becomes a public good if it expresses the actions, events, or consequences they generated. Although all four categories of portraying the memory of the Second World War are active today, democratic societies are not indifferent to which of them is recognized as exemplary and promoted in the public sphere. Jacques le Goff is right in his observation that collective memory is both a tool and an objective of the state. Memory is a message for the present and future—this highlights its educational role; its public use resides in the fact that "it saves the past so as to serve the present and future. Let's make it so that collective memory serves the liberation, not the subjugation of people,"[18] concludes the French historian. The studies included in this volume are inspired by this affirmation.

Focus on Romania

In Romania, as elsewhere, the fall of the communist regime created favorable conditions for the development of an institutionalized civil society that found its expression in the emergence of a public sphere less controlled by the state, and the development of an education system freed from any ideology. How was the past approached in this new social and political order? How is the Holocaust remembered in the postcommunist Romanian society?

Most of the topics explored in this volume were formulated following national surveys, repeated five times between 2007 and 2015,[19] that examined the impact of the *Final Report* of the International Commission on the Holocaust in Romania (2004). These surveys aimed to reveal public perceptions of Marshal Antonescu, the leader of 1940s fascist Romania, the Holocaust in Romania (victims, perpetrators, bystanders), and the social distance separating the Romanian majority and the ethnic minorities. The distribution of answers on a scale with "good" and "bad" memories of the Holocaust at each extreme offers clues about the efficacy of educational policies and public memory constructed after 2004. The results are not encouraging. In the public sphere, the "good" memory of the Holocaust still competes with insistent attempts by some social actors to impose the memory of Romanian fascism as a model for a civic Romanian society. Similar developments are found in many other countries of the former Soviet bloc. Consequently, the approach we propose is comparative. As Romania is not unique with regard to the recuperation of history and the construction of the memory of the recent past, we were interested in identifying where we stand when compared to countries that share not only the same historical experience, as former members of the Soviet bloc, but also common mentalities.

Following the analysis of the survey results, some of which are discussed in chapters of the present volume, we constructed an analytical model that guided the individual research projects brought together within it. Following this analytical line of inquiry, we identify certain facets of the mentality of Romanian society as crucial for understanding the distorted perception of the Holocaust in Romania. Our theoretical approach regards the construction of a mobilizing identity narrative as fundamental for understanding the development of mnemonic practices with a restrictive effect upon Holocaust memory. Within this theoretical model, three factors were considered most relevant in minimizing the tragedy of the Jews: ethnocentrism, nationalism, and anticommunism. The weight of these factors and their interaction are described in chapter 1, as the author configures the matrix of the values that sustain public expressions of the bad memory of the Holocaust.

The following studies explain the ways in which this matrix that brings together ethnocentrism, nationalism, and anticommunism manifests itself in diverse spaces of public communication, overshadowing the memory of the Holocaust, including the mnemonic narrative proposed by the intellectual elite active in radical commentary on Ceaușescu's regime, where one easily finds an antisemitic tone; the nationalist historiography that promotes the myth of Ion Antonescu as a saving hero; and the civic activism that aims to rehabilitate the Legionary Movement (the interwar Romanian fascist movement) and war criminals, despite the legislative apparatus that prohibits the promotion of such persons or symbols in the public sphere.

The volume has two parts. The studies included in the first part, "Competing Memories and Historical Obfuscation," identify and evaluate diverse public expressions that range from minimization to plain denial of the Holocaust. The analysis is carried out by examining data from various public spheres: cultural, historiographic, political, juridical, and so on.

Chapter 1, "Ethnocentric Mindscapes and Mnemonic Myopia" by Ana Bărbulescu, follows two premises. On the one hand, in 2004 the Romanian state assumed responsibility for the Holocaust of the Romanian Jews, establishing an annual commemorative day remembering the victims, and a monument dedicated to them in downtown Bucharest. On the other hand, seventy years after the end of the Second World War, 69 percent of the Romanian population still hold Germany responsible for the Holocaust of the Romanian Jews. Yet, according to the available evidence, the responsibility for the Holocaust of the Romanian Jews lies with the Romanian authorities of the time. Acknowledging this inconsistency in Romanian society's public memory of the Holocaust, Bărbulescu attempts to identify and reconstruct the social processes that explain how mnemonic myopia operates: why does Romanian society have difficulty acknowledging the Holocaust of the Romanian Jews? In formulating an answer, the chapter follows two distinctive directions.

The analysis turns first to Eviatar Zerubavel's theory of the concept of "social mindscapes," social constructions through which communities classify the world. With this approach, the research demonstrates that within the Romanian symbolic universe, the Jews never had the chance to become Romanians; the Romanian identity is constructed in terms of ethnicity, and consequently the Jew remains the radical Other, unable (or, it has been claimed, unwilling) to integrate. This exclusion, according to the author, has consequences for the way the Second World War is remembered in Romanian historiography, where the Jews are not included in the historical narratives describing the Romanian losses during the war. The message is that they are not really us, so when we talk about the Romanian victims of the war, we will not include the Jewish victims on our list. The Holocaust of the Romanian Jews is not considered to be part of Romanian history, and consequently its memory is conveniently obliterated.

The analysis then addresses Festinger's classical theory of cognitive dissonance. Traditionally, Romanian historiography has portrayed the Romanian people in superlative terms, a position acknowledged and supported at the societal level. As social memory operates in a structural manner, the great achievements of Romanians from the past and the fate of the Romanian Jews during the Second World War become ideas relevant to each other. They are equally part of the clusters of mnemonic narratives that legitimate the identity model of the Romanian people. Therefore, because there is need for internal consistency between relevant ideas, the author demonstrates that the Holocaust is bound to become a dangerous memory that is either discarded as irrelevant and thus forgotten, or reconstructed in a manner that does not disturb the special image of the Romanian nation.

Chapter 2, "Postcommunist Romania's Leading Public Intellectuals and the Holocaust" by George Voicu, explores how the post-1989 leading Romanian public intellectuals (the Romanian intellectual elite) relate to the Holocaust in general, and to its Romanian chapter in particular, starting from the premise that their positions on these issues have a powerful impact on public opinion. The first finding demonstrates that in the intellectual debates of postcommunist Romania, the Holocaust has never been a stand-alone subject of reflection or research, even if it was—and still is—a most sensitive one. Although there are numerous references to the catastrophe experienced by Romanian and European Jews during the Second World War, they actually occur in a separate debate: the one about communism and the horrors of the political regimes of communist origin. It is when this debate touches upon the issue of communist crimes that the comparative references to Nazism, fascism, legionarism, and, predictably, the Holocaust usually emerge. In short, the notion of the Holocaust is clarified within the scope of this debate on a separate subject.

The chapter detects two attitudes that characterize the strategy adopted by Romanian intellectuals. The first, which is by far the more prevalent in public discourse, equates the crimes of communism with the Holocaust following a strictly equalizing logic whereby the conclusion is always the same: the Holocaust and the Gulag are ostensibly alike, as there is nothing that essentially differentiates them. According to this view, the two totalitarian ideologies that inspired the two series of crimes are almost identical in nature (even with regard to antisemitism and racism). This martyrological equalization does not satisfy all intellectuals; for some, the Gulag hangs heavier in the balance of horrors than the Holocaust. The judgment that communism represents an "absolute evil" is justified by invoking the presumably more pronounced evilness of this ideology (relative to fascism), or more commonly, by reference to statistical considerations that indicate that the crimes of fascism pale in comparison to communism's. These two attitudes usually go hand in hand with a strong sense of frustration that the memory of the two types of victims is allegedly one-sided, that the Gulag does not hold the place it deserves in history. In conclusion, Voicu highlights the distortions to the concept of the Holocaust as a consequence of these parallel-competitive approaches.

Chapter 3, Alexandru Climescu's "Law, Justice, and Holocaust Memory in Romania," examines the relationship between law and Holocaust memory, based on the postcommunist trials for war crimes and Holocaust denial and fascist propaganda. The analysis focuses first on the retrials in which Romanian war criminals initially convicted between 1945 and 1989 were acquitted after 1989. A second type of criminal prosecution examined by the author is that which fell under Emergency Ordinance 31/2002, which banned Holocaust denial, fascist propaganda, and the public cult of war criminals; most of these cases were dismissed, with decisions to not indict.

The research starts from the frequent criticism that criminal trials are inadequate means of representing traumatic history. According to the critics, history, literature, and psychoanalysis explore collective traumas in a more satisfactory manner, as these approaches are not constrained by the structural parameters of justice. Oversimplifications of history justified by the need to establish what is provable rather than probable; distinctions between legal and historical types of evidence; the focus on individual culpability for collective crimes; and judicial notice which allows the judges to accept well-known facts without the need for evidence—all of these inevitably contribute to inaccurate representations of the Holocaust during criminal trials.

The first objective of this research was to establish to what extent the outcomes of the criminal cases were determined by the structural parameters of the legal system. How were the acquittals of war criminals whose crimes are well documented by historical records possible? What are the historical representations of the Holocaust in Romania, its perpetrators, and its victims that the magistrates took for granted? Under what notion of responsibility for war crimes did the judges operate? Did postcommunist courts maintain a strict distinction between legal evidence and historical proofs? Next, Climescu explores why charges that clearly fall under Emergency Ordinance 31/2002 were dismissed by magistrates. Analyzing the decisions issued by judges and prosecutors, the author examines their understanding of Romanian fascism and the meaning of the term *Holocaust*, and attempts to determine whether the ethnocentric version of Holocaust memory dominant during the first years of the postcommunist transition represented a configuring factor of law.

A second objective of chapter 3 is to establish whether the acquittals of war criminals and the failures to enforce Emergency Ordinance 31/2002 were due to judicial factors alone. Climescu shows that in both cases, the separation between law and justice on one side and history and memory on the other constitutes a fiction. He demonstrates that these cases represented a framework of expression for the dominant version of Holocaust memory, and that the law's structural parameters are a secondary factor in explaining the magistrates' decisions.

Michael Shafir in chapter 4, "Romania: Neither 'Fleishig' nor 'Milchig': A Comparative Study," considers that the radical shift in Romania's attitudes to its "dark past" is clearly connected to its efforts to join NATO and the EU. These efforts led to, among other things, the establishment in October 2003 of the International Commission on the Holocaust in Romania chaired by Elie Wiesel. The Commission's *Final Report* (October 2004) included a number of recommendations, most of which were implemented, including observation of a national Holocaust Memorial Day (October 9, the day deportation of the Jews to Transnistria began); establishment of a governmental institute for the study of the Holocaust; and the erection of a Holocaust memorial in central Bucharest. Nonetheless, the 2002 law prohibiting denial of the Holocaust was not enforced, and many Romanian historians denied or trivialized Romania's participation in the Holocaust, or, as in many other East European countries, practiced Holocaust "obfuscation," arguing that the Gulag was as bad as or worse than the Holocaust. A second version of the law, adopted in 2015, is thus far meeting the same fate. At work here is a good deal of "simulated change," which is not necessarily connected with antisemitism, but rather part and parcel of a long tradition of discrepancies between "legality" and "reality," or "forms without essence." When compared with the situation in other East European countries where antisemitism is almost officially condoned (Hungary being the best example), postcommunist antisemitism in Romania we have a mixing of victims and perpetrators memories,—to the dissatisfaction of both sides.

The last chapter of part 1 is chapter 5, "'Wanting-Not-to-Know' about the Holocaust in Romania: A Wind of Change?" by Simon Geissbühler. The author considers the dichotomies of "knowing" and "not-knowing," "remembering" and "forgetting," and "remembered" and "forgotten," arguing that there are many shades of gray between these respective extremes. To uncover these shades of gray, he applies Paul Ricoeur's concept of "wanting-not-to-know" to post-1990 Romania (and, to a lesser degree, to northern Bukovina/Ukraine and the Republic of Moldova), where poll data indicates that there is some basic knowledge about the Holocaust in Romania, superimposed by an active strategy of avoidance and "wanting-not-to-know." For a majority of Romanians, the Holocaust is not seen as an event that has any relevance to them and to Romania, an attitude aided by the fact that the Holocaust perpetrated by Romania happened mostly in areas that are no longer part of the Romanian state.

Geissbühler approaches his study in two ways: (a) through an analysis of the presentations of their own histories by towns and villages in Romania, the Republic of Moldova, and Ukraine on the internet (websites); and (b) through a discussion of the representation or nonrepresentation of the Holocaust in their public spaces (e.g., monuments, inscriptions). Finally, factors that amplify or undermine the strategy of "wanting-not-to-know" are discussed—for example, international research and pressure; increased education about the Holocaust in schools and universities; educational efforts of civil society institutions; and Romania's presidency of the IHRA. The author concludes that in 2016, Romania lags behind other nations in dealing with the Holocaust, but there are also some positive developments, especially in comparison with other East European countries.

The volume's second part—"National Heroes, Outstanding Intellectuals, or Holocaust Perpetrators?"—approaches the discussion about memory from a more applied perspective. For example, the last chapter looks at the way the young generation perceives the perpetrators, bystanders, and victims of the Holocaust, examining the information or messages used to create human typologies. Two other chapters offer insights into the way images of historical figures are reconfigured in the public sphere, where there are various attempts to reinvent the past through glorification of the "bad" memory of the Holocaust. In these circumstances, forgetting the tragedy of the Holocaust is a side effect of the intensification of nationalist and chauvinist feelings. These trends are sustained mainly by nationalist mythology, as well as a refusal to revisit the ideological and cultural values of the Legionary Movement, the main interwar Romanian fascist organization.

In Western Europe, for many decades, the public memory of the Holocaust has recognized two main categories of victims: the Resistance, that is, persons who fought against fascism, and the Jews, who were the main targets of extermination. In Romania the memory of the victims, which had been forgotten for a long time, is being gradually rebuilt since 1990, when the transition to democracy, pluralism, and freedom of speech began.

Yet, there is controversy and rivalry between the memories of those responsible for the Holocaust and those of its victims, and although Romania adopted democratic values when it joined NATO and the EU, the symbolism of interwar right-wing extremism is still on the public agenda.

Chapter 6 by Alexandru Florian, "Mircea Vulcănescu, a Controversial Case: Outstanding Intellectual or War Criminal?," argues that in Romania, the reconstruction of the memory of Holocaust victims is divided between public memory and public-private memory. Moreover, the public memory of the victims is sometimes given lower priority than the cultural patrimony that was either discriminated against or forbidden during communism. Another obstacle to an adequate Holocaust memory is the absence of a democratic civic culture, which leads to a role reversal that promotes the perpetrators and obscures the memories of the victims. In spite of Romania's fifteen-year-old law forbidding Holocaust denial and the promotion of persons convicted for war crimes, statues of persons convicted for war crimes are still being erected. Their political pasts are forgotten as their "patriotism" or certain intellectual "exceptional traits" are publicly promoted. Often, these events are supported by public institutions. The case of Mircea Vulcănescu, philosopher of the intellectual group close to the Legionary Movement and member of the government of Romania between January 1941 and August 1944, generates controversial answers to an apparently simple question: whose statues, symbols, or messages must be included in the public memory of a democratic society?

Chapter 7 by Marius Cazan, "Ion Antonescu's Image in Postcommunist Historiography," discusses the results of several public surveys conducted after 1989 that dealt with issues such as antisemitism, perception of the Holocaust, and right-wing extremism. The results show that in Romanian society, intolerance of foreigners and misconceptions and clichés about them are widespread. In addition, each of the surveys has a question about Ion Antonescu, and the answers indicate that respondents were more likely to associate him with positive characteristics than with the criminal side of his leadership. For instance, in 2015, 52 percent of the respondents said Antonescu was a "great strategist," and only 23 percent agreed that he was a "war criminal." This chapter considers this incongruence that exists between the perception of the past and the historical truth that Antonescu was in fact convicted in 1946 as a war criminal.

How does distortion operate? And what are the tools used to legitimize it? Starting with these questions, the author analyzes the dynamics of the postcommunist historiographical discourse about Antonescu and the impact of popular Romanian historians' works on the general public. The author focuses on the discourse of the Romanian historians who are most visible in the public domain, appearing on television and writing both books and articles in popular historical magazines. The chapter's narrative is chronological, with a brief section about the historiographical revival of Marshal Antonescu during the last two decades of communism; a second section that focuses on the evolution of Antonescu's image in the 1990s and attempts at rehabilitation; and a final section that examines the impact on the historiographical field of Emergency Ordinance 31/2002 and the 2004 *Final Report* of the International Commission on the Holocaust in Romania.

The last chapter of the volume is "Rethinking Perpetrators, Bystanders, Helpers/Rescuers and Victims: A Case Study of Students' Perceptions," by Adina Babeș. The author defines public memory as the relationship with the past expressed in the public space via institutionalized instruments that connect it to the public space, such as memorials, speeches, books, courses, and so on. Babeș focuses on how Holocaust discourse is perceived by those exposed to those instruments, particularly the younger generation. Her objective is to frame a typology that describes how young people relate to the behavior of individuals who played significant roles in the Holocaust, and how they use Holocaust discourse to understand the variety of human behaviors and the attitudes of victims, rescuers, bystanders, and perpetrators in the Holocaust.

The research group consisted of students enrolled in social sciences and humanities programs who were exposed to Holocaust studies in different fields of study including history, sociology, political science, and culture studies. The research shows how prevailing discourses on the Holocaust affect students' attitudes and behaviors and their understanding of the Holocaust, as well as their understanding of how personal choices and changing circumstances can affect persons' decisions and actions, rendering them victims, rescuers, bystanders, or perpetrators.

The chapters of this volume reveal a symbolic reality specific to a small corner of Europe. In its recent past, Romania experienced two totalitarian regimes, one fascist (1940–1944) and a second, communist (1948–1989), with a short break in between. During both these periods, nationalistic ideologies and mentalities prevailed. When viewed from the perspective of the political and social reconfigurations that occurred, the reinvention of democracy after 1989 also involved a critical approach to our recent past. The diversity of the political and social actors who were participants in the public discourse certainly influenced the public memory of the Holocaust. From this perspective, everything started, and it still continues, under the impact of two different agendas: promotion of the memory of the victims, and rehabilitation of the perpetrators who were morally, politically, and legally responsible for the destruction of the Jewish and Roma population in Romania. This second agenda is supported by public expressions nurtured by the view that in Romania there were two totalitarian regimes, and the communist one was longer and had terrible consequences for the Romanians. The Holocaust is more or less acknowledged, but many position it in second place in the hierarchy of twentieth-century human tragedies. Meanwhile, Romanian fascists who were morally or juridically convicted after 1945, including political dignitaries and intellectual and military elites, are publicly acclaimed by some social actors.

Is there any way out of this mnemonic dilemma that is so visible in the public sphere? This volume provides more than one answer, but they all converge toward the same solution. The present mixture of memories implicitly leads to sterile debates about civic values and generates chaos within the civic cultures acknowledged by the new generation. Young people attend events where they meet and talk with Holocaust survivors, and the next day, they participate in public events where they are taught that we owe a debt of gratitude to the legionaries for their fight against communism. An active state memory that acknowledges the responsibility of the Ion Antonescu government for the Holocaust represents the main channel for recalibrating the public memory of this human tragedy.

Alexandru Florian

Notes

1. Le Goff, *Histoire et memoire*, 161.
2. Chaumont, *La concurrence des victimes*, 58.

3. Ibid., 63.

4. My phrase "good memory of the Holocaust" applies to public events that refer to the Holocaust without revisionism; by contrast, "bad memory" consists of symbolic expressions that directly or indirectly glorify the memory of those responsible for the Holocaust, as well as values or leaders of interwar right-wing extremism.

5. Nora, "Mémoire collective," 398–401.

6. Le Goff, 170. Italics in the original.

7. Werner, "Deux nouvelles mises en scènes de la nation allemande," 97.

8. Torres, "Les usages politiques de l'histoire en Espagne," 132.

9. Ibid., 132–133.

10. "Temele 'legii antilegionare' din perspectiva eticii memoriei" by Gabriel Andreescu, a human rights activist, surveys the various reactions to the law. It is a biased and polemical work critical of the law, in which the author argues in favor of "ethnicisation" of the ethics of memory. Another work from the far right is the book *Eroii anticomuniști și sfinții închisorilor reincriminați prin legea 217/2015*, edited by Cezarina Condurache and published by the pro-legionary publishing house and the George Manu Foundation, which contains a *damnatio memoriae* against Emergency Ordinance 31/2002 signed by Sorin Lavric, a Romanian Academy award-winning author. Andrei Pleșu, an influential public intellectual after 1990, turns the debate to ridicule when he writes that he may not be able to include in his library works by "the inoffensive old man" Nichifor Crainic, a far-right extremist and author of the thesis of the ethnocratic Romanian state; see Pleșu, "Mărturii pentru cercetări viitoare." Finally, in the summer of 2015 the channel Realitatea TV broadcast several biased debates against the law built upon the false premise that the law entails censorship of interwar authors who were members of or sympathetic to the Legionary Movement. The aim was to set public opinion against Law 217/2015.

11. Todorov, *Abuzurile memoriei*, 17.

12. Ibid., 23.

13. Ibid., 17.

14. Ibid., 28

15. Ibid. Italics in the original.

16. Ibid., 31.

17. Ibid., 41.

18. Le Goff, 177.

19. Institutul Național pentru Studierea Holocaustului din România, "Sondaje," accessed March 10, 2016, http://www.inshr-ew.ro/ro/proiecte/sondaje.html.

References

Andreescu, Gabriel. "Temele 'legii antilegionare' din perspectiva eticii memoriei." *Noua revistă de drepturile omului* 4 (2015): 3–43.

Chaumont, Jean-Michel. *La concurrence des victimes. Génocide, identité, reconnaisance*. Paris: La Découverte, 2010.

Condurache, Cezarina, ed. *Eroii anticomuniști și sfinții închisorilor reincriminați prin legea 217/2015*. Bucharest: Editura Evdomikos, Fundația George Manu, 2015.

Institutul Național pentru Studierea Holocaustului din România Elie Wiesel. "Sondaje." Accessed March 10, 2016. http://www.inshr-ew.ro/ro/proiecte/sondaje.html.

Le Goff, Jacques. *Histoire et mémoire*. Paris: Gallimard, 1988.
Nora, Pierre. "Mémoire collective." In *La Nouvelle Histoire*, edited by Jacques Le Goff, 398-401. Paris: Retz.
Pleşu, Andrei. "Mărturii pentru cercetări viitoare." *Adevărul*, August 10, 2015.
Todorov, Tzvetan. *Abuzurile memoriei*. Timişoara, Romania: Amarcord, 1999.
Torres, Ruiz Pedro. "Les usages politiques de l'histoire en Espagne. Formes, limites et contradictions." In *Les usages politiques du passé*, edited by François Hartog and Jacques Revel, 129–156. Paris: Éditions de l'École des Hautes Études en Sciences Sociales, 2001.
Werner, Michael. "Deux nouvelles mises en scènes de la nation allemande. Les expériences du Deutsches Historisches Museum (Berlin) et du Haus der Geschichte der Bundesrepublik Deutschland (Bonn)." In *Les usages politiques du passé*, edited by François Hartog and Jacques Revel, 77–97. Paris: Éditions de l'École des Hautes Études en Sciences Sociales, 2001.

HOLOCAUST PUBLIC MEMORY IN POSTCOMMUNIST ROMANIA

Part 1

COMPETING MEMORIES AND HISTORICAL OBFUSCATION

CHAPTER ONE

ETHNOCENTRIC MINDSCAPES AND MNEMONIC MYOPIA

Ana Bărbulescu

Between 1940 and 1944 the Romanian authorities imposed broad antisemitic legislation that led to the exclusion of the Jewish minority from all levels of society. The Jews from the Old Kingdom of Romania were subjected to two major outbreaks of violence: the pogroms in Bucharest (January 1941) and Iași (June 1941). The pogrom in Bucharest led to the killings of 125 Jews, while the one in Iași resulted in as many as 14,850 Jewish deaths.

In late summer 1941 Transnistria was transferred under Romanian authority and Ion Antonescu ordered the deportation of the Jews from Bessarabia and Bukovina to these newly acquired territories. Prior to deportation, between 45,000 and 60,000 Jews were shot by the Romanian and German troops. Of those who were deported to Transnistria, between 105,000 and 120,000 Romanian Jews died of starvation, cold, and diseases. In addition, between 115,000 and 180,000 Jews were killed, mainly in Odessa and the Golta and Berezovka districts. Of the 25,000 Roma sent to Transnistria, 11,000 perished before repatriation. In the summer of 1942 the Romanian and German authorities reached an agreement regarding the deportation of the Jews from the Old Kingdom to the Belzec extermination camp. The first transport was scheduled for October but it never took place, as Antonescu changed his mind and decided not to implement the plan. The reasons for this decision remain unclear. In April and May 1944 around 132,000 Jews from Northern Transylvania were deported to Auschwitz by the Hungarian authorities. Most of those deported never returned.

If we put together these pieces of information, we get the full scope of the human tragedy that occurred during those years, when between 280,000 and 380,000 Jewish men, women, and children were killed or died of illness, hunger, or cold in territories under Romanian control. All these historical facts were absent from the communist historiography, where the Holocaust of the Romanian Jews remained a taboo subject. Fifteen years after the regime change, in 2004, the Romanian state acknowledged responsibility for the Holocaust of the Romanian Jews, accepting the conclusions of the *Final Report* of the International Commission on the Holocaust in Romania. Furthermore, this acceptance was externalized into the public domain: there is a commemorative day remembering the victims, and a monument dedicated to them in downtown Bucharest. However, this official acknowledgment of the not so distant past is not shared by the majority of the Romanian population, as demonstrated by a survey on the representation of the Holocaust, conducted in the summer of 2015 on a national representative sample.[1]

According to this research, 73 percent of the respondents declared that they had heard about the Holocaust, and among those, 78 percent associated it with the extermination of the Jews during the Second World War, 59 percent with the Nazi concentration camps, and 46 percent with the gas chambers. Only 20 percent of the Romanians who had heard about the Holocaust associated it with the deportations of the Jews to Transnistria. The discriminatory policies directed against the Roma population are remembered by only 18 percent of the respondents. When the questions were asked in a more explicit manner, the Romanian population's perception of the Holocaust proved to be equally distorted. Thus, when the respondents were asked to indicate the territory they associated with the Holocaust, 73 percent of them pointed to Nazi Germany and only 28 percent to Romania. Even more importantly, when they were asked to indicate what association they make with the Holocaust, of the 28 percent of respondents who indicated Romanian territory as the place where the Holocaust took place, 80 percent associated the Holocaust with the deportation of the Jews to the camps controlled by Nazi Germany, while the fact of the deportations to Transnistria was acknowledged by only 28 percent of those who located the Holocaust in

Romania. When the questions address who was responsible, we get a similar picture: 86 percent of the respondents identified Nazi Germany as the main perpetrator. The Antonescu government was identified as responsible by 58 percent of the respondents, while 15 percent indicated the Soviet Union and 5 percent pointed to the Jews.

These results are quite surprising given that in the last twenty-five years some important works on this topic were published in Romania, and that, as mentioned above, more than ten years ago the Romanian state assumed responsibility for the anti-Jewish measures imposed during the Holocaust.[2] Recognizing this inconsistency that characterizes the public memory of the Holocaust within Romanian society, my aim is to identify and reconstruct the social processes that explain how mnemonic myopia operates: why is it difficult for Romanian society to acknowledge the Holocaust of the Romanian Jews? In my opinion, the answer lies in a deficient historiographic socialization where, due to the dialectic relation between identity and memory, the Holocaust is presented in a distorted manner in order to remain consonant with the generic image ascribed to the Romanian people.

To develop this hypothesis, I turn to the main vectors of historiographic socialization that can be identified within postcommunist Romanian society and consider two categories of sources: the textbooks of Romanian history edited in postcommunist Romania and historiographical syntheses published after 1989 by four well-known Romanian historians (Florin Constantiniu, Neagu Djuvara, Dinu C. Giurescu, and Ioan Aurel Pop).

Postcommunist Historical Narratives of the Holocaust

When trying to determine from the history textbooks published in postcommunist Romania the mnemonic narrative associated with the Holocaust of the Jews in Romania or in territories under Romanian authority, we first need to consider that although Romania's transition to democracy started in December 1989, another ten years had to pass before Holocaust-related issues were included in the school curricula for contemporary and Romanian history. This change occurred only in 1999, with Decision 3001 of the Romanian Ministry of Education. Furthermore, despite this requirement, the Romanian educational system is characterized by the use of alternative textbooks, and as a consequence, the specific content of each lesson can vary from one textbook to another.

Considering this, and turning to the history textbooks, six different ways of recounting the events become apparent: mention of the Holocaust is completely absent (model A); Romania is depicted as a savior of Jews (B); mention of discrimination but not deportations (C); mention of deportations to camps, but the victim groups are not specified (D); mention of deportations but not the Final Solution (E); discussion of the Romanian Holocaust, including discrimination, pogroms, and deportations (F). These six models have been discussed at length in a previously published article,[3] and therefore I will only outline here the specifics of each discursive model.

In the first model (A),[4] the lessons make no reference to the Romanian case. This discursive narrative is found in textbooks published between 1993 and 2006. In these textbooks there is no mention of the actions perpetrated by the Romanian authorities against the Jewish population in either the territory of the Old Kingdom or the territories under Romanian control after June 1941.[5] When the authors discuss the allies of the Third Reich and the fate of the Jews who lived in the territories under their control, the Romanian state is once again ignored. This approach erases Romania from the list of countries that were allied to Nazi Germany, and in doing so, implicitly denies the participation of the Romanian authorities in any rights infringements imposed upon the Jews under Romanian authority.

According to the second model (B),[6] in Romania there were no discriminatory laws, camps, pogroms, or deportations. Consequently, there were no victims. The only association of Romania with the Holocaust is as one of the countries that saved their Jewish populations or participated in saving Jews who had escaped from other areas. This approach not only is silent on Romania's participation in exterminatory policies directed against the Jewish minority, but also transforms Romania into a positive actor on the international stage by including it among the countries that saved their Jews.

The textbooks following the third model (C)[7] contain several objective facts regarding the status of Romanian Jews between 1938 and 1944. The information is not false but incomplete, and therefore the past is reconstructed in a distorted manner. Thus, in a textbook issued in 2000 we read about the Iron Guard and its antisemitic program, the existence of anti-Jewish discriminatory laws in Romania, and how many Jews were living in Romanian territory at the end of the war (about 300,000).[8] All three of these things are true, but the authors do not state how many Jews were living in Romania at the beginning of the war, and what happened to those that constitute the difference in the prewar and postwar numbers. More importantly, in this version of history, the deportations to Transnistria are mentioned in a mere line and a half, with no attribution of responsibility, as Antonescu's regime is presented as opposing the "extermination of the Romanian Jews."[9] A textbook from 1999 follows the same model, adding that the anti-Jewish legislation enforced by the Antonescu regime was simply a "takeover" of laws promulgated by the Iron Guard during the National Legionary state.[10]

The fourth model (D),[11] which mentions deportations of unspecified victims, recounts the historical facts in a most original manner: there is a short note on anti-Jewish legislation; there is a reference to the number of Romanian Jews at the beginning of the war (800,000), but we never learn how many were still alive at the end of it; and there is a short reference to the situation of the Jews from Northern Transylvania under the "Horthyist government." More importantly, we learn that the Romanian government built camps and ordered deportations.[12] The examples provided are historical ones—Vapniarka, Bogdanovka, Dumanovka—but the authors do not explain who the victims were. As long as there is no causal connection made between Jewishness and the probability of being interned in such a camp, this information allows the reader to conclude that the political regime in Romania between 1940 and 1944 was nondemocratic, without understanding the situation of the Romanian Jews during the same period.

In the fifth discursive model (E),[13] the description of the events is more complete and is accompanied by a more thorough description of the discriminatory legislation; the pogroms in Iași and Odessa and the mass deportations to Transnistria (directed explicitly against the Jews) are also mentioned. The main characteristic of this discourse is not its more detailed description of the events but its development of a comparative dimension. Thus, the authors emphasize Antonescu's decision in October 1942 to not deport the Jews from the Old Kingdom to the Belzec extermination camp, comparing the fate of the Jews from the Old Kingdom with those from Northern Transylvania. The strategy is evident in a textbook that was first issued in 2000. The authors accept the reality of the deportations to Transnistria, in which several thousands of the 100,000 deportees died, but for these authors, what is essential is "the fact that as a result of Antonescu's decision, 292,149 Jews remained alive in August 1944."[14]

In the last model (F),[15] the information provided to the students is quite extensive. They learn about Romania's antisemitic legislation, the pogroms in Dorohoi, Bucharest, and Iași, the deportations to Transnistria, and the massacre of the Jews in Odessa by the Romanian army, as well as the cessation of the deportations after 1943. Antonescu's position on the Final Solution is presented from the double perspective of ante- and post-October 1942. Thus, the authors record not only the breakdown of the agreement with the Germans after October 1942, but also the period before, when the Romanian authorities accepted the deportations of the Jews from the Old Kingdom to the Belzec extermination camp. The situation of the Jews from Northern Transylvania is also taken into consideration, but without emphasizing a comparison between the two cases (Antonescu and Horthy) and consequently diminishing the responsibility of the Romanian authorities.

In conclusion, the contents of the analyzed textbooks vary greatly, ranging from a complete lack of information on the Holocaust (model A) to a thorough reconstruction of the historical events (model F). Between the two extremes, we have identified several models that fail to reconstruct the historical events, either by omitting important information (models B, C, and D) or by choosing to emphasize particular decisions of the Romanian authorities while ignoring others (model E).

Turning to the main historiographic syntheses edited in postcommunist Romania, we encounter a not-so-different scenario in the works of four mainstream historians: Florin Constantiniu, Neagu Djuvara, Dinu C. Giurescu, and Ioan Aurel Pop.

Probably the most popular synthesis of Romanian history published after 1989 was Florin Constantiniu's *O istorie sinceră a poporului român* (An honest history of the Romanian people). The volume was published in 1997 and reedited four times up to 2016. Constantiniu dedicates 100 of the 500 pages of his work—one-fifth of it—to Romania's participation in the Second World War. Within this generous space we find a half-page description of the legionary rebellion in late January 1941, another half-page description of the pogrom in Iași, and two inserts regarding the deportations to Transnistria—all together, amounting to no more than eleven lines.[16]

With regard to the legionary rebellion we learn that there were 118 Jewish victims and that Ion Antonescu reestablished order, an approach that portrays the Romanian leader in a positive light, even if indirectly. The pogrom in Iași is presented in a more elaborate manner. According to the author, in order to get the correct picture, we first need to put it in the right context, meaning that we have to consider the intensifying actions of the Soviet agents and the collective fear of "Judeo-communists"; this, explains Constantiniu, is the context of the attack of June 29 against the Jewish population of the city. In the course of the next day, two convoys of the Romanian army were attacked, so the Romanian and German soldiers proceeded to carry out summary executions. Next, at the request of the Germans, the Jewish population of the city was evacuated under inhumane conditions, and thousands ended up dying. We learn nothing about the random arrests made on the streets of Iași, about the civilians, including small children, who were killed in those streets, or about Antonescu's order to evacuate the Jews from the city. The main perpetrators seem to be either the Legionary Movement or the German troops, an approach that omits mention of the Romanian authorities and thus diminishes their responsibility.

Transnistria is discussed in connection with the beginning of Antonescu's regime, which is described as nonfascist because it was not backed up by a fascist party. Constantiniu accepts that Antonescu's regime had an antisemitic component, mainly evident, according to the historian, between 1940 and 1942, but he provides no examples of the antisemitic legislation promulgated after January 1941. There is also no mention of the massacres in Bessarabia and Bukovina, but the author accepts the reality of some 200,000 Jewish victims.

Constantiniu sees Romania's position as paradoxical: "In a Europe heavily hit by war, Romania remained an island of prosperity and peace, where strange things happened. King Michael was visiting the American prisoners, comfortably detained in the Prahova Valley, ... and while in Europe the putting into practice of the Final Solution (*Endlösung*) led to the death of millions of Jews in the German camps, in Bucharest the Jewish theater *Baraşeum* was functioning."[17]

Romania was surely not an island of prosperity and peace to its deported Jewish citizens who were awaiting repatriation, or for those already dead in territories under Romanian authority. Moreover, the Jews from the Old Kingdom—not deported, but severely affected by the Romanianization policy—would find it difficult to regard the Romania of the time as an island of prosperity. Not less importantly, Constantiniu fails to explain the survival of the Baraşeum Theater, and chooses not to acknowledge the dismissal of all Jewish actors from state theaters across the country. The Baraşeum Theater continued to exist during Antonescu's regime as a compromise following the dismissal of Jewish actors from state theaters. However, there were several conditions that limited its activities: Yiddish became a forbidden language, the actors being allowed to play only in Romanian, and they were not remunerated by the Romanian state, their financial gains being strictly determined by ticket sales.

Synthesizing this mnemonic narrative, it appears that the author is aware of the main events that he must mention in order for his account of the Holocaust to be seen as "honest": the Bucharest and Iaşi pogroms, the antisemitic legislation, and the deportations to Transnistria. However, the Bucharest pogrom is presented as the responsibility of the Iron Guard alone; the Iaşi pogrom is analyzed in the context of the Soviet threats and the fears of "Judeo-communism," an approach that implicitly rationalizes the anti-Jewish measures taken in June 1941 in Iaşi, in terms similar to those used by the authorities of the time. Moreover, the killings are presented as having been prompted by some attacks carried out against the Romanian and German armies, and the evacuation of the Jewish population is presented as having been demanded by the German ally—it is as if Antonescu had nothing to do with them. Antonescu's regime is described as nonfascist, and its antisemitic policies are represented as having existed only until 1942. There were deportations to Transnistria and about 200,000 Jews died, but in territories under Romanian authority there was no Final Solution. The Final Solution is not put on a par with the Transnistria deportations and massacres, but is pitched against the existence of the Baraşeum Theater in Bucharest, a strategy that allows the author to describe Romania as "an island of peace and prosperity."

In 1999 Neagu Djuvara published *O scurtă istorie a românilor povestită celor tineri* (A short history of the Romanians narrated to the young), which quickly became very popular and was reissued in five editions through 2016.

In its pages, the author proposes an account of the Holocaust on Romanian territory even more ambiguous than Constantiniu's. According to Djuvara, the organization responsible for the anti-Jewish legislation was the Legionary Movement, whose members savagely attacked the Jews and tried to confiscate their wealth through Romanianization; the Romanian state seems not to have been involved, as the goods confiscated from the Jews were shared by the legionnaires among themselves.[18] Nothing is said about the anti-Jewish legislation imposed by Ion Antonescu after January 1941. However, Djuvara explains, Antonescu considered that the Jewish population from Bessarabia and Bukovina was pro–Soviet Union, so he decided to deport them beyond the Dniester.[19] Some 150,000 Jews and Roma shared this fate, but Djuvara argues that it is next to impossible to estimate the total number of dead or missing. Why?—because they were in a war zone, and the brutality of the advancing German army is well known. The Romanian authorities are completely missing from this scenario, and consequently, there is almost no responsibility assigned to them. Antonescu deported the Jews, yes, but it was the Germans, or the war, that killed them. How many were killed? It is impossible to calculate.

Along the same lines, we learn that after 1942, Antonescu changed his position on the Jews, and in spite of Germany's repeated insistence that Romania hand over the local Jews, he not only steadfastly refused but also helped some Western and Transylvanian Jews to escape persecution. Djuvara emphasizes that nothing of the kind happened in neighboring Hungary, where the Jews were handed over to the German authorities and deported to concentration camps.[20] This comparative approach implicitly puts the Romanian authorities in a better light, and I regard it as an instrument to diminish their responsibility. I note Djuvara's lament with regard to the unfairness of life (or perhaps history): "Despite the fact that the Hungarians handed over their Jews to the Germans and they were exterminated in gas chambers, still, the vast majority of the international Jewry rather sympathize with Hungary and not with Romania."[21] It is quite surprising to read these two and a half lines in which one of the best-known Romanian historians makes reference to an all-encompassing category—"international Jewry"—a term often found in traditional antisemitic discourse. Then Djuvara goes a step further, drawing a comparison with Hungary that allows him to cast the Romanian people as victim: the Hungarians sent their Jews to

Auschwitz, but the "international Jewry" unfairly sympathizes with Hungary and not with Romania.

In 2008, the ninth volume of the main synthesis of Romanian history edited after 1989, covering the period 1940–1947, was issued as part of a collection published under the authority of the Romanian Academy. The volume, *Istoria românilor. România în anii 1940–1947* (The history of the Romanians: Romania between 1940–1947), was authored by another well-known historian, Dinu C. Giurescu, who takes great care to cover the main events regarding the fate of the Jews in territories under Romanian authority, but fails to provide a clear account of these events.

If we take, for example, the pogrom in Iași, we learn that it started as a result of provocations by Iron Guard members. Jews were killed in the streets by the German army and in police headquarters by the same German soldiers.[22] There is an admission that there were some other killings in the streets of the city, but we are given no information about the perpetrators. Nothing is said about the civilians who participated in the killings, but in the following paragraph, the author lists the Romanian civilians who were killed while trying to save Jews. According to Giurescu, the order to evacuate the Jews from Iași was given by the Romanian commander of the Fourth Division, which implicitly leaves Antonescu out of the equation. The total number of victims is (under)estimated to have been 2,521.[23]

In discussing the fate of the Jews from Bessarabia and Bukovina in the summer of 1941, the author uses minimizing terms—"raids," or "summary executions"—to describe the massacres that occurred in these territories when the Romanian army entered the war. The massacre in Odessa is described in the same minimizing manner, and the total number of victims is once again underestimated, as 5,417.[24] The mass executions in Bogdanovka, Dumanovka, and Acmecetka are presented as the joint responsibility of some German special units and Ukrainian militias.[25] No less importantly, the historian maintains that Romania did not participate in the Final Solution, because no deportation trains departed to Poland from the territories under Romanian authority. And, he points out, the same cannot be said about neighboring Hungary, where the local authorities closely cooperated with the Nazis.[26] When discussing the total number of victims,[27] the author is careful to present no fewer than five different estimates, but fails to indicate which is his own. His conclusion, while politically correct, is an exercise in ambiguity: "The murder remains murder. The total number of victims varies based on the documentary evidence. The record and analysis of the tragedy represent a priority and are mandatory. For the future generations to understand and not to forget. For such things, not to happen again, nowhere, never."[28] In spite of this declaration, it is not clear who is responsible for the crimes; the responsibility of the Romanian authorities is never made explicit, and when it is hinted at, the events are minimized.

Ioan Aurel Pop's synthesis of Romanian history, *Istoria românilor* (The history of the Romanians), was published in 2010. In this work, too, we find an ambiguous approach to Romania's participation in the Holocaust. The author acknowledges that Romania imposed antisemitic legislation between 1938 and 1940, but he presents this as merely the observation of a European practice of the time, or a means by which the Romanian authorities attempted to gain the favor of the German government.[29]

Similarly, Ion Antonescu is portrayed as having had Anglo-French sympathies, and becoming Germanophile only by necessity. Moreover, he is credited as the leader who dislodged the Legionary Movement from power so that, unlike in other countries, in Romania the profascist party remained in power for only five months.[30] As in Constantiniu's book, here, the ideological content of Antonescu's government is analyzed through a sole indicator—its relationship with a fascist party. Thus, the substance of Antonescu's own policies becomes irrelevant, and his government is praised for dislodging the Legionary Movement, even though it continued to impose its own anti-Jewish measures.

The Transnistria deportations are discussed in a short paragraph in which the context of the antisemitic and anti-Roma policies defines the military collaboration between the German and Romanian armies on the eastern front.[31] Although responsibility for the deportations seems to be shared, we have already learned in the preceding pages that at the time, the Germans were the true masters of Europe. The description of the historical events is minimalist, and we are given no estimate of the numbers of victims. Again, the antisemitic policies imposed by the Romanian authorities are presented in a comparative perspective. In Romania, writes Pop, "the antisemitic policy continued and made many victims, although Romania refused to send its Jews to the German extermination camps and, in 1943–1944, in order to solve 'the Jewish problem,' envisaged their emigration to what would become the Israeli state."[32]

All four mnemonic narratives discussed above acknowledge the existence of some anti-Jewish measures and also some outbreaks of violence directed against the Jewish minority in Romania. Yet, the anti-Jewish legislation is mainly attributed to the period of the legionary state, and Antonescu is credited for having dislodged from power this fascist party (see Constantiniu and Pop). The pogrom in Bucharest was provoked by Iron Guard members, and the one in Iași by the Germans (Constantiniu) or the legionnaires (Giurescu). Nothing is said about Antonescu's order to evacuate the Jews from the city, or about the participation of the local population in killing their Jewish neighbors. All four narratives acknowledge the fact of the deportations to Transnistria, but the responsibility for those who were killed lies with the Germans and the war (Djuvara) or with Romania's collaboration with the German ally on the eastern front (Pop); Constantiniu and Giurescu are not interested in assigning responsibility.

Importantly, all four mnemonic narratives develop a comparative analysis, emphasizing the fact that in territories under Romanian authority, in contrast to neighboring Hungary, there was no Final Solution. The mass executions in Bessarabia and Bukovina and in Transnistria and the policy of extermination directed by the Romanian authorities against the deported Jews are not seen by these historians as on a par with the Final Solution, so Romania's participation in the Holocaust is minimized, allowing the authors to show Romania in a better light. When the Hungarian authorities were deporting their Jews to Auschwitz, the Romanian authorities, explains Pop, were solving the Jewish problem through "emigration." According to Constantiniu, the situation was even better than that, because while the Hungarian Jews were being deported to the Nazi extermination camps, Romanian Jews had a whole theater just for themselves.

Returning to the models identified when analyzing the history textbooks published in Romania after 1989, the mnemonic narratives proposed by Constantiniu, Djuvara, and Giurescu belong to the fifth model, as all three authors emphasize that Romania did not participate in the Final Solution, and they choose not to discuss the Bessarabia massacres or Transnistria deportations in terms of extermination policies. Pop combines the fifth model with the second, for according to his narrative, not only there was no Final Solution in Romania, but after 1943, Antonescu solved the "Jewish problem" through emigration, and in this way helped many Jews to escape persecution.

Framing the Realm of Social Forgetting: Social Mindscapes and Cognitive Dissonance

The dialectical relationship that links social identity and collective memory is well known.[33] Both concepts are fundamental for understanding what Schutz calls the "symbolic universe,"[34] and what Zerubavel, following the theoretical line opened by Berger, calls "optical community"—the social unit from within which the world is perceived in a similar way.[35] Both these approaches fall within the domain of the sociology of knowledge, and both regard reality as a social construct. Within the process of social construction, the boundaries constructed to create meaningful entities have a major role in establishing a social world, and therefore, examining the way the boundaries are drawn is fundamental to understanding any social order.[36]

Any optical community, affirms Zerubavel, contains a set of impersonal mindscapes shared by its members. They are by no means universal, but specific to "the thought community we happen to belong to."[37] These socially shared mindscapes define the lenses we use to "see" our environment, ourselves, and all others. They are defined by cognitive norms, and internalized through socialization. Through them, we are taught how and on what to focus our attention, how to frame our experience, when it is legitimate to generalize, and what is morally relevant or irrelevant. Consequently, if we want to understand how the world is seen by a specific community, we first need to acknowledge how these lenses are configured. More importantly, any symbolic framework is internally coherent, and the nucleus of this construction defines the identity narrative associated with the in-group. The world we inhabit is read and interpreted according to the identity narrative we assume for ourselves. All other groups we acknowledge alongside us are attributed meaning and consistency only in relation to the identity narrative of the group to which we belong.

The differences between symbolic worlds, according to Goodman, derive from the distinctive manner of constructing the categories considered relevant within those specific worlds.[38] The emphasis proposed by Goodman is quite helpful for understanding how social attribution operates, and consequently how the border separating "us" from all others is constructed. This is the first and foremost discrimination, and the way we construct "us" influences our manner of perceiving, interpreting, and acknowledging the Other. Beyond this primary discrimination, to understand how a particular symbol is represented by a given community, we must first understand how it is related to other symbols already in use.[39] Or, using Brubaker's conceptualization, any symbol we try to recover needs to be analyzed within the "frame alignment" to which the respective symbol belongs.[40] The generic framework that configures the symbolic system we share as members of the same community and the positioning of the analyzed symbol within the framework are equally important for the correct understanding of the symbol.

Leon Festinger helps us understand the principles that allow the construction of the frame alignment in a coherent manner, demonstrating that our opinions and attitudes tend to exist in clusters that are internally consistent.[41] According to Festinger, cognitive dissonance occurs when people believe that two of their psychological representations are inconsistent with each other.[42] The relation between any two cognitions is either one of irrelevancy or relevancy. In the first case, the two cognitions exist and are used independently from each other; in the second instance, when the two cognitions are relevant to each other, they share a common root, and any new input involving one of them will necessarily transform the other. Considering this dependency, Festinger argues that the state of cognitive dissonance occurs only between two or more cognitions that are relevant to each other.[43] To reduce the dissonance, a person can try to lower the discrepancy between the cognitions, or add cognitions to reduce the total magnitude of the dissonance.[44] Either way, he will avoid situations and information that are likely to increase the dissonance.[45]

The need for internal consistency, diligently proved by Festinger and his followers, functions not only at the individual but also at the social level, where the relationship among the cluster of symbols structuring a symbolic universe is also one of coherency, this consistency being confined to the generic frame circumscribing the symbolic universe.

As Mary Douglas has demonstrated, all cultures are inherently coherent, and meaning is constructed and maintained in areas that contain all domains of reality.[46] One of the most important tools for structuring the symbolic universe in a coherent manner is the dialectical relationship that exists between social identity and collective memory. The social environment we share as social beings and the mindscapes characteristic of it influence not only the ways we mentally process the present but also, as Zerubavel shows, the manner in which we remember the past.[47] When, for example, we imagine the core of our identity in terms of lineage, we are in fact accommodating collective agendas of inclusion and exclusion. Tracing descent always involves certain norms of selective remembrance,[48] because when we identify our ancestors we are identifying the past that we accept as ours, and by doing so, we are creating a community of belonging from which all who do not share this past are excluded. The pasts of all those who do not belong are relegated to the out-of-frame domain and become meaningless for the definition of reality shared by those who do belong.

All communities construct their own norms of historical focus that dictate what should be mnemonically attended to and what can be largely ignored, and thus forgotten.[49] Moreover, as Irwin-Zarecka pointed out, when we talk about forgetting we are actually talking about replacing one version of the past with another[50]—another, I might add, that is more suitable to the generic mindscapes shared as members of the same community. Consequently, if we wish to understand how mnemonic distortion operates, we need to first identify the borders that the analyzed community attributes to itself, and then consider what Zerubavel calls "free mnemonic associations," the framework through which community members read the world, and identify the cognitive dissonance raised by a potential alternative reading of the past.

Given this dialectical relationship that exists between social identity and collective memory, between what a community assumes it represents and the ways it remembers its past, I consider the identity narrative ascribed to the Romanian people as the main factor in understanding the mnemonic myopia of Romanian society with regard to the Holocaust. How is this identity narrative constructed? Does it allow for complexity, or does it enforce unity? Does it integrate minorities, or does it exclude them?[51]

I propose an explanatory model in which the answer to the question I began with—why is it difficult for Romanian society to acknowledge the Holocaust of the Romanian Jews?—rests with the generic mindscapes shared by Romanian society, or more specifically, with the ways Romanian identity is constructed and internalized through socialization.

As Constantin Iordachi diligently proves,[52] traditionally, Romanian historiography has been dominated by themes of nation-building and the creation of the Romanian state. Romania's present form is an outcome of the Second World War; the territorial unity that is today taken for granted does not have a long history. Apart from the fleeting and controversial actions of Mihai Viteazul, the Wallachian king who united the principalities of Moldavia, Wallachia, and Transylvania for just one year, in 1600, the first lasting act of union occurred only 159 years ago, when Wallachia and Moldavia unified in 1859. After the First World War, the young Romanian state acquired three new territories: the former Russian province of Bessarabia, the former Austrian province of Bukovina, and the regions of Transylvania, Maramureș, and Banat, which had been part of the Hungarian half of the Habsburg monarchy.[53] After the Second World War Romania lost the provinces of Bessarabia and Bukovina, a territorial reconfiguration that resulted in the borders we have today.

Beginning in the nineteenth century, the much cherished concept of the homogeneity of the Romanian people was constructed by the development of three main ideas: common origin; unity and continuity; and a shared national specificity. Common origin was claimed by three distinctive theories: the Latinist position,[54] the Dacianist alternative,[55] and the Daco-Roman compromise.[56] The premise of ancient origins goes hand in hand with the second burden of the Romanian historiography—the thesis of unity and continuity. The main idea is simple: people living on Romanian soil at any given moment are just like those who lived there 2,000 years before, as there is a continuous line that links all generations living in the territory. All historical contacts with migratory peoples and the influence of the Slavic peoples are set aside to maintain the purity of the line linking current generations with their ancestors.[57]

Furthermore, continuity is provided by the existence of a common essence shared throughout history by all those who have inhabited the Romanian territories, incarnated not just in the great historical figures from the past, but in each individual.[58] This discursive approach started in the nineteenth century but gained momentum in the twentieth century as the main representatives of Romanian culture followed the same narrative. For example, Nicolae Iorga wrote about a unitary Romanian civilization, and portrayed the nation itself as a living being that follows its inner ways.[59] Constantin Rădulescu-Motru pointed toward the existence of a collective conscience within the Romanian ethnos, a set of typical manifestations that each individual inherits at his birth.[60] Lucian Blaga, one of the most prominent Romanian philosophers, identified a matrix specific to the inalienable Romanian ethnic soul.[61] For Nichifor Crainic, this essence, ethnically defined, was provided by the Orthodox tradition, as he saw the Orthodox faith as inherent to the Romanian soul. This essentialism was further expressed in the sharing of a common blood, a common language, and a common land.

Consequently, up to the middle of the twentieth century, Romanian historiography was constructed on primordialist and ethnocentric claims.[62] The emphasis was placed on common origins, unity and continuity, and the existence of a common essence shared by those defined as members of the group. Given the emphasis on common origins and continuity, both which have as a corollary the idea of a homogenous community, all these mnemonic narratives created a community with impenetrable boundaries, where citizenship (which after 1923 was granted to minorities) would fail to confer belonging.

Turning to the communist period, we can identify two distinct approaches to the Romanian past: up to 1960, the historical narrative was de-ethnicized as class struggle was emphasized, and afterwards, the Romanians were once again cast as the main actors of their history.[63] The Program of the Romanian Communist Party edited in 1974 and published one year later contains a thirty-eight-page synthesis of Romanian history[64] that became the main source for the authors of history textbooks used in schools, the main instrument of historical socialization for every citizen.[65] The main themes developed in the document were the ancient roots of the Romanian people, the continuity on the same territory, the unity of the people throughout history, and Romanians' continuous struggle for independence.[66] In this second phase of the communist regime, the emphasis was on the notion of a national consciousness, defined as the specific way of feeling and reacting that was characteristic of the ethnic community.[67] The nation was thus defined not only as a community that was historically constituted but also, and foremost, as an ethnic community[68] that generated a specific manner of feeling and reacting shared by all its members.[69]

What changed after the regime change in 1989? The fourth article of the Romanian Constitution states that Romania is the common homeland of all its citizens, irrespective of race, nationality, ethnic origin, language, religion, gender, opinion, political affliation, wealth, or social origins. The good news is that we have no discriminatory politics against different categories of Romanian citizens. But is the fourth article enough to put to rest the ethnocentric frameworks of constructing the Romanian identity?

Identity Narratives in Postcommunist Romanian Historiography

To answer this question, it is useful to look again at the four main syntheses of Romanian history discussed above. Florin Constantiniu opts for the Daco-Roman synthesis to explain the origins of the Romanians. The most important element for explaining the synthesis are the Roman colonists, who, like the locals, were farmers. From the interactions of these groups, the Geto-Dacians became Romans, then Romanics, and in the end, Romanians.[70] Elsewhere, Constantiniu calls these early Romanized populations proto-Romanians, who integrated to the Roman culture brought by the colonists. The second important factor in "the ethno-genesis of the Romanians" is Christianity. Although Constantiniu rejects the traditional explanation that attributes the spread of Christianity in Romanian territories to St. Andrew the Apostle, he does present Christianization as fundamental "in the formation of this people."[71]

Importantly, the ethnogenesis of the Romanians was already complete by the end of late antiquity, and although there are almost no sources of evidence pertaining to the fourth to the eleventh centuries, according to Constantiniu, this does not suggest discontinuity. The locals were still there, but were veiled by populations coming from the steppe: "Sometimes the veil was lifted, and through the ruptures we are able to see the natives."[72] According to this identity narrative, Romanians are the heirs of the people resulting from the Christianized Daco-Roman synthesis. Significantly, there was a continuous line stemming from these common roots, as the locals—replicas of this inheritance—were always there.Throughout history, they were attacked, robbed, dominated, occupied, exploited—in other words, they were *victims* who learned to adapt to different conquerors but remained faithful to their roots.

In Neagu Djuvara's *O scurtă istorie a românilor povestită celor tineri* (1999), the cradle of the Romanian kin (*neamul românesc*) is Transylvania, and our ancestors are the Daco-Romans.[73] Yet, this binominal ancestry only partially explains the origins of the Romanian people; to get the full picture we need to consider two more groups: the Slavs and the Western Asian peoples who arrived in the region. All four, affirms Djuvara, are part of the ethnogenesis of the Romanian people,[74] though he emphasizes the Romanians' Latinity, as on the north side of the Danube the Slavs were Romanized, whereas on the southern side the locals were Slavicized.[75]

Interestingly, Djuvara tries to overcome the old obsession of Romanian historiography that emphasizes common origins and the unity–continuity dyad, but proposes instead an identity narrative where the old ambiguities are still present and continuity is still pursued through the artificial overlapping of the narrative categories. Thus he affirms that an analysis of the formation of the Romanian people must consider, in addition to the four groups associated with its ethnogenesis, all "foreign" groups that shared the same territory with the Romanians (Armenians, Roma, Jews).[76] This is a position that should theoretically lead to the inclusion of these groups in the national community. However, Djuvara's use of the Daco-Romans–Wallachians (*valahi*)–Romanians triad implicitly points toward common belonging and continuity: the Geto-Dacians are our ancestors;[77] after Romanization, they became Daco-Romans; the descendants of the Daco-Romans are the Wallachians; and the Wallachians are the ancestors of the Romanians.[78] Within this identity narrative, the Armenian, Jewish, and Roma minorities are still kept outside the border of the national community, because they do not have roots that go back to the Romanians' Daco-Roman ancestors.

To prove continuity, Djuvara uses his own triad, common ancestry–territory–language, with the emphasis on language.[79] Consistent with this approach, the Jewish minority is regarded as the Other—"We were speaking Romanian, they Yiddish"[80]—and their quest to gain Romanian citizenship in the second half of the nineteenth century is discussed from the perspective of the Romanian majority.[81] For Djuvara, Romanian politicians' opposition to the naturalization of the Jews was consistent with the national interest, as it was understood at the time; the main force pressing for citizenship for the Jews was the Freemasons, and more precisely, its significant Jewish membership.[82]

The first two volumes of the largest synthesis of Romanian history edited after 1989 were published in 2001 by the Romanian Academy. In both volumes—*Istoria românilor. Moștenirea timpurilor îndepărtate* (The history of the Romanians: The heritage of past times) and *Istoria românilor. Daco-romani, romanici, alogeni* (The history of the Romanians: Daco-Romans, Romanics, aliens)—the authors dwell extensively on the origins of the Romanian people. As Alexandru Nicolescu points out, the main plot of the first volume unfolds along the lines of the assumption of a compact inhabitation of the national territory, from the beginnings of the Neolithic, by "an interrupted genealogy of archeological cultures," a continuity that creates a "strong and pervasive dichotomy" between the locals, who will "continuously evolve to become Romanians, and the foreign peoples."[83]

The sociohistorical process that defines "the emergence of the Romanian people on the historical arena" is Romanization,[84] or the synthesis of the native Dacians with the Roman colonists. The thesis is not new, but the way it is used in this twenty-first-century synthesis is appalling. The particularities of this sociohistorical process, that is, Romanization, are conferred by the place, the time, and the ethnic basis on which it was grafted.[85] Consequently, the Romanization process had two components: the territorial colonization of Latinophonic populations, and the assimilation of the native population, who not only adopted the Latin language and the Roman way of living, but also changed their mentality and ethnicity.[86] From this Roman graft onto the ethnic core of the native Dacians, a new unity was born. This unity needs to be understood in linguistic and ethnic terms, and it takes the form of a spiritual habitus, seemingly understood as an inner predisposition shared by those who originate from this common stem.[87] The natives were assimilated, but the Romanization was carried out on this autochthonous ethnic fundament.

The migratory peoples passing through these territories had no influence upon the local population because "the Roman graft on the Dacian trunk proved strong and viable despite the historical vicissitudes."[88] At this stage, the autochthonous people are described as Latinophones and Christians who, by keeping their inner being and identity, constituted the basis of the historical process in the former Roman provincial space.[89] According to this narrative, the migratory peoples had no role in the ethnogenesis of the Romanians; instead, they were all integrated and assimilated within the Romanized, and then proto-Romanian, population.[90] Consequently, according to this perspective, the sociohistorical processes that led to the formation of the Romanian people had a twofold ethnic character: first, there was a Roman element grafted on the Dacian ethnic trunk, and second, this synthesis created a unitary community sharing an ethnocultural core, a linguistic legacy, and an original spiritual habitus. These are the grounds on which Romanianness (*românitatea*) rests.

In the last work, published in 2010, Ioan Aurel Pop starts with a question similar to mine: who are the Romanians? Romanians, he says, "could be defined, in a hurry, as the inhabitants of Romania, only that the facts are not so simple."[91] Why is this not sufficient to be considered a Romanian? First, because the Romanians existed in history long before an official state called Romania appeared on the map; and second, because although all people living in Romania could be called Romanians, they are seen as Romanian only with regard to their citizenship, as their nationality may not be Romanian.[92] In other words, there are two kinds of Romanian citizens, the "true Romanians"—that is, the Romanian citizens of Romanian nationality—and the Romanian citizens of other nationalities. According to this narrative, the Romanians of Romanian nationality were here long before the formation of the Romanian state. They are portrayed as the heirs of the Romans from 2,000 years ago, and Trajan's Column in Rome represents the birth certificate of the Romanian people.[93]

Like all Latin peoples, the Romanians have two main ethnic elements: the pre-Roman autochthonous element (the Dacians) and the Latinophonic element of the conqueror (the Romans). In addition to these, a third one, the migratory element (the Slavs), should also be considered.[94] However, in the case of the Romanians, the Slavic influence was minor and occurred after the formation of the Romanian people was almost complete,[95] so the Slavs slowly melted into the mass of "early Romanians."[96] Again, Romanianness is constructed in ethnic terms; we are the heirs of the Daco-Romans, identified by Pop as *strǎromâni* (ancient Romanians), and this ethnic core was already defined before the arrival of the Slavic element. Pop's approach to the Union of 1918 reveals the same autochthonic understanding of Romanian identity. The author acknowledges that at the time of union, more than one quarter of the population belonged to a national minority, but "unfortunately, the borders could not follow the sinuous line of the ethnic groups."[97] Strictly speaking, they are members the group, but they belong only because of the unfortunate manner in which the borders were drawn. Consequently, they are Romanian citizens but not really Romanians, since within this model citizenship does not translate into belonging.

Turning again to the history textbooks edited after 1989, we find two different ways of constructing the identity narrative ascribed to the Romanian people. The first is associated with the aforementioned golden triad of Romanian historiography (common roots, unity, continuity), and its discussion of common origins emphasizes the Dacian legacy, the Roman descent, or the Christian core. The second method goes back to the Daco-Roman roots but does not correlate them with the unity–continuity dyad, and therefore it does not offer a continuous reading of history expressed in a common essence shared by the entire people.

A textbook from the mid-1990s that follows the first of these models states that the Romanians are the unique heirs of the Geto-Dacian people and the descendants of the Latin element from the eastern side of the Roman Empire.[98] With regard to Mircea cel Bătrân, a Wallachian king from the late fourteenth to the beginning of the fifteenth century, we learn that through the common efforts of his family "the eternal body of the country was born," and its unity is deeply rooted in kin consciousness (*conștiința de neam*). Moreover, emphasize the authors, the continuity of the state and the defense of our independence are defining features of our existence, an expression of the creative power of the Romanian people and of its long-lasting fulfillment.[99] It must be noted that between Mircea cel Bătrân's "long-lasting fulfillment" and contemporary Romania there were six centuries of history, and more than half of the territory of present-day Romania was never under Mircea's authority. The same textbook states that when Mihai Viteazul two centuries later united Wallachia, Moldavia, and Transylvania under his authority, he was following the call of his kin (*chemarea neamului*) and the old plan of the Dacians.[100] Thus, what we encounter in this narrative is not only a common essence shared by all the people inhabiting the Romanian territories, but a living force that transcends history and is embodied in each individual and in the great leaders from the past who were all fighting for the same goal of territorial unity.

Another textbook describes the 1848 revolutionary movement in the three principalities as profoundly democratic and an expression of the ideological core shared by all Romanians—*daco-românismul* (Daco-Romanianism).[101]

Here, the Dacian origins explain not only the common roots and the transhistorical quest for unity, but also a propensity for democracy exhibited by the Romanian people throughout history.

A second approach to the common origins paradigm emphasizes the Roman legacy. In a textbook published in 2015 the argument runs as follows: the ancestors of the Romanians are the Romans; the Daco-Romans and the Romanians had a continuous existence in the Dacian territory; consequently, the population living on this territory has a threefold unitary character, with regard to its kin (*neam*), territory, and language.[102] What we have here is once again a classic definition of Romanianness in ethnic terms: common descent, territory, unity and continuity. The best expression of the latter two, explain the authors, is the Romanian language, with its incontestable Latin character.

According to the third model identified in the textbooks, the inner trait specific to the Romanian people is explained not through our common Dacian or Roman origin but by an inherent Christian nature. The common Daco-Roman origins are still acknowledged, but the emphasis is on our inborn Christian core. This is a return to the old paradigm most popular during the interwar period, according to which the Romanian people were born Christian and did not need to be converted. According to this interpretation, the Orthodox Church is rooted within the very being of the people,[103] and consequently, in the northern region of the Danube, Christianity spread naturally, without any political interference.[104] The inborn Christian nature of the Romanian people explains their resistance against the Ottoman Empire exhibited during the Middle Ages, and also their Europeanness.[105]

Regardless of how the common roots are explained (Roman legacy, Dacian heritage, or inner Christian core), all these textbooks construct the identity narrative attributed to the Romanian people in ethnic terms and emphasize the existence of a transhistorical collective force that transcends all individuals and at the same time inhabits every one of them. It is the expression of common origins and the proof of continuity. This collective consciousness creates what Zerubavel calls "historical continuity,"[106] a powerful discursive tool that allows, on the one hand, the linking together of virtually noncontiguous points in time, and on the other, the creation of a "seemingly coherent, constant identity."[107]

Furthermore, in addition to using the golden triad of Romanian historiography, all these textbooks reconstruct the history of the Romanian people in spectacular terms. The Romanians are the heirs of the oldest European communities, and perhaps even the heirs of the first human beings identified on the European continent;[108] their ancestors created one of the oldest civilizations in Europe (Cucuteni-Ariușd);[109] and during the Iron Age, the Geto-Dacians constituted a powerful civilization exhibiting a unitary and original culture.[110] Faithful to the inner Christian core, the Romanian principalities were the East European actor in the fight against the Ottoman Empire, representing an advanced stronghold of Christianity.[111] Ștefan cel Mare was the greatest fighter of his century against the Ottoman enemy;[112] Iancu de Hunedoara was the most brilliant exponent of the late crusaders;[113] and Mihai Viteazul, when he united the principalities, was recreating the anti-Ottoman front.[114]

Following this model, common territoriality and extraordinary ancestry are combined to create a different type of continuity. Territorial consistency is used to create what Zerubavel calls "mnemonic bridging,"[115] a discursive strategy that allows one to create a sense of sameness by filling the gap between noncontiguous points in history. Continuity is conferred by the shared territory, and when that territory is populated with great fighters, true defenders of Christianity, the result is a people whose history is truly great. It must be noted that although the emphasis on territoriality should theoretically open the symbolic border, restricting its use to the paradigm of common origins makes it a tool to prove vertical homogeneity rather than legitimate horizontal solidarity.

The second model identified in the textbooks offers a nonheroic reconstruction of Romanian history, and the representation of the nation as a living entity is completely absent. However, the identity narrative ascribed to the Romanian people is still constructed in terms of descent, and therefore the authors are still very interested in proving the common origins of the Romanian people. Following this line of thought, a textbook published in 2007 emphasizes the Daco-Roman origins of the Romanian people and their formation in Dacia under Trajan's rule.[116] In another example, where the emphasis is on the Roman legacy,[117] we learn that while the German peoples referred to the people living in these territories as *w(a)lach*, "*vlahii* probably called themselves Romanians (*români*), meaning Romans (*romani*)."[118] By bringing together the three denominations in the same sentence, the authors suggest the unitary character of the populations sharing these territories and their common Roman ancestry.

Consequently, in postcommunist Romanian historiography, the identity narrative of the Romanian people is still constructed in ethnic terms, with the emphasis, in the vast majority of the investigated sources, on three things—common origins, unity, and continuity—an approach that constructs the Romanian identity in essentialist terms. The common origins are portrayed in Dacian, Roman, or Daco-Roman terms, while unity is imagined in terms of common language, religion, or territory. Regardless of how these terms are combined, common origins and unity always result in continuity and create a community of belonging from which those who do not share these traits are implicitly excluded.

Brubaker's approach to ethnicity helps us understand the importance of this symbolic construction. According to his interpretation, ethnicity, alongside race and nation, should be analyzed not in terms "of substantial groups of entities but in terms of practical categories, ... cultural idioms, cognitive schemas, discursive frames."[119] Thus, ethnicity is not a thing that exists in the world but a perspective on the world, structuring the principles of vision and division of the world.[120] In other words, ethnicity, though imagined, is not imaginary.[121] When it is the main element used to construct the identity narrative of the in-group, it generates a cognitive perspective shared by those socialized within the community. It becomes the template used to represent and organize social knowledge, to filter and shape "what is noticed and unnoticed, relevant or irrelevant, remembered or forgotten."[122]

Furthermore, ethnicity configures the border between the insiders and the outsiders, and consequently the categories used by social actors to interpret reality. In doing so, it creates the optical lens theorized by Zerubavel, consisting of the fundamental factors that determine what individuals consider to be relevant within their present and what from the past is worthy of being remembered. This prompts a final question: how does the Holocaust of the Romanian Jews fit with this ethnic narrative attributed to the Romanian identity?

Ethnocentric Mindscapes and Mnemonic Myopia

The question that frames this chapter deals with Romanian society's difficulty in acknowledging the persecutions, deportations, and massacres perpetrated against the Jews under Romanian authority during the Second

World War. My theoretical model approaches this question from the perspective of social constructivism, regarding the Holocaust of the Romanian Jews as belonging to the cluster of symbols configuring the symbolic universe assumed within the Romanian social space. As the core of any symbolic universe defines the image ascribed to the in-group, the rest of the items populating the symbolic narrative are configured in ways that are consistent with this primary attribution.

Starting from these presuppositions, my aim was to uncover how this primary attribution functions in the Romanian case and how it aggregates with the perception of the Holocaust. As we have seen, the Romanian identity was traditionally constructed in terms of ethnicity, with the emphasis on common origins, unity, and continuity. Together, these create a community of belonging, understood in essentialist terms, founded on common descent. All of the peoples who arrived later to the territories shared by this community of descent are not really Romanians, though they are granted citizenship. This long-standing tradition of explaining the Romanian identity in essentialist terms enters the realm of taken-for-granted knowledge and creates, as Brubaker explains, a perspective on the world, the template individuals use to decipher reality. It creates the mindscapes shared by those who are socialized within the community, and determines "ethnicized ways of seeing (and ignoring), of constructing (and misconstruing), of inferring (and misinferring), of remembering (and forgetting)."[123]

The upgrading of the ethnic stance specific to the Romanian identity pattern within the domain of taken-for-granted knowledge is best seen in its embedding in the Romanian language, where the term *popor* (people)—theoretically, a term that includes all the citizens of the Romanian state—is in fact synonymous with *neam* (kin) and *națiune* (nation),[124] both of which point toward an idea of common descent and shared consciousness. This ethnic stance determines what Zerubavel calls "sociomental structures" grounded in culturally and historically specific cognitive traditions.[125] These sociomental structures are learned during the process of cognitive socialization and generate specific ways of perceiving, attending, associating, and remembering.[126]

The second explanatory variable of the theoretical model I propose is the dialectical relationship linking social identity and collective memory. Acquiring a group's memories, and in this way identifying with its collective past, is part of any process of acquiring social identity. Those who share the same identity model, and consequently the same mnemonic framework, will also share what Zerubavel calls "free mnemonic associations,"[127] historical landmarks internalized through socialization that create our sense of belonging and provide the tools that symbolically construct the border between us and the Others. The Others are outsiders because they are not part of the mnemonic narrative we share as a group, and they are not to be included within the same mnemonic narrative because of their status as outsiders. In other words, we carry the sociomental structures acquired through socialization within our daily lives, and use them to decipher the events occurring in our present and to remember those from the past of our community. Due to the stability of the cognitive categories, their representations of present and past events will be internally consistent, as will be their ascribed relation to the present and past members of the in-group. Put differently, individuals are prone to find in the past the same categories that are acknowledged in the present, and to approach these categories in similar ways. Consequently, due to this cognitive socialization, we will read participants in past events in terms of "us" and "them," and we will be more interested in learning about the sufferings of our ancestors and less prone to elaborate on the anguish of others.

Within the mnemonic space specific to Romanian society, there are three possible approaches to Jewish suffering during the Second World War: one could consider the war a national catastrophe, and consequently regard the Jews as victims belonging to the Romanian people; one could dissociate from the actions of the Romanian authorities of the time and regard the Jews as victims of the Romanian state; or one could regard the Jews as victims of others.

The ethnocentric mindscapes specific to Romanian historiography exclude the Jews from the community of belonging, and, I would say, this exclusion has consequences for the ways Jewish suffering during the Second World War is remembered or forgotten within Romanian society.

Given the ethnic narrative specific to the Romanian identity, Jews never had the chance to become true Romanians, so they remained a radical Other, unable (or allegedly unwilling) to truly integrate. As they do not really belong to the Romanian people, the Jews are not included in the historical narratives describing the Romanian losses during the Second World

War. As they are not really Romanian, the Jewish victims of the period, though Romanian citizens, are not part of Romanian history, and consequently their memory is conveniently set aside. Put differently, due to the ethnic narrative specific to the Romanian identity, there is no "free mnemonic association" between being Jewish and being a Romanian victim, and so the Holocaust of the Romanian Jews is set aside as not belonging to Romanian history.

Equally important, a second correlation seems to exist between the historiographical discourse that explains community in ethnocentric terms and the distorted recollection of the Holocaust. The old triad of common roots, unity, and continuity creates a historical discourse where the identity narrative ascribed to the Romanian people is constructed in terms of historical continuity. In my opinion, here lies the problem. As it is true that emphasizing common roots provides a sense of belonging, it is equally true that deriving one's identity from one's ancestors is a double-edged sword, since we inherit not only our forefathers' assets but also the liabilities associated with being their descendants, which translates into what Zerubavel calls "guilt by genealogical association."[128]

Zerubavel's conceptualization is fundamental for understanding why the Holocaust becomes in this case a dangerous memory, while Festinger helps us identify how this dangerous memory is dealt with. When common belonging is used to create a sense of community and this community is understood in homogenous terms, the relationship between the present and the past becomes dialectical. Each generation is a replica of former generations; people living today are similar (in different ways) to those who lived in former times, and by proxy, those from the past must have been like us. Consequently, the (hi)story of each generation must remain guiltless so that we do not step into the realm of what Festinger calls cognitive dissonance.

When the identity narrative of the Romanian people is constructed in terms of historical continuity, then our noble origins, our inner Christian core, and our great achievements from the past and the fate of the Romanian Jews during the Second World War become cognitions relevant to each other. They are equally part of the clusters of mnemonic narratives that legitimate the identity model ascribed to the Romanian people. Therefore, as the need for internal consistency operates only between relevant cognitions, the

Holocaust becomes a dangerous memory that is either discarded as irrelevant and thus forgotten, or reconstructed in a manner that does not disturb the special image of the Romanian nation.

During the communist regime the Holocaust was a taboo subject, and the responsibility of the Romanian authorities for the hundreds of thousands of victims was never acknowledged as such. Within this mnemonic narrative the Holocaust was completely absent, an approach that we find in some of the history textbooks edited after 1989 (model A). The authors of the four main syntheses of Romanian history published after 1989 solve the dissonance by reconstructing the events in a manner that diminishes the responsibility of the Romanian authorities for the killing of hundreds of thousands of Jews. According to the narrative proposed by these four historians, there were some discriminatory measures and even deportations, but in Romania there was no Final Solution. While in the rest of Europe Jews were killed in extermination camps, the Romanian authorities solved the "Jewish problem" through emigration; or, in Bucharest a Jewish theater was operating, so Romania could legitimately be labeled "an island of peace and prosperity." A similar emphasis on nonimplementation of the Final Solution is found in some of the history textbooks (model E). In other textbooks, the dissonance is attenuated by ignoring the more problematic decisions taken by the Romanian authorities, by arguing that in Romania there were no deportations (model C), or failing to acknowledge who the victims were (model D). In some textbooks the dissonance is completely eliminated by counting Romania among the countries that saved their Jews (model B).

In a smaller number of the textbooks, although the identity narrative ascribed to the Romanian people is constructed in ethnic terms, this is not accompanied by a continuous reading of history. There is no shared feature to explain Decebal's victories against the Romans, Mircea cel Bătrân's victories against the Ottoman Empire, or Mihai's struggle for territorial unification. Therefore, the victory of Ștefan cel Mare at Podu Înalt and the Holocaust of the Romanian Jews become cognitions irrelevant to each other; they can belong to the same discursive model because between mutually irrelevant cognitions the rule of cognitive consonance does not apply. For the authors of these textbooks, the participation of the Romanian authorities in the anti-Jewish and anti-Roma policies that led to the deaths of hundreds of thousands of children, men, and women is a historical fact (model F) included among those considered to be historically relevant and worthy of collective remembrance.

Revisiting Brubaker's conceptualization of ethnicity, the construction of group identity in ethnic terms proves to be most important for understanding how mnemonic myopia operates, as the ethnic stance conditions the mnemonic narrative associated with the in-group in two distinctive manners. First, the borders of the ethnic community delineate the relevant past, the past worthy to be remembered, and the realm beyond these borders is destined for mnemonic myopia. Second, the past acknowledged for the ethnic community is configured in terms that are consistent with the image ascribed to it. When the community is described in glorious terms, or history is read in a continuous manner, past events are rememorized in ways that do not disturb this special image ascribed to the in-group.

Regarding the perception of the Holocaust in Romania today, the ethnocentric mindscapes used to frame reality, which indicate a deficient historiographic socialization, make Romanian society unable to approach the recent past in an objective manner, and create space for mnemonic myopia. This operates on two levels. On the first level, because the Jews were placed outside of the national community, Jewish suffering during the Second World War is not seen as belonging to Romanian history. Consequently, although the Jews were citizens of the Romanian state, the Holocaust is read as belonging to Jewish history, not Romanian history, and therefore the Holocaust is relegated to the out-of-frame background—to oblivion. Here, an induced vertical dissimilarity works against horizontal solidarity. On the second level, the construction of the Romanian identity in ethnic terms and the reading of history in a continuous manner transform the Romanian people into a transhistoric being that cannot be held guilty of such a crime. In this respect, vertical homogeneity works against horizontal dissimilarity so that no guilt is assigned to the Romanian authorities of the time, in order not to spoil the great image ascribed to the Romanian people.

Consequently, if the Jews cannot be remembered as victims of the Romanian state, or, because they are Romanian citizens, as Romanian victims of the war, only one solution remains: to account for them as victims of some other group. Therefore, consistent with the ethnic narrative of the Romanian identity, Romanian society externalizes this dangerous memory outside its borders, making the Germans responsible for the deaths of the Jews.

Ana Bărbulescu is researcher at the Elie Wiesel National Institute for the Study of the Holocaust in Romania. She is editor of the volume *Munca forțată a evreilor din România* and author of *Evreul înainte și după Cristos. O analiză a genezei anti-iudaismului.*

Notes

1. Institutul Național pentru Studierea Holocaustului din România "Elie Wiesel," "Sondaje." The survey was conducted in May to June 2015 on a national representative sample, maximum sampling error ± 3.0%.
2. See, for example, Ioanid, *Evreii sub regimul Antonescu*; Ancel, *Contribuții la istoria românilor*; Ioanid, *Holocaustul în România*; Ancel, *Distrugerea economică a evreilor români*.
3. See Bărbulescu, "Discovering the Holocaust."
4. See Mureșan et al., *Istorie universală modernă și contemporană, manual pentru clasa a X-a*; Mitu et al., *Istorie, manual pentru clasa a XI-a*; Bușe and Rădulescu, *Istorie, manual pentru clasa a XI-a*; Băluțoiu, *Istorie, manual pentru clasa a XI-a*; Oane and Strat, *Istorie, manual pentru clasa a XI-a*.
5. Mureșan et al., *Istorie universală modernă și contemporană, manual pentru clasa a X-a*.
6. See Ciupercă and Cozma, *Istorie, manual pentru clasa a XI-a*; Ciupercă, Cristian, and Cozma, *Istorie, manual pentru clasa a XI-a*; Cristescu et al., *Istoria românilor—epoca modernă și contemporană, manual pentru clasa a VIII-a*.
7. See Oane and Ochescu, *Istorie, manual pentru clasa a XI-a* or Brezeanu et al., *Istorie, manual pentru clasa a XII-a*.
8. Oane and Ochescu, *Istorie, manual pentru clasa a XI-a*, 103.
9. Ibid., 101.
10. Brezeanu et al., *Istorie, manual pentru clasa a XII-a*, 198.
11. See Manea and Teodorescu, *Istorie, manual pentru clasa a XII-a* or Manea and Teodorescu, *Istoria românilor de la 1821 până în 1989, manual pentru clasa a XII-a*.
12. Manea and Teodorescu, *Istoria românilor de la 1821 până în 1989, manual pentru clasa a XII-a*, 339.
13. See Scurtu et al., *Istoria românilor din cele mai vechi timpuri până astăzi, manual pentru clasa a XII-a*; Barnea et al., *Istorie, manual pentru clasa a X-a*; Oane and Ochescu, *Istorie, manual pentru clasa a VIII-a*; Dumitrescu et al., *Istoria românilor, manual pentru clasa a XII-a*.
14. Dumitrescu et al., *Istoria românilor, manual pentru clasa a XII-a*, 164.
15. Selevet, Stănescu, and Bercea, *Istorie, manual pentru clasa a X-a*; Băluțoiu, *Istorie, manual pentru clasa a X-a*; Stan and Vornicu, *Istorie, manual pentru clasa a XI-a*; Petre et al., *Istorie, manual pentru clasa a XII-a*.
16. Constantiniu, *O istorie sinceră*, 382, 385, 392, 397.
17. Ibid., 411.
18. Djuvara, *O scurtă istorie a românilor*, 221.
19. Ibid., 222.
20. Ibid.
21. Ibid., 173.

22. Dinu C. Giurescu, *Istoria românilor*, 397.
23. Ibid., 398.
24. Ibid., 425.
25. Ibid. 437.
26. Ibid., 399, 447.
27. Ibid., 446.
28. Ibid., 448.
29. Pop, *Istoria românilor*, 166.
30. Ibid., 167.
31. Ibid., 168.
32. Ibid.
33. Halbawchs, *On Collective Memory*, 22. See also Gillis, "Memory and Identity: The History of a Relationship," 3.
34. Schutz, *The Phenomenology of the Social World*, 114.
35. Zerubavel, *Social Mindscapes*, 33.
36. Zerubavel, *The Fine Line*, 2.
37. Zerubavel, *Social Mindscapes*, 9.
38. Goodman, *Ways of Worldmaking*, 8.
39. Zerubavel, *Social Mindscapes*, 72.
40. Brubaker, *Ethnicity without Groups*, 80.
41. Festinger, *A Theory of Cognitive Dissonance*, 1.
42. Ibid., 13.
43. Ibid., 6–7. See also Cooper, *Cognitive Dissonance*, 6.
44. Cooper, *Cognitive Dissonance*, 8.
45. Festinger, *A Theory of Cognitive Dissonance*, 3.
46. Douglas, *Rules and Meanings*, 249.
47. Zerubavel, *Social Mindscapes*, 81.
48. Zerubavel, *Ancestors and Relatives*, 10.
49. Zerubavel, *Time Maps*, 27. See also Zerubavel, *Social Mindscapes*, 87.
50. Irwin-Zarecka, *Frames of Remembrance*, 118.
51. Assmann, "Europe's Divided Memory," 38.
52. Iordachi and Trencsényi, "In Search of a Usable Past: The Question of National Identity in Romanian Studies, 1990–2000," 419.
53. For the conflicts generated by the union after 1918 see, for example, Livezeanu, *Cultural Politics in Greater Romania*.
54. The locals were either killed (see, for example, Bălcescu, "Românii sub Mihai Voevod Viteazul," 12) or they fled after the Roman conquest (see, for example, Maior, *Istoria pentru începuturile românilor în Dachia*, 98–109, 146).
55. This second identity narrative makes the Romanians the direct descendants of the Dacians, and Dacia becomes the cradle of this specific civilization. The main proponent of this narrative was Nicolae Densușianu, whose volume *Dacia preistorică* (Prehistoric Dacia) became and has remained the main textbook of Dacist autochthonism.
56. Here, the Romanians are neither entirely Dacians nor Romans, but an original combination of the two. For some authors, the ancestries are equally weighted (see Petriceicu Hașdeu, "Pierit-au dacii?," 78–106), whereas for others, the Roman ancestry is more valorized (Tocilescu, *Manual de istoria românilor*, 22, 34; Xenopol, *Istoria românilor*

din Dacia Traiană, 163, 307). The two main historians of the first half of the twentieth century, Nicolae Iorga and Vasile Pârvan, opt for this third model to explain the origins of the Romanian people. For Iorga, the Roman element was more powerful, while for Pârvan, both ethnic legacies are equally weighted. See Iorga, *Istoria românilor pentru poporul românesc*, 16, 26, and Pârvan, *Dacia*, 150–151.

57. See, for example, Petriceicu Hașdeu, *Istoria critică a românilor*, 278–281. For the same conclusion, see Iorga, *Istoria românilor pentru poporul românesc*, 33, and Constantin C. Giurescu, *Istoria românilor*, 247, 260.

58. Mihai Eminescu's emphasis on the genius of the Romanian people (Cf. Panu, *Amintiri de la Junimea din Iași*, 99–100) or Vasile Conta's racial approach—we have the same blood, and consequently we share the same beliefs, feelings and ideas—are just two examples of this development.

59. Iorga, *Istoria poporului românesc*, 9.
60. Rădulescu-Motru, *Etnicul românesc*, 35.
61. Blaga, *Spațiul mioritic*, 165–166.
62. Ibid., 429.
63. Petrescu and Petrescu, "Mastering vs. Coming to Terms with the Past," 315.
64. See *Programul Partidului Comunist Român*.
65. Petrescu and Petrescu, "Mastering vs. Coming to Terms with the Past," 316.
66. Ibid., 317.
67. Marinescu and Tănase, *Conștiința națională și valorile patriei*, 206.
68. Rebedeu, "Cu privire la fizionomia spirituală a națiunii," 316.
69. As Cristian Roiban proves, the problem of ethnic minorities was solved by the invention of a specific concept—"the patriotic national conscience" (*conștiința națională patriotică*)—that circumscribes "the feelings, ideals, and aspirations common to all working class, irrespectively of their nationality, of our entire people." It is an all-inclusive concept, a sum of feelings shared by "the nation and all co-inhabiting nationalities (*naționalități conlocuitoare*)." See Roiban, *Ideologie și istoriografie: Protocronismul*, 270.

70. Constantiniu, *O istorie sinceră*, 46.
71. Ibid., 53.
72. Ibid., 49.
73. Djuvara, *O scurtă istorie a românilor*, 1, 4.
74. Ibid., 2.
75. Ibid., 31.
76. Ibid., 8.
77. Ibid., 4.
78. Ibid., 26–28.
79. Ibid., 167.
80. Ibid., 173.
81. Ibid., 169–170.
82. Ibid., 173.
83. Niculescu, "Archaeology and Nationalism in the History of the Romanians," 237–238.
84. Protase, "Romanizarea," 159.
85. Ibid.
86. Ibid., 160.

87. Ibid., 165.
88. Protase, "Sfârșitul stăpânirii romane în Dacia. Retragerea aureliană. Cauze și consecințe," 267.
89. Ioniță, "Populația locală în secolul al IV-lea în regiunile extra-carpatice," 604.
90. Ibid., 603.
91. Pop, *Istoria românilor*, 10.
92. Ibid., 11.
93. Ibid., 13, 25.
94. Ibid., 26–27.
95. Ibid., 42.
96. Ibid., 27.
97. Ibid., 160.
98. Manea, Pascu and Teodorescu, *Istoria românilor din cele mai vechi timpuri până la revoluția de la 1821, manual pentru clasa a XI-a*, 5.
99. Ibid., 229.
100. Ibid., 298. See also Dumitrescu et al., 42.
101. Ibid., 53.
102. Băluțoiu and Grecu, *Istorie*, 10.
103. Scurtu et al., *Istoria românilor din cele mai vechi timpuri până astăzi, manual pentru clasa a XII-a*, 30.
104. Oane and Ochescu, *Istorie*, 36.
105. Oane and Strat, *Istorie*, 15. For a similar idea, see Oane and Ochescu, *Istorie, manual pentru clasa a XI-a*, 143.
106. Zerubavel, *Time Maps*, 40.
107. Ibid.
108. Oane and Strat, *Istorie, manual pentru clasa a XI-a*, 15; Manea, Pascu and Teodorescu, *Istoria românilor din cele mai vechi timpuri până la revoluția de la 1821, manual pentru clasa a XI-a*, 5.
109. Oane and Ochescu, *Istorie, manual pentru clasa a VIII-a*, 21.
110. Scurtu et al., *Istoria românilor din cele mai vechi timpuri până astăzi, manual pentru clasa a XII-a*, 6.
111. Dumitrescu et al., *Istoria românilor, manual pentru clasa a XII-a*, 37.
112. Manea, Pascu and Teodorescu, *Istoria românilor din cele mai vechi timpuri până la 1821, manual pentru clasa a XI-a*, 259.
113. Dumitrescu et al., *Istoria românilor, manual pentru clasa a XII-a*, 39.
114. Oane and Ochescu, *Istorie, manual pentru clasa a VIII-a*, 72.
115. Zerubavel, *Time Maps*, 40–41.
116. Barnea et al., *Istorie, manual pentru clasa a XII-a*, 9.
117. Petre et al., *Istorie*.
118. Ibid., 7.
119. Brubaker, *Ethnicity without Groups*, 11.
120. Brubaker, *Grounds for Difference*, 81.
121. Jenkins, *Social Identity*, 123.
122. Brubaker, *Ethnicity without Groups*, 81.
123. Ibid., 16.
124. See Neumann, "Neam și popor: noțiunile etnocentrismului românesc," 384, 389.

125. Zerubavel, *Social Mindscapes*, 113.
126. Ibid.
127. Zerubavel, *Time Maps*, 3.
128. Zerubavel, *Ancestors and Relatives*, 25.

References

Ancel, Jean. *Contribuții la istoria românilor. Problema evreiască 1933–1944*. Bucharest: Hasefer, 2003.
———. *Distrugerea economică a evreilor români*. Bucharest: INSHR–EW, 2008.
Assmann, Aleida. "Europe's Divided Memory." In *Memory and Theory in Eastern Europe*, edited by Uilleam Blacker, Alexander Etkind, and Julie Fedor, 25–41. New York: Palgrave Macmillan, 2013.
Barnea, Alexandru, Vasile Manea, Eugen Palade, Mihai Stămătescu, and Bogdan Teodorescu. *Istorie, manual pentru clasa a X-a*. Bucharest: Corint, 2005.
———. *Istorie, manual pentru clasa a X-a*. Bucharest: Corint, 2008.
Barnea, Alexandru, Vasile Manea, Eugen Palade, Bogdan Teodorescu. *Istorie, manual pentru clasa a XII-a*. Bucharest: Corint, 2014.
Bălcescu, Nicolae. *Românii sub Mihai Voevod Viteazul*. Bucharest: Litera Internațional, 1998.
Băluțoiu, Valentin. *Istorie, manual pentru clasa a XI-a*. Bucharest: Editura Didactică și Pedagogică, 2000, 2012.
———. *Istorie, manual pentru clasa a X-a*. Bucharest: Editura Didactică și Pedagogică, 2005, 2012.
Bărbulescu, Ana. "Discovering the Holocaust in Our Past: Competing Memories in Post-Communist Romanian Textbooks." *Holocaust Studies* 21, no. 3 (2015): 139–156.
Blaga, Lucian. *Spațiul mioritic*. Bucharest: Humanitas, 1994.
Brezeanu, Stelian, Adrian Cioroianu, Florin Müller, Sorin Rădulescu, and Mihai Retegan. *Istorie, manual pentru clasa a XII-a*. Bucharest: RAO Educational, 1999.
Brubaker, Rogers. *Ethnicity without Groups*. Cambridge, MA: Harvard University Press, 2004.
———. *Grounds for Difference*. Cambridge, MA: Harvard University Press, 2015.
Bușe, Constantin, and Sorin Rădulescu. *Istorie, manual pentru clasa a XI-a*. Bucharest: All Educational, 2000.
Ciupercă, Ioan, and Elena Cozma. *Istorie, manual pentru clasa a XI-a*. Bucharest: Corint, 2001.
Ciupercă, Ioan, V. Cristian, and Elena Cozma. *Istorie, manual pentru clasa a XI-a*. Bucharest: Corint, 2006.
Constantiniu, Florin. *O istorie sinceră a poporului român*. Bucharest: Editura Univers Enciclopedic, 2008.
Conta, Vasile. *Opere complecte*. Bucharest: Editura C. Sfetea Librăria Școalelor, 1914.
Cooper, Joel. *Cognitive Dissonance: Fifty Years of a Classic Theory*. New York: Sage, 2007.
Crainic, Nichifor. *Ortodoxie și etnocrație*. Bucharest: Cugetarea, 1937.
Cristescu, Octavian, Vasile Păsăilă, Bogdan Teodorescu, and Raluca Tomi. *Istoria românilor—epoca modernă și contemporană, manual pentru clasa a VIII-a*. Bucharest: Editura Didactică și Pedagogică, 1992, 1994, 1995, 1998.

Densușianu, Nicolae. *Dacia preistorică*. Bucharest: Institutul de Arte Grafice Carol Göbl, 1913.
Djuvara, Neagu. *O scurtă istorie a românilor povestită celor tineri*. Bucharest: Humanitas, 2002.
Douglas, Mary. *Rules and Meanings: The Anthropology of Everyday Knowledge*. London: Routledge, 2003.
Dumitrescu, Nicoleta, Mihai Manea, Cristian Niță, Adrian Pascu, Aurel Trandafir, and Mădălina Trandafir. *Istoria românilor, manual pentru clasa a XII-a*. Bucharest: Humanitas Educational, 2000.
Eliade, Mircea. *Les Roumains. Précis historique*. Bucharest: Roza Vânturilor, 1992.
Eminescu, Mihai. *Opere*, vol. 9: Publicistica, 1870–1877, Bucharest: Editura Academiei Republicii Socialiste România, 1980.
Festinger, Leon. *A Theory of Cognitive Dissonance*. Stanford, CA: Stanford University Press, 1962.
Gillis, John. "Memory and Identity: The History of a Relationship." In *Commemorations: The Politics of National Identity*, edited by John Gillis, 3–25. Princeton, NJ: Princeton University Press, 1994.
Giurescu, C. Constantin. *Istoria românilor*, vol. 1. Bucharest: Fundația Regală pentru Literatură și Artă, 1946.
Giurescu, Dinu C. *Istoria românilor*, vol. 9, *România în anii 1940–1947*. Bucharest: Editura Enciclopedică, 2008.
Goodman, Nelson. *Ways of Worldmaking*. Indianapolis, IN: Hackett, 1978.
Halbawchs, Maurice. *On Collective Memory*. Chicago: University of Chicago Press, 1992.
Hitchins, Keith. "Orthodoxism: Polemics over Ethnicity and Religion in Interwar Romania." In *National Character and National Ideology in Interwar Eastern Europe*, edited by Ivo Banac and Katherine Verdery, 135–156. New Haven, CT: Yale Center for International and Areas Studies, 1995.
Institutul Național pentru Studierea Holocaustului din România "Elie Wiesel." "Sondaje." Accessed January 15, 2016. http://www.inshr-ew.ro/ro/proiecte/sondaje.html.
Ioanid, Radu. *Evreii sub regimul Antonescu*. Bucharest: Hasefer, 1997.
———. *Holocaustul în România: distrugerea evreilor și romilor sub regimul Antonescu. 1940–1944*. Bucharest: Hasefer, 2006.
Ioniță, I. "Populația locală în secolul al IV-lea în regiunile extra-carpatice." In *Istoria românilor*, vol. 2, *Daco-romani, Romanici, Alogeni*, edited by Dumitru Protase and Alexandru Suceveanu, 617–637. Bucharest: Editura Enciclopedică, 2001.
Iordachi, Constantin, and Balázs Trencsényi. "In Search of a Usable Past: The Question of National Identity in Romanian Studies, 1990–2000." *East-European Politics and Societies* 17(2003): 415–453.
Iorga, Nicolae. *Istoria poporului românesc*, vol. 1. Bucharest: Editura Casei Școalelor, 1922.
———. *Istoria românilor pentru poporul românesc*, vol. 1. Bucharest: Editura Minerva, 1993.
Irwin-Zarecka, Iwona. *Frames of Remembrance: The Dynamics of Collective Memory*. New Brunswick, NJ: Transactions, 2009.
Jenkins, Richard. *Social Identity*. London: Routledge, 2004.
Livezeanu, Irina. *Cultural Politics in Greater Romania: Regionalism, Nation Building, and Ethnic Struggle, 1918–1930*. Ithaca, NY: Cornell University Press, 2000.

Maior, Petru. *Istoria pentru începuturile românilor în Dachia*, vol. 1. Bucharest: Albatros, 1970.
Manea, Mihai, Adrian Pascu, and Bogdan Teodorescu. *Istoria românilor din cele mai vechi timpuri până la revoluția de la 1821, manual pentru clasa a XI-a*. Bucharest: Editura Didactică și Pedagogică, 1996.
Manea, Mihai, and Bogdan Teodorescu. *Istoria românilor de la 1821 până la 1989, manual pentru clasa a XII-a*. Bucharest: Editura Didactică și Pedagogică, 1998.
———. *Istorie, manual pentru clasa a XII-a*. Bucharest: Editura Didactică și Pedagogică, 1995.
Marinescu, Gheorghe. *Națiunea și conștiința națională în lumea contemporană*. Iași, Romania: Junimea, 1986.
Marinescu, Gheorghe, and Alexandru Tănase. *Conștiința națională și valorile patriei*. Iași, Romania: Junimea, 1986.
Mitu, Sorin, Lucia Copoeru, Ovidiu Pecican, Virgiliu Țârău, and Liviu Țîrău. *Istoria românilor, manual pentru clasa a XII-a*. Bucharest: Sigma, 2000.
———. *Istorie, manual pentru clasa a XI-a*. Bucharest: Sigma, 1999.
Mureșan, Camil, Vasile Cristian, Vasile Vesa, and Eugen Vârgolici. *Istorie universală modernă și contemporană, manual pentru clasa a X-a*. Bucharest: Editura Didactică și Pedagogică, 1993, 1995, 1996, 1998.
Neumann, Victor. "Neam și popor: noțiunile etnocentrismului românesc." In *Istoria României prin concepte*, edited by Victor Neumann and Armin Heinen, 379–400. Iași, Romania: Polirom, 2010.
Niculescu, Gheorghe Alexandru. "Archaeology and Nationalism in the History of the Romanians." In *Selective Remembrance: Archaeology in the Construction, Commemoration, and Consecration of National Past*, edited by Philip L. Kohl, Mara Kozelsky, and Nahman Ben-Yehuda, 127–159. Chicago: University of Chicago Press, 2007.
Oane, Sorin, and Maria Ochescu. *Istorie, manual pentru clasa a VIII-a*. Bucharest: Humanitas Educational, 2000, 2012.
———. *Istorie, manual pentru clasa a XI-a*. Bucharest: Humanitas Educational, 2000.
Oane, Sorin, and Cătălin Strat. *Istorie, manual pentru clasa a XI-a*. Bucharest: Humanitas Educational, 2006.
Panu, George. *Amintiri de la Junimea din Iași*, vol. 1. Bucharest: Editura Remus Cioflec, 1942.
Pârvan, Vasile. *Dacia*. Bucharest: Editura Științifică, 1972.
Petre, Zoe, Carol Căpiță, Alin Ciupală, Ecaterina Stănescu, Florin Țurcanu, Ecaterina Lung, Laurențiu Vlad, Ligia Livadă-Cadeschi, and Sorin Andreescu. *Istorie, manual pentru clasa a XII-a*. Bucharest: Corint, 2007.
Petrescu, Cristina, and Dragoș Petrescu. "Mastering vs. Coming to Terms with the Past: A Critical Analysis of Post-Communist Romanian Historiography." In *Narratives Unbound: Historical Studies in Post-Communist Eastern Europe*, edited by Sorin Antohi, Balász Trencsényi, and Péter Apor, 311–408. Budapest: CEU Press, 2007.
Petriceicu Hașdeu, Bogdan. *Istoria critică a românilor*, vol. 1. Bucharest: Imprimeria Națională, 1873.
———. "Pierit-au dacii?" In *Scrieri istorice*, vol. 1, edited by Aurelian Sacerdoțeanu, 78–106. Bucharest: Albatros, 1973.
Pop, Ioan Aurel. *Istoria românilor*. Chișinău, Moldova: Litera, 2010.

Programul Partidului Comunist Român de făurire a societății socialiste multilateral dezvoltate și înaintare a României spre comunism. Bucharest: Editura Politică, 1975.

Protase, Dumitru. "Romanizarea." In *Istoria românilor*, vol. 2, *Daco-romani, Romanici, Alogeni*, edited by Dumitru Protase and Alexandru Suceveanu, 159–168. Bucharest: Editura Enciclopedică, 2001.

———. "Sfârșitul stăpânirii romane în Dacia. Retragerea aureliană. Cauze și consecințe." In *Istoria românilor*, vol. 2, *Daco-romani, Romanici, Alogeni*, edited by Dumitru Protase and Alexandru Suceveanu, 263–272. Bucharest: Editura Enciclopedică, 2001.

Rădulescu-Motru, Constantin. *Etnicul românesc, comunitate de origine, limbă și destin; Naționalismul, cum se înțelege și cum trebuie să se înțeleagă.* Bucharest: Editura Albatros, 1996.

Rebedeu, Ion. "Cu privire la fizionomia spirituală a națiunii." In *Națiunea și contemporaneitatea*, edited by Ioan Ceterchi, Damian Hurezean, and Eleonora Nechita, 273–320. Bucharest: Editura Științifică, 1971.

Roiban, Cristian. *Ideologie și istoriografie: Protocronismul.* Timișoara, Romania: Editura Universității de Vest, 2014.

Schutz, Alfred. *The Phenomenology of the Social World.* Evanston, IL: Northwestern University Press, 1967.

Scurtu, Ioan, Marian Curculescu, Constantin Dincă, and Aurel C. Soare. *Istoria românilor din cele mai vechi timpuri până azi, manual pentru clasa a XII-a.* Bucharest: Petrion, 1999, 2000.

Selevet, Mihaela, Ecaterina Stănescu, and Marilena Bercea. *Istorie, manual pentru clasa a X-a.* Bucharest: Corint, 2002, 2008.

Stan, Magda, and Cristian Vornicu. *Istorie, manual pentru clasa a XI-a.* Bucharest: Niculescu, 2007.

Tocilescu, Grigore. *Manual de istoria românilor.* Bucharest: Tipografia Corpului Didactic C. Ispănescu & G. Brătănescu, 1899.

Xenopol, D. Alexandru. *Istoria românilor din Dacia Traiană*, vol. 1. Iași, Romania: H. Goldner, 1888.

Zerubavel, Eviatar. *Ancestors and Relatives: Genealogy, Identity, and Community.* New York: Oxford University Press, 2012.

———. *The Fine Line: Making Distinctions in Everyday Life.* Chicago: University of Chicago Press, 1993.

———. *Social Mindscapes: An Invitation to Cognitive Sociology.* Cambridge, MA: Harvard University Press, 1999.

———. *Time Maps: Collective Memory, and the Social Shape of the Past.* Chicago: University of Chicago Press, 2003.

Chapter Two

POSTCOMMUNIST ROMANIA'S LEADING PUBLIC INTELLECTUALS AND THE HOLOCAUST

George Voicu

The Subject of Research

How do Romania's most influential intellectuals after 1989 relate to the Holocaust in general and to its Romanian chapter in particular? Given the powerful impact of their views on the public opinion in the country, one could say that the answer to such a question unveils to a great extent the very foundation of the social perception of the catastrophe experienced by the European Jews during the Second World War. Undeniably, this preliminary assumption does not simply imply a cause-effect relationship between those who articulate the mainstream public discourse and the larger society to which they belong; in many respects, those who shape society are, in their turn, shaped themselves—by intellectual traditions or paradigms, by commonplace representations, some of which unconscious, and sometimes by the very expectations of those whom the opinion makers address—but, all in all, the balance of influences leans nevertheless toward the major opinion leaders.

Undoubtedly, any attempt to identify the public intellectuals with the strongest impact on public opinion can always be questioned, for this exercise seems to involve a value judgment, something that automatically triggers disagreements. In order to prevent such susceptibilities, at least partially, it must be stated from the very beginning that the first reasonable criterion by which these intellectual figures can be identified is their social perception. In other words, this criterion is related to the echoes generated by their public interventions and, ultimately, by the degree to which they succeed in shaping public opinion. Certainly, to a large extent, a major impact has to do with Romanians' nearly unanimous value judgments—overwhelmingly positive and sometimes superlative—of the works of these authors who have assumed the position of public intellectuals, as these pave the way for their opinions to have social effects. This might explain why the most prominent public intellectuals are also perceived as forming Romania's intellectual elite, a title granted to them by numerous media sources and accepted—and sometimes claimed—by those concerned.

Therefore, one can identify several personalities who in recent decades have acquired considerable social prestige, which has made them influential, both socially and politically. From this perspective, the intellectual triumvirate Andrei Pleșu–Gabriel Liiceanu–Horia-Roman Patapievici already enjoys a privileged place on the Romanian cultural map of the last quarter of a century. In addition to these philosophers, there is also a host of writers, led by Nicolae Manolescu, the literary critic and historian who is also the president of the Romanian Writers' Union. Various groups of intellectuals who emigrated from Romania during the communist period also enjoy a special place in this circle, such as the Parisian group, with Monica Lovinescu and Virgil Ierunca at the forefront (who, while both no longer among us, continue to influence through their works the public opinion in the country), and the American group, with Vladimir Tismăneanu as the most visible intellectual figure. Certainly, there are others, but Romanian public intellectuals remain an elitist club, small in numbers.

This deserves an explanation. Indisputably "voted in," these intellectuals seem to have organized in a distinct and inaccessible—or exclusivist—social body that exists and functions according to its own set of internal norms and conditions. Among these, the mutual recognition of the members' value seems to be decisive (a veto from one member is sufficient to block the accession of a newcomer). In addition, the members of this circle must have conducted themselves in a certain way before 1990, espousing outspoken anticommunism (for those who resided outside Romania), or at least a discernible resistance—even if only symbolic—to the ideological constraints of that time (for those who resided inside Romania). After the fall of the communist regime, their postcommunist anticommunism had to have become unrestrained and unshakable, omnipresent and intransigent, even visceral. Surely, there are other conditions of membership, including a certain group loyalty that must have passed the test of time. To summarize, the circle of prominent Romanian public intellectuals behaves like a club with closed membership; that is why accession to this group took a long time for some people, such as Vladimir Tismăneanu, who was suspected for a long time of not meeting the "membership requirements" and who, even today, may not be considered a full member. For all these reasons, the circle of prominent Romanian intellectuals remains small. (This might explain why important Romanian opinion makers such as Ion Cristoiu and Cristian Tudor Popescu remain outside.)

There is one more aspect that deserves closer inspection: while this club is very exclusivist, it attracts many "satellites" who gravitate in orbits at various distances from the center. They tend to align themselves to the positions of the established intellectual figures, just as iron filings align to a magnet, especially in the political and social matters deemed sensitive. Because the top intellectuals of contemporary Romanian culture are perceived not only as epistemic authorities but also as possessors of important resources and as reliable launching pads, the considerable number of kindred spirits is understandable. Among this host of intellectuals orbiting the nucleus, some have established profiles (such as Gheorghe Grigurcu and Mircea Mihăieș), others are at the beginning of their careers, eager to ingratiate themselves with the top Romanian public intellectuals. All in all, most of those who publish at the Humanitas publishing house, in magazines such as *Revista 22* (Magazine 22) and *România literară* (Literary Romania), or in other periodicals under the patronage of the Romanian Writers' Union such as *Acolada* (The Accolade) and *Orizont* (The Horizon), in *Dilema veche* (The Old Dilemma), and sometimes even in some of the daily newspapers such as *Evenimentul zilei* (The Story of the Day), and on various electronic platforms (contributors.ro or inliniedreapta.net, for example), most of these authors usually (with some exceptions) serve "the cause" of those considered to be the leading public intellectuals.

Once this outer orbit is taken into account, the contours of the map of the intellectuals who matter to public opinion become much more uncertain;

now, it is not just the narrow circle outlined above, but also its rearguard, which is considerable in numbers. In their public expressions, they act as the "spokespersons" of the top intellectuals. They are, in a sense, extensions of the presence and position of the inner circle. This situation compels us, as we examine the social effects of the positions adopted by the leading public intellectuals, to also keep in mind those from the secondary echelons.

With such a "mechanism" in place (whereby a few personalities set the course, which is immediately assumed by a cohort of voluntary columnists), these public intellectuals exert a considerable cultural influence on Romanian society. Despite the criticism coming from outside this intellectual perimeter, which in many cases proved to be inconsistent (with the critics calling the leading public intellectuals, sometimes ironically, "the elite"), their role in the postcommunist period never diminished; on the contrary. And their significant influence can be detected in many debates, including the one regarding the Holocaust.

Nonetheless, it should be noted that in intellectual debates in postcommunist Romania, the Holocaust was not a distinct subject of reflection or research, even if it was—and still is—one of the most sensitive. References by the intellectual elite to the tragedy of European and Romanian Jews during the Second World War, while numerous—and sometimes even abundant—originated from another debate: the one about communism and the horrors of the political regimes of communist origin. Usually, comparative references to Nazism, fascism, legionarism, and the Holocaust tend to appear once the debate touches upon the crimes of communism. In most cases, intellectuals' interpretations of the Holocaust emerge during this debate. This consequent, even reactive situation has left its mark on the public representation of the Holocaust. This status, secondary where reflection and research are concerned (yet very significant), is responsible for the simplifications and distortions in the public portrayal of the terrible Jewish tragedy, as it constantly sacrificed and ignored the identity traits of the Holocaust.

In 2002 Gabriel Liiceanu summarized quite accurately the state of mind of the majority that today forms the core of the Romanian public intelligentsia when dealing with the great tragedy of the European Jews during the Second World War:

Is it really that hard to understand that you must first deal with *the evil that you knew*, which disrupted your life, hijacked your history, and whose consequences you cannot escape even after a decade since its exit from the stage? And that only through an analogy with this one you can understand *all* the shapes of evil, and you can open up towards a suffering that you would have otherwise found harder to understand? My way to Shoah goes through the trauma of communism, and precisely for this reason I can look at any Jew—with his fears, hatred, and memory of the suffering of his people—as a brother of mine. Is it that much to expect a symmetrical treatment?[1]

In more than twenty-five years of debates about communism, all too often there has been an irresistible pull toward drawing a parallel with the Holocaust, and each time the debate has concluded that the crimes of the communism were at least as serious, but for ignoble reasons they are overlooked or even absolved. Sometimes this frustration that the crimes of communism have been downgraded leads to a conditional recognition of the Holocaust.

Within these parallels, according to the adopted strategy and especially the outcome, one can detect two solutions. The first one, by far the most common in public discourse, is that where the crimes of communism are weighed against the Holocaust in accordance with a strictly equalizing logic, the conclusion is always the same: the Holocaust and the Gulag are the same, as there is nothing essential that differentiates them. Second, in the postcommunist intellectual landscape it is not unusual to find attempts to rank the two destructive phenomena in terms of gravity and drama and conclude that the "absolute evil" is to be found in communism. From the outset, it must be said that these two approaches have a lot in common, and that the boundary separating them is in many cases difficult to establish; what sets them apart, ultimately, is the different emphases in their conclusions.

Communism = Fascism; Holocaust = Gulag

The attempt to place the two totalitarian ideologies of the twentieth century and their criminal outcomes on the same historical, political, and memorial level seems to be the common denominator of those who belong to the circle of leading public intellectuals in Romania.

However, this effort is not confined to the members of this circle. The idea that in recent history there was another destructive phenomenon no less serious that the Holocaust is all too prevalent in the intellectual circles of present-day Romania. Beginning in the 1990s the notion of a "red Holocaust" (or a "communist Holocaust") was forged in order to establish—including at the level of terminology—the similarity of the two tragedies.[2] The concept of Holocaust, specific to the history of European Jews (and Roma people and other social categories), was thus extracted from its customary register and used to define a different historical experience with its own specific traits. Leon Volovici rightfully condemned the abusive use of this concept as an attempt to "usurp" and undermine a symbol specific to the history of European Jews.[3] As many of those who use the term "red Holocaust" (and other terms along the same lines, such as "the Holocaust of Romanian culture" and "the Holocaust of Romanian people") do so with antisemitic rancor, claiming that the authors of this "Holocaust" are none other than the Jews, the reason for the hijacking of the term becomes clear: to place the blame on Jews and to manufacture an alternate history.[4]

It should be noted that the intelligentsia at the top of Romanian culture does not use the expression "red Holocaust" systematically, but rather accidentally. Gabriela Adameșteanu and Rodica Palade, for instance, once considered this syntagma an innocent "metaphor" that could be used legitimately and fruitfully in the debate about the crimes of the communist regime.[5] However, the two journalists—who at the time they supported this syntagma were at the helm of *Revista 22*—did not use the expression in later publications. From time to time, the syntagma was used by other intellectuals, too,[6] but most of them have recognized its traps and intentions. Yet, while it is no longer part of their usual vocabulary, something of its spirit is still present in the positions they adopt.

Before we explore these potential affinities in more detail, it should be noted that virtually all members of the prestigious circle of public intelligentsia of postcommunist Romania see no major differences between what happened at Auschwitz, Belzec, Buchenwald, and Majdanek and what happened in the camps and colonies of the Gulag; rather, they see them as fully equal, or if not so, then perfectly equivalent. Consequently, the crimes committed would have shared the same ideological grounds in both totalitarian systems. Any attempt to distinguish between the two destructive phenomena would be—according to the proponents of this theory—prone to failure. This representation of the ostensibly identical exterminatory finality of the two totalitarian systems can be found in a large number of cases. The Romanian intellectuals' plea to place the two series of crimes on equal footing often takes a self-glorifying rhetorical form, with those concerned depicting themselves—or being depicted by their supporters—as having the courage to defy a dogma. In one of her diaries, Monica Lovinescu, who played a major role in establishing the landmarks of this debate, mentioned her tireless and courageous fight to place the two phenomena—the Holocaust and the communist crimes—"on the same level of horror," proudly claiming that she thus "broke the taboo of the uniqueness of the Shoah," and promising that she will continue to do so.[7]

If the destructive effects of fascism and communism are deemed to be identical, this would be the result of their profound ideological affinities, which would ostensibly blur their distinctions or make them superfluous. For instance, not even the criterion of antisemitism would be sufficient to make a pertinent differentiation between the two ideologies, given that—as Nicolae Manolescu, referencing Marx's atheism, which sometimes took the form of anti-Judaism, pointed out—the founder of communism was himself an antisemite, a position adopted by his followers (such as Stalin and Ceaușescu).[8] His opinion is shared by Andrei Pleșu, for whom the author of *Das Kapital* exhibited "radical forms of antisemitism."[9] In addition, according to the same author, Hitler and Mussolini learned a great deal from Soviet communism (which might be accepted to a certain extent, but not affirmed in absolute terms). Previously, Manolescu had expressed his view that not even the criterion of racism was revealing enough to distinguish between Nazism and Stalinism, given that "just like Hitler, Stalin was racist."[10] Even Vladimir Tismăneanu voiced his conviction that the term "racism" applies equally to both totalitarian ideologies, one of which exhibits a "biological racism," the other a "social racism."[11] Such jugglery with terminology was undoubtedly meant to demonstrate that what is defining for Nazism, namely its racist credo, is also applicable to communism, thus erasing one of the fundamental distinctions between the two ideologies with a simple act of lexical manipulation.

The profound similarities between the two—which would presumably make any differentiation undesirable—are often explained by invoking their common origin, as communism and fascism are considered kindred systems. In order to demonstrate this deep kinship, the leading intellectuals of Romanian culture often use in their discourse a metaphor coined by prestigious intellectuals (Hannah Arendt and François Furet) that they consider to be deeply persuasive, calling the two totalitarian ideologies "twins." Adopting this figure of speech, Horia-Roman Patapievici argued that communism and fascism "are twins because they originated from the same idea, namely from the radical revolutionary socialism of the late 19th century and early 20th century."[12] The fact that the leader of the Italian fascist movement, Benito Mussolini, had initially been a socialist, and the fact that the name of Hitler's party included terms of the left ("socialist" and "workers") seem to him irrefutable arguments of the deep resemblance of the two totalitarianisms and the ideologies that animated them. Some intellectuals, not satisfied with the twins metaphor, have advanced even more radical tropes such as "Siamese twins" and "genocidal twins."[13]

For the most visible intellectuals of contemporary Romania, there is no substantive difference between fascism and communism, but rather resemblance, compatibility, or even complementarity. Moreover, the end was the same in both cases: criminal. Consequently, to consider communism as different from fascism is a terrible mistake and one that goes against historical evidence, as Mircea Mihăieș pointed out, given that "it is one and the same phenomenon, the same ideological and resentful 'devilish inciting' that was spitting fire from twin guns," resulting in "the perfect political and practical overlapping of the two biggest ideologically motivated killings of the 20th century."[14] Mihăieș, the author of the "Contrafort" section of *România literară* (Literary Romania), went on with his indictment, attacking those who obstinately continue to see an opposition between the two ideologies, and revealing the careerist and ignoble motives that push them to such an antithesis:

The myth of "anti-fascism" vs. "pro-communism" still functions in Romanian society. Lucrative academic, journalistic, and political careers are still being forged on the basis of the huge diversion—in fact, an ideological fraud of planetary proportions—according to which the two political formulas that gave expression to populist and authoritarian collectivism, deeply rooted in the mystique of the providential leader, would somehow be antithetical. Not even close. Even from a distance, they seem complementary, and, if you have enough guts to go down and analyze the political practice, you will see that they are as alike as two droplets of water. The Romanian version of Stalinism, whose representatives still continue to play important roles—directly or through the cohorts of protégées and former doctoral students—exhibited the exact same methods as fascism. And vice versa. The hate between the tags hanging on the militants' chests came from the inevitable competition over resources, group particularities, and professions. Otherwise, they were identical.[15]

When formulating this idea, Mihăieş claimed to have faithfully summarized Vladimir Tismăneanu, whom he considered an outstanding authority in this field, and Tismăneanu seemed to confirm this, republishing the article and returning the praise, both on his personal blog and in his column in *Evenimentul zilei*.[16] The logical conclusion of such public interventions would be the abolishment of any distinction between fascism and communism, with the notion of socialism ostensibly encompassing them both; after all, it would be pointless to talk about the crimes of the Holocaust and communism without discussing the crimes of socialism, as it was socialism that made them both possible.

Despite this deep resemblance they identify between the two totalitarian ideologies, and especially between their criminal outcomes, the leading public intellectuals in Romania claim that the horrors of communism remain unknown or underestimated, in Romania, in the West, and, generally speaking, internationally. It is hard to find anyone from the elite core of Romanian culture who did not decry this asymmetry and who did not consider it a blatant injustice. Therefore, any examples are prone to be selective and, in a way, random. Horia-Roman Patapievici, for instance, in a text published in the mid-1990s, talked openly about the "double standard" by which the two totalitarian systems of the previous century are measured in political and intellectual circles. "It is still believed, I suppose"—the philosopher satirized—"that the idea on whose behalf the left killed is in fact honorable (class equalization), while the idea on whose behalf the right killed is completely discredited (race equalization)."[17] In this text, Patapievici also acknowledged his bitterness that *"the international public opinion is far from understanding that the communist idea is as pernicious as the Nazi idea."*[18] The statistics provided by the author seem to support this thesis, if not the criminal preeminence of communism: "Numerically speaking, between the crimes committed by the Nazis and those committed by the communists there is a difference by an order of magnitude (from 6 to 60 million) in 'favor' of the communists, who exterminated more people, although by a less systematic criterion (but equally absurd: for those murdered, it did not make too big of a difference if they were exterminated as 'Jews,' 'kulaks,' or 'enemies of the people')."¹⁹ In the same "numerical" vein, in a text bearing the suggestive title "Două măsuri și un morman de cadavre" (Two measures and one pile of corpses), Patapievici ridiculed the selective-dogmatic sensitivity of the contemporaries at home or abroad: "However, as the [N]azi crimes are more unforgivable than the communist crimes, it results that 10 bodies produced by the left are significantly less important than 1 body produced by the right."²⁰

Twenty years later, Patapievici voiced the same frustration, criticizing Western intellectuals as well as members of the European Parliament and the Venice Commission for facilitating the emergence and maintenance for decades of "the problem of asymmetry in perception between fascism/Nazism and communism."²¹ According to Patapievici, the manner in which the Western intellectuals and politicians incriminate fascism is legitimate, displaying what he calls "moral clarity," but where communism is concerned, they suffer from a reprehensible obnubilation.

Many contemporary Romanian intellectuals identify with the words and ideas of Horia-Roman Patapievici. Almost all of them decry the injustice of the "asymmetry" in perception between fascism and communism, which is supposedly proven by the fact that communist symbols, as opposed to fascist ones, are banned by law almost nowhere in the civilized world. When some national parliaments attempted to pass laws in this regard, an international body voiced its opposition—in the case of the Republic of Moldova in 2012, the Venice Commission—which scandalized those who placed on equal footing the two series of crimes. Mircea Mihăieș protested: "I am not sufficiently knowledgeable to draw an informed parallel with the banning of fascist or Nazi symbols—but more competent people than me do it, bringing overwhelming evidence. I can only take note that a virulent ideological plague, which exterminated over one hundred million human beings, benefits from an unexplainable clemency. I wonder how many more should have died in order to prompt the minds empty of empathy of the various decision makers to say: that's enough!"²²

When Romania passed a law in 2015 banning extreme right organizations and symbols and incriminating the "cult" of those guilty of crimes against humanity and war crimes, voices from the circle of the leading public intellectuals immediately claimed that "if the condemnation of fascism is needed, it is unacceptable not to talk, in the context of this law, about the bloody symmetrical catastrophe, namely communism."[23] Nicolae Manolescu decried the omission: "Law 217 continues to ignore, absolutely inexplicably, communist events and personalities."[24] The director of the Institute for the Investigation of Communist Crimes and the Memory of the Romanian Exile criticized with similar rigor the fact that this normative act avoided "the condemnation of communism," which presumably leads to "memorial obscenity."[25] Thus, many seem to think that it is mandatory that the same law should criminalize in the same manner the acts inspired by the communist credo, as if two separate laws cannot be passed, each with its properly defined object of incrimination, according to its particularities. Of course, according to the opinion makers there are no such particularities, given that between the two totalitarianisms there is a perfect "symmetry"; that is, the crimes of the communism necessarily and exclusively mirrored the Holocaust, and vice versa.

The result of this injustice—according to the supporters of the equality thesis—is that the memory of only one category of victims is cultivated. Thus, as Nicolae Manolescu once claimed, a "monopoly" over suffering is established that excludes recognition of the torment inflicted by the communist regimes:

It is as if the discovery that a gulag existed would put into question the existence of the Holocaust. Who is afraid to lose the monopoly over the revealing of the crimes against humanity? An indirect proof supporting my hunch is the trial of Garaudy in France, who never claimed that the Holocaust had not existed, but only that a terrible lobby sprang up in its aftermath. Well, it is the loss of this monopoly over this kind of lobby that seems unnerving to some. However, it is incorrect and immoral to silence the mouths of those who decry the millions of victims of communism solely from the fear that there will not be many left to decry the millions of victims of Nazism.[26]

Vladimir Tismăneanu promptly recognized the gaffe contained in this allegation and criticized it.[27] Years later, he himself pointed the finger at what he called the "unidimensionality of memory," which he described as a "scientific, political, and moral error."[28] For Tismăneanu, if in one case humanity is right to feel obliged to preserve and cultivate the memory of the victims, then its failure to do the same in the other case it looks amnesiac. According to the supporters of the equalization thesis, this is how a selective and unjust victimology emerged. As Liiceanu put it, historical memory was occupied abusively by the "unique victim": "Have the lives *systematically* mutilated for

45 years gained the right to one single tear? Since when does one suffering risk losing its aura of suffering just because another one exists? Why the egotistical rejection of cohabitation in suffering? From where does this entitlement to the condition of unique victim come from, why doesn't it admit to be contradicted?"[29]

Those who formulate such clamorous interrogations do not feel the least bit obliged to clearly state whom they have in mind when they point the finger at the creators of a "monopoly" over suffering or the cult of the "unique victim." It seems that they do not need to specify the perpetrators, to name them, to quote them in regard to what they allegedly support, or to reveal the sources they have in mind, for their readers "know" to whom they refer. Their readers "know" because on other occasions, these same authors have pointed out, sometimes transparently but more often allusively, to whom they refer.

Let us take a closer look at the intellectual who points the finger at the cult of the "unique victim." In explaining the hypermnesia concerning the Holocaust and, unsurprisingly, the amnesia with regards to the crimes of communism, Liiceanu advanced the idea that Jews have an interest in keeping the historical memory in the terms they choose because the "unique victim" (a term he coined) was not just a victim during the Holocaust, but also, during the communist regime, its opposite: an executioner. For this reason, according to Liiceanu, historical interpretation by the victim-turned-executioner must be regarded with caution. When referring to a text about nationalistic and antisemitic ideas in Romanian culture, its editor, Liiceanu, after pointing out that it is a book "written, not by accident, by a Jewish author," concluded, "it is hard to image that the historical figures can be reconstructed through the discourse of those who are always ready to speak from the posture of victims, but who forget to acknowledge themselves as executioners."[30] In other words, Jews, by not acknowledging their role as executioners, create a distorted view of recent communist history. Liiceanu's thesis is that Jews from a country such as Romania, after experiencing the Holocaust, enlisted in the repression apparatus of the newly established communist regime promptly and voluntarily, becoming coauthors, or even the main authors, of the regime's crimes. Liiceanu considered this a sort of axiomatic truth that does not need any proof. The supposed transformation of Jewish victims into Jewish executioners was invoked by Liiceanu several times in the 1990s, sometimes in pompous literary forms, giving tropes a central role in his discourse: "how is it possible that he who, in a certain moment of history, had worn the victim's uniform, now puts on the executioner's uniform?"[31]

Gabriel Liiceanu is not the only one who thinks this way. Although his discourse on this topic is rather cryptic—and sometimes a little too much so—there are others who "translate" what the philosopher tried to convey. Gheorghe Grigurcu, for instance, wrote in a review that:

Numerous Jewish analysts simply cannot come to terms with the analogy, which arises naturally from the perspective of cruelty and responsibility, between the Holocaust and the Gulag. This corresponds to an inappropriate protection of the red totalitarianism. Despite its longer tenure in our country than the rule of the extreme right, and with a myriad of consequences that we can still feel today, this totalitarianism sees itself retroactively protected by the spirit of a standard "correctness," not least because of the Jewish collaborators that played a part. To reconstruct it and to condemn it often represents for them or for their coreligionists a reprehensible act.[32]

The idea that the communist regime in Romania was, in considerable measure, the work of the Jews, who now after the fall of communism have an interest in opposing its condemnation, appears in other texts by Grigurcu, a literary critic. In a literary review of the book *Cuvinte din exil* (Words from exile) that included an interview with its author, Jewish Romanian writer Norman Manea, the director of *Acolada* mentioned to his readers "the thesis, not without its logic, that the Jews 'are not really interested in the Gulag, for many of them were communists and would do anything to preserve the memory of the Holocaust as the largest genocide in history and to help it prevail over other historical tragedies.'"[33]

The widespread opinion in Romania's intellectual circles is that this distorted version of history has prevailed worldwide—especially in the West, but also in Eastern Europe—thanks to the tireless Jewish "lobby."[34] Intellectuals as well as politicians and international bodies (such as the Venice Commission, the European Court of Human Rights, and the European Parliament—that is, decisions makers who are able to change how the victims of communism are remembered) have all supposedly submitted to this view of history. Even the Vatican has surrendered to this dominant perception, as the Pope's statements mention only the Stalinist crimes and not, as some think would be appropriate, all communist crimes.[35]

But it is not only this conformism that stands accused. It is alleged that the fact that many intellectuals from the West had communist sympathies in their pasts prevents them from recognizing the true magnitude of the crimes of the Gulag; one such person, according to Liiceanu, was André Glucksmann.[36] In addition, communism still attracts, still twists the minds of many: "Communism's parlor prestige managed to systematically outlive its historical crimes. What we lived as reality and they as ideological self-indulgence has no common measure."[37] Under such circumstances, many intellectuals decry a censorship that obstructs the disclosure of the horrors committed by the communist regimes: "It sometimes happens that we want to recount the hallucination in which we had to live. But, as Monica [Lovinescu] put it, 'we are not allowed to.'"[38] It is never clear who the persons are who issue interdictions, but the rhetorical figure of speech produces the desired effect, as the choir of persistent complaints and accusations confers on this supposed censorship an air of veracity. In his turn, Vladimir Tismăneanu asked himself demonstratively: "Are we allowed to compare communism with fascism?"[39] The question was purely rhetorical, given that the author himself had made this comparison countless times—including in the respective article (in which his comparative exercise went only halfway, identifying only the similarities and avoiding any differences)—but its placement in the title of the article was clearly meant to insinuate that those who oppose such analyses are powerful and numerous; then again, if they do exist, they should have been named.

Others, however, do not hesitate to name the culprits. Often without producing a single piece of evidence, they accuse political actors, for instance, of interfering with the research objectives of the institutes in this field in order to block recognition of the communist disasters, as this is the only way to preserve the amplitude of the Holocaust from competition.[40] Predictably, this atmosphere triggers vindictive impulses. The calls for a "trial of communism" that would produce the "de-communization" of contemporary Romanian society, tainted by the legacy of the communist morbus, have always been on the agenda. Many invoke the precedent of the Nuremberg trial, proposing it as the model of action because it presumably led to the denazification of postwar German society, though that is far from the truth.[41] Most of the pleas for "justice," however, take a profoundly inquisitorial shape. Adam Michnik, while lecturing at the Romanian Athenaeum and taking note of the vigilante-style postcommunist anticommunism that was haunting one of his interlocutors (Gabriel Liiceanu), saw in Liiceanu's attitude the attributes of a "prosecutor" driven by ideological passions, and rightly warned him that "When politics enters a court, justice exits on the backdoor."[42] His words, however, produced no results; quite the opposite. Many Romanian intellectuals, maintaining their anticommunist intransigence intact, criticized Michnik for his "conciliatory" attitude.[43]

Communism—The "Absolute Evil"

In reference to the comparison between the two totalitarianisms, another solution was put forward, endorsing the idea that if an "absolute evil" did exist in history, it was not fascism (Nazism, legionarism), but communism. Consequently, the Holocaust appears as a lesser crime, overshadowed by the horrors of communism.

Although it is less widespread in the public interventions that compare the Gulag and the Holocaust, this supremacist view seems to have appeared before the equalization thesis. However, it is not an independent direction of thought; on the contrary, these two tendencies are intertwined, mutually validating each other, and sometimes the very same authors seem to embrace both. Ultimately, what sets the two theses apart is the different emphases on the gravity of the two tragedies.

The paradigm that sees communism as "the absolute evil" began to be constructed in the very early years of postcommunism. In a text published in 1992, Gabriel Liiceanu rejected the usual distinction made between Hitler and Stalin based on the criterion of racism, because—as he acknowledged—Stalin "comes out better" from this comparison, though the murders in the name of "class" are not more pardonable than the murders in the name of "race"; likewise, neither the number of victims (a factor he would later revisit) nor their "quality" seemed to him criteria solid enough for a relevant comparative approach meant to mark the essential distinctions between the two totalitarian ideologies. For that reason, Liiceanu proposed a single distinction between Hitler and Stalin, that is to say, between fascism and communism, which seemed to him definitive:

> Such a comparison—between two terrible murderers—prevents us from making the only true comparison that needs to be done: between two monstrosities of history, between the Nazi dictatorship and the communist totalitarianism. Between the two,

there is indeed a major difference, which, because of our persistent preoccupation to equalize or to compare the horrors committed by Hitler and Stalin, we constantly lose sight of: Nazism did not explicitly aim at destroying the fundament of society, which is private property; communism did, and succeeded. Placed side by side, Nazism and communism intersect until becoming indistinct from the perspective of their infinite crimes and aggression against the human being; but they do not overlap when it comes to the destruction of society's last resorts. Once Nazism was annihilated, society continued to function in a manner that had remained intact and whose effectiveness had been tested by mankind's long experience. The *brain* of the German society had been damaged, but its body remained untouched.[44]

That is how Gabriel Liiceanu explained the rapid economic recovery of postwar Germany. It is not hard to notice that, in the implicit value judgment issued by the disciple of Constantin Noica, the Nazi evil appears to be significantly less than the communist evil, and this is only because Nazi fascism seemingly did not attack private property. This argument is especially vulnerable when confronted with the historical facts of the "aryanization" of Jewish property during the Third Reich and the "Romanianization" practiced by Ion Antonescu, as well as the fact that private property continued to subsist in part under the communist regimes.

In the opinion of the same intellectual, the asymmetries do not stop here. Although it can be inferred from the quote above that in 1992 Liiceanu considered that, from the perspective of the crimes committed, the two totalitarian systems were virtually identical, in other interventions he abandoned this equalizing judgment. Over the years, Liiceanu seemed preoccupied with what he saw as communism's criminal character par excellence. In his view, "the communist crime ... beat all of mankind's records in crime."[45] Always tempted to make a comparison with fascism, he saw the crimes committed in the name of the ideology of the extreme left as having an extra degree of steadfastness and perhaps even an extra degree of inevitability when weighed against those committed under the impetus of fascist ideology:

Unlike the sinister criterion of race, the criterion of class offers crime an infinite scope, as it can be activated at any time and in any society on the globe. That is why communism is the *universal crime waiting to ambush*, the crime that can be triggered and fomented precisely because it is based on the eternal natural inequality between individuals and on the frustrations derived from the latter. When the hierarchy between inferior and superior is lost, the inferior can easily transform into an element of the "revolution."[46]

Certainly, if one takes into account the Leninist theory of revolution, with the privileged place it grants to violence and all the consequences that brought to political practice, it can be concluded after even a superficial examination of its ideas that the communist ideology is far from spotless. Furthermore, the injustices, abuses, and crimes committed by communist regimes at various points in time represent irrefutable evidence in this respect. At the same time, it is hard not to notice that Liiceanu's emphasis on the "universal" character of crime under communism results in the (albeit partial) exoneration of the other side in the comparison (Nazi racism), which transgresses historical truth and even common sense.

All these flagrant exaggerations have but one purpose: to demonstrate that the communist regimes were worse than the fascist ones. Sometimes the political left in general—and communism, as its relative—is given a demonic image. On one occasion, Andrei Pleșu—who usually considers the left to be legitimate—delighted his listeners and readers with a decoding of the left's "genome" that explained the aberrations of this political orientation.[47] And Liiceanu focuses not only on the crimes that communism ineluctably entailed, but also on the society and individuals who directly experienced this political system. In the wake of the communist regime, all that was left was "human rubble," for this political order severely damaged the moral attributes of those who lived under its grip.[48] Then again, crime represented the culmination of this human degradation. The historians and, in general, the Western intellectuals who perceive Nazism as the "absolute evil" are corrected in a superior tone:

> I read a stupefying claim by a British historian (Tony Judt) . . . : "When it comes to the incarnation of absolute evil, Nazism remains unmatched. Communism continues to represent the greatest danger because it is not compromised." However, what he should have said is the following: when it comes to the incarnation of absolute evil, communism remains unmatched (for *one hundred million victims* do represent an *incarnation*, don't they?). Despite all these, it remains uncompromised. And that is exactly why it still represents the greatest danger.[49]

In brief, for Liiceanu, communism represents history's "absolute evil." He did not voice this thesis many times, but every once in a while he did it bluntly: "With communism, we have experienced"—he noted in 2002 and repeated *ad litteram* in 2015, as a proof of his consistency—"the fulfillment on a global scale of the most terrifying dark utopia."[50] In the fabric of this judgment, one can detect a sort of doubt that goes much further: if Nazism was not as evil as communism, then the Holocaust does not deserve the special place in memory it is usually granted. It should be noted that the Romanian philosopher does not explicitly express this doubt, but it can be detected in his comparative relativizing about the sort of evil represented by fascism. This probably explains why Liiceanu sometimes treated the suffering of Jews as something exterior that did not concern him directly, as when he referred to "your Holocaust" during his dialogue with Amos Oz.[51]

Not many intellectuals openly subscribed to the thesis claiming communism's supremacy in terms of evil, but Liiceanu was not completely alone either. From time to time this martyrologic classification was invoked by other intellectuals, including Horia-Roman Patapievici, who gave voice to the same idea when he wrote that "the most terrible genocidal trauma that history has ever known (80 million dead, as a minimum figure) is tied to Marx's revolutionary ideas and instigations."[52] Moreover, the rearguard of these intellectuals is always ready to confirm and reassure them. When a journalist working for *Revista 22* affirmed that communism was "by far the most terrible flagellum that has fallen upon mankind," he did nothing other than emulate the judgments of the aforementioned philosophers, deeming them foolproof.[53]

Distortions of the Concept of the Holocaust

It can be concluded that most of the leading public intellectuals in today's Romania acknowledge the historical fact of the Holocaust, but do not individualize it enough to reveal its own irreducible characteristics. Views that deviate from this "syntax" of the debate, that focus only on the tragedy of the Jews during the Second World War, are exceptionally rare. One person who adopted this approach was Petru Creția (1927–1997):

Like any individual with some basic knowledge, I know all too well that the 20th century was and still is defiled by other forms of genocide, some absolutely atrocious. But I consider—and I shall consider so until the end—that the Holocaust, of which, over the years, I came to have a deeper understanding, is and will remain in history as *something special*. As something that makes some processes irreversible, some words sacrilegious, some self-indulgences of man towards man, where the image of the self is concerned, immoral.... Those who deny the Holocaust know all too well what they are doing, and perhaps their attempt is the most eloquent proof that something irreparable did happen to the history of mankind. Something that makes the reading of Dante's *Inferno* less painful, given that, as a matter of fact, the latter is all about punishment for some wrongdoings determined within a clearly defined reference system. But to erect with lucidity and determination a thorough penitential system operating outside the notion of *guilt* is something monstrous and proves that, deep down, our human nature secretly harbors something monstrous.[54]

These exemplary words about the uniqueness of the Holocaust, written in 1997, remained without echoes among Romania's leading public intellectuals, even though their author was undoubtedly close to them, having numerous affinities with the philosophical triumvirate mentioned earlier. Creția's statement was neither contradicted directly nor accepted, but ignored, as if it had never existed. In other words, it went unnoticed by those at the top of Romanian culture.

As we have seen, the only manner in which the leading Romanian intellectuals accept a discussion of the two totalitarian ideologies, communism and fascism, and of their criminal outcomes, the Gulag and the Holocaust, is by comparative approach. In principle, such a perspective seems legitimate; one cannot find any reasonable argument against it. However, it must be noted that to most of our intelligentsia, to compare simply means to liken, to make correlations, to equalize—not to make distinctions; furthermore, in their obstinate search for similarities they often force things, finding similarities where there are none. This causes severe distortions in the representations of both horrors.

And this is how the distinctive, individual characteristics of the Holocaust are completely ignored. Romanian public intellectuals—and I have in mind especially those with a philosophical bent—do not seem in any way willing to scrutinize the significance of the location of the epicenter of the Holocaust. The fact that it started in the heart of European civilization and that it took, so to speak, "modern" and "civilizational" forms (seen in its "hygienic" and "industrial" aspects, and in the bureaucratic and systematic character of the exterminations) seems to mean very little to them. Obsessively preoccupied with finding resemblances and equivalences, and sometimes even with demonstrating the martyrological supremacy of the Gulag, they ignore not only what proved to be the shallowness of European civilization, but also the anthropological—and even metaphysical—lesson on "how it was possible" for the Holocaust to take place in this part of the world, which truly reveals that, as Creția wrote, "deep down, our human nature secretly harbors something monstrous."

But, *nota bene*, the Gulag took place at the periphery of European civilization, if not plainly outside it, and this has consequences for its significance. Even though a substantial part of the Holocaust (including its Romanian episode) also happened at the periphery, taking the "standard" forms of barbarism (bullets, hunger, disease, etc.), its "legitimizing" and the subsequent shockwave came from the very center of Europe, where "industrial" extermination was the norm. It is true, of course, that the communist idea also had European origins, but there is one major distinction: the materialization of the communist idea occurred in states outside the perimeter of Western civilization, and the local conditions cannot and should not be ignored. Numerous researchers have revealed the continuities between the tsarist empire and the Soviet Union, between the profound Russian culture and the communist idea.[55] Moreover, in the opinion of some historians, the Gulag itself had deep tsarist roots, as sentencing people to forced labor in Siberia, the *katorga* prison camps, was a notorious practice of the tsarist regime inaugurated by Peter the Great and continued by all his successors. In fact, the *katorga* system was a veritable "house of the dead," as Fyodor Dostoyevsky described it in the middle of the nineteenth century after being found guilty and sentenced for being a *narodnik*; before the October Revolution of 1917 there were several tens of thousands of convicts in the *katorga* system.[56] Andrew Genetes, a meticulous researcher of the practice of forced labor in tsarist Russia, noted that "continuities existed between tsarist *katorga* and the Soviet Gulag."[57] Between the two punitive systems there were certainly also major differences, Genetes pointed out, one of which was that the Bolsheviks "perfected" (in terms of cruelty) the old system. This does not mean, however, that the precedent—and, in a way, the source of inspiration—must be ignored. Undoubtedly, the Gulag remains a powerful symbol of Soviet and, by extension, of communist oppression (as depicted by Solzhenitsyn), but to present it as the exclusive product of a single ideological seed represents a distortion of the historical facts.

The communist regimes elsewhere had their own autochthonous "signatures" that were sometimes even more pronounced; for instance, the Khmer Rouge were only minimally influenced in their criminal acts by the communist credo, which Vladimir Tismăneanu himself acknowledged in a moment of sincerity: "Pol Pot and his clique were a strange mixture of ideological criminals, barely bound to the classical dogmas of Marxism, Leninism, Maoism, or Castro-Guevarism."[58] Despite this, Romanian intellectuals still talk about "the communist genocide in Cambodia."[59]

History and local sociology, through which the communist precepts have been filtered, must be considered, because the crimes of Stalin, Mao, Pol Pot, and others could not have been possible by ideology alone. But most analyses do not take this into account at all. Often this is due to ignorance, but there are also cases when intellectuals well aware of these academic disciplines choose to avoid them, considering this the "healthy" attitude given the Romanian cultural and ideological climate, as the rationalization is significantly easier in the absence of this "complication." By invoking the 60 or 100 million victims of communism (in most cases reflexively, that is, ideologically, without any documentary foundation), the criminal outcome of the Gulag becomes overwhelming when compared to the 6 million Jews exterminated during the Second World War. The Holocaust thus becomes somewhat secondary. This remark is not meant to exonerate communism of responsibilities and faults, of brutal oppression and crimes, but to introduce certain nuances that any judgment regarding history must take into account. Alternatively, by forcing such "quantitative" comparisons, one can lose sight of the particularities of the crimes committed by the communist regimes; and, at the same time, the image of the Holocaust is once again distorted.

The distortions do not end here. The inability to recognize the specificity of the Holocaust is not merely the result of tendentious statistics and a failure to reflect on the significance of the geographical area where the Final Solution was conceived and put into practice. On this last point, Romanian intellectuals might be excused for their inattention, given the great distance from the epicenter of the Holocaust and the peripheral position of the Romanian chapter of this tragedy. However, there is something more that they ignore, with no mitigating circumstances: the role of antisemitism in preparing, unleashing, and supporting the Holocaust. Antisemitism was without a doubt a distinct fundamental characteristic of the enormous Jewish tragedy, for no other mass murder in history had such a strong cultural foundation. Manifested in a virulent or persuasive intellectual fashion, the hatred against Jews has persistently occurred almost everywhere in Europe, reaching its peak in Germany, but also in France and Romania, just before and during the Second World War, when it became state-sanctioned antisemitism in Hitler's Germany, Pétain's France, and Antonescu's Romania. To separate antisemitism from the Holocaust, to ignore antisemitism, as often happens, or to inappropriately diminish its significance, as some of Romanian intellectuals do, represents a failure to understand an essential characteristic of the unique Jewish tragedy that makes it unprecedented and unmatched, irreducible.[60] Nevertheless, for the leading philosophers and writers in present-day Romania, the temptation to downplay the antisemitism of the intellectuals from the interwar period is a defining trait. There are also quite a few attempts to discredit people who testified about the ordeals they endured under raging antisemitism and those who make antisemitism an object of research.[61] Occasionally, some intellectuals do take aim at what Julien Benda before the Holocaust called "the intellectual organization of political hatreds," and do empathize accordingly, but this is so rare that these positions are barely visible.[62]

The failure of the public discourse in postcommunist Romania to grasp the specificity of the Holocaust has to do with the role of these public intellectuals and the special place they hold in contemporary Romanian culture. They are the ones who imposed, categorically, the thesis that equates communist crimes with fascist crimes, sometimes going so far as to claim that the crimes of the Gulag were worse than those of the Holocaust. Any departure from this canonical "principle" is promptly attacked; if an intellectual wants recognition in the Romanian public space, there is no other way but to conform.

Thus, it is no wonder that in the quarter century that has passed since the fall of communism, a number of intellectuals who used to think differently eventually converted, embracing this tenet. Among them is Vladimir Tismăneanu, professor of Political Science at the University of Maryland, who in the 1990s and up until the early 2000s pointed out frequently and emphatically—and quite often, memorably—the uniqueness of the Holocaust, but later become silent on this issue, especially after April 2006, when he became the head of the Presidential Commission for the Study of the Communist Dictatorship in Romania; his current discourse focuses exclusively on the similarities between the criminal outcomes of the two systems, a stance that comforts the partisans of equivalence. Previously, in the 1990s

Tismăneanu went so far as to castigate Gabriel Liiceanu because his book *Cearta cu filosofia* (The quarrel with philosophy), in which he discussed Emil Cioran extensively, made "no mention of his fascist past."[63] Toward the end of the 2000s, the political scientist completely changed his position, adopting a fawning attitude toward the author of *Apel către lichele* (A plea to scoundrels). Other young intellectuals in the service of the leading public intellectuals benefitted from the same treatment from Professor Tismăneanu, despite their revisionist claims about the Legionary Movement; they include Radu Preda and Mihail Neamțu, contributors to the neolegionary publication *Puncte Cardinale* (Cardinal points), and Sorin Lavric, who in one of his books sympathized with the legionary tribulations of Constantin Noica—all these intellectuals are equally intransigent in their anticommunism as their mentors.[64] Finally, when an author criticized Law 217/2015 for avoiding the "communist genocide," ostentatiously using the controversial and compensatory term "communist Holocaust," Tismăneanu unreservedly agreed with the article, finding it "touching," and reiterated the thesis according to which "social racism" is synonymous with "class struggle."[65] Such prestidigitations, coming from an academic authority, further fuel the confusion in the public discourse with regards to the alleged overlapping of the two totalitarian ideologies and their destructive outcomes.

Indeed, the domination of the public space by Romania's leading intellectuals could also be seen during the media frenzy sparked by the adoption of Law 217/2015 that amended and supplemented the government's Emergency Ordinance 31/2002, which banned fascist, racist, and xenophobic symbols and organizations and the cult of the individuals found guilty of crimes against peace and humanity. Whereas the adoption of the ordinance thirteen years ago went unnoticed, and its subsequent approval by the parliament in 2006 drew little attention, the law passed in 2015 generated an earthquake in Romania's cultural circles, despite the fact its changes do not affect in any way the spirit of the normative acts of 2002 and 2006. Why the sudden shift from indifference to indignation? For one simple reason: Law 217/2015 was initially criticized by a leading intellectual, Andrei Pleșu, giving a "green light" to wage war not only against the new law, but also for the "return of the repressed." In quick succession, various media outlets—television channels, magazines, newspapers, blogs—took up the subject, giving the floor to individuals, some with open legionary sympathies, to criticize the law and its supporters (often cast as "traitors") as they invoked the indisputable authority of the intellectual who had launched the debate.

Finally, there is one more thing that deserves discussion: the interminable outcry of Romanian intellectuals on the subject of the "unique victim" and the alleged ban that denies victims of communism their rightful place in the memory of posterity. It is often insinuated—sometimes allusively, sometimes openly—that the Jews, and especially their intellectuals, bear responsibility for the one-sidedness of memory. A reader unfamiliar with the subject might conclude that intellectuals such as Leon Volovici and Norman Manea are guilty of such sins, but that would be wrong. Moreover, it is nearly impossible to find among the Jewish intellectuals who have distinguished themselves in the study of the Holocaust, even among those who do not have Romanian origins, anyone who is unsympathetic to the memory of the victims of communism. In the straightforward words of Yehuda Bauer, a prominent Israeli researcher of the Holocaust, "one certainly should remember the victims of the Soviet regime, and there is every justification for designating special memorials and events to do so."[66] Bauer is the honorary president of the International Holocaust Remembrance Alliance, with thirty-one member states including Romania, and his statements carry heavy weight in terms of what the Holocaust meant not only for Jews, but for all mankind. It is easy to spot the diversion when some voices claim that those who keep the memory of the Holocaust alive are opposed to the memory of the victims of communism. Of course, if a failure does exist in this respect, it must be investigated in the Romanian perimeter, in the manner in which the leading Romanian intellectuals understand the duty to commemorate those who suffered under the communist regime, with confused, amalgamated, and vindictive demands addressed to external bodies on which the memory of the victims of communism depends.

Conclusions

This chapter has explored how the post-1989 leading Romanian public intellectuals (the Romanian intellectual elite) relate to the Holocaust in general, and to its Romanian chapter in particular, starting from the premise that their positions on these issues have a powerful impact on public opinion. First, the research found that in the intellectual debates in postcommunist

Romania, the Holocaust has never been a stand-alone subject of reflection or research, even if it was—and still is—a most sensitive one. References to the catastrophe experienced by Romanian and European Jews during the Second World War, while numerous—and occasionally abundant—in the public discourse of the intellectual elite, actually occur in a separate debate: the one about communism and the horrors of the political regimes of communist origin. It is when this debate touches upon the issue of communist crimes that the comparisons to Nazism, fascism, legionarism, and, predictably, the Holocaust usually emerge. In most cases, the notion of the Holocaust with which the leading Romanian intellectuals operate is clarified within the scope of this debate.

Within these approaches, according to the strategy adopted by these intellectuals, but also to the conclusions they reach, this study detected two main attitudes. The first, and by far the more prevalent in the public discourse equates the crimes of communism to the Holocaust following a strictly equalizing logic whereby the conclusion is always the same: the Holocaust and the Gulag are ostensibly alike, as there is nothing that essentially sets them apart. In the opinion of these intellectuals, the two totalitarian ideologies that inspired the two series of crimes are almost identical in nature (even with regard to antisemitism and racism).

However, this martyrological equalization, while very prevalent, does not satisfy all of the aforementioned intellectuals. For some—though notably fewer—the Gulag hangs heavier in the balance of horrors than the Holocaust. The value judgment that "absolute evil" can be found in communism is supported by pointing to the supposedly more pronounced evilness of this ideology (relative to fascism), or more commonly, to statistics that indicate that the criminal record of fascism pales in comparison to that of communism.

These two attitudes usually go hand in hand with a strong sense of frustration that the memory of the two types of victims is allegedly one-sided, that the Gulag does not have the place it deserves in the consciousness of posterity. Finally, the research highlights the distortions of the concept of the Holocaust as a consequence of these parallel-competitive approaches.

(Translated by Alexandru Voicu)

George Voicu is Professor of Political Science at the National University of Political Studies and Public Administration (SNSPA), Bucharest, Romania. He is author of *Zeii cei răi. Cultura conspirației în România postcomunistă*.

Notes

1. Liiceanu, *Ușa interzisă*, 257. Emphasis in original.
2. The first use of the term was by Florin Mătrescu, who published an ample volume with this title; see Mătrescu, *Holocaustul roșu*. The volume has been reedited several times (1998, 2009).
3. Volovici, "Antisemitism in Post-Communist Eastern Europe: A Marginal or Central Issue?," 15.
4. Such expressions are used especially by radical nationalists, most of them of traditionalist or national-communist origin. See, for example, Ungheanu, *Holocaustul culturii române* or Buzatu, *Așa a început holocaustul împotriva poporului român*.
5. Adameșteanu and Palade, "Fascism și Comunism."
6. A few examples: Tudoran, "Nepoții gorniștilor (II)," *România literară* 12 (1998); Popovici, "Revizionismul de stânga," *Orizont* 3 (1418); Vrancea, "Disocieri și incompatibilități față de memoria 'sovietologică' a holocaustului negru și roșu," *România literară* 10 (2002).
7. Lovinescu, *Jurnal*, 321.
8. Manolescu, "Antisemitismul lui Marx," *Adevărul*, May 15, 2015.
9. Pleșu, "A treia zi a comunismului?," 30.
10. Manolescu, "Ce înseamnă să fii rasist," *România literară* 19 (1998).
11. Tismăneanu, "Avem voie să comparăm comunismul cu fascismul?"
12. Patapievici, "Oamenii trăiesc într-o societate în care nu este fericirea pe stradă, dar măcar poți trăi fără să fii urmărit zilnic."
13. Tismăneanu, "Papa Benedict, universul concentraționar și Declarația de la Praga," *Evenimentul zilei*, August 19, 2009.
14. Mihăieș, "Al treilea val," *România literară* 10 (2013).
15. Ibid.
16. Tismăneanu, "Centrul și periferia: Despre un articol de Mircea Mihăieș," *Evenimentul zilei*, March 10, 2013.
17. Patapievici, *Politice*, 201. The text referenced here, "Refuzul memoriei," was first published in *Revista 22* 40 (1995): 10–11.
18. Ibid., 202. Emphasis in original.
19. Ibid.
20. Ibid., 212.
21. Patapievici, "Memoria divizată. Reflecții asupra comunismului: efectele lui și defectele noastre," 114.
22. Mihăieș, "Liber la comunism!," *Evenimentul zilei*, March 11, 2013.
23. Pleșu, "O dezbatere blocată," *Adevărul*, August 3, 2015.
24. Manolescu, "Legea 217 și numele de străzi," *Adevărul*, August 28, 2015.
25. Preda, "Obscenitatea memorială: Cui îi este, într-adevăr, frică de condamnarea comunismului," *Adevărul*, September 2, 2015.

26. Manolescu, "Holocaustul și Gulagul," *România literară* 9 (1998).
27. Tismăneanu, "Sunt fascismul și comunismul frați siamezi?," *Cuvântul* 5, no. 253 (1998).
28. Tismăneanu, "Inteligența morală în acțiune. În numele celor uciși in zori . . . ."
29. Liiceanu, *Ușa interzisă*, 257. Emphasis in original.
30. Liiceanu, "Nota editorului," 7. This unexpected and incomprehensible note by Liiceanu, found right at the beginning of the volume, reminds us in its placement and attitude of the foreword by Nae Ionescu for *De două mii de ani* by M. Sebastian.
31. Liiceanu, "Sebastian, mon frère."
32. Grigurcu, "Un spirit curajos," 3.
33. Grigurcu, "Ne dăm seama," 3.
34. See, for instance, Manolescu, "Holocaustul și Gulagul."
35. Vladimir Tismăneanu and Marius Stan, after eulogizing the current pontiff for his attitude toward major historical tragedies, including the ones committed by Stalinism, considered it necessary to correct what was said by the head of the Catholic Church: "Nevertheless, we dare to ask ourselves whether the formulation 'Stalinism' is encompassing enough to include the *communist crimes* of the past century, including those of Maoism. These crimes against humanity were genocidal" (Tismăneanu and Stan, "Genocidul armean și etica neuitării" (emphasis in original). Nor did the pontiff's predecessor escape a similar judgment—after Benedict condemned the Nazi concentration camps as "the symbols of hell on earth," Tismăneanu promptly admonished him for an omission: "I think it would be appropriate and just if the pontiff describes the Gulag too as the embodiment of hell" (Tismăneanu, "Papa Benedict, universul concentraționar și Declarația de la Praga," *Evenimentul zilei*, August 19, 2009). Yet, in the late 1990s, Tismăneanu was satisfied with the attitude of the Holy See, expressed in the document *Shoah: Ne amintim*, which did not explicitly mention "the victims of communism." See supra, Tismăneanu, "Sunt fascismul și comunismul frați siamezi?"
36. Meditating on the "major difference" between "human and anti-human" (and rhetorically asking himself, "Is [the criminal] human? Is the torturer human?"), Liiceanu claimed that Glucksmann's words ("Hitler c'est moi. Stalin c'est moi. Mao c'est moi.") are completely foreign to him, and accused the French philosopher of thinking in such a manner because of his Maoist youth (Liiceanu, *Ușa interzisă*, 115–116).
37. Liiceanu, *Ușa interzisă*, 307.
38. Ibid., 306–307.
39. Tismăneanu, "Avem voie să comparăm comunismul cu fascismul?"
40. The Romanian government—we are told in such interventions—ostensibly stopped the activity of the Institute for the Investigation of Communist Crimes aimed at discovering new victims (the excavations at Aiud and Târgu Ocna) because "such an action would . . . represent a competition to the Holocaust, namely, an equalization of the communist crimes with the Holocaust." See Oprea, "La mulți ani?," *Observator cultural*, December 12, 2014.
41. About the myth of "denazification," see Shafir, "The 'Second Nürnberg': Legend vs. Myth in Postcommunism (I)."
42. Tita, "Michnik: Generalizarea anticomunistă este inacceptabilă."
43. Manolescu, "Când n-am mai fost de acord cu Adam Michnik," *România literară* 7 (2011).
44. Liiceanu, "Prostia ca încremenire în proiect. Câteva exemple." Republished in Liiceanu, *Apel către lichele*, 113–114. Emphasis in original.

45. Liiceanu, "Gânduri despre comunism," 86.

46. Ibid., 84–85. Emphasis in original. This text assembles fragments by Liiceanu from *Uşa interzisă* (2002), *Întâlnire cu un necunoscut* (2008), and an interview from 2013.

47. Andrei Pleşu "uncovered" the origin of today's left in a character from the Bible, who in chapter 12 of the Gospel of John objected to Mary Magdalene's washing the feet of Jesus Christ and anointing them with myrrh, because of the expense: "At this point, one character comes up and says: 'Too bad the money was spent on myrrh. We should have sold it and given the money to the poor.' In other words, you are looking at the saviour of mankind, your God—at least that is the idea in the context of the Gospel—but you are more preoccupied with making money for the poor. This represents the original act of 'commitment.' And Jesus replies: 'I will not be long with you, this occasion is unique.' But our man says: 'No, we have to look after the poor, not after ourselves, not after our redemption, but after the others.' The character who makes this intervention and who is, by coincidence, the most mercantile character from the Gospel, is Judas. I contend that what we have here is the original phenomenon of the 'generous' left." See Pleşu, "A treia zi a comunismului?," 26.

48. Liiceanu, "Gânduri despre comunism," 94. It may appear that although communism deformed people on a grand scale, the author of these lines seems to have escaped its dissolving power. Unlike his fellow countrymen who were largely affected, Gabriel Liiceanu, by his own confession, came out of this political experience with substantially strengthened aptitudes and knowledge: "I feel superior to many intellectuals from the West in what concerns the understanding of human nature, of the realm of history, of the meanings of right and left in politics." Liiceanu, "Gânduri despre comunism," 97.

49. Ibid., 92. Emphasis in original.

50. Liiceanu, *Uşa interzisă*, 307. See also Liiceanu, "Gânduri despre comunism," 79.

51. Apud Chiriţoiu, "Amos Oz şi Gabriel Liiceanu la Ateneu," *România literară* 9 (2012).

52. Patapievici, *Omul recent*, 349.

53. Pretor, "De cine ascultă preşedintele."

54. Creţia, "Despre antisemitism," *Realitatea evreiască* 4 (1997). Emphasis in original.

55. For example, Pipes, *Scurtă istorie a revoluţiei ruse*.

56. According to one researcher, in 1916 Russia there were 28,600 convicts in the *katorga* system. See Merritt Miner, "The Other Killing Machine," *New York Times*, May 11, 2003.

57. Gentes, "Katorga: Penal Labor and Tsarist Siberia," 83.

58. Tismăneanu and Stan, "Neo-totemism secular: Mai are totalitarismul un viitor?"

59. Patapievici, "Memoria divizată . . . ," 122.

60. When referring to the "antisemitic idea," Patapievici wrote: "Had the Armenians been the intellectual and financial minority deemed by the ethnic Germans as having taken over Germany's key jobs, then the Armenians would have been the scapegoats instead of the Jews" (Patapievici, *Omul recent*, 165–166). Similar judgments can be found in the writings of some of those who gravitate around the intellectual elite. For example: "Isolated from the bulk of the Romanian population, Jews have turned over time into a social caste of economic and financial magnates, which in the eyes of Romanians, increasingly resembled an occult society whose members were pulling the strings of the Romanian destiny." See Lavric, *Noica şi mişcarea legionară*, 24.

61. For a more detailed analysis of these attempts, see Voicu, "L'attitude des intellectuels roumains face à la Shoah et à sa mémoire dans la Roumanie postcommuniste," 583–618.

62. One example was a broadcast of the television show *Înapoi la argument* by TVR Cultural on April 8, 2010, moderated by H.-R. Patapievici, about the Jewish Romanian poet Benjamin Fondane. Gabriel Liiceanu, too, had a revelation of the horrors of antisemitism—this is what he wrote on the cover of the book *A fi evreu după Holocaust* by Imre Tóth, published by Humanitas in 2015: "You cannot avoid encountering this book without leaving your own self in disarray. And those who do encounter it cannot escape the shame. A shame that is—how to put it?—prior to you. But in the end, this feeling is the only remedy to the manner in which we let ourselves be inhabited, at one moment or another of our existence, by the most tenacious and humiliating prejudice that was passed on us by our ancestors." There are other examples. Liiceanu also demonstrated sensitivity—sometimes expressed movingly—to other victims of antisemitism, but the exercise in empathy that seemed so promising was soon ruined by his subsequent writings about the metamorphosis of the victim into executioner (see Liiceanu, "Sebastian, mon frère").

63. Tismăneanu, "Romania's Mystical Revolutionaires."

64. Tismăneanu, "Noica și revoluția legionară," *Evenimentul zilei*, February 20, 2008.

65. Lalu, "Holocaustul comunist," *contributors.ro*, September 3, 2015. See also Tismăneanu's comment on this article.

66. Bauer, "Remembering the Holocaust Accurately," *The Jerusalem Post*, January 26, 2014.

References

Adameșteanu, Gabriela, and Rodica Palade. "Fascism și Comunism." *Revista 22* 7, no. 417 (1998): 16.
Bauer, Yehuda. "Remembering the Holocaust accurately." *The Jerusalem Post*, January 26, 2010.
Buzatu, Gheorghe. *Așa a început holocaustul împotriva poporului român*. Bucharest: Majadahonda, 1995.
Chirițoiu, Ana. "Amos Oz și Gabriel Liiceanu la Ateneu." *România literară* 9 (2012).
Creția, Petru. "Despre antisemitism." *Realitatea evreiască*, no. 4 (1997).
Gentes, Andrew. "Katorga: Penal Labor and Tsarist Siberia." In *The Siberian Saga: A History of Russia's Wild East*, edited by Eva-Maria Stolberg, 41–61. Frankfurt am Main: Peter Lang, 2005.
Grigurcu, Gheorghe. "Ne dăm seama." *Acolada* 2 (2013): 3.
———."Un spirit curajos."*Acolada* 12 (2010).
Ionescu, Nae. "Prefată." In *De două mii de ani*, by Mihail Sebastian, 7–24. Bucharest: Hasefer, 1995.
Lalu, Rasvan. "Holocaustul comunist." *contributors.ro*. September 3, 2015. http://www.contributors.ro/editorial/holocaustul-comunist/.
Lavric, Sorin. *Noica și mișcarea legionară*. Bucharest: Humanitas, 2007.
Liiceanu, Gabriel. *Apel către lichele*. Bucharest: Humanitas, 1992.

———. "Gânduri despre comunism." In *O idee care ne suceşte minţile*, edited by Andrei Pleşu, Gabriel Liiceanu, and Horia-Roman Patapievici, 71–102. Bucharest: Humanitas, 2014.

———. *Întâlnire cu un necunoscut*. Bucharest: Humanitas, 2008.

———. "Nota editorului." In *Ideologia naţionalistă şi "problema evreiască" în România anilor '30*, edited by Leon Volovici, 5–8. Bucharest: Humanitas, 1995.

———. "Prostia ca încremenire în proiect. Câteva exemple." *Revista 22* 4, no. 105 (1992): 5; 5, no. 106 (1992): 5.

———. "Sebastian, mon frère." *Revista 22* 17, no. 135 (1997): 10–11.

———. *Uşa interzisă*. Bucharest: Humanitas, 2002.

Lovinescu, Monica. *Jurnal: 1998–2000*. Bucharest: Humanitas, 2006.

Manolescu, Nicolae. "Antisemitismul lui Marx." *Adevărul*, May 15, 2015.

———. "Când n-am mai fost de acord cu Adam Michnik." *România literară*, no. 7, February 18, 2011.

———. "Ce înseamnă să fii rasist." *România literară*, no. 19, May 20–26, 1998.

———. "Holocaustul şi Gulagul." *România literară*, no. 9, March 11–17, 1998.

———. "Legea 217 şi numele de străzi." *Adevărul*, August 28, 2015.

Mătrescu, Florin. *Holocaustul roşu*. Bucharest: Ericson, 1994.

Mihăieş, Mircea. "Liber la comunism!" *Evenimentul zilei*. Accessed March 13, 2012.

———. "Al treilea val." *România literară*, no. 10 (2013).

Oprea, Marius. "La mulţi ani?" *Observator cultural* 752 (2014).

Patapievici, Horia-Roman. "Memoria divizată. Reflecţii asupra comunismului: efectele lui şi defectele noastre." In *O idee care ne suceşte minţile*, edited by Andrei Pleşu, Gabriel Liiceanu, and Horia-Roman Patapievici, 105–155. Bucharest: Humanitas, 2014.

———. "Oamenii trăiesc într-o societate în care nu este fericirea pe stradă, dar măcar poţi trăi fără să fii urmărit zilnic." *Gândul.info*. Accessed December 21, 2014. http://www.gandul.info/interviurile-gandul/h-r-patapievici-la-25-de-ani-de-la-revolutie-oamenii-traiesc-intr-o-societate-in-care-nu-este-fericirea-pe-strada-dar-macar-poti-trai-fara-sa-fii-urmarit-zilnic-13729329.

———. *Omul recent. O critică a modernităţii din perspectiva întrebării "ce se pierde atunci când ceva se câştigă."* Bucharest: Humanitas, 2001.

———. *Politice*. Bucharest: Humanitas, 1996.

———. "Refuzul memoriei." *Revista 22* 40 (1995):10–11.

Pipes, Richard. *Scurtă istorie a revoluţiei ruse*. Bucharest: Humanitas, 1998.

Pleşu, Andrei. "A treia zi a comunismului?" In *O idee care ne suceşte minţile*, edited by Andrei Pleşu, Gabriel Liiceanu, and Horia-Roman Patapievici, 13–52. Bucharest: Humanitas, 2014.

Popovici, Vasile. "Revizionismul de stânga." *Orizont* 3 /1418 (2000): 30–31.

Preda, Radu. "Obscenitatea memorială: Cui îi este, într-adevăr, frică de condamnarea comunismului?" *Adevărul*, September 2, 2015.

Pretor, Şerban. "De cine ascultă preşedintele." *Revista 22* 1326 (2015).

Shafir, Michael. "The 'Second Nürnberg': Legend vs. Myth in Postcommunism (I)." *Holocaust. Studii şi cercetări* 1, no. 7 (2014): 109–144.

Tismăneanu, Vladimir. "Avem voie să comparăm comunismul cu fascismul?" *contributors.ro*. August 15, 2015. http://www.contributors.ro/global-europa/avem-voie-sa-comparam-comunismul-cu-fascismul/.

———. "Centrul și periferia: Despre un articol de Mircea Mihăieș." *Evenimentul zilei*, March 10, 2013.

———. "Inteligența morală în acțiune. In numele celor uciși in zori . . ." *contributors.ro*. August 3, 2015. http://www.contributors.ro/global-europa/inteligenta-morala-in-actiune-in-numele-celor-ucisi-in-zori/.

———. "Noica și revoluția legionară." *Evenimentul zilei*, February 20, 2008.

———. "Papa Benedict, universul concentraționar și Declarația de la Praga." *Evenimentul zilei*, August 19, 2009.

———. "Romania's Mystical Revolutionaries." *Partisan Review* 4 (fall 1994): 600–609.

———. "Sunt fascismul și comunismul frați siamezi?" *Cuvântul* 5/253 (1998).

Tismăneanu, Vladimir, and Marius Stan. "Genocidul armean și etica neuitării." *contributors.ro*. April 12, 2015. http://www.contributors.ro/global-europa/genocidul-armean-o-crima-absoluta-un-eseu-de-vladimir-tismaneanu-si-marius-stan/.

———. "Neo-totemism secular: Mai are totalitarismul un viitor?" *contributors.ro*. May 20, 2015. http://www.contributors.ro/global-europa/neo-totemism-secular-mai-are-totalitarismul-un-viitor-un-eseu-de-marius-stan-%c8%99i-vladimir-tismaneanu/.

Tita, Teodor. "Michnik: Generalizarea anticomunistă este inacceptabilă." *contributors.ro*. February 15, 2011. http://www.contributors.ro/editorial/michnik-generalizarea-anticomunista-e-inacceptabila/.

Tóth, Imre. *A fi evreu după Holocaust*. Bucharest: Humanitas, 2015.

Tudoran, Dorin. "Nepoții gorniștilor (II)." *România literară* 12 (1998).

Ungheanu, Mihai. *Holocaustul culturii române: 1944–1989*. Bucharest: D. B. H., 1999.

Voicu, George. "L'attitude des intellectuels roumains face à la Shoah et à sa mémoire dans la Roumanie postcommuniste." *Revue de l'histoire de la Shoah* 194 (2011): 583–618.

Volovici, Leon. *Antisemitism in Post-Communist Eastern Europe: A Marginal or Central Issue?* Jerusalem: Hebrew University of Jerusalem, Vidal Sassoon International Center for the Study of Antisemitism, 1994.

Vrancea, Ileana. "Disocieri și incompatibilități față de memoria 'sovietologică' a holocaustului negru și roșu." *România literară* 10 (2002).

Chapter Three

LAW, JUSTICE, AND HOLOCAUST MEMORY IN ROMANIA

Alexandru Climescu

The fall of communism in 1989 created favorable conditions for various versions of the past to be promoted by public actors. Holocaust denial and the public worship of Marshal Ion Antonescu, Romania's dictator during the Second World War, whose rehabilitation began during the period of national communism,[1] became common discourses among politicians, historians, military officials, and representatives of civil society. The rehabilitation of the Legionary Movement, Romania's main interwar fascist organization, was also supported by some historians, Orthodox priests, and various nongovernmental organizations.

After 1989, historiographical works, political discourses, and commemoration activities meant to rehabilitate the Antonescu regime were complemented by legal actions. In 1994 the general prosecutor of Romania announced that steps were being taken to initiate an extraordinary appeal to overturn Ion Antonescu's conviction for war crimes, following requests from several ultranationalist organizations.[2] Eventually, the legal rehabilitation of Antonescu was halted after concerns were expressed by representatives of the US Congress. Instead of trying to acquit Antonescu, the Prosecutor's Office initiated extraordinary appeals of the convictions of other members of Antonescu's government, fascist ideologists, and military personnel involved in the extermination of Jews. In 1995, at the request of the General Prosecutor's Office, the Supreme Court of Romania retried and acquitted most of the antisemitic ideologists who had been convicted during the Journalists' Trial in 1945 for supporting Nazism or fascism. In 1997 the General Prosecutor's Office made another request for the acquittal of eight members of Antonescu's government. In 1998 and 1999 the Supreme Court of Romania acquitted Radu Dinulescu, chief of the Second Section in the General Staff of the Romanian Army, and his assistant, Gheorghe Petrescu. They had been convicted for, among other things, organizing and carrying out the deportations of Jews from Bukovina and Bessarabia, a crime that led some researchers to refer to Dinulescu as "the Eichmann of Romania."[3] In 2004 the General Prosecutor's Office overturned the conviction of Ion Pănescu, former commander of the Czernowitz airport, who had used the regime of Jewish forced labor to his own advantage.

Following the recommendations of the European Court of Human Rights and criticisms of Romania's extraordinary appeal procedure, which had been used in both civil and criminal cases, it was eliminated from Romanian legislation in 2004, narrowing the legal means to acquit former Holocaust perpetrators.

The early 2000s saw the decline of an ethnocentric version of Holocaust memory in Romania. In 2002, amid negotiations for Romania's accession to NATO, after repeated concerns expressed by US officials regarding the cult of Marshal Ion Antonescu, the Romanian government adopted Emergency Ordinance 31.[4] In its original version, the document, bearing the basic features of criminal law, punished Holocaust denial, fascist propaganda, and the public cult of persons convicted for crimes against peace or humanity. As a result of the adoption of this legislation, the Holocaust and fascism once again became a topic of judicial reasoning in the years that followed.

Although judicial memory generated an authoritative representation of the history of Romania, it should be noted that the state's record with regard to Holocaust remembrance is not limited to the version promoted by magistrates. In 2004 the International Commission on the Holocaust in Romania, established under the authority of Romanian president Ion Iliescu, published its final report,[5] which underlined the responsibility of the Romanian state with regard to the persecution and extermination of Jews, as well as the deportation and killing of part of the Roma community.

That same year, the government established October 9 as National Holocaust Commemoration Day. One year later, following the recommendations of the Commission, the Romanian government established the Elie Wiesel National Institute for the Study of the Holocaust in Romania, which was tasked with carrying out educational programs, research projects, and commemoration activities. Since then, state officials have regularly offered public apologies and expressed regret for the persecution and extermination of Jews by the Romanian state during Antonescu's dictatorship. In 2009 a memorial dedicated to the victims of the Romanian Holocaust was erected with the support of the Romanian state.

The purpose of trials for war crimes and crimes against humanity is a matter of dispute, particularly since Hannah Arendt argued that trials should refrain from attempting to serve pedagogical aims and concentrate on delivering justice.[6] However, Arendt's perspective has been contested by scholars who have proved that criminal trials may satisfactorily fulfill both legal and extralegal aims. In this context, one cannot ignore the fact that the prosecution of Holocaust perpetrators has effects that extend beyond the legal system. In his plea for a rigid separation of history and law, Henry Rousso argued that trials constitute vectors of memory, of means through which society's representations about the past and its relationship to it are organized.[7] Michael Shafir argued that the Nuremberg trials served as a mobilizing myth meant to raise awareness about war crimes, genocide, and crimes against peace and humanity.[8] The trials themselves may constitute sites of remembrance, capitalized differently by various carriers of memory. In Romania, whereas Holocaust victims view the convictions for war crimes and crimes against humanity as an official acknowledgement of their suffering under Antonescu's dictatorship, those who identify themselves as victims of the communist regime see these trials as a traumatic event that saw esteemed members of the political, military, and intellectual elite of Romania sent to prison.

Kim Priemel and Alexa Stiller observed that the Nuremberg trials were frequently a target of criticism from both historians and jurists. While historians based their criticisms on the trials' failure to "account for historical complexity and bring about adequate justice," jurists were circumspect with regard to "the historical agenda of the trials" and to the historians' oversight of these trials as "legal institutions governed by established procedures and operating their own logic."[9]

According to such criticisms, the failure of criminal trials to accurately represent complex traumatic history is contrasted by the more satisfactory ways in which history, literature, and psychoanalysis explore collective traumas, as Lawrence Douglas argues.[10] The absence of procedural norms and legal reasoning from literary, historical, and psychological approaches ensures a certain interpretative freedom that justice, constrained by various structural parameters, does not enjoy. Richard J. Evans showed that evidentiary standards are differently treated by law and history, and that frequently, those who interpret and enforce the law "cannot take for granted what in history would count as common knowledge."[11] For Donald Bloxham, in the Nuremberg trials organized by the United States and Great Britain, the legal imperative to focus on what is provable and not probable, restrictions on the cumulative use of evidence, judicial notice, and court simplifications of the past resulted in the distortion of the Holocaust narrative.[12] As such, the number of victims was minimized, evidence regarding the extreme nature of some killings contradicted the common knowledge displayed in court, judgments did not capture broad complicities and the local developments of the center-directed killing policy, and the complexity of the forced labor regime was overlooked.

This chapter addresses the relationship between Holocaust memory and law during the postcommunist period in Romania. What is the narrative of the Holocaust in Romania, of its perpetrators and victims, that results from the legal treatment of the Holocaust in Romania? How do we explain the acquittal of major criminals responsible for the Holocaust in Romania, and the judiciary's tolerance of fascist propaganda and Holocaust denial? Is it only the inherent structural limitations of trials that were responsible for this? This chapter focuses on a perverted effect of transitional justice, namely, the acquittal of Holocaust perpetrators by Romanian courts of law, and also examines the judicial treatment of contemporary manifestations such as fascist propaganda, Holocaust denial, and the public cult of persons convicted for war crimes and crimes against humanity.

Retrials of Persons Convicted for War Crimes and Crimes against Humanity

The Armistice Convention signed by the Romanian government and representatives of the Soviet Union, the United States, and the United Kingdom on September 12, 1944, obliged the Romanian state to cooperate with the Allied (Soviet) High Command in the apprehension and trials of persons accused of war crimes. Most of the perpetrators prosecuted for their involvement in the Romanian Holocaust were brought to court under two laws, repeatedly amended between 1945 and 1948. Law 312/1945 for the prosecution and sanctioning of those guilty for the country's disaster and war crimes provisioned the sanctioning of acts such as participation in the war against the Allied forces and the Soviet Union.[13] It also established punishments for inhumane treatment of war prisoners, civilians in the confrontation zones, and other persons, based on racial and political reasons or support for fascism through propaganda.

After the People's Tribunals, which tried the most important political and military leaders until 1946, beginning in 1947 the organization of trials came under the authority of courts of appeal. Law 291/1947 was much closer to the Charter of the International Military Tribunal at Nuremberg, as it was not limited to establishing and defining war crimes based on the international rules regarding war and the treatment of war prisoners.[14] Crimes against peace and humanity, included explicitly in this new law, were defined as granting permission to the German army to enter the Romanian territory, or repressions for political and racial reasons, such as deportations, forced labor, the establishment of ghettos or camps, abusive treatments, violent acts, and acts of torture.

As in the Nuremberg trials, the convictions of Holocaust perpetrators in Romania after the Second World War did not succeed in fully capturing the scale of the genocide or the ramifications of the complicity that made it possible. However, the International Commission on the Holocaust in Romania demonstrated that, despite attempts by accusers and judges to politicize the process, especially during the trial of Antonescu, the courts carefully documented and assessed individual culpabilities based on official documents issued by Romanian authorities during the war, as well as testimonies of witnesses and perpetrators.[15]

Convictions for war crimes were punished by imprisonment and, frequently, confiscation of properties. Hence, the acquittals of war criminals after 1989 entailed not only clearing their criminal records, but also restitution of their confiscated properties, to them or to their descendants. Such were the cases of Radu Dinulescu and Gheorghe Petrescu, former chiefs of the Second Section within the General Staff of the Army, whose requests for acquittal were submitted to the general prosecutor by their families in 1995 and 1996, respectively.

As officers of the Second Section, Dinulescu and Petrescu were convicted in 1953 for crimes against humanity and war crimes, including involvement in the Iași pogrom, deportation of Jews from Bessarabia and Bukovina to Transnistria, and inhumane treatment of civilians. The evidence presented by the prosecutor during their trials included declarations from military officials regarding the officers' involvement in the preparation of the Iași pogrom by ensuring the liaison between Marshal Ion Antonescu and the Special Information Service, which organized the pogrom; documents that indicated that the Second Section had sent instructions for the internment of Jews in ghettos; orders and telegrams sent by the two officers regarding ethnic cleansing acts; and declarations of witnesses regarding the involvement of Petrescu on the ground in the organization of the Czernowitz ghetto.[16]

Dinulescu's legal situation was complicated by the communist regime's need for legitimacy, and his original conviction for crimes against humanity was overturned by the Supreme Tribunal in 1956. In 1957 the Bucharest Military Tribunal convicted him again for the same acts on different legal grounds stipulated by the amended criminal code: intense activity against the working class and the revolutionary movement.[17] Essentially, according to this new conviction, the victims of Dinulescu were not Jews, but communists and members of the revolutionary movement. This decision brought into legal practice the communist regime's plan to remove Jews from the position of main victims of Antonescu's regime, a process referred to by some authors as "Holocaust de-Judaization."[18]

Although the later conviction of Dinulescu under a law that sanctioned "intense activity against the working class and the revolutionary movement" differs from the conviction of his subordinate Petrescu for war crimes and crimes against humanity, the two cases cannot be separated. Both men were officers of the same army section, and cooperated to enact persecutions, deportations, and killings of Jews. Their trials after 1989 were closely linked, since the prosecutor initiated a single acquittal request for both of them, and the prosecutor and judges used similar arguments in acquitting them both.

In his memorandum submitted to the Supreme Court of Justice, the general prosecutor argued that the official prerogatives of the Second Section made it impossible for Dinulescu to act in a systematic and constant manner against the working class and for Petrescu to be involved in war crimes and crimes against humanity. In making this case, the prosecutor relied on a military regulation that established the responsibilities of the Second Section, which appeared to be a structure concerned only with the gathering of intelligence and counterintelligence. To prove Petrescu's innocence, the prosecutor also presented the declaration of an officer from the Special Information Service who also had been convicted of war crimes for his involvement in the Iași pogrom, and who denied any involvement of the Romanian authorities in the massacre of Jews.

In addition to using the testimony of a convicted person who had a clear self-interest in denying the Romanian state's responsibility for the pogrom, the prosecutor himself engaged in what some authors have called deflective denial, by blaming the SS for the bloody acts in Iași.[19] Given the judges' acceptance of this argument, the decisions in the retrials of these two war criminals were partly based on a form of Holocaust denial that does not reject that the crimes occurred, but "transfers culpability for these crimes to the members of other nations."[20] Although during the 1990s it was common for politicians and historians to put the entire blame for the Iași pogrom on German soldiers or members of the Legionary Movement, one should keep in mind that prosecutors and judges had access to the documentary evidence in the criminal files of persons who had been convicted for war crimes or crimes against humanity. Petrescu's file contained a declaration by Eugen Cristescu, chief of the Special Information Service, admitting that the massacres in Iași were carried out by his organization in cooperation with the Second Section, Radu Dinulescu, and Gheorghe Petrescu.

The prosecutor and judges not only ignored this piece of evidence, but also overlooked the most persuasive evidence—documents signed by the two officers that proved their direct involvement in the persecution and extermination of Jews. These were the orders by which Dinulescu and Petrescu requested the ethnic cleansing of the eastern front, the internment of Jews in camps near the river Bug, and the mandatory wearing of the yellow star by the Jews in Moldova, Bukovina, and Bessarabia.[21]

A similarly selective discussion and interpretation of evidence had been evident earlier in the retrials of ten persons convicted in 1945 for war crimes in what was known as the Journalists' Trial.[22] The members of the journalists' group, known fascists and antisemitic propagandists, were originally found guilty for two crimes: "leaving the national territory in order to serve Hitlerism and Fascism and attacking the country through writings, public speech, or any other means" and "serving, through their own acts, Hitlerism and Fascism, contributing to their political aims or to the economic enslavement of the country at the expense of the Romanian people's interests."[23] The evidence brought against the journalists in the 1945 trial included articles they had written that had been published in extreme right-wing publications, while the indictment examined in detail their antisemitic and profascist ideas.

In his request for acquittal, the general prosecutor downplayed the importance of the convicted journalists' writings, arguing that they represented errors of analysis and political prognosis, and that the original conviction was based on a truncated and tendentious interpretation of these texts, which were protected by the freedom of speech. Neither the prosecutor nor the judges addressed in a systematic way the content of the texts published by those journalists, some of which explicitly praised the persecution of Jews by the Antonescu regime.

Other arguments advanced by the general prosecutor after 1989 in the defense of convicted war criminals relate to factors that relieved them of responsibility for harmful acts. In the case of Dinulescu and Petrescu, the prosecutor argued that they could not be held responsible for delivering and enforcing orders issued by their superiors. The order to deport the Jews in Czernowitz—which was issued by Ion Antonescu, passed along by Dinulescu, and enforced by Petrescu, who was dispatched to supervise the deportations and the establishment of the ghetto—was not considered a relevant piece of evidence against the two officers. According to the prosecutor, "even if such an order were illegal," they could not be held liable for it because it had been first issued by Ion Antonescu. As such, the memorandum that supported their acquittal depicted Dinulescu and Petrescu as disciplined officers who acted according to their duties and the legal provisions in force during war.

A similar reasoning about responsibility for war crimes formed the basis of an earlier attempt by the general prosecutor in 1997 to obtain the acquittals of eight members of Ion Antonescu's cabinet. In that case, the prosecutor argued that the dictatorial features of the regime voided the accountability of ministers and secretaries of state, because the absolute power of decision belonged to Ion Antonescu. If this argument had been accepted, the convicted officials would have been held liable for neither the decisions taken collectively by the government nor the particular measures enforced by each of them under their portfolios. This was highly significant because the persecution of Jews was decided not only through joint cabinet resolutions, but also through measures taken by each minister in his respective policy field. Such was the case of Minister of Justice Gheorghe Docan, who adopted a law regarding crimes against the existence and interests of the state that discriminated against Jews by doubling for them the punishments given to ethnic Romanians for the same crime. Another request for acquittal pertained to the Minister of Education, Religions, and Arts, Radu Rosetti, who had banned Jews from converting to other religions, and ordered that Jewish actors and technical staff be discharged from theater and opera companies. Following public debate, and concerns expressed by two congressmen from the United States, the general prosecutor withdrew all of the acquittal requests except one, for Toma Petre Ghițulescu, former undersecretary of state in the Ministry of Economy.

In the case of the journalists formerly convicted for war crimes, their responsibility for the antisemitic and fascist propaganda they wrote was mitigated by the fact that these were the dominant ideas in the era. The Supreme Court concluded that the ideas expressed in their writings "were conventionally tolerable in that era and socio-political regime."[24] According to its decision, the Court had to consider "the nature of the profession of the convicted persons, the ideas which usually circulated in the era ..., the contextual factors which might have influenced them, and the manner in which the journalists, according to their training and conception, could have represented the national interest."[25]

The postcommunist trials of Holocaust perpetrators also indicated that the judiciary neglected information about the persecution and extermination of Jews, though both the prosecutors and judges seemed willing to engage in historical reasoning. When justifying the acquittal of journalists convicted for war crimes, the Supreme Court stated that the journalists had expressed harmful ideas which, "appreciated in relation with the following historical periods, were more or less or even obviously harmful to the interests of the Romanian people."[26] Although they vaguely conceded the misconduct of the journalists, the judges failed to acknowledge explicitly that they had incited hatred against Jews in an era when Jews were subjected to persecutions, deportations, and exterminations. Furthermore, in the plea for Dinulescu's acquittal, the General Prosecutor's Office expressed doubts about the illegality of the order issued by Dinulescu for the deportation of the Jews in Czernowitz.

Ion Pănescu's acquittal in 2004 clearly shows that the judiciary was unfamiliar with the different phases of the Holocaust in Romania.[27] Pănescu, former commander of the Czernowitz airport, was convicted in 1950 based on Decree 207/1948, for "unlawfully appropriating state or privately owned properties from the territories where the war was fought or, in the same conditions, acquiring wealth, in an unlawful manner, by taking advantage of his official status or of his relations with other official persons."[28] In 1941 and 1942 he used the forced labor of several Jews in a clock and jewelry workshop he rented, and according to the testimonies of his victims, he extorted them under threat of deportation to Transnistria. During the postcommunist trial the court and the prosecutor did not take into consideration that the establishment and functioning of Pănescu's rented workshop was made possible by the regime of forced labor, which was a persecutory policy officially justified during that period solely by the ethnicity of the workers, and which had a profound punitive nature.[29] Eventually, Pănescu was acquitted because the prosecutor proved that the convicted did not manage to accumulate great wealth from the business of the workshop.

Enforcement of Ordinance 31/2002

Ordinance 31, issued by the Romanian government in 2002 and revised repeatedly by the parliament, established a special system to deal with hate crimes based on ethnic, racial, and religious criteria.[30] Until 2015, this act incriminated and punished three types of expressions: the promotion of fascist, racist, or xenophobic symbols and ideologies through propaganda; the public cult of persons convicted of crimes against humanity; and Holocaust denial. According to the law, fascist, racist, or xenophobic organizations are defined as those that promote hatred based on ethnic, religious, or racial criteria, race supremacy, antisemitism, violence in order to change the constitutional order, or extreme nationalism. Persons guilty of crimes against peace and humanity are those who were convicted of these crimes by a Romanian, foreign, or international court of law. The Holocaust is defined as the "systematic state-sponsored persecution and annihilation of Jews by Nazi Germany and its allies and collaborators between 1933 and 1945." The definition also refers to the genocide of the Roma, stating that "during the Second World War, a part of the Roma population was subjected to deportation and annihilation." The sanctions provisioned by this law include imprisonment or criminal fines. The ordinance was adopted during a period when Holocaust denial and the cult of Marshal Antonescu were prevalent in the public space and state institutions, but the main incentive for its adoption came in the context of Romania's candidacy for NATO accession, which required that it take some steps to combat xenophobia, Holocaust denial, and extremist propaganda.

Between 2002 and 2015 the Prosecutor's Office initiated criminal investigations of violations of Emergency Ordinance 31/2002 in 302 cases, either ex officio or after receiving complaints. Only thirteen of these cases were brought to trial, while the prosecutor dropped charges or dismissed the complaints for the rest of them. The case that drew the widest public attention was the trial of Grigore Oprița in 2003 to 2005 for chauvinistic propaganda and distribution of fascist, racist, or xenophobic symbols.[31] At that time, this trial was of paramount importance to the Romanian far right, since what was at stake was the acknowledgement of the Legionary Movement's legality. As such, Șerban Suru, self-proclaimed leader of the Legionary Movement, Ion Coja, a known Holocaust denier, Tudor Ionescu, president of the Noua Dreaptă (New Right) organization, members of the Partidul pentru Patrie (Party for the Fatherland),[32] and other extremist activists showed solidarity and supported Grigore Oprița and acted as witnesses on his behalf.

The evidence that prompted the trial of Grigore Oprița included several publications in which he praised the Legionary Movement. In addition, a company founded by the defendant and registered under the name "Arbeit MF" published and sold the *Asalt* (Assault) magazine and CDs that included legionary songs, speeches of Horia Sima, and writings of Corneliu Zelea

Codreanu. Furthermore, authorities found in Opriţa's possession thousands of items of propaganda material including flyers and magazines advertising the Legionary Movement, writings of Horia Sima and other legionary ideologists, and brochures that contested the figure of six million Holocaust victims.

Initially, Opriţa was convicted in 2003 by a tribunal and given a prison sentence of two and a half years. In 2005 the court of appeal, after reexamining the first sentence, acquitted the defendant, holding that the organizations that support the Legionary Movement, its doctrine, symbols, and songs represent "a reality which cannot be ignored" and a "manifestation of the freedom of speech."[33] The judges also reasoned that the circulation of several publications by different authors who praise the Legionary Movement, as well as the public use of symbols such as the Celtic cross, proved that Opriţa's acts were not crimes and were not unique to Romania. Such publications had been previously submitted to the court by Şerban Suru, who appeared in front of the judges dressed in a legionary uniform.

Most of the court's reasons for acquitting Opriţa were based on interpretation of the European Court of Human Rights jurisprudence. The decision mentioned that a preference for a certain political movement or ideology is protected by Article 10 of the European Convention on Human Rights, and that respect for other persons' rights is an obligation associated with the freedom of speech, but some exaggeration must be tolerated. In defense of this thesis, the Romanian judges invoked several decisions in which the European Court of Human Rights had established that Article 10 of the Convention had been violated by certain states. However, these decisions did not refer to persons convicted by states for hate speech, but to journalists who were either subjected to violence and threats or sanctioned for defamation, distribution of erotic content, or false allegations. In one of the cases, a Danish journalist was convicted for broadcasting an interview that included racist comments,[34] though the interview was meant to portray the mentality and social background of racists and not to support their views.

The acquittal of Grigore Opriţa was a foundational moment for Romanian jurisprudence with regard to the promotion of legionary symbols and ideology. Despite the fact that legal precedents are not binding in Romania, this decision has been invoked in other trials dealing with the same issue. Furthermore, mass media portrayed the Opriţa decision as a tacit acknowledgment that it is legal to publicly display the symbols and promote the ideology of the Legionary Movement.

Following Oprița's acquittal, the Prosecutor's Office was reluctant to prosecute apologists of legionarism, and as a consequence, legionary symbols were frequently displayed in public. A few kilometers from Bucharest, where the founding leader of the Legionary Movement was executed in 1938, adepts of legionarism built a roadside cross and placed next to it a fence and a flag bearing the symbol of the interwar organization. The site became a common destination of parades organized by extreme right organizations and adepts of the Legionary Movement, who regularly gathered there dressed in legionary uniforms to sing songs, perform the fascist salute, and commemorate Corneliu Zelea Codreanu. On several occasions, right-wing extremists from Germany (NPD), Sweden (SVP), and Italy (Forza Nuova) joined their Romanian counterparts at these ceremonies.

In 2012 the Elie Wiesel National Institute for the Study of the Holocaust in Romania notified the general prosecutor attached to the High Court of Cassation and Justice that this site permanently displays the logo of the Legionary Movement and a photograph of Corneliu Zelea Codreanu, symbols that are forbidden according to Ordinance 31/2002. That same year, after investigating the evidence submitted by the Institute, the prosecutor issued a decision that no crime had been committed.[35] The first of several reasons for this decision was that Corneliu Zelea Codreanu had not been convicted for crimes against peace and humanity, which is true—no such conviction could have been issued since he died in 1938, seven years before crimes against peace or humanity were established for the first time in criminal law. This reasoning also ignores the fact that Codreanu might be seen as a symbol of fascism, anti-Semitism, or xenophobia. The prosecutor's second reason was that the ensemble that included the symbols considered to be fascist, antisemitic, or xenophobic is not propaganda, and as such, does not fall under the provisions of the law. Finally, the prosecutor referred to an exception stipulated by Ordinance 31/2002 that the public use of fascist, racist, or xenophobic symbols is allowed if it serves an educational, academic, or artistic purpose. The prosecutor decided that there were no indications that symbols of the Legionary Movement were placed there to promote fascist, racist, or xenophobic ideas, rather than to serve a scientific or educational purpose. Eventually, the mayor's office established that the flagpole and fence did not have a construction permit and removed them, but the spot still serves as a pilgrimage site for Romanian and foreign adepts of fascism.

The case of Șerban Suru, who proclaimed himself the leader of the Legionary Movement after 1989, represented another occasion for prosecutors and judges to assess whether legionarism constitutes a version of fascism and consequently falls under the provisions of Emergency Ordinance 31/2002. In 1994 Suru established a "Legionary Library" in Bucharest where he held meetings and where sympathizers of the Iron Guard, dressed in traditional legionary uniforms, participated in ceremonies and took oaths. In 2013, the Elie Wiesel Institute notified the Prosecutor's Office that several fascist symbols were displayed on flags and signboards attached to the building where the Legionary Library and Suru's Legionary Movement had its headquarters. Suru declared to the prosecutor that he was a founding member and leader of the "Legionary Movement," an organization without legal standing that had been functioning continuously since 1994. He also stated that the symbols of the Legionary Movement do not have any fascist, xenophobic, or antisemitic connotations, but only anticommunist ones.

As a consequence, the prosecutor tried to establish whether the Legionary Movement falls under the provisions of Ordinance 31/2002 regarding fascist, racist, or xenophobic symbols and ideas. At his request, the Romanian Academy issued an opinion on the matter, which stated that "not all extremist right-wing organizations in Europe can be considered exclusively fascist; without any doubt, there are common elements between them, but not enough to draw a radical conclusion; each movement had its own peculiarities."[36] This led the prosecutor to conclude that the nature of the Legionary Movement is subject to controversy, and that any characterization of this organization is an open issue. Yet, the Romanian Academy did not refer explicitly to the Legionary Movement. Furthermore, the Academy did not deny the fascist nature of extremist right-wing organizations, but instead stated that fascism is not the only feature of these organizations, that in addition to their fascist nature, they also have special features that allow for differentiation among them. A complaint was also addressed to the chief prosecutor of Bucharest, who upheld his colleague's opinion and established that the legionary symbols do not fall, beyond any reasonable doubt, under the provisions of Ordinance 31/2002.

A complainant who seeks the initiation of a criminal prosecution may, as a last resort, appeal to a court of law, which can force the prosecutor to start criminal investigations. The Institute resorted to this solution and brought to the attention of the court a previous opinion of the Romanian Academy, expressed in the Romanian explicative dictionary, that legionarism is a category of fascism. Furthermore, the Institute referred to a wide range of academic perspectives, from textbooks approved by the Ministry of Education to scholarly works, which confirmed the fascist nature of the Legionary Movement. Despite this evidence, the judge maintained the conclusion that the Legionary Movement is a subject of controversy and that Ordinance 31/2002, which does not explicitly refer to legionarism, is not understandable and legally certain with regard to legionary ideology.[37] As such, the public display of legionary symbols was considered an expression that is not punishable according to the criminal provisions in place. In addition to rejecting the argument that the Legionary Movement is fascist in nature, the magistrates did not take into account the fact that legionarism, even if it does not fall under the legal category of fascism, could be considered xenophobic, and as a consequence, fall under the incidence of Ordinance 31/2002.

The magistrates' interpretation of Emergency Ordinance 31/2002 demonstrates the similarities between the legal treatment of Romanian fascism and the legal treatment of discourses that deny the existence of the Romanian Holocaust. In 2005 Professor Corvin Lupu published an elaborate article in *Transilvania*, a cultural publication financed by the Sibiu County Council, in which he denied the existence of a Holocaust in Romania. The prosecutor attached to the Sibiu Tribunal considered that the article did not represent Holocaust denial under the terms of Ordinance 31/2002 because as an academic endeavor, it could not have been written in bad faith, based on antisemitic reasons, or with the intention of denying the existence of the Holocaust. Furthermore, the prosecutor established that Lupu did not deny or contest the Holocaust in its entirety, but only discussed its dimension and existence in Romania. Hence, the prosecutor's reasoning suggests that denial of the Holocaust is punishable only if a person denies the European Holocaust as a whole.

These cases prove that magistrates did not enforce Ordinance 31/2002 when dealing with expressions that promoted the Romanian version of fascism or denied the Romanian chapter of the Holocaust. However, prosecutors and courts of law had a different approach with regards to cases that involved National Socialism. In 2004 the Department for Combating Organized Crime in Alba County learned that an extremist organization called the Gebeleizis Society, founded in 2003, had launched a website that disseminated fascist, racist, and xenophobic content, such as Aryanist ideas, marches and songs of the National Socialist Party and SS, and various fascist symbols. On December 21, 2004, law enforcement authorities raided the Dacian fortress of Costești where the members of the Gebeleizis Society gathered, and seized propaganda materials. Additionally, the police confiscated from Vasile Molnar, one of the society's members, racist materials including posters of Adolf Hitler, printed depictions of fascist symbols, and copies of a publication titled *Noua Dreaptă* (The new right), which was characterized by prosecutors as a collection of antidemocratic, racist, and antisemitic articles. According to the prosecutors, Molnar's computer and CDs contained racist publications, images, and texts that advocated against the rights of Roma and Jews, tape cases referring to Nazi marches, and texts advertising the brochure "Did Hitler Really Kill 6 Million Jews?" (It is worth mentioning that copies of this same brochure and the *Noua Dreaptă* publication were also confiscated from Grigore Oprița's house during his trial.)

Based on this evidence, in 2007 Vasile Molnar was convicted and given a two-year suspended sentence for possession with intent to distribute and public use of fascist, racist, or xenophobic symbols; promotion of fascist, racist, or xenophobic ideas; and Holocaust denial.[38] The same year, another court gave him a one-year suspended sentence for offenses committed in 2003 during a music festival, when police searched his backpack and found dozens of racist and fascist propaganda materials that he intended to distribute.[39] In both cases, magistrates established that the materials were connected to National Socialism, Adolf Hitler, and the SS.

Concern about the public promotion of National Socialism was similarly expressed by prosecutors and judges in 2006, when Marius Trancă, previously convicted for drawing a swastika on a building, was sentenced to five months in prison for displaying his SS tattoo, performing a fascist salute ("Heil Hitler"), and disseminating the swastika through his racist website. In its decision, the court relied on the opinion issued by the National Committee of Heraldry, which established that the SS logo and the swastika are

Nazi symbols associated with racism and the extermination of the Jews and Roma.[40] Hence, the court established that Trancă was guilty of the public use and distribution of fascist symbols and the promotion of fascist, racist, or xenophobic ideologies.

The most recent example of the asymmetric enforcement of Emergency Ordinance 31/2002 was in 2015, when the Sighișoara Court of Law sentenced an ethnic Hungarian to pay a criminal fine for the public cult of a person convicted for crimes against peace and humanity. In 2014 Ferenc Toth had organized a commemoration ceremony and unveiled a statue of Albert Wass, installed on the exterior wall of his house, which prompted law enforcement authorities to take notice ex officio about this event and start investigations on the same day. Count Albert Wass, a Hungarian noble, had been convicted for war crimes in 1946 by the Cluj People's Tribunal under Law 312/1945 for "ordering or carrying out collective or individual repressions, with the aim of persecuting the civilian population for political or racial reasons."[41] In 1940, after Northern Transylvania came under the control of the Hungarian state, Wass acted as an instigator for the killing of seventeen persons, including a Jewish merchant and his family.

The fact that Wass had been convicted for war crimes was not an obstacle to punishing his public cult under Emergency Ordinance 31/2002, which at that time incriminated the public cult of persons convicted for crimes against peace or humanity, not war crimes; the judges held that Wass's acts, initially considered war crimes, fell under the category of crimes against humanity according to the criminal code then in force. The presence of statues of Wass in several towns in Transylvania had been repeatedly denounced, especially by journalists and intellectuals who emphasized the anti-Romanian nature of his acts. But there is a lesser concern with regard to the public cult of Marshal Ion Antonescu. In 2015 the Argeș History Museum portrayed Antonescu as a great, patriotic, and disciplined leader, several streets bore his name, and the town council of Târgoviște refused to withdraw the title of "post mortem honorary citizen" awarded to him in 1996.

THE LEGAL NARRATIVE OF THE HOLOCAUST: BETWEEN STRUCTURAL LIMITATIONS AND DELIBERATE CONSTRUCTION

The acquittals of persons convicted for war crimes or crimes against humanity and the enforcement of Emergency Ordinance 31/2002 share a common narrative about the Holocaust and are based on kindred arguments, but they performed different functions and did not develop in the same context. The acquittal requests initiated by the General Prosecutor's Office were backed by the convicted persons' families as the only way they could secure property restitution. At the same time, acquittals of high-profile persons convicted after 1945 represented symbolic reparation for what were perceived as abuses of the communist regime. Since 1990, lawmakers were aware of the problems that could arise from granting compensation to former members of the Legionary Movement or to Holocaust perpetrators convicted after 1945 for war crimes, crimes against peace, or crimes against humanity. Right after the Romanian Revolution, the Provisional Council of National Union adopted Decree Law 118/1990 granting some rights to persons persecuted by the communist dictatorship for political reasons.[42] The law implied that those who qualified as victims would be entitled to a monthly payment for each year of their detention, internment, mandatory residence, or resettlement. Individuals who were convicted for crimes against humanity or who were proven to have carried out fascist activities within an organization or movement could not qualify for reparations under this law. This important distinction was maintained in Emergency Ordinance 214/1999, repeatedly amended between 2000 and 2006, which established that individuals who participated in activities of armed opposition or forced overthrow of the communist regime between 1945 and 1989 are entitled to be granted the status of "fighter in the anticommunist resistance" and can benefit from the provisions of the previous law.[43] Again, persons who were convicted for crimes against humanity or for carrying out fascist activities within organizations or movements are excluded from benefiting from the provisions of the law.

The acquittals of Holocaust perpetrators represented a legal operation performed on the past in order to redress what was seen as an abuse and to grant the anticommunist narrative a legal acknowledgement. This became obvious in 1997, when the General Prosecutor's attempt to acquit members of Antonescu's cabinet provoked an intellectual debate, and established historians supported this legal endeavor.[44] On the contrary, the enforcement of Ordinance 31/2002 should have been an operation performed on the present, in order to establish a different narrative about the traumatic fascist past of Romania, but both legal maneuvers ended up serving the same narrative.

For example, the claim that the pogrom in Iași had been carried out by the SS and not by Romanian authorities, argued by the prosecutor during the retrials of Radu Dinulescu and Gheorghe Petrescu, can be coupled with the magistrate's refusal to prosecute Corvin Lupu under Ordinance 31/2002 for denial of the Romanian Holocaust. In contrast, judges convicted Vasile Molnar for Holocaust denial because his offense was related to Nazi propaganda and the cult of Adolf Hitler.

In the acquittals of propagandists initially convicted in the Journalists' Trial, although the court did not explicitly address the fascist and antisemitic content disseminated by them, it concluded that propaganda that would be considered wrong by the criteria of today was common before and during the war. According to the prosecutor who requested the acquittal, the convicted journalists' writings were protected as free speech. Similarly, the failure to enforce Emergency Ordinance 31/2002 in the case of Grigore Oprița, apologist of the Legionary Movement, was supported by the judges' observation that his acts were not unique; that is, the fact that various organizations drew inspiration from the Legionary Movement and numerous authors were favorable to this organization represented, from the court's point of view, a manifestation of the freedom of speech.

The failure of magistrates to establish the fascist nature of the Legionary Movement, a fact almost unanimously ascertained by foreign scholars, was contrasted by the convictions of persons involved in disseminating propaganda materials linked to a foreign version of fascism, namely National Socialism.[45] Likewise, in 2015 authorities promptly reacted against a planned commemoration of Albert Wass attended by ethnic Hungarians. Yet, magistrates neglected cases when the cult of Marshal Ion Antonescu, who has the same legal status as Albert Wass, was promoted through writings, religious iconography, and the naming of streets.

Considering the two types of jurisprudence under discussion, the postcommunist legal narrative about the Holocaust in Romania is structured along several main coordinates. Thus, military personnel who followed orders to persecute and exterminate Jews, as well as propagandists who followed the dominant ideology and incited antisemitic hatred, cannot be held responsible for their crimes. Responsibility for the pogrom in Iași and the killings in Northern Transylvania lies with foreigners, be they members of the SS or ethnic Hungarians. The regime of forced labor imposed on Jews during the war did not constitute a form of persecution per se. According to the magistrates' assessment of the Legionary Movement, Romania did not experience a local version of fascism. Indeed, legionary ideology is not antisemitic or xenophobic, either, since it withstood the test of a law that sanctions not just fascist propaganda, but also the promotion of xenophobic or racist ideologies.

What remains to be clarified is the degree to which this narrative was made possible by the inherent structural limitations of the trials. We should note that common knowledge played an important role in both the acquittals of Holocaust perpetrators and the enforcement of Emergency Ordinance 31/2002. In all the retrials of persons convicted for war crimes or crimes against humanity, magistrates relied on their own understanding of history, without resorting to the expertise of historians. Under these conditions, the denial of the Romanian authorities' responsibility for the pogrom in Iași, the doubts expressed about the illegal nature of the deportation of Jews from Czernowitz, and the failure to recognize forced labor as a phase of the Holocaust went unchallenged during the trials. Similarly, in Grigore Oprița's trial based on Emergency Ordinance 31/2002, the lack of an expert opinion made it possible for apologists of the Legionary Movement to act as witnesses and submit to the court writings that distorted the history of the organization. As a consequence, judges did not consider the crimes committed by the Legionary Movement or the nature of its ideology.

In contrast, in the case of Șerban Suru's public use of fascist symbols, the prosecutor asked the Romanian Academy to issue an opinion regarding the fascist nature of the Legionary Movement. However, it is problematic to claim that this expert opinion convinced the prosecutor to conclude that legionarism is not a version of fascism, because the Academy did not deny the fascist ideological affiliation of the Legionary Movement. This prosecutor's position was instead a manifestation of a strategic behavior that can be observed in other cases, too. In the case of the public cult of Albert Wass, judges also engaged in strategic argumentation when they convicted Ferenc Toth for promoting the commemoration of a war criminal, based on an article that incriminated the public cult of persons convicted for crimes against humanity. Returning to the 1997 attempt to acquit members of Ion Antonescu's cabinet, the general prosecutor argued that the criminal responsibility of secretaries and undersecretaries of state derives from their political responsibility, and since political responsibility belonged solely to the dictator Ion Antonescu, his subordinates should not have been held accountable for the policies to which they contributed. What the general prosecutor did not acknowledge was that political responsibility was obsolete, given the fact that Antonescu governed in the absence of a constitution and elections, and the parliament had been dissolved.

The simplifications of the past that emerged during the trials to acquit Holocaust perpetrators may have been caused partly by reliance on common knowledge, which had been adulterated by the communist regime's efforts to distort or minimize the Holocaust in Romania. However, evidence suggests that in some cases, magistrates preferred to simplify the legal narrative regarding the Holocaust and Romanian fascism. In the retrial of the journalists convicted in 1945, neither the prosecutor nor the judges referred to the antisemitic content of their articles. The same selectivity in the interpretation of evidence was manifested in Ion Pănescu's retrial, where the court ignored the victims' testimonies given during the original trial. In the postcommunist trials of Radu Dinulescu and Gheorghe Petrescu, the court relied heavily on a regulation of the Second Section that established its formal duties, and did not consider other official documents included in the criminal file that attested to the Second Section's role in the Holocaust. In another case, the evidence on which Vasile Molnar was convicted for Holocaust denial (among other offenses) consisted of texts that advertised the brochure "Did Hitler Really Kill 6 Million Jews?," and yet, two years earlier, Grigore Oprița, who possessed 46 copies of the actual brochure, had been acquitted of any crime under Emergency Ordinance 31/2002.

The difference between the judicial version of Holocaust memory and other recollections of this tragic episode is a matter of hierarchy. Invested with public authority and having a self-referential nature, Romanian justice performed both a retributive and distributive function based on its own recollection of the Holocaust. As vectors of memory, the trials discussed in this chapter imposed a narrative of the past that suited a nationalist agenda. However, in the summer of 2015 the Romanian parliament adopted several amendments to Emergency Ordinance 31/2002. The new version explicitly incriminates the promotion of legionary ideology and symbols and the public cult of persons convicted for war crimes, and includes a separate definition of the Holocaust in Romania. In the explanatory memorandum, the initiators made direct reference to the inadequacy of the previous version of the Ordinance with regard to legionary expressions. It remains to be seen whether the new version of the law will bring a change in the hierarchy of memories.

> Alexandru Climescu is a researcher at the Elie Wiesel National Institute for the Study of the Holocaust in Romania. His research interests include legal approaches to right-wing extremism, Holocaust public memory, and the acquittals of war criminals during postcommunism.

NOTES

1. National communism, one of the defining features of Nicolae Ceaușescu's regime (1965–1989), represented a syncretism of nationalism and communism.
2. Shafir, "Reabilitarea postcomunistă," 400–465.
3. Ioanid, "Un criminal de guerre réhabilité?," Le Monde, March 2, 2007.
4. Shafir, "Memory, Memorials," 67–96.
5. International Commission, Final Report.
6. Arendt, Eichmann, 253.
7. Conan and Rousso, Vichy, 74–76.
8. Shafir, "Nürnberg II," 87–104; Shafir, "The Second Nurnberg," 109–144.
9. Priemel and Stiller, introduction, 4.
10. Douglas, Memory of Justice, 1–7.
11. Evans, "History, Memory," 326–345.
12. Bloxham, Genocide on Trial, 221–222.
The topic of this section was developed in two previously published articles: Climescu, "Post-Transitional Injustice," 145–157; Climescu, "Holocaust on Trial," 307–320.
13. Law 312, Monitorul Oficial no. 94 (1945): 3362.
14. Law 291, Monitorul Oficial no. 189 (1947): 7423.
15. International Commission, Final Report, 313–331.
16. NCSSA, dos. P639, vol. 4.
17. Decree-law 62 (1954), NCHA SC, dos. 2/1954, vol. 1, and Decree-law 358 (1954), NCHA SC dos. 6/1954.
18. Shafir, "Radical Politics."
19. Shafir, Între negare și trivializare, 47–85.
20. Ibid., 49.
21. Carp, Cartea neagra, 104, 143; Trașcă, "Chestiunea evreiască," 179, 215, 311.
22. In 1945 the People's Tribunal convicted Pamfil Șeicaru, Grigore Manoilescu, Ilie Rădulescu, Romulus Seișanu, Ilie Popescu-Prundeni, Gabriel Bălănescu, Pantelimon Vizirescu, Aurel Cosma, Nichifor Crainic, Stelian Popescu, Ion Dumitrescu, Romulus Dianu, Alexandru Hodoș, and Radu Demetrescu-Gyr for war crimes. Grigore Manoilescu,

Ilie Rădulescu, Ilie Popescu-Prundeni, and Radu Demetrescu-Gyr were not acquitted in 1995.

23. Law 312, *Monitorul Oficial* no. 94 (1945): 3362, articles j and o.

24. NCSSA, dos. P 77, vol. 34, 117–119, The Supreme Court of Justice, Decision no. 17/8, May 1945.

25. Ibid.

26. Ibid.

27. NCSSA, dos. P076520, vol. 1.

28. Decree no. 207/1948 for the amendment of Law 291/1947, *Monitorul Oficial* no. 2546 (1948), article b.

29. Bărbulescu, "Muncă obligatorie," 59–70.

30. Emergency Ordinance no. 31, *Monitorul Oficial* no. 214 (2002).

31. Brașov Court of Appeal, Decision no. 284/2005.

32. This party was founded in 1993 by former members of the Legionary Movement and identified itself with the legionary symbols and ideology.

33. Brașov Court of Appeal, Decision no. 284/2005.

34. Jersild v. Denmark no. 15890/1989 [1994] ECHR.

35. Prosecutor's Office attached to the Buftea Court of Law, Resolution 2596/P/2012.

36. Prosecutor's Office attached to the Bucharest Court of Law, Sector 1, Ordinance no. 1161/II–2/2014.

37. Bucharest Court of Law, Decision no. 23010/299/2014.

38. Criminal Section of the High Court of Cassation and Justice, decision no. 1646/13, May 2008.

39. Criminal Section of the High Court of Cassation and Justice, decision no. 1750/20 May 2008.

40. Court of Appeal in Ploiești, decision no.788/09, October 2008.

41. Law 312, *Monitorul Oficial* no. 94 (1945), article e: 3362.

42. Decree-law no. 118/1990, republished in *Monitorul Oficial* no. 631 (2009).

43. Emergency Ordinance no. 214, *Monitorul Oficial* no. 650 (1999).

44. "Sentințe și apel," 8–12.

45. With respect to the writings of foreign scholars who studied the Legionary Movement, see, for instance, Payne, *A History of Fascism*, 277–289, 281–282; Laqueur, *Fascism*, 18; Paxton, *Anatomy of Fascism*, 97; Morgan, *Fascism in Europe*, 45; Griffin, *Nature of Fascism*, 218.

References

Arendt, Hannah. *Eichmann in Jerusalem: A Report on the Banality of Evil*. New York: Viking, 1965.

Bărbulescu, Ana. "Muncă obligatorie în România anului 1941: ideologie vs. randament economic." *Holocaust. Studii și cercetări* 2 (2009): 59–70.

Bloxham, Donald. *Genocide on Trial: War Crimes Trials and the Formation of Holocaust History and Memory*. New York: Oxford University Press, 2001.

Carp, Matatias. *Cartea neagra*, vol. 2. Bucharest: Societatea Națională de Editură și Arte Grafice "Dacia Traiană," 1948.

Climescu, Alexandru. "The Holocaust on Trial: Memory and Amnesia in the Case of Romanian War Criminals." *Holocaust. Studii și cercetări* 8 (2015): 307–320.

———. "Post-transitional Injustice: The Acquittal of Holocaust Perpetrators in Post-Communist Romania." *Holocaust. Studii și cercetări* 7 (2014): 145–157.

Conan, Eric, and Henry Rousso. *Vichy: An Ever-Present Past.* Hanover, NH: University Press of New England, 1998.

Douglas, Lawrence. *The Memory of Justice.* New Haven, CT: Yale University Press, 2001.

Evans, Richard J. "History, Memory, and the Law: The Historian as Expert Witness." *History and Theory* 3 (2002): 326–345.

Griffin, Roger. *The Nature of Fascism.* New York: Routledge, 1993.

International Commission on the Holocaust in Romania. *Final Report.* Edited by Tuvia Friling, Radu Ioanid, and Mihail E. Ionescu. Iași, Romania: Polirom, 2004.

Laqueur, Walter. *Fascism: A Reader's Guide.* Los Angeles: University of California Press, 1976.

Morgan, Philip. *Fascism in Europe, 1914–1945.* New York: Routledge, 2003.

Paxton, Robert. *The Anatomy of Fascism.* New York: Random House, 2005.

Payne, Stanley. *A History of Fascism, 1914–1945.* Madison: University of Wisconsin Press, 1995.

Priemel, Kim C., and Alexa Stiller. "Introduction." In *Reassessing the Nuremberg Military Tribunals,* edited by Kim C. Priemel and Alexa Stiller, 1–21. New York: Berghahn Books, 2012.

"Sentințe și apel în cabinetul Antonescu." *Revista 22* (December 2–8): 1997.

Shafir, Michael. *Între negare și trivializare. Negarea Holocaustului în țările postcomuniste din Europa Centrală și de Est.* Iași, Romania: Polirom, 2002.

———. "Memory, Memorials, and Membership: Romanian Utilitarian Anti-Semitism and Marshal Antonescu." In *Romania Since 1989. Politics, Economics and Society,* edited by Henry F. Carey, 67–96. Lanham, MD: Lexington Books, 2005.

———. "Nürnberg II? Mitul denazificării și utilizarea acestuia în martirologia competitivă Holocaust-Gulag." *Caietele Echinox* 13 (2007): 87–104.

———. "Radical Politics in East-Central Europe: Part IX: The Romanian Radical Return (B)." *Radio Free Europe/Radio Liberty East European Perspectives.* January 24, 2001. http://www.rferl.org/a/1342522.html.

———. "Reabilitarea postcomunistă a mareșalului Antonescu: *Cui bono?*" In *Exterminarea evreilor români și ucraineni în perioada antonesciană,* edited by Randolph L. Braham, 400–465. Bucharest: Hasefer, 2002.

———. "The Second Nurnberg: Legend vs. Myth in Postcommunism (I)." *Holocaust. Studii și cercetări* 7 (2014): 109–144.

Trașcă, Ottmar. "*Chestiunea evreiască" în documentele militare române. 1941–1944.* Iași, Romania: Institutul European, 2010.

Chapter Four

ROMANIA
Neither "Fleishig" nor "Milchig": A Comparative Study

Michael Shafir

Right after the change of regime in December 1989, Romania displayed some features that were common to most postcommunist East-Central European countries in regard to antisemitism, as well as some specific features of its own. Freed from ideological and censorship constraints, latent antisemitism erupted in the public space, and after a while it became a cross-party phenomenon. This does not mean that political parties had all put antisemitism on their banners; it rather means that regardless of ideology, both antisemitic prejudice and, above all, the perception of Romania's "dark past"[1] of the interwar period and the Second World War, as well as the role Jews had allegedly played in the early stage of communism, figured in similar shades, if not intensity, in all political formations. The "dark past" was by and large ignored and occasionally justified, while the claim about the Jews was overemphasized in what turned out to be a renaissance of the "Judeo-Bolshevik" myth.[2] All of these elements were common to most East-Central European countries.

This is not to say that differences between attitudes were not noticeable. One could, for example, distinguish between: (a) self-exculpatory nostalgic antisemitism, or parties and movements of a "radical return" to models of the interwar radical right; (b) self-propelling antisemitism, or what I have called parties and movements of a "radical continuity," based on models provided by exacerbated Ceaușescu-era national communism; (c) neopopulist mercantile antisemitism, in which antisemitism is either utilized or discarded according to what "sells" and what does not at both national and international levels; (d) utilitarian antisemitism, which shares some characteristics with neopopulist mercantile antisemitism but is distinguished by the fact that it is employed by parties, movements, and personalities who are on record as being "anti-antisemitic"; (e) reactive antisemitism, which is basically explained in terms of a "competitive martyrdom" between the Holocaust and the Gulag; and (f) vengeance antisemitism, represented by those who are driven by the simple hatred of Jews for whatever they do or refrain from doing.[3] For this chapter, utilitarian antisemitism is of special relevance, for it unwillingly and unwittingly triggered significant shifts in the official narrative on antisemitism and the Holocaust. However, that official narrative is not necessarily accompanied by a similarly extensive shift in unofficial practices and attitudes. This is best examined by observing how reactive antisemitism replaced Holocaust denial and/or trivialization with "Holocaust obfuscation"[4] within the general East-Central European trend of competitive martyrdom.

From the Antonescu Cult to Ordinance 31/2002

With Romania banging on NATO's doors, and against the background of protests in the United States and Israel triggered by the Ion Antonescu cult in Romania, in 2001 former Romanian president Ion Iliescu attended a ceremony commemorating the 1941 Iași pogrom, where he felt compelled to declare that "no matter what *we* may think, international public opinion considers Antonescu to have been a war criminal."[5] This was as honest an admission as Iliescu was capable of that Romanian and Western memory of the Second World War did not coincide.

By early 2002 Romania had been bluntly told by US officials that the conditions for its acceptance into NATO included facing its Second World War past, and that it would have to put an end to the Marshal Antonescu cult that had been thriving in Romania since 1990.[6] Although the cult's main promoters were people associated with the Greater Romanian Party (Partidul România Mare, PRM), its spectrum was in fact far wider, cutting across party lines and involving prominent historians and other intellectuals. Between six and eight statues had been erected in memory of the Marshal, twenty-five streets and squares had been renamed after him, and in Iași even the "Heroes" military cemetery carried the dictator's name.[7] On March 18, 2002, the Defense Ministry launched a syllabus on the Holocaust at the National Defense College in Bucharest, and in a message to participants, Prime Minister Adrian Năstase said that "the future cannot be built on falsification and mystification," and that the 1941 pogroms in Iași and the decimation of Jews in liberated Bessarabia and Bukovina, as well as the later deportation of Jews to Transnistria, had been "in no way different from . . . the Nazi operation known under the name of the Final Solution." In his message, Năstase announced that the government had approved an emergency ordinance prohibiting the display of "racist or fascist symbols," the erection of statues or plaques commemorating those convicted in Romania or abroad for "crimes against peace" and "crimes against humanity," and the naming of streets and other places after those personalities.

Emergency ordinances become effective upon their issuance, but must eventually be approved by the parliament in order to become laws. Lengthy debates in parliamentary commissions showed that this was by no means to be taken for granted, as it took four years for the Romanian parliament to approve the new law.[8] The procrastination was obviously intentional. As approved, the new law employed the definition of the Holocaust included in the report issued by the International Commission on the Holocaust in Romania (see infra)—"the state-sponsored systematic persecution and annihilation of European Jewry by Nazi Germany, *its allies and collaborators* between 1933–1945"—adding to it that the country's Roma population had also been subjected to "deportation and annihilation."[9]

A Presidential Blunder Gives Rise to a Commission

The setting up of the Commission has its own peculiar saga. It followed a blunder by Ion Iliescu in an interview with a journalist from the Israeli daily *Haaretz*.[10] Engaging in "Holocaust trivialization," the president told the interviewer that "the Holocaust was not unique to the Jewish population in Europe. Many others, including Poles, died in the same way." But only Jews and Gypsies, the interviewer observed in reaction, had been "targeted for genocide" at that time. To which Iliescu responded, "I know. But there were others, who were labeled communists, and they were similarly victimized."

Although Iliescu admitted that massacres of Jews had been perpetrated on Romania's territory proper and observed that "the leaders of that time are responsible for those events," he insisted "it is impossible to accuse the Romanian people and the Romanian society of this. When Germany declared [*sic*] the Final Solution—a decision that was obeyed by other countries, including Hungary—Antonescu no longer supported that policy. On the contrary, he took steps to protect the Jews. That, too, is historical truth." In an attempt to hush the international scandal created by the interview, the president proposed the setting up of what became known as the Elie Wiesel Commission, after the name of its chairman.

Established in October 2003 and ending its work one year later, the Commission's achievement proved to be a milestone in the official narrative of the Holocaust in Romania. Its members included several recommendations in their *Final Report*.[11] In what follows, I examine to what extent these recommendations were heeded or sidestepped, and how, and I briefly discuss the reactions that they triggered in society.

In order to improve the public awareness of the Holocaust, the government "should issue an official declaration acknowledging the report of the Commission and adopting the entirety of its contents and conclusion." This recommendation was promptly implemented and the entire report was placed on the website of the Romanian presidency. Similarly implemented in full was the recommendation that "once accepted and endorsed by the president of Romania," the report be published in full in Romanian and English. Under the same heading, the Commission also recommended that the "full report be distributed throughout the country to all libraries, schools, universities, and other educational and research institutions." This recommendation was never put into practice. While the written media carried some rather perfunctory items on the Commission's conclusions, and while some of these items were often accompanied by dismissive comments by readers, most reactions (particularly on the internet) were negative and had antisemitic tones.[12]

The Commission remarked that "many Romanian textbooks currently in use that do refer to the Holocaust present incomplete or even factually incorrect information." It therefore recommended that "the Ministry of Education create a working group in cooperation with experts of the Commission and appropriate international institutions, with the purpose of reviewing, correcting, revising and drafting appropriate curricula and textbook material on the Holocaust based on the findings of the Commission's report."[13]

The Commission was referring to the textbooks used by schools since 1999, when, following the 1998 initiative of Education Minister Andrei Marga, Holocaust education was introduced in the national curricula as a mandatory subject (to be tackled in two to four hours) in the larger framework of the history of the Second World War (which is taught in the seventh, tenth, eleventh, and twelfth grades). The first textbooks to include the topic were published in 1999, but due to the lack of reliable resources and a unitary view on recent Romanian history, many of them included wrong or biased information, usually in a clear attempt to exonerate the Romanian authorities from any responsibility for their wartime wrongdoings. As a result of the Commission's recommendation, things appeared to take a turn for the better, and with a few exceptions, the textbooks published after 2004 were generally more coherent and accurate.

Concerning higher education, the Commission recommended that "universities and the Romanian Academy should be called on to organize conferences and symposia on the Holocaust in Romania." It also said "colleges and universities should be encouraged to establish courses on the subject, not only for their students but also for professional, cultural, and public opinion leaders in this country." Four universities (the Babes-Bolyai University of Cluj-Napoca, the University of Bucharest, the Alexandru Ioan Cuza University of Iași, and the National School for Political and Administrative Studies—SNSPA of Bucharest) heeded the recommendation.

The Romanian Academy, mentioned in the report's recommendations, is another story altogether. Packed with members appointed under the national-communist regime of Ceaușescu (as membership in this institution is for life), as well as with historians with links to the former Iron Guard (the Legionary Movement) and/or the communist secret police, the Academy is a bastion of nationalist tradition.[14] After repeated postponements, on February 17, 2014, Romania's most prestigious scientific forum hosted a special public debate titled "Historical Information and Testimonies Concerning the Holocaust in Romania." The meeting was organized in collaboration with the Federation of Jewish Communities in Romania (FCER) and the Elie Wiesel National Institute for the Study of the Holocaust in Romania

(INSHR-EW) as part of the events marking International Holocaust Remembrance Day (January 27). Academy president Ionel Haiduc, who apologized for having to leave early due to other engagements, chaired the meeting. At that point, one of his deputies, historian Dan Berindei, stepped in for Haiduc. Berindei commented that although the forum had heard "interesting things," it was "a pity that the historical context had not been taken into account."[15] Though reminiscent of German historian Martin Broszat's advocacy of "historicization (*Historiesierung*),"[16] which warned against demonizing Nazism by judging it outside its actual historical context, Berindei's remark was a lot more than that. It had all the ingredients of what has been called "Holocaust obfuscation," which is based on the "Double Genocide" theory that claims that the Holocaust was part of the reaction to (as well as an emulation of) the provocations posed by Bolshevism within what Holocaust trivializer[17] Ernst Nolte called the "European Civil War" (see infra).[18]

Returning to the Commission's conclusions, it was said that "the government of Romania has adopted October 9 (2004) as the official date of Holocaust commemoration."[19] The choice of October 9 followed the suggestion of the Commission, whose work was ongoing at that time, and it took legal form with Government Decision no. 672 of May 5, 2004. The day marks the beginning of deportations to Transnistria of Romanian Jews from Bukovina. The Commission also recommended that "a national memorial to the victims of the Holocaust should be erected on public property in Bucharest."[20] After considerable procrastination, the monument was finally inaugurated on October 8, 2009. Since then, annual ceremonies are held at the site on October 9, attended by either the head of state or his representatives, governmental officials, and members of the diplomatic corps accredited in Bucharest.

The Commission drew attention to the existence of "several mass graves of Holocaust victims... (most notably victims of the Iași pogrom [June 1941]), that should be properly identified and maintained by the government of Romania."[21] A first and important step in this direction was made in 2010, when an INSHR-EW team headed by historian Adrian Cioflâncă identified at Popricani, a locality situated at a short distance from Iași, a mass grave in which thirty-six victims of the Holocaust (among them, twelve children and nine women) had been buried.[22] A case file was opened with the Prosecutor's Office in Iași, which then relinquished competence in favor of the local Military Prosecutor's Office. In February 2012 the Military Prosecutor's Office attached to the Bucharest Court of Appeal took over the inquiry, as the investigations had established that it was a case of genocide. In an unprecedented decision, the investigators announced in April 2014 that the Romanian army had committed genocide in 1941 in the forest of Popricani.[23] Furthermore, as of 2017, the same team was searching for mass graves at locations in the Republic of Moldova, and had already discovered sites where the Romanian army had similarly executed Jews at the outset of the Second World War.[24]

The Commision also noted the necessity of "reversing the rehabilitation of war criminals." In this connection it named "the noted war criminals Radu Dinulescu and Gheorghe Petrescu, whose 'rehabilitation' was recently upheld by the Supreme Court."[25] Colonel Dinulescu, chief of the Second Section of the General Staff, and his deputy within the same section, Colonel Petrescu, had been exonerated by the Supreme Court in 1998 and 1999, respectively. They had been sentenced in 1953 to fifteen years of hard labor and ten years of civic degradation (Dinulescu) and ten years of hard labor and a similar period of civic degradation (Petrescu), and to the confiscation of their assets.[26] They had been found guilty of having participated in the preparations for the Iași pogrom; of organizing the deportations to Transnistria; and of mistreating prisoners of war and a part of the civil population in Bessarabia.[27]

Romania's then Prosecutor General, Ilie Botoș, initiated a procedure called "extraordinary appeal," whereby prosecutors may appeal unjustified sentencing. The whole affair was kept secret. In both Dinulescu's and Petrescu's cases, the Prosecutor General claimed that the Iași pogrom had never involved participation of the General Staff's Second Section, and that it had been organized by German SS troops. The position adopted here clearly corresponds to what elsewhere I described as that variety of "deflective negationism" that, by placing all guilt on the Germans alone, is in fact attempting to exonerate not merely individuals such as Dinulescu and Petrescu, but states and local collaboration.[28]

The Commission also mentioned the need for "correcting and enforcing legislation on Holocaust denial and public veneration of Antonescu."[29] The reference was to Emergency Ordinance 31/ 2002, which eventually became Law 107/2006. The problems with this law were manifold. First, mention should be made of the traditional Romanian propensity for ignoring legislation. Second, however, the judiciary (prosecutors and tribunals alike) have tended to interpret the legislation forbidding the denial of the Holocaust as if it referred to denial of the genocide having taken place elsewhere (although many such cases were also ignored), not in Romania. In this respect, the report has been a failure, despite having been accepted by the authorities. According to official statistics, between 2002 and 2015, only fourteen cases led to indictments for violating the provisions of Ordinance 31/2002. How many were actually convicted is not known. Between 2007 and 2015, out of a total of 294 complaints to the Prosecutor General's office for violations of the provisions of Law 107/2016, prosecutions were launched in seven cases, involving nine persons. In 2005 a Brașov-based tribunal convicted Iron Guard apologist Gheorghe Oprița to thirty months in prison, but the sentence was quashed on appeal in 2006.[30]

Under these circumstances, it became clear that the law had to be amended to address both its main lacunae. First, the legislation had to clarify that denying the Holocaust also referred to Romania and its own contribution to the perpetration of the Shoah; and second, the interdiction on propaganda and display of symbols in the public space had to specifically refer to the Iron Guard. After significant pressure from abroad and intensive lobbying by the INSHR–EW, this was achieved with the approval of Law 217 in July 2015.[31] The amendment was initiated by three parliamentarians representing the Partidul Național Liberal (PNL, National Liberal Party), one of whom, Crin Antonescu, had presidential ambitions at the time.[32] According to malicious comments in the media, Antonescu was thereby hoping to enlist US support for his candidacy; true or not, this reflected the notorious canard according to which Romania was ruled by the United States and the United States, in turn, was ruled by Jews. Sadly, Crin Antonescu subsequently confirmed the existence of a huge discrepancy between the official and the unofficial narratives on the Holocaust.

Whereas Ordinance 31/2002 had prompted many negative reactions denying Romania's role in the Holocaust and Ion Antonescu's role in particular,[33] this time around, reactions tended to focus on the Iron Guard, but had ramifications for the more general ongoing debates in East-Central Europe about the crimes committed by the two totalitarian regimes of the twentieth century—Nazism and communism. Both times, the debates triggered what Rafał Pankowski, when discussing the case of Jedwabne and the "Auschwitz Crosses" in Poland, calls a "by-product" that "led to antisemitic views being expressed more loudly than before and with more mainstream legitimacy, especially in the broadly conceived right-wing conservative spectrum."[34]

Double Genocide, Holocaust Obfuscation, Competitive Martyrdom

These reactions fall in line with three main and intertwined characteristics of postcommunist attitudes to memory and the "dark past," found elsewhere in the region as well. The first characteristic is the repeated use of the Double Genocide theory. In a nutshell, the Double Genocide theory places the Gulag and its local derivates on par with the Holocaust. In its more benign form, it calls for "symmetry" in condemning the two atrocities of the last century, which it casts as equally repulsive, and for a similar "symmetry" in punishing those guilty for them. In its (rather common) aggressive form, it insists on the role played by Jews in communization, which in the eyes of the theory's partisans should exculpate local collaboration with the Nazis. This latter form has many elements in common with deflecting the guilt for the Holocaust onto the Jews themselves.

The second characteristic, Holocaust obfuscation,[35] channels the debate toward the alleged guilt of the Jews for bringing communism to power, with the purpose of justifying local participation in the perpetration of the Shoah, which is by and large ignored, while autochthonous resistance against communism is grossly exaggerated. With this purpose in mind, no distinction is made between the Nazi genocide and the Stalinist crimes against humanity, in spite of the fact that according to international legislation both are exempt from the statute of limitations.

This prompts the third and last characteristic, namely, "competitive martyrdom."[36] In its search for positive heroes to replace the ousted and artificial communist symbolism, and against the background of communist Holocaust neglect and/or distortion, the Double Genocide approach is fast becoming in all these countries the master commemorative narrative, one in which the myth of anticommunist resistance finds both hero-models and exculpation for the past. Within the framework of a century dominated by the Holocaust as a paradigmatic genocide, competitive martyrdom is the synthesis of all these elements. It strives to provide an alternative dominant narrative, not an alternative paradigm, for the paradigm remains genocidal. In the substituted narrative, the collective trauma of denationalization and Sovietization prevails over any attempt to draw attention to the suffering of Jews and Roma during the Holocaust, the more so as Jews continue to be perceived as instruments of communization.

The Double Genocide theory was first advanced in the Baltic states (to be more precise, in Lithuania) soon after the fall of communism. Lithuania was also the first state to grant Double Genocide institutional recognition, by passing legislation that prohibits the denial of both Nazi and communist "genocides" in 2010.[37] It was followed in the same year by similar legislation in Hungary. The denial of communist crimes was also introduced in the penal codes (albeit in different forms) in Latvia, the Czech Republic, Poland, Moldova, and Ukraine.[38]

Expectedly, publications with overt Iron Guardist profiles denounced the amendment without mincing words. The legionary veterans' journal *Permanențe* (Consistencies), printed irregularly since 1998, published a special edition entirely dedicated to the new version of the law. The main contribution was a three-page-long article titled "Abuzul statului împotriva drepturilor cetățeanului—încă posibil în România" (The abuse of the state against the citizen's rights—still possible in Romania). The article ended with an "appeal" supported by nearly all organizations, foundations, and Orthodox Church organizations with legionary sympathies—no less than fifteen in total.[39] The "appeal" had been issued before the approval of Law 217, in the hope of dissuading the legislature from proceeding. Nothing that followed (apart from some injurious attacks on INSHR–EW and its director, and some rather melodramatic outbursts) added anything new to the arguments of the legionaries and their sympathizers. It is therefore sufficient to examine the initial reaction, expressed by the article.

First, it was argued that Law 217/2015 represented an attack on the constitutional provision guaranteeing freedom of expression and of assembly. This was little more than an emblematic illustration of the reactions of extremists (left and right) whenever their own antisystemic capability to undermine democracy is circumvented. To "demonstrate" this contention, the article made use of a syllogism: since all previous postcommunist attempts to outlaw the legionaries and their offshoots had failed, this was proof that they had always acted strictly within democratic procedure. This neglects to mention that the failures were due to a great extent to the fact that Ordinance 31/2002 and Law 107/2006 do not specifically refer to the Iron Guard.

The article also utilized as an argument the hoax that the Nuremberg Tribunal had allegedly exonerated the Iron Guard in respect of all accusations. The hoax is not very original, having also been utilized by sympathizers of Monsignor Jozef Tiso in Slovakia.[40] In reality, the tribunal never dealt with any fascist movements anywhere except in Nazi Germany. It was also claimed in the article that the purpose of the amendments included in Law 217 was to introduce a new form of censorship similar to that introduced by Stalinist rule in late 1947 and early 1948. This old-new censorship would allegedly outlaw the reading, studying, and dissemination of works by Romanian intellectuals who at one point or another had sympathized with the Iron Guard (including Mircea Eliade, Emil Cioran, and poet Radu Gyr, author of the Iron Guard anthem "Holy Legionary Youth"). In actual fact, the amendment specifically referred to propaganda aimed at exonerating Iron Guard ideology; to organizing pro-Guard events; to the dissemination of legionary symbols; and to utilizing public space for the promotion of the cult of personalities sentenced for war crimes after the Second World War. The new law did not mention and was not intended to prohibit the republication of works by former Iron Guard sympathizers when it came to their literary, philosophical, or sociological publications, as critics (and not only declared Guard sympathizers) had insinuated. Finally, the article gave full vent to the Double Genocide theory and to competitive martyrdom. The Iron Guard, it claimed, had been at the forefront of the struggle against communism, and its leaders and sympathizers imprisoned by the communists were the martyrs of the nation, as proved by the numerous priests with Iron Guard sympathies (known for some time as *Sfinții Închisorilor*, or "Prison Saints").

The Prison Saints phenomenon is not unique to Romania. In Serbia, the dominant Orthodox Church had transformed the virulently antisemitic Bishop Nikolaj Velimirović (1880–1956) from "traitor," as he was dubbed by the communists, into a "saint."[41] Slovak attempts to bring about the beatification of Bishop Ján Vojtaššák were thwarted after Israeli historians wrote to Pope John Paul II, showing that the bishop had been a Nazi sympathizer and had participated in a meeting of the Slovak National Council in March 1942 where plans to deport 58,000 Jews (most of whom perished in extermination camps) had been discussed. Vojtaššák was Deputy Chairman of the council headed by Tiso himself in the clerical fascist state. He was sentenced in 1950 to twenty-four years in prison and released in 1963 under an amnesty. Vojtaššák died in 1965 and his conviction was quashed in 1990. The Slovak Bishops Conference continues to press for his canonization.[42] Croat Archbishop Alojzije Viktor Stepinac, who was Ante Pavelić's spiritual advisor under the Ustaša Nazi puppet regime and supreme military vicar of the army of the Independent State of Croatia, is a third example. One of the initiators of the forcible conversion of the Orthodox Serbs, Stepinac was beatified by Pope John Paul II in 1998 and declared a "martyr," and to the chagrin of the Serbs, he might soon be canonized. Stepinac was tried by the communist regime and sentenced to sixteen years in prison for treason and collaboration with the Ustaša regime, but later was released, confined to his home village, and made a cardinal by Pope Pius XII in 1952.[43]

Returning to Romania, the Prison Saints phenomenon deserves further examination. The incarcerated priests were all, or nearly all, former Iron Guardists, some of whom had been imprisoned already by Marshal Antonescu for having participated in the legionary rebellion against him in January 1941. Their pasts as members of the Iron Guard are seldom mentioned, and if they are, no mention is made of the Guard's antisemitism. On the contrary, heroic deeds have been attributed to some of them (e.g., Valeriu Gafencu) that prove their "love" for Jews who were also incarcerated, though these alleged deeds are never mentioned in the prison memoirs of the Jews themselves (e.g., Pastor Richard Wurmbrand).[44]

It is not an accident that authors known for their previous attempts to rehabilitate the Iron Guard and its members, including founder Corneliu Zelea Codreanu, edit many of these books that follow a similar goal. For example, a volume edited by Răzvan Codrescu (one of the first to attempt to rehabilitate Codreanu) contains articles by himself, by Sorin Lavric (author of a eulogistic volume on philosopher Constantin Noica and the Iron Guard[45]), and by Radu Preda, who in May 2014 was appointed Director of the Institute for the Investigation of Communist Regime Crimes and the Memory of the Romanian Exile (IICCMER). His predecessor, the young historian Andrei Muraru, had carefully avoided any association of IICCMER with competitive martyrdom and links to Iron Guard promoters, and when he left to become a presidential counselor to newly elected president Klaus Iohannis, his departure radically changed IICCMER's face. Immediately upon his appointment, Preda, a theologian by training, stated that it was his "obligation" to place "the case of the 'Prison Saints' on the agenda of the institute."[46] In the aforementioned volume, he authored two articles: "Mercenarii memoriei" (Memory's mercenaries) and "Memoria ca obligație" (Memory as an obligation). Lavric's contribution was titled "Nevoia de martiri" (The need of martyrs), while Codrescu himself wrote "Martirologia temnițelor comuniste" (The martyrology of communist jails) and reported on the recently held "First Symposium of Martyrdom."[47] In the former tract, he placed anticommunist militant and Radio Free Europe journalist Monica Lovinescu and Corneliu Coposu, the leader of the Partidul Național Țărănesc Creștin Democrat (PNȚCD, Christian Democratic National Peasants' Party), side by side with Codreanu and legionary police chief Alexandru Gyka. As Alexandru Climescu formulated it, this was disingenuous "organized confusion."[48]

Apologists of the Guard were also at the vanguard of attacks on the INSHR–EW and its director, Alexandru Florian, since INSHR–EW and Florian, personally, had long pressed lawmakers to amend Law 217. Examples abound and can be easily found by a search of the internet. Under the auspices of the Professor George Manu Foundation—one of several organizations specializing in Iron Guard cleansing—Cezarina Condurache (a member of *Permanențe*'s editorial board) published in 2015 a volume titled *Chipuri ale demnității românești. Eroi ai neamului și Sfinți ai Închisorilor* (Faces of Romanian dignity: heroes of the nation and saints of prison) and edited another tome titled *Eroi anticomuniști și Sfinții Închisorilor reincriminați prin Legea 217/2015* (The anticommunist heroes and saints of prison reincriminated by Law 217/2015).[49] Lavric's contribution to the latter volume says a lot about the purpose of this exercise. Titled "Damnatio memoriae" (Latin for condemnation of memory), it lists fourteen "traits" of the "persecutor." From the very first trait, it becomes clear that this is a stereotypical antisemitic endeavor of Holocaust obfuscation: "The persecutor's first trait is that he descends from the clique [*tagma*] of those who brought communism to Europe. The group of allogeneic conspirators who dreamt of enthroning the Bolshevik revolution in all European countries..., that group represents the grandfathers of those persecuting us today."[50]

The second trait, according to Lavric, is in fact a metaphor borrowed from the history of the Roman Empire, where the names of those fallen from grace were banished from even being mentioned, so that "two generations on, nobody knew anymore who that or that person had been." Similarly, "after having physically exterminated his enemies in communist prisons, the persecutor seeks to kill them for a second time, destroying their posthumous effigy. The destruction goes from symbolic diabolization to elimination from the annals of collective memory."[51] According to Lavric, this is precisely what the partisans of Law 217 seek to do.

According to the third trait Lavric attributes to the persecutor, he always poses as a representative of the law. The author then spends over half a page clarifying to readers the distinction between legality and legitimacy, without even once mentioning the name of Max Weber, the real author of the distinction. But when he comes to the fourth trait, he duly mentions the Nazi constitutional and international relations theoretician Carl Schmitt, citing as illustration Schmitt's diary, written between 1947 and 1951, when he was prohibited from publishing. According to Lavric, this illustrates the "humiliating posture of him whose right to reply has been taken away."[52]

One need not read all fourteen traits, for they are actually summarized in the thirteenth, where Lavric unwittingly confirms the counternarrative nature of competitive martyrdom: "The thirteenth trait is that the persecutor atavistically hates those dignified examples that might belittle his acquisitive influence. This is precisely why the persecutor is seized with defiling frenzy (*frenezie profanatoare*) when he hears about heroes (partisans), martyrs (victims of communist prisons) or saints (clerical figures with power of attraction over the masses). These figures are the totemic capital whose symbol upsets him beyond measure..... This is why these words ... have a 'democratic' smell driving the persecutor mad, why the zeal with which he seeks to annihilate their memory touches a draconic threshold."[53]

One of Condurache's edited volumes is extensively cited in an article published by Professor Gabriel Andreescu, who joined the attacks against Florian, making personal family allegations for which he was forced to apologize when threatened with a lawsuit.[54] Andreescu, who was among the first to embrace "symmetry," that is, the Double Genocide argument in Romania, and for this (and other) reasons opposed Ordinance 31/2002,[55] also honored the author of this chapter with a few paragraphs in which he reproached me for lack of compassion for the Iron Guard victims.[56]

However, Andreescu was neither the most prominent nor the most influential of the "mainstream" intellectuals to express misgivings about or outright opposition to the amended law. The list is too long to reproduce in full, but two names deserve mention in particular, although, metaphorically speaking, oceans divide the quality of their products: Andrei Pleşu on the one hand, and Oana Stănciulescu on the other. We shall deal with both when discussing "liberal negationism."

The Extreme Right's Parliamentary Antechamber

In September 2014 the Bucharest Court of Appeals rejected the objections of the Prosecutor General's Office against registering the Everything for the Country Party (Partidul Totul pentru Ţară, TpŢ).[57] The first attempt to register a party under that name—which was also the name of the Iron Guard after 1934—dates back to 1993, when due to the rejection of that bid the group registered instead under the name Everything for the Fatherland (Totul pentru Patrie). Among its leaders (first as vice chairman and later as chairman) was Ion Gavrilă Ogoranu, who was posthumously transformed into a "hero-model" for having fought against the communist regime at the head of a group of Iron Guardist partisans. A motion picture about him titled *Portretul luptătorului la tinereţe* (Portrait of the fighter as a young man), produced in 2010, did not once mention the Iron Guard "detail."[58] Yet, when Ogoranu died in 2006, his casket was wrapped up in the Legion's flag, for he had never abandoned his legionary ideas; Premier Călin Popescu Tăriceanu (PNL) saw fit to send a wreath to the burial ceremony.[59] Similarly, in Latvia, Herberts Cuckurs, the deputy commander of the murderous Arājs Commando unit that played a leading role in the mass annihilation of the Jews in Riga and elsewhere in Latvia and Belarus, was transformed into the hero of a 2014 musical depicting his brave deeds as an aviator.[60]

In Croatia, the 2016 release of a documentary by film director Jakov Sedlar titled *Jasenovac—The Truth* that minimized the number of victims at the concentration camp prompted the Coordinating Committee of Jewish Communities in Croatia to boycott the yearly commemoration that takes place on April 22 at Jasenovac, where at least 83,000 prisoners (Serbs, Jews, Roma, and anti-Nazi Croats) were killed by the Ustaša regime. Instead, a separate vigil was held on April 13 at the site of the former death camp. The decision to boycott the ceremonies was joined by the Serbian National Council in Croatia. Sedlar told Croatian Radio–Television HRT that the number of victims was exaggerated as a result of "non-scientific Yugoslav historiography," and that the actual figure was 20,000 to 40,000. Culture Minister Hasanbegović (see infra) supported his claims.

Returning to the TpȚ, its electoral success was meager, as it managed to elect just a few local councilors. The party reregistered under its original name in 2011, and this time around, the Bucharest Tribunal accepted the registration despite the party's obvious (and hence illegal) roots in the fascist formation established in 1934 as successor formation of the Iron Guard.[61] The Prosecutor General's Office failed in several attempts to have the party dissolved on grounds of "fascist ideology." Yet, the TpȚ was erased from the list of parties in 2015, because it did not comply with legal provisions concerning the functioning of political formations. Among other provisions, the law stipulated that political formations must have at least 25,000 members registered in eighteen counties and obtain a minimum of 50,000 votes in county, local, or parliamentary elections. The tribunal rejected the TpȚ's argument that it had failed to meet this requirement due to harassment by the Prosecutor General's office.[62] However, an initiative for changing that legislation on political parties to allow registration with just three members was approved soon after, and it would not be surprising if the TpȚ reapplies for registration as a legally functioning formation. The initiators of the change were not sympathizers of the extreme right. Rather, as civil society activists, they claimed that the current requirements were far too strict and hence undemocratic. The TpȚ, of course, supported this initiative.[63]

Another political formation on the ultranationalist spectrum entered officially into political competition in 2015, after the change in the law on political parties. This is the New Right (Noua Dreaptă, ND). Its roots are in the New Right Association set up by lawyer Tudor Ionescu in 2000. At that time, and in the fascist tradition, the ND defined itself a "movement" rather than a political party. Antisemitism was more implicit than emphasized among the expressions of its members, who often wore green t-shirts with Codreanu's portrait and displayed the Celtic cross characteristic of the neofascists.[64] Considerably more emphasized were (and continue to be) anti-Roma and anti-Hungarian attitudes and homophobia, alongside an ethnocratic affiliation to the Romanian Orthodox Church and (more recently) an antirefugee posture, a subject on which the ND identifies with the positions of Hungary and Slovakia.[65] It has also expanded its activity in the neighboring Republic of Moldova. Soon, the ND also became involved in the apparently lucrative business of marketing Codreanu (and Prison Saints) t-shirts, CDs with ultra-right racist rock bands, and symbols of the Legionary Movement. It was clearly following models from elsewhere in Eastern Europe, for example, Poland in the early 1990s.[66] Perhaps the best and most concise description of the ND is the following: "They are few, but they are vocal. They are religious and march with icons, but they also wear military clothes. They love God, but hate refugees and minorities. They believe they defend their country, but regularly flaut its laws."[67]

A third neolegionary formation that appeared after the change in the law on political parties initially called itself the Group for Romania (Grupul pentru România, GpR). This name was no coincidence, for the central figure in the new formation is Marian Munteanu, the leader of the first neolegionary formation set up after 1989, the MpR (Movement for Romania). Furthermore, the group includes sociologist Ilie Bădescu, who chaired the "senate" of the MpR—a body that copied the legionaries' "senate."[68] Another prominent member is actor Dan Puric, known for his unconcealed admiration for the Iron Guard. The GpR spokesman, Florin Zamfirescu,[69] who is also an actor, first introduced the group to the public on January 13, 2016, on the private TV station Realitatea.

Employing classical fascist palingenetic terminology,[70] Zamfirescu began by stating that the main purpose of the GpR was "Romania's salvation." That meant, above all, "reestablishing the property right of Romanians over their [own] country," as Marian Munteanu put it in a separate interview on Realitatea TV the next day.[71] Zamfirescu said the new group appeals to "all Christians" to join it; the implication was opaque but nonetheless reflected the nativist-ethnocratic mind of the group's organizers. Anyway, according to Florin Colceag, another GpR founding member, Romania was the cradle of European civilization, and its people were "the Dacians, who always lived here."[72] It was consequently necessary, according to Munteanu, "to defend the identity values of Romanian civilization."[73] The GpR, Munteanu also said, intended to become at the next (2016) elections a "significant parliamentary party of at least 100 members," that is, the third-largest parliamentary group in the legislature after the Social Democratic Party and the PNL.[74]

On March 28, again on Realitatea TV, Munteanu suddenly came up with a new name and a new manifesto for the envisaged formation. Apparently warned about the association with the MpR the GpR had stirred, he singlehandedly changed the name to Our Alliance Romania (Alianța Noastră România, ANR).[75] Its manifesto circulated on the internet the same evening under the title "Proclamation."[76] He called for a "mobilization of insurrectional dimensions," carefully adding that he had in mind a "civic insurrection" of all those who put "loyalty" to Romania above any other interest. Some of the formulations utilized in the ANR manifesto were purposely designed to mislead. Among other things, the document said the ANR will "discourage any xenophobic or anti-Romanian actions, blocking any attempts to change Romania's current political-administrative profile through various forms of coercion—whether ethnic, cultural or religious."[77]

It was noble of Munteanu to distance the ANR from xenophobia, but literary critic Alex I. Ștefănescu, one of his supporters, explained why xenophobia and anti-Romanian actions had been put on the same footing. In Romania, Ștefănescu said, natives are in the minority when it comes to interest promotion. The time had come to correct this situation: national minorities should be respected, but represented in proportion to their numbers. In other words, denouncing xenophobia turned out to be a veiled call for introducing a *numerus clausus*. It must be said that promoting "Romanianism" and combating its alleged enemies had been an idiomatic form by which the interwar extreme right displayed its phobias;[78] and it must also be said that in 2001 Romania's chief Holocaust denier and Iron Guard exalter Ion Coja had set up the League for Combating Anti-Romanianism. It was also Coja who disseminated the hoax that half a million Jews had secretly acquired Romanian citizenship as part of a plan to transfer Israelis to Romania and transform Romania itself into a Jewish state, and that the secret plan called for one million.[79] Hence, the promise to resist alleged attempts to change the administrative profile of the country, including its culture and ethnicity.

The Liberal Negationism

Radu Preda might have been the first to claim that the new law was discriminatory, calling it "procommunist" because it ignored crimes committed by the communist regime,[80] but the most influential person to make this claim was aesthetician, philosopher, and former minister of culture and foreign affairs Andrei Pleșu. Though Pleșu and Andreescu are known personal adversaries, they were on the same "wavelength" vis-à-vis the amended legislation. In the spirit of Double Genocide and Holocaust obfuscation, Pleșu called for "symmetry" in addressing legally the two totalitarian legacies and claimed the tribunals that had sentenced wartime Romanian intellectuals had been under communist influence.[81] Starting with the initial reactions to the amendment published by *Permanențe* (see supra), this was one of the leitmotifs shared by radical right, conservative, and even some liberal critics of Law 217/2015. As in other former communist countries, there is a predominant sentiment in Romania that the trauma of communist rule is neglected by the West, which imposed on the new postcommunist regimes a memory that is not their own. Sometimes (in Andreescu's, but not Pleșu's case) the implication is that this imposition is instrumentalized by the Jews. In the preface of a book published by Pleșu in 2014 jointly with philosopher Gabriel Liiceanu[82] and conservative author Horia Roman Patapievici,[83] the authors wrote that European reunification has been pursued "exclusively through the westernization" of the East. This, however, had imposed on the region a "new iron curtain." Unlike the former curtain, the new one is "no longer dividing Europe in line with a geographic axis running—as the old one did—from Szczecin to Trieste, but one that runs through the soul of every European, dividing his memory and dissociating his sensibility." Those who lived behind the former Iron Curtain, they write, "have other memories, are *marked by other traumas*, remember differently." Postcommunist Westernization has meant the transformation of its memory (the allusion to the Holocaust is clear) into a common memory. Yet, "the other memory, the memory of communism and of the totalitarian trauma that did not last a decade but half a century, is still not common."[84]

Oana Stănciulescu is altogether another cup of tea. A rather inglorious journalist, she is editor in chief of *Express magazin*, one of Romania's numerous weeklies without readership whose survival remains a mystery. She is also a TV journalist. Participating in a talk show called *Power Games* anchored by Realitatea TV director Rareş Bogdan, she repeated the Double Genocide argument that criticized Law 217 for not simultaneously forbidding communist propaganda. She displayed onscreen a few publications authored by interwar intellectuals with Iron Guard sympathies, claiming that the new law aimed to wipe them out of Romania's history. She also spoke admiringly and at length about Radu Gyr. Furthermore, Stănciulescu displayed an appalling lack of familiarity with (or perhaps ill will toward) the background of the amended legislation; no one, she claimed, has ever denied the Holocaust in Romania. Her aggressive tone was complemented by the anchor with readouts from an article by Pleşu that reiterated the obviously distorted argument that the literary and philosophical production of interwar authors with Iron Guard sympathies would be taken out of circulation; this would, Pleşu wrote, be tantamount to deleting from the world cultural patrimony the works of Ezra Pound, Louis-Ferdinand Céline, and Martin Heidegger.[85]

On her blog, Stănciulescu gave vent to her views without any restriction. She posted a message received from one of her readers, commenting that she entirely identifies with it. Among other things, the reader wrote, "when in Majadahonda, I am proud [of] Moţa and Marin," two prominent Iron Guardists killed at Majadahonda while fighting on Franco's side. At other times, he went on, I am Nae Ionescu "and suffer for the white race." An ideologist of the Guard (though apparently never a registered member), Ionescu is famous for his ethnocratic views. Finally, the message went on to say, "I am Ion and Ică [Mihai] Antonescu, caught between Moscow and Berlin." Ică Antonescu was the Marshal's deputy, and was executed together with him in 1946. Congratulating the author of the message, Stănciulescu wrote: "I feel the same. Maybe there are more like ourselves."[86] On one occasion, she publicly stated that the promoters of the law intended to remove from public space figures who were her "moral guide marks."[87] In January 2016 Stănciulescu participated alongside leaders of the legionary "Ion Gavrilă Ogoranu" Foundation in a symposium dedicated to the memory of a prominent Iron Guard leader, Gogu Puiu, who had committed suicide while in prison.[88] One could hardly find a better example of "heroization" utilized for the purpose of competitive martyrdom and Holocaust obfuscation. This partly explains why Octav Bjoza, president of the Association of Former

Political Prisoners in Romania (AFDPR), called Stănciulescu "our adoptive daughter."[89]

Stănciulescu, as well as other intellectuals with similar sentiments, bitterly attacked INSHR–EW director Alexandru Florian. Florian and the Institute had been the driving force behind the initiative to amend Law 107/2006. Once that was achieved, he was adamant that it be enforced in public spaces, demanding that the names of streets and squares named in honor of persons sentenced by Peoples' Tribunals in the late 1940s for war crimes be changed, and statues erected in their honor be demolished. He also insisted that honorary citizenships bestowed on them be annulled. This made him the target of a hate campaign that included death threats. The case of exiled writer Vintilă Horia, who is on record for having been an admirer of Adolf Hitler, was particularly bitter, for Horia had achieved some notoriety in exile,[90] and it became even more bitter after Horia's birthplace (Segarcea) acquiesced in withdrawing the honorary citizenship it had bestowed on him.

Yet, as long as the Romanian cultural and historical establishment remains packed with overt and covert admirers of the Iron Guard, and as long as the judiciary writ large either ignores current legislation or interprets it in a distorted manner, the capabilities of INSHR–EW remain constrained. One example should suffice: in 2014 Florian received a reply from the Prosecutor General's Office in regard to his protests concerning the toleration of neofascist groups in Romania. As in many other instances, Romanian prosecutors said they decided not to initiate legal proceedings against one of the several revived Legionary Movement organizations, which was openly displaying the Iron Guard insignia on the building of its headquarters in Bucharest. The prosecutors specified that the decision was partly based on the testimony of Şerban Suru, the organization's leader, who claimed that the Iron Guard emblem was not an infringement of the law prohibiting the display of fascist symbols, as it merely symbolized opposition to Soviet expansion. The second basis on which the prosecution refused to pursue the complaint was the opinion of one of the Romanian Academy's vice chairmen, who said historians are divided over whether the Iron Guard was a fascist organization. The prosecutor did not reveal the name of this person, but he is more than likely to have been Dan Berindei, the only historian who occupies that position (see supra).[91]

The 2015 change to the law does not appear to have moved things further—at least not for now. When INSHR–EW again contacted the Prosecutor General's Office about the display of Iron Guard insignia and provocative Nazi salutes made right in front of the INSHR–EW office by leader Suru, with video posted on his organization's webpage, the response was that the offense may have been committed before Law 217/2015 went into force, and the legislation does not apply retroactively. A similar response was received concerning the case of outright Holocaust denier Vasile Zărnescu,[92] whose latest opus is by no means different from those authored in the West by the likes of David Irving, Arthur Butz, and Robert Faurisson.[93] The author is a retired cadre of the Romanian Information Service (the Romanian intelligence service), with the rank of colonel.[94] So far, the only instance when the Prosecutor General's Office initiated the prosecution of offenders against the legislation prohibiting fascist-like manifestations was in 2014, and this was against members of the Hungarian minority exalting Hungarian irredentism.[95] This can hardly be accidental.

There is, consequently, little reason for optimism. Indeed, shortly after Stănciulescu's display of solidarity with, and admiration for, the interwar extreme right, she was nominated by the PNL for membership on the Administrative Council of public Romanian TV. And while the appointment triggered a letter of protest addressed to the party's leaders and signed by prominent intellectuals, it also triggered a counterresponse by her supporters.[96] What is more frightening, Stănciulescu's colleagues from Realitatea TV called the signatories of the former letter "traitors" in the service of the KGB, the Mossad, and the Freemasons. Remininiscent of the Nazi and Iron Guard zoologic vocabulary that depicted adversaries as repulsive creatures, they were called "worms," and journalist Octavian Hoandră said he could well understand support for the new law coming from Jews, but not from ethnic Romanians.[97] Thus, not only had the Judeo-Bolshevism legend returned, but so had the Iron Guardist image of the "Yiddized" (*Jidovit*) being more dangerous than the Jew. The station's main shareholder, Cosmin Guşă, announced on the same program that he would never let Stănciulescu's critics set foot in the studio again.[98] Judging by the Stănciulescu precedent, Realitatea TV might be striving to become a Romanian version of the Polish Radio Maryja, for the discourse of Guşă and his employees on March 17, 2016, reminded one of the statements of Roman Giertych, the leader of the League of Polish Families (LPR).[99] And just as Radio Maryja played a crucial role in the rise of the extremist LPR in 2001,[100] Realitatea TV engaged in promoting Marian Munteanu's comeback to politics (see infra).

The new Administrative Council including Stănciulescu was validated by Parliament on March 22, 2016, with an overwhelming majority of 312 votes in favor and 21 against. FCER president Aurel Vainer explained why Stănciulescu's positions on the Iron Guard disqualified her from taking up the post, and Markó Belá, former chairman of the Hungarian Democratic Union of Romania, announced that his group would boycott the vote in view of eulogies for the Legionary Movement having been uttered in Parliament for the first time in the postcommunist period. This referred to the speech by Cristina Anghel, a senator representing the Conservative Party, who had reiterated the hoax about the Legionary Movement's exoneration at Nuremberg; she also used the occasion to launch an attack on the Hungarian minority. Justifying the PNL's nomination of Stănciulescu to the Administrative Council, PNL deputy chairman Puiu Hașotti misleadingly said that Stănciulescu had not been defending the Iron Guard and had only referred to cultural figures who were sympathetic to the Guard and should not be eliminated from the country's national patrimony. By example, he said that Radu Gyr had been the author of not just the legionary anthem but also other patriotic verse, from which he recited. However, the quoted verse had been authored by someone else—long-forgotten nationalist poet Mircea Rădulescu.[101]

Following two failed designations of candidates for the post of Bucharest mayor in the local elections due to be held on June 5, 2016, the PNL announced on April 13 that it had designated Marian Munteanu as its candidate for the post.[102] The two PNL cochairpersons, Alina Gorghiu and Vasile Blaga, told the media that Munteanu would be joining the party, and Blaga affirmed that he was "unaware of any dubious spot in Munteanu's past." Apparently, for the PNL leadership, being founder of the first postcommunist legionary party was not a "dubious spot." Instead, emphasis was placed on Munteanu's leadership of the anticommunist protest in Bucharest's University Square following Ion Iliescu's election as Romania's first postcommunist president, which ended in his brutal beating by the miners called to the capital by the president. There was an obvious trace of "competitive martyrology" in this as well.

Initially, pundits and politicians who criticized the candidacy tended to refer only in passing or not at all to Munteanu's legionary past. This was another illustration of the dominance of the Double Genocide approach, albeit an indirect one. A notable exception was Bucharest University professor Ioan Stanomir, who immediately pointed out the ethnocratic character of Munteanu's unchanged positions.[103] But most of the critical commenators distanced themselves from Munteanu due to his alliance with former Romanian Information Service (SRI) director Virgil Măgureanu ahead of the 2000 elections.[104]

However, the ignoring of Munteanu's activity in the early 1990s quickly ended. On April 14, several NGOs demanded that the PNL withdraw its support from Munteanu, pointing out that he "had and continues to have sympathies for currents of fascist orientation," and that he "is promoting a discourse entrenched in Orthodox-fundamentalist values, incompatible with democratic and even constitutional values."[105] On April 15, the Group for Social Dialogue began gathering signatures on a protest letter addressed to the PNL that stated that although the PNL was free to designate as candidate for the mayoralty whomever it pleased, it must be aware of the fact that Munteanu's designation compromises liberal values, with which he has nothing in common: "The leap Marian Munteanu makes today... is just as stupefying as that made from the values of University Square to those of the Movement for Romania [which were] impregnated with ideologies that ravaged twentieth-century Europe."[106] Noting that as a governmental institution the INSHR–EW must refrain from interfering in elections, its director general Alexandru Florian reacted only when Munteanu declared on April 13 on the Antena 3 private TV channel that Law 217/2015 was "antisemitic" because it generated antisemitism.[107] This argument, blaming Jews for the existence of antisemitism, is as old as antisemitism itself—and in fact, an oblique justification for it. FCER president Vainer's reaction to the designation was this time more cautious than what one might have expected or wished. He said he was "somewhat worried," but "for now we place question marks, to avoid utilizing exclamation marks." It was, however, "hard to believe" the choice was the best possible one, in view of the fact that "the movement to which he belonged in the past was very nationalist-oriented." Nonetheless, Munteanu "might respond and show that he has changed."[108] Finally, MCA director Marco Katz asked Munteanu to clarify his present position vis-à-vis the Legionary Movement, Law 217/2015, and "the atrocities committed by the Antonescu regime." According to "information we received, in the 1990s you led a pro-legionary, pro-Zelea Codreanu party, called Movement for Romania," said Katz in a letter addressed to Munteanu and published by the negationist and antisemitic *Rost Online*.¹⁰⁹

In his response to Katz, Munteanu claimed the MpR had never been an Iron Guardist party, a "label" attached to it by the then ruling National Salvation Front in order to discredit it and hide its own communist roots. The MpR ideology, he claimed, had been democratic and inspired by what he dubbed the "conservative-popular" ideology of Nicolae Iorga's National Democratic Party and by French and British conservative parties.¹¹⁰ He also wrote that he was ready to send Katz the MpR's party statutes to demonstrate his arguments. But those statutes demonstrate exactly the opposite, as I proved in several articles written at that time. Sadly (or ironically), the title of one of these tracts was "Marginalization or Mainstream? The Extreme Right in Postcommunist Romania"; looking back, I wish my prediction had failed.¹¹¹

Acknowledging that he had participated in meetings with veterans of the Legion, Munteanu claimed that this was only to show respect for those incarcerated in communist prisons, and that he was later attacked by them precisely because he would not identify with their ideology. Memory must have failed him. Yes, the Timișoara-based wing of the Iron Guard that was linked to Codreanu's successor, Horia Sima, and published *Gazeta de vest* (Western Gazette), had indeed criticized him, but the MpR publication *Mișcarea* (The Movement) openly and repeatedly hailed Codreanu, and its rivals concurred. He also "forgot" to mention that a photo of Codreanu photo hung in his office.¹¹² He no less conveniently omitted to mention his open letter to the former members of the Legion in which he wrote that different times call for different strategies, but added: "we are all streams in one and the same river."¹¹³

He also wrote in the letter to Katz: "I never was and will never be an antisemite. I am not, and will never be, a xenophobe. I am in solidary with the suffering of the Jewish people hit by the holocaust [sic] provoked by Nazism, just as the suffering of Romanians marks me and other peoples hit by Bolshevik terror." Leaving the Double Genocide premise aside, one wonders how Munteanu explains the repeated publication in *Mișcarea* of negationist articles translated from other languages;[114] or his own statement that Jews inflated the number of Holocaust victims in order to "obtain illicit money from Romanian people through disinformation and manipulation of public opinion, with the complicity of treacherous elements who infiltrated the Romanian institutional structures."[115]

The rest of the letter merely repeats the claims already found in *Permanențe* and many other publications concerning Law 217/2015. Unlike in Western Europe, where "those who had instigated to crimes, those who took decisions and ordered executions were identified and their deeds were punished and criminalized," Romania's case is different. The rise to power of "the Bolsheviks" right after the war "superposed and toxically interfered with the natural process of sentencing decision makers guilty of crimes and abuses." That natural process was replaced by one aimed at "cleansing a whole political and cultural class" out of pursuit of "power interests." According to Munteanu, "a great many number of people and cultural productions were labeled [by the regime] *'fascist,' 'legionary,'* or, more vaguely, *'reactionary element,'* despite having nothing in common with events or decisions of criminal nature." Such "unjustified trials and the traumas of affected families left deep sensibilities among those affected, inclusive of a background of vulnerabilities." The time that has passed "is too short and the mixed emotions stirred by such still living traumas have not yet settled." This, Munteanu concluded, "convinced me to evaluate Law 217/2015 as a Trojan Horse in some of its aspects," one that "serves the interests of groups or directions contrary to those entertained by yourself and me, namely, the building of a stable and powerful society around values and fundamental democratic benchmarks."[116] In short, this was a considerably more sophisticated formulation of the same "Jews generate antisemitism" claim, and at the same time a veiled warning.

In an interview with the Mediafax independent news agency on April 17, Munteanu was asked whether he considered that Codreanu had been a criminal. He answered that "Romanian justice has said 'no,'" referring to the trial in which Codreanu was acquitted by a panel of sympathetic judges for killing Iași prefect Constantin Manciu in 1924. Pressed by the interviewer to speak in his own name rather than in the name of "Romanian justice," all Munteanu was able to come up with was: "I do not know, I have long been waiting for historians, for the justice system, to clarify that." The interviewer confronted him with a citation from his own earlier writings where he had said: "The historic experience of the Legionary Movement enriches the national Romanian patrimony, presenting it with a valuable model for the purity of its spiritual message, the firmness of its political discourse, the performance of its organizing techniques and above all its elevated capacity of national and Christian experience." Did he maintain that claim? Obviously embarrassed, Munteanu once again provided a typical "competitive martyrdom" reply: "Only inasmuch as it refers to the sacrifice of those imprisoned, who were fighting against Bolshevik occupation."[117]

The PNL's reaction was similar, only a lot less sophisticated. Defying all evidence, in an "open letter" addressed to those contesting Munteanu's candidacy, the Liberals said the accusation about "the alleged proximity of Mr. Marian Munteanu to the extreme right was nothing but a myth" originally launched by former president Iliescu in 1990. Nowadays, however, the accusations stem from "organizations and people who apparently think they have a monopoly over the idea of civil society..., part of a propagandist political discourse often encountered in the politicking game."

The Gorghiu-Blaga PNL leadership's decision to promote Munteanu at the head of the party's Bucharest local elections campaign eventually began to be questioned and challenged from within the party's own ranks. One might have expected former PNL chairman Crin Antonescu, as initiator of Law 217, to take the pole position in this quest. Not only did Antonescu fail to do so, but he called criticism directed at the decision "agitation with hysterical accents." The former chairman said that one could "say anything about [Munteanu], but not that he is an uninteresting person," and that Munteanu's role in the 1990 University Square protests "triggers in me positive emotions."[118] The first dissenting voice unexpectedly came from former culture minister Alexandru Paleologu, who bluntly stated that he was not going to vote for Munteanu.[119] Petre Roman, today a PNL member (he was Iliescu's premier in the tumultuous days of 1990), revealed that in an article published in April 1994 in *Mișcarea*, Munteanu had called Liberal premier I. G. Duca (shot by an Iron Guard squad on December 29, 1933) an "assassin." Duca had outlawed the Iron Guard. The PNL leadership, Roman said, had called for proof that Munteanu had legionary sympathies. What better proof than this article?, he asked. The revelation prompted historian and journalist Ion M. Ioniță to publish an appeal to PNL honorary chairman Mircea Ionescu-Quintus titled "Domnule Quintus, nu girați întoarcerea României in anii `30!" (Mr. Quintus, do not endorse Romania's return to the 1930s!). The nonagenarian honorary chairman (the only person to have abstained in the vote for Munteanu's designation) found himself in an awkward position, for Duca had been a friend of his family, and his assassination prompted his own decision to join the party.[120]

Even worse for the PNL leadership was the announcement made by two Bucharest administrative sector candidates (eventually joined by a third) that their own electoral campaigns would be conducted separately from Munteanu's. Ovidiu Raețchi, the party's sector 5 candidate, said, "I have heard [Munteanu] saying he did not know whether Zelea Codreanu had been a criminal or not.... I myself am certain he was one. I have also seen things written [by Munteanu] about the importance and the positive elements of the Legionary Movement. I believe ... it was a terrorist movement that killed three premiers."[121]

A real danger of a split seemed to be looming over the PNL. Under these circumstances, on April 20 the leadership of the PNL announced it was "withdrawing" Munteanu's candidacy, replacing him with Bucharest PNL chairman Cătălin Predoiu. On April 23, Munteanu announced he intended to set up a new political formation, with the purpose of changing the government. The executive, he said, must put the country "on a new path," where Romanians "would not be ashamed of being Romanians." The government, he added, must "respect our values, our identity."[122] In turn, Predoiu announced that the PNL had eliminated Munteanu from its list of Bucharest municipal councilor candidates, where he once had occupied the first spot.[123]

What prompted the PNL leadership to rally behind Stănciulescu and then Munteanu is yet unclear. One possibility is that with the December 2016 general elections approaching, the party feared that Crin Antonescu's "sin" would be sanctioned by the nationalist segment of the electorate. In a talk show on Antena 3 on April 14, PNL deputy chairman Atanasiu offered as an explanation that the party hoped to enlist the nationalist electorate of the PRM, left leaderless after the death of Corneliu Vadim Tudor. However, the PNL's traditional electorate (upper-middle-class successful businesspeople) and the PRM's (losers of the transition, pseudo-intellectuals of the former regime, and former secret police operatives and collaborators) are in many ways mutually exclusive. Another possibility is that the PNL hoped to sail the populist-nationalist winds blowing in other East European countries (but also in Western Europe) such as Hungary, Poland, Croatia, and Slovakia.[124] In any case, within the PNL the unofficial narrative on the Holocaust and its perpetrators had once more prevailed over its official version. The fact that a significant segment of civil society proved capable of rejecting that discourse is the good news. Finally, it must be mentioned that in the parliamentary elections on December 11, 2016, the poor performance of the PNL forced Gorghiu to submit her resignation (Blaga had resigned earlier, under suspicion of taking bribes). The "Munteanu adventure" alone does not explain the party's failure in the elections. But it obviously contributed to it.

Conclusion: Not the Best and Not the Worst

Since the 2004 elections, no political party in Romania deserving to be labeled antisemitic has held seats in the legislature. Compared with neighboring Hungary, where the extremist, ultranationalist, antisemitic, and anti-Roma Jobbik (Jobbik Magyarországért Mozgalom, or Movement for a Better Hungary) first gained parliamentary representation in 2010, this is remarkable. Jobbik went on to do even better in the 2014 elections,[125] when ballot returns made it the third-strongest force in the parliament. No Romanian party has attempted to create paramilitary organizations, as Jobbik did when it set up the Magyar Gárda, which functioned from 2007 until it was banned in 2009. In spited of the ban, at the swearing-in ceremony of the newly elected legislature in 2014, Gábor Vona, the commander of the Magyar Gárda and the leader of Jobbik, threw off the jacket he had worn during the ceremony and displayed the Guard's fascist-like uniform.[126]

To be sure, the Hungarian Guard is not the only organization to march the streets of East-Central Europe in uniforms reminiscent of the Nazis. Estonian Waffen SS veterans march annually, and are referred to as "freedom fighters." Latvian veterans of the former Latvian Legion parade in Riga every year on March 16 (Latvian Fighters Day), while in Lithuania admirers and apologists of the Lithuanian Activist Front march twice a year in Kaunas and Vilnius to commemorate their predecessors' wartime defense against the USSR; some of them wear modified Nazi symbols.[127] But these are either very old people or a handful of members of the young generation—not a paramilitary organization engaging in regular training. Still, they enjoy the support of some political parties and prominent politicians.

Even if reluctantly and under foreign pressure, Romania has by and large respected commitments it made on renouncing the initial Antonescu cult. In Hungary, by contrast, there is an uninterrupted promotion of the Miklós Horthy cult in which the ruling FIDESZ–Hungarian Civic Alliance (Fidesz–Magyar Polgári Szövetség) not only collaborates with Jobbik, but also very often leads in cleansing the admiral's regime and its members of any trace of responsibility for the fate of the Jews during the Second World War. Hand in hand, Premier Viktor Orbán and his supporters utilize the Double Genocide theme to obfuscate the Holocaust and to transmogrify perpetrators into respected intellectual and political historical figures.[128] Two recent attempts (in 2015 and 2016) involved statues honoring historians Bálint Hóman, one of the drafters of Second World War–era anti-Jewish legislation, and György Donáth, a racist and supporter of the same legislation, whose life-sized bust was placed just around the corner from Budapest's Holocaust Memorial Center, to add insult to injury. Competitive martyrdom also played a role, for Donáth had been executed by the communist regime in 1947 on trumped-up charges, while Hóman was sentenced in 1946 to life in prison and died in jail in 1951. The unveiling of Donáth's bust stirred a public protest, and the ceremony had to be interrupted. Leaving the site, FIDESZ deputy chairman Gergely Gulyás said that while he did not agree with views that exclude minorities, Donáth was a martyr and deserved to have a statue in Budapest.[129] Vojtech Tuka, the Slovak prime minister largely responsible for the deportation of the Jews in clerical fascist Slovakia, is also considered to be a "martyr" by his contemporary admirers.[130]

Just as worrisome as the transformation of wartime criminals into martyrs is the reaction to Jewish protests against these attempts by pundits close to the official ruling circles. For example, Zsolt Bayer, a FIDESZ founding member notorious for his antisemitism, as well as a personal friend of Prime Minister Orbán, wrote shortly after the Donáth incident in the daily *Magyar Hírlap* (Hungarian News): "Why are we surprised that the simple peasant whose determinant experience was that the Jews broke into his village, beat his priest to death, threatened to convert his church into a movie theater, why do we find it shocking that twenty years later he watched without pity as the gendarmes dragged the Jews away from his village?" This was but one of numerous attempts by Bayer to deflect onto Jews the guilt for what happened in Hungary during the Holocaust. In Bayer's opinion, there is no justification for denying cultural figures the likes of Hóman and Donáth their rightful place for having contributed to Hungarian culture. As for their views on Jews, Bayer cites Zsigmond Móricz, a rampant antisemite of Transylvanian origins: "Their noses and ears are big, their mouths strange, the lower lip is swollen: the kind of mouth I always see with disgust so that I have to avert my eyes. Such a mouth makes my throat nauseous."[131] As Eva Balogh pointed out, in the eyes of the pundit, antisemitism in Hungary after 1919 was a "natural" state of mind "because of the Jewish preponderance in the leadership of the Soviet Republic. And with this assertion he absolves all anti-Semitism between the two world wars."[132] This is nothing short of Holocaust obfuscation.

As we have seen, Romania has almost clandestinely rehabilitated some war criminals. Yet, attempts to rehabilitate Ion Antonescu and some of those executed with him in 1946 (Transnistria governor Gheorghe Alexianu, for example) have failed.[133] Neighboring Serbia, in contrast, rehabilitated in May 2015 Chetnik leader Dragoljub ("Draža") Mihailović, executed in May 1946 for high treason and collaboration with the Nazis. A court of justice in Belgrade ruled that his trial at the hands of Tito's communist regime had been "political and ideological," and said serious legal errors had been committed in its course.[134] Worse still, the rehabilitation of the wartime Nazi puppet regime head Milan Nedić appears to be imminent. The procedure was started by his family and has enlisted the support of the Association of Political Prisoners and Victims of the Communist Regime. Under Nedić's regime, Belgrade became the first capital city in the world to be declared *Judenrein*. By the end of the war, some 90 percent of Serbia's Jewish population had been murdered by the Nazis. Nedić's legal successors argue that his trial had been politically motivated. His apologists go even further, claiming that his suicide (in prison, in 1946) was actually murder, and that while acting as the head of the government, Nedić had given refuge to some 600,000 Serbs from all over the Balkans and thus helped Serbs survive Nazi occupation.[135]

Expectedly, Croatia has protested against these steps,[136] but Croatia has problems of its own. Under former presidents Stjepan Mesić (elected in

2000 and reelected in 2005) and one-term successor Ivo Josipović (2010–2014), Croatia successfully dismantled much of the legacy of its first postcommunist head of state, Franjo Tuđman. This meant that negationism, among other things, was out, and so was the glorification of the Nazi puppet state under Ante Pavelić. The victory of Kolinda Grabar-Kitarović in the presidential runoff on February 19, 2015, and the subsequent return to power of a coalition government in which the Tuđman-founded Croatian Democratic Union (HDZ) is the most powerful member changed the change. Leaving other worrisome signs aside, one indication of what seems to lie ahead was provided by the appointment as culture minister of historian Zlatko Hasanbegović.

Apparently a protégé of President Grabar-Kitarović, Hasanbegović is known to have belonged in his youth to the Croatian Liberation Movement (Hrvatski oslobodilački pokret, HOP), a party founded in exile by Pavelić in the 1950s and officially registered in postcommunist Croatia in 1992. At that time, as revealed after his appointment, he wrote extensively for the HOP publication *Nezavisna Država Hrvatska* (*NDH*, Independent State of Croatia), an Ustaše-cleansing journal. Photos showing Hasanbegović wearing the beret of the Ustaša (Pavelić's criminal fascist guard) also emerged. Nowadays a member of the HDZ, Hasanbegović had made the transition via another far-right formation, the Croatian Pure Party of Rights (Hrvatska Čista Stranka Prava, HČSP), founded in 1992, whose youth wing he headed. Hasanbegović is also a member of the Bleiburg Honorary Platoon, an NGO that honors the Ustaše executed by Tito's partisans in 1945. It is not an accident that soon after being sworn in, the presidency of the parliament elected in November 2015 decided to reinstate sponsorship of the Bleiburg commemoration, which had been withdrawn in 2012—a move Hasanbegović had harshly denounced. In articles published in *NDH*, he called the Ustaše "heroes" and "martyrs," in the best spirit of what would later emerge as Holocaust obfuscation. And in the same spirit, after his appointment as minister, he rejected criticism and calls for his resignation, saying that antifascism was just "an empty phrase," and arguing that "Stalin, Tito, and Pol Pot were all antifascists" who after victory went on to establish dictatorships in their countries. Double Genocide has thus come to power in Croatia.[137]

Apparently, so has the heroization of the Ustaše, and, what is more, this enjoys the support of the crowds. At a friendly soccer match with Israel in

March 2016, the Ustaša slogan "Za dom spremni" (Ready for the homeland) was chanted by the local team supporters in the presence of former premier Tihomir Oresković, who did not see fit to react.[138] Similarly, at the match with Norway in March, supporters at the Maksimir stadium in Zagreb also chanted "Za dom spremni," and the slogan was shouted by Croatian player Josip Simunić after a game with Iceland in November 2013, which led to his suspension from the World Cup in Brazil.[139] A huge swastika appeared on the pitch at the Euro 2016 qualifier match between Croatia and Italy at Stadion Poljud in Split.[140] Even more worrisome, at an official event in April 2016 marking the setting up of the Knight Rafael Boban unit in 1991, master of ceremony Colonel Marko Skejo, a former commander of that unit and head of its veterans' association, invited those in attendance to chant "Za dom spremni" in the presence of Deputy Defense Minister Ivan Vukić and other military officials including Generals Zeljko Glasnović and Mile Dedaković, and called for the salute to be legalized (previously, an appeal to make it the official chant of the Croatian army had been signed in August 2015 by several thousand people, but rejected by President Grabar-Kitarović). The Knight Rafael Boban unit was named after Ustaša commander Rafael Boban, who fought alongside the German-allied Axis states on the eastern front during the Second World War. The ceremony was held at a memorial for the unit that had been defiantly inaugurated in Split by the local mayor on May 9, 2014, Croatia's national Day of Victory over Fascism. Sejko's speech on the occasion notably was marked by Holocaust obfuscation and competitive martyrdom: "The Croatian dream briefly became a reality in 1941 with the creation of the Independent State of Croatia," he said, but "unfortunately, due to the treason of part of the Croat nation [i.e., Tito's Partisans], the NDH was crushed and Croatia fell into the darkest communist darkness in which every Croat word and idea was persecuted."[141]

Thus far, Romania has been spared similar incidents, but with some additional effort from the likes of Oana Stănciulescu, the day might be closing in when Bucharest stadium crowds will sing again "Holy Legionary Youth." For the time being, however, Romanian stadiums are used to "just" anti-Roma racist slogans, such as "One million crows, a single solution: Ion Antonescu."[142]

No figures as controversial as Hasanbegović[143] are (or were) members of the Romanian cabinet. Inaugurated in November 2015, the government headed by Premier Dacian Cioloș included as minister of communication the sponsor of a right-wing online publication with occasional forays to the extreme right—*În linie dreaptă* (The Right Line). For a communication minister, however, Marius Bostan was graciously silent, and in any case was dismissed by the premier after just a few months in office. Cioloș's predecessor, Victor Ponta, had included in his cabinet in several positions his personal friend Dan Șova. In March 2012 Șova said in an interview on the private television channel Money Channel that Jews in Romania never suffered during the Holocaust and they have to thank Marshal Antonescu for that. After the INSHR–EW protested, Șova apologized and was "sanctioned" by the premier by being dispatched to the United States Holocaust Memorial Museum in Washington, DC, to "learn the facts."[144] To find a genuine Holocaust denier in a Romanian cabinet one has to look back to 1993, when PRM member Mihai Ungheanu served as a deputy minister of culture. Among other (mis)deeds, Ungheanu participated in and spoke at the ceremony unveiling a statue honoring Antonescu in the town of Slobozia, which also happened to be his birthplace.[145]

Compared with cabinets in other former communist countries, this is neither impressive nor very frightening. In Poland, for example, the 2015 return to power of the Law and Justice Party (Prawo i Sprawiedliwosc, PiS) with an absolute parliamentary majority resulted in the designation of Antoni Maczierewicz as defense minister. Described as a "leading protagonist of the nationalist populist radical right," Macierewicz had moved to PiS from the League of Polish Families (Liga Polskich Rodzin, LPR), an ultranationalist and antisemitic party with which PiS ruled in coalition alongside the radical nationalist antisemitic populists of Self-Defense (Samoobrona) between July 26, 2006, and November 2007. Nowadays, Macierewicz is one of PiS's deputy chairmen. He is on record for having said in an interview with Radio Maryja in July 2002 (while still an LPR member and editor of its radical right publication *Głos* (The Voice) that he had read *The Protocols of the Elders of Zion* and considered the well-known forgery to be "very interesting." He added, "Some say it is authentic, some say it's not. I am no specialist. Experience shows that there are such groups in Jewish circles."[146]

Macierewicz is not the only extremist LPR member to be coopted into the high ranks of PiS. So was university professor Richard Bender, an LPR founder who accused former president Aleksander Kwaśniewski of having sold out to Jewish influence because he had participated in the July 2001 ceremonies commemorating the massacre at Jedwabne. Bender also denied the pogrom in an electoral television spot.[147] Bender, who taught history at the Catholic University of Lublin, had been a member of the communist-appointed parliament in the 1970s, and in the 1980s a member of the communist-led Patriotic Movement of National Rebirth (PRON), as a proregime Catholic representative. Later, he switched allegiance to the right and was for some time an LPR senator and the chairman of the State Council on Radio and Television. He came to the defense of Holocaust denier Dariusz Ratajczak. This record did not impede the Sejm from appointing him as a judge representing his party on the State Court of Justice. In the 2007 elections Bender was elected to a seat in the Senate as a PiS representative.[148] Upon his death in 2016 he was eulogized by the entire right-wing spectrum, including Radio Maryja's daily show *Nasz Dziennik* (Our Daily).[149]

PiS itself had an evolution that was similar to FIDESZ's in Hungary. It started as a classical centrist formation and "absorbed the populist radical right surge through its own appeal to illiberal democracy."[150] Viewed from this perspective, Viktor Orbán might have been the first to utilize "illiberal democracy" as a positive term of reference,[151] but the Kaczyński brothers in Poland were the first to apply it in practice. It is also true that Poland, as Jarosław Kaczyński himself has put it, was overtaken by Budapest and is now trying to catch up. Right after losing the 2011 parliamentary election, Kaczyński was reported to have said: "I am deeply convinced that the day will come when we will have Budapest in Warsaw."[152] The 2015 PiS victory seems, indeed, to be a step in that direction. Should the PNL pursue its 2016 course, Romania might one day join this undistinguished club. After all, the founding father of the PNL, Ion C. Brătianu, shares some traits with Józef Klemens Piłsudski, whose road the PiS follows. Both have great merits, but neither was a democrat in the current sense of the word.

Be that as it may, the collaboration of PiS with the LPR in the 2006 to 2007 government impacted the major coalition partner more than it did the two minor members of the coalition. As Pankowski puts it, this formation "started as a moderate conservative party in 2001, but the strategic alliance with Radio Maryja in 2005 meant a growing acceptance of the radical nationalist and Catholic fundamentalist ideology." This is what opened the door to the 2006 to 2007 coalition, and "by 2007, the Piłsudski party [had] largely absorbed the previous popular support of Self-Defense and the

LPR."[153] Viewed from this angle, the fact that the election was lost was less important than the move from Piłsudski's etatist and nationalist (but still civic) ideology to the exclusivist, antisemitic, and integral nationalist ideology of the interwar Endecja led by Roman Dmowski.

Lech Kaczyński was elected head of state in December 2005, but his twin brother Jarosław became premier only in July 2006. Whether or not the same model was followed in 2015, when Jarosław chose lawyer Beata Szydło to step into the premier's shoes after the PiS ballot victory, remains to be seen. Szydło had earlier organized the ballot victory of little-known PiS presidential candidate Andrzej Duda. During the electoral campaigns, PiS strove to display as little as possible of LPR-like positions. During their (short-lived but significant in the long term) partnership, the LPR was led by Roman Jacek Giertych, who was deputy premier and minister of education (in this position, he was directly in charge of education on the Holocaust!). Roman Giertych was the grandson of the notorious interwar antisemite Jędrzej Giertych. Together with his father Maciej, he had reestablished in 1989 Roman's National Party (Stronnictwo Narodowe).[154] Maciej Giertych previously had represented the LPR in the European Parliament, where he caused several uproars due to his extreme homophobia and his racist publications directed against non-Europeans.[155]

Two (apparently contradictory, but on closer inspection, complementary) symbolic gestures were made by President Duda not long after taking office. On the one hand, he participated in March 2016 in the ceremony of the inauguration of a museum honoring Polish Righteous among the Nations[156] opened in the southeastern town of Markowa.[157] Earlier, however, Duda had initiated the rescinding of the Order of Merit from Polish-American historian Jan Gross, for allegedly insulting Poles in an article published in the German conservative publication *Die Welt*.[158] In fact, the article referred to the attitude of East-Central Europeans in the ongoing refugee crisis, and Poland was mentioned only in this particular connection, but in the harshest possible terms—as a country whose citizens might have killed more Jews than Nazis during the Second World War. The Order of Merit had been bestowed on Gross in 1996 for his books on the underground structures of the state during the Second World War and on Polish children sent to Siberia, for his personal record of opposing communism as a young man in his native country, and for his support of the independent resistance movement after his emigration in 1969 to the United States, where he became a professor at Princeton University.[159] But that was all before Gross shattered Polish self-delusions about their behavior toward Jews during the war and in its aftermath.[160] While a decision on withdrawing the Order of Merit is still pending, in April 2016 Gross was interrogated in Katowice by a prosecutor, under suspicion of insulting the Polish nation—an offense punishable by up to three years in prison.[161]

While campaigning for the presidency, Duda criticized his rival, incumbent Bronisław Komorowski, for allowing Poles to be "wrongfully accused by others for participating in the Holocaust." He asked why the president had failed to defend the good name of Poland when he did not reject the accusations that Poles had burned alive their Jewish neighbors in Jedwabne.[162] After his electoral victory, Duda proclaimed a "new historical policy strategy" to enhance Poland's image in the world.[163] Reminiscent of Hungary's first postcommunist premier, József Antal, Duda's "new strategy" for dealing with Holocaust-related problems apparently consists of emphasizing the role of the (honorable, but few in number) Polish Righteous among the Nations, while denouncing critical inquiries into Polish society during and after the war. Or, as I put it when discussing Antal's case, "symbolic history" is to replace real history and play the role of communist "socialist realism," only in reverse: if for Stalin and Andrei Zhdanov the "typical hero in typical circumstances" existed in a fictitious present, Antal (and now Duda) placed him in an almost fictitious past.[164] But there might be more to that. The Poles are well known to see themselves as the eternally victimized "Christ of Nations," and one cannot help but remark that competitive martyrdom ultimately leads to the substitution of *imitatio Christi* by *imitatio Judae*. As Polish historian Witold Kukla put it, "in the past, the Jews were envied for their money, qualifications, positions and international contacts—today they are envied for the very crematoria in which they were incinerated."[165] The "Auschwitz Crosses" saga[166] is but one example among many, and Poland itself is but one among many East European competitors for victimhood.

These comparative remarks should not end without discussion of the possibly emblematic case of Slovakia. In the parliamentary elections of March 2016 an openly neo-Nazi party, the Ľudová strana Naše Slovensko (L'SNS, People's Party—Our Slovakia), led by the governor of the Banská Bystrica region Marian Kotleba, garnered 8.1 percent of the votes and entered the legislature with fourteen deputies out of 150 in the Národná rada. The ĽSNS has also sent to the legislature the youngest member of the new parliament, Milan Mazurek. Aged only twenty-two, Mazurek is an admirer of Adolf Hitler, denies the Holocaust, and is known for his involvement in anti-Roma and antiimmigrant incidents.[167]

Soon after, Kotleba said he intends to utilize the subsidy from the state budget to which the ĽSNS was entitled as a parliamentary party (some 5 million euro) to set up a militia modeled on the Magyar Gárda. After the elections, members of the militia began boarding trains, allegedly to ensure the passengers' safety. In fact, a paramilitary formation linked to the ĽSNS already existed in Slovakia; unlike the Hungarian Guard it does not yet march on the streets to intimidate the Roma population, but it trains in the woods. Occasionally, it surfaces in towns, marching in uniforms and carrying torches, according to Slovak president Andrej Kiska. The formation is called Akčná skupina Vzdor (Action Group Resistance), and Kotleba's close collaborator Richard Holtan set it up.[168] Kotleba and the Akčná are linked to Slovenská pospolitosť (Slovak Brotherhood), set up in 1995, whose members wear the fascist uniform of the Hlinka Guard—the militia of the Slovak clerical fascist state between 1938 and 1945. In 2003 Kotleba became the leader of the far-right Slovak Solidarity–National Party (Slovenská pospolitost–Národní strana),[169] which the Slovak Supreme Court dissolved in 2006. As leader, Kotleba was charged for having ended a speech delivered on the seventieth anniversary of the establishment of the Slovak fascist state with the official salute of that state—"Na stráž!" (On guard!). The charges were dropped by the prosecution in 2009 on the strange grounds that it could not be proven that the use of the slogan was meant to display sympathy for extremism.[170] As a member of parliament in April 2016, Kotleba proposed that the house observe a minute of silence in Tiso's memory. "Today is the sixty-ninth anniversary of an abominable judicial murder [of Tiso] that is rightly seen by every patriot as a martyr of Slovakia's sovereignty and a defender of Christianity against Bolshevism," Kotleba said in an open letter addressed to parliamentary speaker Andrej Danko.[171]

According to Cas Mudde, the entrance of the ĽSNS into parliament is mainly explained by Premier Robert Fico's campaigning on a nativist, anti-Islamic, and antirefugee campaign that legitimized the positions that Kotleba had long been advocating.[172] This is probably accurate, but only in part. After all, Kotleba had been elected as governor already in 2013, and his activity at the head of far-right organizations dated back to the 1990s. There is more to an electoral performance than just its immediate outcome. I have in mind what Pankowski calls the "cultural resources."[173]

The cultural resources of the Slovak extreme right are well rooted, and so, I dare add, are those of its Romanian counterpart. Viewed from this perspective, the "solution" the Slovaks came up with as a result of the election is both short-term and ironic. Its main pillar seems to be the Slovak National Party (Slovenská národná strana, SNS), which has entered into coalition with Fico's Smer–SD (Smer–sociálna demokracia) and, surprisingly enough, with the Slovak-Hungarian Bridge (Most–Híd) and the centrist Sieť (Network).[174] But the SNS is an ultranationalist formation, whose members had been exalting Tiso's interwar Slovakia and calling for his rehabilitation long before the ĽSNS.[175] Though it is true that the SNS is nowadays led by new parliamentary speaker Andrej Danko rather than the embarrassingly flamboyant Ján Slota, whom Danko replaced at the head of the party in 2012, one wonders if he can change a party that used to threaten to send tanks to Budapest (Slota). The Progressive Alliance of Socialists and Democrats in the European Parliament twice in the past suspended Smer for entering into a coalition with the SNS, and is warning it once more against the partnership.[176] For now, however, Fico does his best to alleviate such apprehensions. On March 14, 2016, the anniversary of the establishment of Tiso's state, he laid a wreath on the monument dedicated to Holocaust victims at the Rybné Námestie square in Bratislava. Three ĽSNS representatives just elected to the new parliament, on the other hand, marked the day at Tiso's grave at the Martinský cemetery in the Bratislava borough of Ružinov.[177]

Far-right and antisemitic organizations are active in the Czech Republic as well, but they are by and large marginal and have little echo in Czech society. Adam B. Bartoš, leader of the extraparliamentarian National Democracy Party, and a fellow member of the party were convicted in early March 2016 for making antisemitic statements at the grave of Agnes Hrůzová. Hrůzová was murdered on Easter 1899, and the Jew Leopold Hilsner (Hülsner) was convicted for the crime in September the same year, in a blood libel.[178] Unfortunately, there haven't been the same legal consequences for the anti-Roma activism that some of these groups also promote, with a lot more success.

The best way to conclude might be to refer to Jewish dietary laws that prohibit mixing meat with milk. Compared to other places in East-Central Europe, Romania is neither the worst plate (meaty, or *fleishig* in Yiddish) nor the best portion (dairy, or *milchig*). It is rather a mixture of the two. And that, without doubt, is not *kosher*.

> Michael Shafir is Emeritus Professor at the Babeș-Bolyai University, Cluj-Napoca, Romania. He is author of *Romania: Politics, Economics, and Society: Political Stagnation and Simulated Change* and *Between Denial and "Comparative Trivialization": Holocaust Negationism in Post-Communist East Central Europe*.

Notes

1. See Himka and Michlic, "Introduction," 1–2.
2. See Geritz, *The Myth of Jewish Communism*.
3. Shafir, "Rotten Apples," 150–187.
4. This term was first utilized by Katz in "On Three Definitions," 259–277.
5. *RFE/RL Newsline*, January 22, 2001. Emphasis mine.
6. On a visit to Romania in February, Bruce Jackson, chairman of the US NATO Committee did not mince words: "Give me a bulldozer and I shall immediately destroy all Antonescu statues," adding that adherence to democratic values includes facing the historical past, and that this adherence is "not negotiable" in the NATO accession process. *România liberă*, February 27, 2002.
7. Currently, and in defiance of the legislation discussed below, a street in the town of Beiuș, Bihor County is still named after the wartime leader, and the local council of Târgoviște, Dâmbovița County, obstinately refuses to annul his honorary citizenship of the locality. See Florian, "Memoria publică a Holocaustului în postcomunism," 35–44. There is also a bust of the Marshal in the regional museum of Argeș County in the town of Pitești. While the law allows this for didactic purposes, it certainly does not allow the eulogies that surround the bust. There is also a monument to Antonescu at Movila lui Burcel (Vaslui County) depicting him giving the order to Romanian soldiers to "cross the river Prut" and liberate Bessarabia in 1941. I owe the latter information to historian Adrian Cioflâncă.
8. Law no. 107 in *Monitorul oficial al României*, no. 377, May 3, 2006.
9. International Commission, *Final Report*, 381. Emphasis mine.
10. *Haaretz*, English edition, July 25, 2003. See also *RFE/RL Newsline*, July 28, 2003.
11. International Commission, *Final Report*, 386–390.
12. See Totok, "Receptarea publicistică a raportului final al Comisiei Wiesel în presa românească și germană," 186–195.
13. International Commision, *Final Report*, 387.
14. See Shafir, "Unacademic Academics," 942–964.
15. The author of this chapter attended the meeting.
16. Broszat, "Plädoyer für eine Historisierung des Nationalsozialismus," 373–385.

17. Gay, *Freud, Jews and Other Germans: Masters and Victims in Modernist Culture*, xi–xii.
18. Nolte, *Războiul civil european*.
19. International Commision, *Final Report*, 388.
20. Ibid., 389.
21. Ibid.
22. See Cioflâncă, "Groapa comună de la Popricani (Iași)"; Florian, "Holocaustul evreilor din România. Un nou document juridic."
23. IHRA, "Holocaust Education, Remembrance, and Research in Romania."
24. Cioflâncă "Gropile comune din nord-est (I–II)."
25. International Commision, *Final Report*, 389.
26. Climescu, "Post-Transitional Injustice," 151. For other rehabilitations of persons condemned under the same legislation, see Climescu, "The Holocaust on Trial," 314–318.
27. Climescu, "Post-transitional Injustice." On the activities of Dinulescu and Petrescu on the eve of and during the Second World War, see also Ioanid, *The Holocaust in Romania*, 64–65, 127–128, 155–156 and passim; Ancel, *Preludiu la asasinat*, 25–26, 29–30, 42, 290–292, 441; Deletant, *Hitler's Forgotten Ally*, 137, 153, 156–157, 320 (note 76); Florian, "Memoria."
28. Shafir, "Between Denial and 'Comparative Trivialization,'" 24–37.
29. International Commision, *Final Report*, 390.
30. *Cotidianul*, June 3, 2006; Clej, "Negarea Holocaustului și activități fasciste—16 inculpați în 14 ani."
31. "Legea nr. 217/2015 pentru modificarea și completarea Ordonanței de Urgență a Guvernului nr. 31/2002 privind interzicerea organizațiilor și simbolurilor cu caracter fascist, rasist sau xenofob și a promovării cultului persoanelor vinovate de săvârșirea unor infracțiuni contra păcii și omenirii," *Monitorul Oficial al României*, July 15, 2015.
32. While Crin Antonescu was a member of the Senate, the other two (Dominic Gerea and Adrian Silviu Scutaru) were members of the lower house.
33. Shafir, "Memory, Memorials," 67–97.
34. Pankowski, *The Populist Radical Right in Poland*, 105.
35. See note 4.
36. For earlier uses of the concept, see Chaumont, *La concurrence des victimes*; Besançon, *Le malheur du siècle*, 138; Bartov, *Mirrors of Destruction*, 71–75; Rosenbaum, "Introduction to First Edition," 2. According to Pankowski, *The Populist Radical Right in Poland*, 109, Western-based Polish sociologist Irineusz Krzemiński published in 2002 an article in which he proposed "an interpretation of contemporary Polish antisemitism without Jews as a result of the competition of two national narratives, both claiming supreme martyrdom, or, in other words, the competition of suffering."
37. In Lithuania, the term *genocide* has been officially "redefined to include victims of Soviet deportations," and the NKVD and the KGB were "officially declared to be criminal organizations, thus bringing them in line with the Nürnberg tribunal's definition of the SS." Bartov, "Conclusion," 668.
38. Andreescu, "Interzicerea negării crimelor comuniste pe plan european," 41–58; Geissbühler, "The Struggle for Holocaust Memory in Romania and How Ukraine Can Learn from It," 1–10; Socor, "Moldova Condemns Communism at Long Last," *Eusasia Daily Monitor* 9, July 12, 2012.
39. *Permanențe*. Ediție specială, no date, 2015.

40. Shafir, "Between Denial and 'Comparative Trivialization,' " 59.
41. See Byford, *From "Traitor" to "Saint": Bishop Nikolaj Velimirović in Serbian Public Memory*; Byford, *Denial and Repression of Antisemitism*.
42. See Webb, *The Routledge Companion to Central and Eastern Europe since 1919*, 156; "Protest against Beatification of 'Anti-Semitic' Bishop. Israeli Historians Have Expressed," *The Tablet*, November 18, 2000; JTA,"Controversial Slovak Bishop May Be Canonized," June 13, 2001; Mešťan, *Anti-Semitism in the Political Development of Slovakia (2000–2009)*, 47 and passim.
43. See Carter, "Once the Ustasha Archbishop Stepinac Is Canonized, He Becomes Officially a Catholic Saint," *There Must Be Justice*, February 13, 2014; Dragojlo, "Serbian Church Demands Vatican Talks over Stepinac," *BalkanInsight*, June 2, 2015; Milekić, "Croatia PM to Push Pope to Canonise Stepinac," *BalkanInsight*, April 7, 2016; "Zuroff: Jews, Serbs Were Victims of Genocide in NDH," *inSerbia*, July 14, 2015; "Croatian Prelate: Pope Francis Believes Blessed Stepinac Is a Saint," *Catholic Culture*, January 22, 2016; "Pope Appoints Members of Commission to Study Cause of Cardinal Stepinac," *Catholic Culture*, March 8, 2016; "Croatian Archbishop Confident that Cardinal Stepinac's Canonization Will Not Be Delayed," *Catholic Culture*, March 9, 2016; "Croatian Leader Meets with Pope, Presses for Canonization of Cardinal Stepinac," *Catholic Culture*, April 7, 2016; Pavlić, "Želimir Puljić, Archbishop of Zadar, Talks about Cardinal Stepinac and Meeting with the Pope," *Total Croatia*, March 8, 2016.
44. A converted Jew and a former communist, Wurmbrand is claimed to have had his life saved by Valeriu Gafencu, but he never mentions that in his autobiographical works. See Wurmbrand, *Tortured for Christ*; Wurmbrand, *With God in Solitary Confinement*; Wurmbrand, *In God's Underground*.
45. Lavric, *Constantin Noica și Mișcarea Legionară*.
46. Preda, "Este de datoria mea să pun pe agenda institutului cazurile Sfinților Închisorilor," *Cuvântul Ortodox*, April 26, 2014.
47. Codrescu, *Cartea mărturisitorilor* and *Sfinții Închisorilor în lumea credinței. Texte alese, prefață și note de Răzvan Codrescu*.
48. Climescu, "IICCMER, centenarul Vintilă Horia și apologia fascismului. 'Diversitate igienică' sau confuzie organizată?," *contributors.ro*, April 8, 2016.
49. Condurache, *Chipuri ale demintății românești*; Condurache, *Eroi Anticomuniști și Sfinții Închisorilor.*
50. Lavric "Damnatio memoriae," 3.
51. Ibid., 4.
52. Ibid., 5–6.
53. Ibid., 8.
54. Nonetheless, Andreescu republished the same article in the Bucharest weekly *Contemporanul* soon after, replacing the original attacks *ad personae* with others, seeking to demonstrate that Florian, "who determines the policy of the Elie Wiesel Institute, promoted under the former regime Lenin's ideas, nourished the Nicolae Ceaușescu cult, and was an active supporter of communist ideology." The references were an obvious effort to discredit the Institute through "guilt by association." In fact, very few social science or history authors had a chance to see their work published if they declined to introduce quotes such as those mentioned by Andreescu. See his "Etica, politica memoriei și 'legea anti-legionară,' " 21–22. By the same (unjustified) token, I could associate Andreescu with

the promotion of the Codreanu cult. Back in 2011, I stopped collaborating with *Contemporanul* following the publication by its editor in chief, writer Nicolae Breban, of excerpts from a book exalting the leader of the Legion. For details, see my "Doamnei Aura Christi, redactor-șef, 'Contemporanul. Ideea Europeană,'" *Acum*, July 15, 2011.

55. Andreescu, "Necesitatea amendării Ordonanței de urgență nr. 31," 8–19.

56. Andreescu, "Temele 'legii antilegionare' din perspectiva eticii memoriei," *Noua Revistă a Drepturilor Omului*, no. 4/ 2015. I found it amusing to be charged with lack of compassion by the author of a volume titled *I Hated Ceaușescu*, as compassion is probably one of the opposites of hate. (See Andreescu, *L-am urât pe Ceaușescu: Ani, oameni, disidență*.) So much for Mr. Andreescu's "ethics"; one might add that such criticism is seldom found in Andreescu's works for foreign consumption.

57. Dinescu, "Partidul legionar Totul pentru Țară a intrat în legalitate."

58. The movie can be watched at http://www.iedb.net/movie/portrait-of-the-fighter-as-a-young-man.

59. See Hategan, "Ion Gavrilă Ogoranu s-a frânt, dar nu s-a îndoit," *România liberă*, May 5, 2006.

60. Zuroff, "The Musical Rehabilitation of a Latvian Mass Murderer," *I24 News*, October 7, 2014; Zuroff, "False Symmetry between Perpetrator and Victim," *The Jerusalem Post*, October 19, 2014; JTA, "Israel Slams Latvian Show Celebrating Life of Alleged Nazi War Criminal," October 23, 2014.

61. Miron, "Oficial: Legionarii revin în forță," *stiripesurse.ro*, September 25, 2014.

62. See the misleadingly titled article by Stoica, "Premieră. Primul PARTID POLITIC desființat în JUSTIȚIE. Partidul 'Totul pentru Țară' a fost acuzat de procurori de FASCISM. Judecătorii au decis să fie dizolvat și radiat din Registrul partidelor politice," *Evenimentul zilei*, May 5, 2015.

63. "TPȚ susține apelul societății civile către parlamentari," *Buciumul*, March 12, 2015.

64. Totok, "Noua Dreaptă (Rumänien)," 453–455; Davis and Lynch, 311; Davis, *The Extreme Right in France*, 127.

65. See the interview with Tudor Ionescu on the private channel Neptun TV, February 10, 2016, conducted by journalist Răzvan Zamfir on the program *Contraziceri*, https://www.youtube.com/watch?v=pO-OoyFHpto.

66. Pankowski, *The Populist Radical Right in Poland*, 99.

67. From the introduction to the documentary "The Faces of Romanian Extremism," produced by RISE Project, and Atlátszó, *Organized Crime and Corruption Reporting*, March 12, 2016. RISE Project was set up by a group of Romanian journalists to investigate organized crime in Romania and other countries in the region and its links to politics. I owe this information to William Totok. Atlátszó is a Budapest-based NGO combining investigative journalism and civic activism to promote transparency.

68. Shafir, "The Inheritors," 70–89.

69. Although initially the spokesman of the group, Zamfirescu ran in the December 2016 elections at the head of the PRM, one of several nationalist formations that failed to gain seats in the legislature.

70. See Griffin, *The Nature of Fascism*, 26–55, and Feldman, "Editorial Introduction," XII–XXVII.

71. Udrea, "Marian Munteanu, despre 'Grupul pentru România': Dorim să apărăm calitatea de proprietari a cetățenilor români în România," *Evenimentul zilei*, January 14, 2016.

72. On "Dacopathy" see Alexe, *Dacopatia și alte rătăciri românești*.

73. Bălașa, "Marian Munteanu anunță coagularea unei a treia forțe politice în România," *Rost Online*, March 4, 2016.

74. Ibid. The ANR (as the GpR was renamed) garnered in the December 2016 elections less than 1% of the votes for either of the two parliamentary chambers.

75. Realitatea TV, 28 March 2016, https://www.youtube.com/watch?v=B7azN4 CKZVQ.

76. http://www.aliantanoastra.ro/Proclamatie-Alianta%20Noastra.pdf; https://translate .google.ro/translate?hl=en&sl=ro&u=http://aliantanoastra.ro/&prev=search.

77. Realitatea TV, March 28, 2016, https://www.youtube.com/watch?v=B7azN4 CKZVQ.

78. For a brief discussion see Boia, *Mihai Eminescu, românul absolut*, 88–89.

79. Coja, "Proiectul 'Israel în România' este în plină derulare," February 6, 2014; Coja, "România, colonie a Israelului?" *Justițiarul*, March 27, 2015.

80. Fati, "Interviu cu directorul ICCMER," *România liberă*, August 23, 2015.

81. Pleșu, "O dezbatere blocată," *Adevărul*, August 3, 2015; Pleșu, "Spiritul civic în acțiune...," *Adevărul*, September 7, 2015; Pleșu, "Greșeală, vină, justiție," *Adevărul*, February 1, 2016; Pleșu, "Memorie înjumătățită," *Dilema veche*, February 18, 2016. For an excellent response, see Ioanid, "Aproximațiile păgubitoare ale domnului Andrei Pleșu," *Adevărul*, February 5, 2016.

82. Gabriel Liiceanu, director of the publishing house Humanitas, was the first to indulge in comparative trivialization of the Holocaust, and may be said to have become the main conservative promoter of the Double Genocide theory in his country. See Liiceanu, *Ușa interzisă*, 256–257, and repeated statements in the collection of interviews in Liiceanu, *Estul naivităților noastre. 27 interviuri 1990–2011*, 77, 83–103, 133–134, 164. On Liiceanu, see Shafir, "Between Denial and 'Comparative Trivialization,'" 70–71; Shafir, "The Man They Love to Hate," 74–75; Shafir, "Strange Bedfellows," 175–177; Laignel-Lavastine, "Fascism and Communism in Romania," 178–179.

83. On Patapievici, see Shafir, "Reconciliation at the Wrong End," 696–701.

84. Pleșu, Liiceanu, and Patapievici, *O idee care ne sucește mințile*, 7–8.

85. See the precedent set by Romanian Writers' Union President Nicolae Manolescu, who made the same claim in 1997, coming out against voices objecting to the publication in Romania of a translation of a negationist book. Shafir, "The Man They Love to Hate," 71. The Realitatea TV program is available on http://www.dailymotion.com/video/x3ocsfg. For the article by Pleșu, see supra, "O dezbatere blocată."

86. http://oanastanciulescu.ro/index.php/2015/08/13/mihai-boeru-sunt/. On this particular point, Pleșu and Manolescu parallel Hungarian antisemite FIDESZ pundit Zsolt Bayer, about whom more is said below. Bayer also insists that the pro-Nazi pasts of figures such as Ezra Pound, Louis-Férdinand Céline, Gerhart Hauptmann, and Knut Hamsun do not detract from their value as writers, as if this was relevant to the discussion. See Balogh, "Zsolt Bayer: It's All the Jews' Fault," *Hungarian Spectrum*, March 14, 2016.

87. https://www.youtube.com/watch?v=-dHBKk_jo9M.

88. "Simpozion memorial Gogu Puiu și rezistența anticomunistă din Dobrogea."

89. "Mesaj pentru Oana Stănciulescu: Ești fiica noastră adoptivă," *Știri sociale*, March 21, 2016.

90. See Hermeziu, "Cazul Vintilă Horia: 'criminal de război'? Interviu cu Basarab Nicolescu," *Adevărul*, January 20, 2016; Bălașa, "Cea mai recentă țintă a Institutului Wiesel: Vintilă Horia," *Rost Online*, January 20, 2016; Hermeziu and Roșu, "Dezbatere. Cazul

Vintilă Horia și memoria culturală. Cum se aplică Legea 217/2015 privind crimele împotriva umanității și crimele de război," *Adevărul*, February 6, 2016; Pleșu, "Greșeală, vină, justiție," *Adevărul*, February 1, 2016; Pleșu, "Adaos la 'cazul' Vintilă Horia," *Adevărul*, February 8, 2016. For responses, see Ioanid, "Aproximațiile păgubitoare ale domnului Andrei Pleșu;" Laszlo, "Andrei Pleșu față cu hitlerismul," *e-leonardo*, February 5, 2016; Varzariu, "Pleșu poate este, dar sigur nu îi place," *Adevărul*, February 8, 2016; Iliescu, " 'Cazul Vintilă Horia' și sofistica zglobie a lui Andrei Pleșu," *Argumente și fapte*, February 28, 2016; Șerban, "Vintilă Horia: un invitat inopinat la masa discuțiilor," *Observator cultural*, March 4, 2016; Climescu, "IICCMER, centenarul Vintilă Horia și apologia fascismului."

91. I owe this information to Alexandru Florian.

92. Ibid.

93. Zărnescu, *Holocaustul. Gogorița diabolică*, vol. 1. On earlier Romanian outright deniers see Shafir, "*Ex Occidente Obscuritas*," 23–82.

94. Iacob, "Scandal de proporții: SRI are dispensă să nege Holocaustul?," *inPolitics.ro*, April 8, 2016.

95. Ministerul Public. Parchetul de pe lângă Înalta Curte de Casație și Justiție, Biroul de Presă. "Comunicat," December 2, 2015.

96. "Protest împotriva desemnării Oanei Stănciulescu ca membră în Consiliul de Administrație TVR," *Observator cultural*, March 17, 2016; Andreescu, "Oana Stănciulescu, scrisoare deschisă de susținere a jurnalistei în CA al TVR," *DC News*, March 19, 2016.

97. See the editorial by Șimonca, "Pentru decență în spațiul public," *Observator cultural*, March 23, 2016.

98. Realitatea TV, Jocuri de Putere, March 17, 2016, https://www.youtube.com/watch?v=XFD8K1WNeSg.

99. "As long as the forces of the Nation do not express themselves in a single strong organization, foreign agents and homegrown traitors will be having a free hand and play on our nose." Cited in Pankowski, *The Populist Radical Right in Poland*, 120–121.

100. See ibid., 111, 119.

101. "Parlamentul a validat noul CA al SRTV," *Romania TV.net*, March 22, 2016; parliamentary debate on https://www.youtube.com/watch?v=mkD0W7EqH78; Totok, "Aufstieg des Legionarismus zur parlamentarischen Leitkultur," *Halbjahresschrift-onlie*, March 22, 2016. The Alliance of Liberals and Democrats (ALDE) published the next day a strongly worded communiqué denouncing the vote in Parliament. See "Comunicat de presă-Daniel Barbu (ALDE)," *Agerpres*, March 23, 2016.

102. Udrea and Vintilă, "Marian Munteanu este candidatul PNL pentru primăria capitalei. BPN a validat în unanimitate candidatura sa. Prima reacție a fostului lider al studenților," *Evenimentul zilei*, April 13, 2016.

103. Stanomir noted that by embracing Munteanu, the PNL "identifies with the ideological line organically leading from Legionarism to Nicolae Ceaușescu's National Stalinism and to the National tribalism of the Romanian Cradle and Corneliu Vadim Tudor." The "common denominator" of these, Stanomir wrote, "is the appeal to autochthonism, to autarchic isolation, and to ethnic messianism." According to Stanomir, "Marian Munteanu is the contemporary image of this hybrid, but no less toxic, formula." Stanomir, "Marian Munteanu—etnocrația ca proiect politic," *contributors.ro*, April 13, 2018.

104. The National Party led by Măgureanu announced the designation of Munteanu as presidential candidate of an alliace of which it was member, but in the end Munteanu did not run for the position.

105. Roşca, "Institutul pentru Politici Publice si alte ONG-uri cer PNL să îl retragă pe Marian Munteanu: 'Are simpatii pentru curente de orientare fascist,'" *HotNews*, April 14, 2016. The list of signatories also included the following NGOs: Romanian Academic Society; Filia Center; Romani Criss; Communitarian Development Agency "Together"; Accept; Euroregional Center for Public Initiative; and European Center for the Rights of Children with Disabilities.

106. "Chiar vreți să ne întoarcem la ideologiile care au făcut ravagii în Europa secolului XX?," *Revista 22*, April 15, 2016.

107. "Declarația Institutului 'Elie Wiesel' în privința candidaturii domnului Marian Munteanu la funcția de Primar al Capitalei."

108. Udrea, "Candidatul PNL la Capitală, pus la zid de ONG-uri și Elie Wiesel," *Evenimentul zilei*, April 15, 2016.

109. All quotations from Katz's letter reproduced from Marincu, "Marian Munteanu răspunde acuzațiilor din ultimele zile," *Rost Online*, April 16, 2016.

110. Ibid.

111. Shafir, "The Movement for Romania," 16–21; Shafir, "The Romanian Extreme Right in the Post-Communist Period, 4–6 (part 1) and 16–17 (part 2); Shafir, "The Inheritors"; Shafir, "The Mind of Romania's Radical Right"; Shafir, "Marginalization or Mainstream?," 247–267.

112. Totok and Macovei, *Între mit și bagatelizare*, forthcoming. Fragment published in *Halbjahresschrift-onlie*, April 18, 2016.

113. *Mișcarea* 1, March 1992.

114. For example, in *Mișcarea* 5, March 1–15, 1995.

115. Cited in JTA, "Bucharest Mayoral Candidate Accuses Jewish Community of Lying about Holocaust Dead," *The Jerusalem Post*, April 18, 2016.

116. Marincu, "Marian Munteanu răspunde acuzațiilor." Emphasis in original.

117. Tița, "Interviu Marian Munteanu," Mediafax, April 18, 2016.

118. "Antonescu: Despre Munteanu se poate spune orice, dar nu că nu este interesant," *Ziare.com*, April 19, 2016.

119. Tița, "Interviu—Paleologu despre conducerea PNL," *Mediafax*, April 14, 2015.

120. Mihalache, "Petre Roman: Munteanu a scris în 1994 că I.G. Duca a fost 'asasin'. Conducerea PNL să spună dacă se dezice de istoria sa," *Adevărul*, April 17, 2016; Ioniță, "Domnule Quintus, nu girați întoarcerea României în anii '30!," *Adevărul*, April 18 2016.

121. Petrariu, "Doi candidați la primăriile de sector se leapădă de Marian Munteanu," *Hotweek.ro*, April 19, 2016; Popa, "Încă un candidat PNL de sector se delimitează de Munteanu," *știripesurse.ro*, April 20, 2016.

122. "După primărie, Munteanu vrea la guvernare: Lucrez la o noua construcție politică," *Ziare.com*, April 23, 2016.

123. *Romanian TV*, April 25, 2016, http://www.romaniatv.net/catalin-predoiu-marian-munteanu-nu-mai-este-pe-lista-pnl-ciprian-ciucu-va-fi-primul-pe-lista-pentru-consiliul-general_288743.html.

124. See Unteanu, "Candidatura lui Marian Munteanu, opțiunea perfectă în direcția unei anumite Europe," *Adevărul*, April 13, 2016; Verseck, "Vormarsch der Nationalisten: Rumänien auf Rechtskurs," *Spiegel Online*, April 26, 2016.

125. Since the number of seats in Parliament was reduced from 386 in 2010 to 199 in 2014, one has to take into account the proportion of the garnered vote rather than the number of won seats. This calculus shows that Jobbik increased its support from 16.67% in

2010 to 20.22% in 2014. According to current polls, the party has become the second-strongest political force in Hungary.

126. Follath, "Europe's Capital of Anti-Semitism," *Der Spiegel*, October 14, 2010. Since its disbandment, the Guard has unsuccessfully attempted to re-register under the name Hungarian Guard Foundation. Members of the Guard or people closely associated with it are suspected to have participated in the 2008 and 2009 murder of Roma minority members, but the suspicion was not proved in court, which sentenced three of the murderers to life in prison and a fourth to thirteen years in 2013. See Verseck, "Justice in Hungary: Neo-Nazis Get Life for Roma Murder Spree," *Der Spiegel*, August 6, 2103; Vágyvölgyi, "On Roma Murders in Hungary," *Open Democracy*, September 5, 2014.

127. Shafir, "A Present of *Chiaroscuro*," 225–250.

128. For a detailed analysis, see Shafir, "Conceptualizing Hungarian Negationism," 265–310.

129. Balogh, "Bálint Hóman Is Rehabilitated," *Hungarian Spectrum*, May 17, 2015; Balogh, "Viktor Orbán, the Man Responsible for the Statue Honoring the Anti-Semitic Bálint Hóman," *Hungarian Spectrum*, December 16, 2015; Balogh, "Another Attempt to Erect a Statue Honoring an Anti-Semitic Racist," *Hungarian Spectrum*, February 25, 2016; Than, "Hungary Protest Prevents Unveiling of Statue for Anti-Jewish World War 2 Politician," *The Star Online*, February 24, 2016.

130. See Mešťan, *Anti-Semitism in the Political Development of Slovakia*, 30.

131. Cited in JTA, "Israel's Ambassador to Hungary Blasts Mainstream Daily's Anti-Semitic Columns," April 14, 2016. On Bayer and previous antisemitic incidents see Shafir, "Strange Bedfellows," 170, and "Conceptualizing Hungarian Negationism," 277.

132. Cited in Balogh, "Zsolt Bayer: It's All the Jews' Fault," *Hungarian Spectrum*, March 14, 2016.

133. Shafir, "Marshal Antonescu's Postcommunist Rehabilitation: *Qui Bono*," 349–410; Shafir, "Polls and Antisemitism," 582, note 4 (Alexianu).

134. "Court Rehabilitates WW2-Era Chetnik Leader Draza Mihailović," *b92*, May 14, 2015; "Draza Mihailović Rehabilitated," *inSerbia*, May 14, 2015; Ristić and Milekić, "Serbia Rehabilitates WWII Chetnik Leader Mihailović," *BalkanInsight*, May 14, 2015.

135. Nicolić, "Rehabilitation of Nazi-Backed Leader Begins in Belgrade," *BalkanInsight*, December 7, 2015; Nicolić, "Nazi-Backed Leader Milan Nedić 'Helped Serbs,'" *BalkanInsight*, February 8, 2016; Nicolić, "Nazi-Backed Leader Nedić 'Saved Serbian Families,'" *BalkanInsight*, March 14, 2016; Sokol, "Serbia Begins Rehabilitating Legacy of Controversial Nazi-Era Leader," *The Jerusalem Post*, December 15, 2015.

136. See Milekić, Ristić, and Dzidić, "Croatian President Slams Chetnik General's Rehabilitation," *BalkanInsight*, May 14, 2015.

137. Milekić, "Croatia Pays Tribute to Jasenovac Camp Victims," *BalkanInsight*, April 27, 2015; Milekić, "Croatia: The Fascist Legacy," *Osservatorio Balcani e Caucaso*, September 3, 2015; Milekić, "Croatia's New Cabinet Draws Mixed Response," *BalkanInsight*, January 22, 2016; Milekić, "Croatian Activists Target 'Reactionary' Culture Minister," *BalkanInsight*, January 28, 2016; Milekić, "Croatia Parliament Backs Controversial WWII Commemoration," *BalkanInsight*, February 5, 2016; Milekić, "Croatian Culture Minister Wrote for Pro-Fascist Journal," *BalkanInsight*, February 11, 2016.

138. Milekić, "Croatia's 'Banal' Fascism on Display at Israel Match," *BalkanInsight*, March 25, 2016.

139. BIRN, "UEFA Punishes Croatia for Football Match Swastika," *BalkanInsight*, July 23, 2015.

140. "Italy Make Complaint to UEFA after Swastika is Spotted on Pitch in Croatia," *The Guardian*, June 12, 2014.

141. Milekić, "Croatian Wartime Unit Celebrates with Fascist Chant," *BalkanInsight*, April 11, 2016; "Croatian Officers Request Legalization of the Salute 'For Home—Ready!,'" *inSerbia* April 11, 2016.

142. Chanted at the Dinamo Bucharest–Rapid Bucharest 1998 match. Rapid Bucharet includes several players of Roma ethnic origin. See "Top 7 mesaje rasiste afișate contra Rapidului," *Ofsaid.ro*, September 25, 2012.

143. Although the government in which Hasanbegović was a member was eventually replaced, he retains a powerful position and much influence as a HZD deputy chairman.

144. "După ce a negat Holocaustul evreilor din România. Șova: Regret și retrag afirmațiile făcute," *Cotidianul*, March 7, 2012.

145. Shafir, "Marshal Antonescu's Postcommunist Rehabilitation," 366.

146. Pankowski, *The Populist Radical Right in Poland*, 61, 121–122.

147. See "League of Polish Families" at http://en.wikipedia.org/wiki/League_of_Polish_Families, and Pankowski, *The Populist Radical Right in Poland*, 121.

148. Pankowski, "From the Lunatic Fringe to Academia: Holocaust Denial in Poland," 78–79; Pankowski, *The Populist Radical Right in Poland*, 121, 187.

149. See "Ludzie odchodzą, ale ich czyny trwają," *Nasz Dziennik*, February 25, 2016.

150. Pankowski, *The Populist Radical Right in Poland*, 191.

151. For an English translation of Orbán's speech of July 26, 2014 at Băile Tușnad (Tusnádfürdő) see *The Budapest Beacon*, July 29, 2014, http://budapestbeacon.com/public-policy/full-text-of-viktor-orbans-speech-at-baile-tusnad-tusnadfurdo-of-26-july-2014/10592.

152. Cited in Chapman, "Poland and Hungary's Defiant Friendship," *politico*, January 6, 2016.

153. Pankowski, *The Populist Radical Right in Poland*, 194.

154. See Grün and Stankiewicz, "Spielarten des polnischen Rechtsradikalismus," 178.

155. Wiatr, "The Rise and Fall of the Polish Radical Right."

156. Gentiles who saved Jews during the Second World War.

157. JTA, "Poland, Grappling over Holocaust Role, Opens Museum for Righteous Gentiles," *The Jerusalem Post*, March 18, 2016. On March 24, 1944, the Nazis executed in this town eight Jews and several members of a family who had hidden them.

158. Gross, "Die Osteuropäer haben kein Schamgefühl," *Die Welt*, September 13, 2015. See also Day, "Polish-American Historian Could Be Stripped of Honours after Claiming Poles Killed More Jews," *The Telegraph*, November 2, 2015; Develey, "La Pologne veut déchoir un historien de la Shoah," *Le Figaro Culture*, February 16, 2016.

159. Bikont, "Jan Gross' Order of Merit," *Tablet Magazine*, March 16, 2016.

160. See Gross, *Neighbors*; Gross, *Fear*; Gross, "After Auschwitz," 66–100; Gross and Gross, *Golden Harvest*.

161. JTA, "Poland: Prosecutor Probes Holocaust Historian Who Said Poles Killed More Jews than Germans," *The Jerusalem Post*, April 14, 2016.

162. Bikont, "Jan Gross' Order of Merit."

163. For the reactions to *Neighbors*, see *Thou Shalt Not Kill: Poles on Jedwabne*; Michlic, *Coming to Terms with the "Dark Past,"* and *The Neighbors Respond: The Controversy over the Jedwabne Massacre in Poland*, edited by Polonsky and Michlic. For the reactions to Gross's *Fear*, see Kornak, "Wstep."

164. See Shafir, "Hungarian Politics and the Post-1989 Legacy of the Holocaust," 262.

165. Cited in Michlic and Melchior, "The Memory of the Holocaust in Post-1989 Poland," 416.

166. See Zubrzycki, *The Crosses of Auschwitz*.

167. "Prosecuted ĽSNS Member Replaced in Parliament by Similar One," *The Slovak Spectator*, March 14, 2006; "Video Footage Shows Recently-Elected Slovak MP Attacking Arab Family Including Children Last Year," *romea.cz*, March 14, 2016.

168. Cuprik, "Kotleba to Spend State Money on Militia," *The Slovak Spectator*, March 30, 2016; "Kiska: Let's Be Clear, Kotleba Is Fascist," *The Slovak Spectator*, April 8, 2016; "Extremists Will Monitor Trains," *The Slovak Spectator*, April 13, 2016; Želinský, *Great Expectations*.

169. On this organization, see Mešťan, *Anti-Semitism in the Political Development of Slovakia*, 199–209.

170. "Czech Republic Should Consider Nazi Electoral Gains in Slovakia a Warning," *romea.cz*, March 7, 2016.

171. Jancarikova, "Far-Right Slovak Party Urges Remembrance of Hanged Nazi-Era President," *Reuters*, April 18, 2016; "Slovakia: Fascist Politician Seeks Minute of Silence in Parliament for WWII–Era Leader, Doesn't Get It," *romea.cz*, April 19, 2016.

172. Mudde, "A Slovak Shocker," *The Huffington Post*, March 5, 2016.

173. Pankowski, *The Populist Radical Right in Poland*, 6, 95–104.

174. Germanova, "Robert Fico Retains Power in Slovakia with New Coalition," *New York Times*, March 17, 2016.

175. Mešťan, *Anti-Semitism in the Political Development of Slovakia*, 37.

176. "Socialists and Democrats Alliance Warns Fico about Coalition with SNS," *Slovak Spectator*, March 17, 2016.

177. "Wartime Slovak State Hailed by Far Right, PM Fico Laid Wreath at Holocaust Monument," *Slovak Spectator*, March 15, 2016.

178. See "Czech Right-Wing Radicals Found Guilty of Inciting Hatred of Jewish People, Will Appeal," *romea.cz*, March 16, 2016. Uhl, "The Jew Hilsner from Polná Was Unjustly Convicted of the Murder of the Christian, Hrůzová," *romea.cz*, January 7, 2016.

References

Alexe, Dan. *Dacopatia și alte rătăciri românești*. Bucharest: Humanitas, 2015.

Ancel, Jean. *Preludiu la asasinat: Pogromul de la Iași, 29 iunie 1941*. Iași, Romania: Polirom and Yad Vashem, 2005.

Andreescu, Gabriel. "Etica, politica memoriei și 'legea anti-legionară.' " *Contemporanul* 4 (2016): 21–22.

———. "Interzicerea negării crimelor comuniste pe plan european: Norme, ideologie, drepturi." *Noua revistă de drepturile omului* 1 (2011): 41–58.

———. *L-am urât pe Ceaușescu. Ani, oameni, disidență*. Iași, Romania: Polirom, 2009.

———. "Necesitatea amendării Ordonanței de urgență nr. 31 privind organizațiile și simbolurile cu caracter fascist, rasist sau xenofob." *Revista română de drepturile omului* 23 (2002): 8–19.

———. "Temele 'legii antilegionare' din perspectiva eticii memoriei." *Noua revistă de drepturile omului* 4 (2015): 3–43.

Bartov, Omer. "Conclusion." In *Bringing the Dark Past to Light: The Reception of the Holocaust in Postcommunist Europe*, edited by John-Paul Himka and Joanna Beata Michlic, 663–694. Lincoln: University of Nebraska Press, 2013.

———. *Mirrors of Destruction: War, Genocide and Modern Identity*. Oxford, UK: Oxford University Press, 2000.

Besançon, Alain. *Le malheur du siècle. Sur le communisme, le nazisme et l'unicité de la Shoah*. Paris: Fayard, 1998.

Boia, Lucian. *Mihai Eminescu, românul absolut. Facerea și desfacerea unui mit*. Bucharest: Humanitas, 2015.

Broszat, Martin. "Plädoyer für eine Historisierung des Nationalsozialismus." *Merkur* (May 1985): 373–385.

Byford, Jovan. *Denial and Repression of Antisemitism: Post-Communist Remembrance of the Serbian Bishop Nikolaj Velimirović*. Budapest: CEU, 2008.

———. *From "Traitor" to "Saint": Bishop Nikolaj Velimirović in Serbian Public Memory*. Jerusalem: Hebrew University of Jerusalem, Vidal Sassoon International Center for the Study of Antisemitism, 2004.

Carter, Grey. "Once the Ustasha Archbishop Stepinac Is Canonized, He Becomes Officially a Catholic Saint." *There Must Be Justice*, February 13, 2014. https://theremustbejustice.wordpress.com/2014/02/13/once-the-ustasha-archbishop-stepinac-is-canonized-he-becomes-an-official-catholic-saint/.

Chaumont, Jean-Michel. *La concurrence des victimes. Génocide, identité, reconnaissance*. Paris: La Découverte, 1997.

"Chiar vreți să ne întoarcem la ideologiile care au făcut ravagii în Europa secolului XX? Grupul pentru Dialog Social reacționează ferm față de candidatura lui Marian Munteanu." *Revista 22*, April 15, 2016.

Cioflâncă, Adrian. "Groapa comună de la Popricani (Iași)." *Pogromul de la Iași*. Accessed April 3, 2016. http://www.pogromuldelaiasi.ro/gropi-comune/groapa-comuna-de-la-popricani-iasi/.

———. "Gropile comune din nord-est (I–II)." *Pogromul de la Iași*. Accessed April 3, 2016. http://www.pogromuldelaiasi.ro/gropi-comune/gropile-comune-din-nord-est-i/ and http://www.pogromuldelaiasi.ro/gropi-comune/gropile-comune-din-nord-est-ii/.

Clej, Petru. "Negarea Holocaustului și activități fasciste—16 inculpați în 14 ani." *Radio France Internationale Romania*, April 19, 2016. http://www.rfi.ro/societate-86399-negarea-holocaustului-si-activitati-fasciste-16-inculpati-14-ani.

Climescu, Alexandru. "The Holocaust on Trial: Memory and Amnesia in the Case of War Criminals." *Holocaust. Studii și cercetări* 7, no. 1 (2015): 307–320.

———. "IICCMER, centenarul Vintilă Horia și apologia fascismului. 'Diversitate igienică' sau confuzie organizată?" *contributors.ro*, April 8, 2016. http://www.contributors.ro/cultura/iiccmer-centenarul-vintila-horia-și-apologia-fascismului-"diversitate-igienica"-sau-confuzie-organizata/.

———. "Post-transitional Injustice: The Acquittal of Holocaust Perpetrators in Post-Communist Romania." *Holocaust.Studii și cercetări* 6, no.1 (2014): 145–157.
Codrescu, Răzvan. *Cartea mărturisitorilor. Pentru o istorie a învrednicirii românești.* Bucharest: Editura Rost and Fundația Sfinții Închisorilor, 2014.
———, ed. *Sfinții Închisorilor în lumea credinței. Din rezistența României creștine împotriva ateismului comunist.* Texte alese, prefață și note de Răzvan Codrescu. Bucharest: Editura Lumea Credinței, 2014.
Coja, Ion. "Proiectul 'Israel în România' este în plină derulare" (blog post). February 6, 2014. http://ioncoja.ro/proiectul-israel-in-romania-este-in-plina-derulare/.
———. "România, colonie a Israelului?" *Justițiarul*, March 27, 2015. http://www.justitiarul.ro/romania-colonie-a-isralelui/.
Condurache, Cezarina. *Chipuri ale demnității românești. Eroi ai neamului și Sfinți ai Închisorilor.* Bucharest: Editura Evdokimos, Fundația Profesor George Manu, 2015.
———, ed. *Eroi Anticomuniști și Sfinții Închisorilor Reincriminați prin Legea 2017/2015.* Bucharest: Editura Evdokimos, Fundația Profesor George Manu, 2015.
Davis, Peter. *The Extreme Right in France, 1789 to the Present: From de Maistre to Le Pen.* London: Routledge, 2002.
Davis, Peter, and Derek Lynch, eds. *The Routledge Companion to Fascism and the Far Right.* London: Routledge, 2002.
Deletant, Dennis. *Hitler's Forgotten Ally: Ion Antonescu and His Regime, Romania 1940–44.* London: Palgrave Macmillan, 2006.
Dinescu, Gabriela. "Partidul legionar Totul pentru Țară a intrat în legalitate." *Puterea.* September 24, 2014.
"The Faces of Romanian Extremism." *Organized Crime and Corruption Reporting.* March 12, 2016. http://reportingproject.us2.list-manage.com/track/click?u=8a7b7dd3a0e2coadfe8fae715&id=15645a6a7a&e=0b99f2f08c.
Feldman, Mathew. "Editorial Introduction." In *A Fascist Century: Essays by Roger Griffin*, edited by Matthew Feldman with preface by Stanley G. Payne, xii–xxvii. Houndmills, UK: Palgrave Macmillan, 2008.
Florian, Alexandru. "Holocaustul evreilor din România. Un nou document juridic." *Sfera politicii* 173 (2013): 168–177.
———. "Memoria publică a Holocaustului în postcomunism." *Polis* 4, no. 1 (2016): 35–44.
———. "Memoria publică și capcanele actului de justiție. Schiță pentru o teorie a actului public în tranziție." *Sfera politicii* 180–181 (2014): 222–246.
Gay, Peter. *Freud, Jews, and Other Germans: Masters and Victims in Modernist Culture.* Oxford, UK: Oxford University Press, 1978.
Geritz, André. *The Myth of Jewish Communism: A Historical Interpretation.* Bern: Peter Lang, 2009.
Geissbühler, Simon. "The Struggle for Holocaust Memory in Romania and How Ukraine Can Learn from It." *Israel Journal of Foreign Affairs* (2016): 1–10.
Griffin, Roger. *The Nature of Fascism.* London: Routledge, 1994.
Gross, Jan T. "After Auschwitz: The Reality and Meaning of Postwar Anti-Semitism in Poland." In *The Holocaust in International Perspective*, edited by Dagmar Herzog, 66–100. Evanston, IL: Northwestern University Press, 2006.
———. *Fear: Anti-Semitism in Poland after Auschwitz.* New York: Random House, 2006.

———. *Neighbors*. Princeton, NJ: Princeton University Press, 2001.
Gross, Jan T., with Irena Grudzińska Gross. *Golden Harvest: Events at the Periphery of the Holocaust*. New York: Oxford University Press, 2012.
Grün, Michaela, and Katharina Stankiewicz. "Spielarten des polnischen Rechtsradikalismus—die Liga der Polnischen Familien und die Selbstverteidigung in ihrem politischen Umfeld." In *Radikale Rechte und Fremdenfeindlichkeit in Deutschland und Polen: Nationale und europäische Perspektive*, edited by Michael Minkenberg, Dagmar Sucker, and Agnieszka Wenninger, 168–196. Bonn: Informationszentrum Sozialwissenschaften, 2006.
Himka, John-Paul, and Joanna Beata Michlic. "Introduction." In *Bringing the Dark Past to Light: The Reception of the Holocaust in Postcommunist Europe*, edited by John-Paul Himka and Joanna Beata Michlic, 1–14. Lincoln: University of Nebraska Press, 2013.
Iliescu, Adrian-Paul. "'Cazul Vintilă Horia' și sofistica zglobie a lui Andrei Pleșu." *Argumente și fapte*, February 28, 2016. http://www.argumentesifapte.ro/2016/02/28/cazul-vintila-horia-si-sofistica-zglobie-a-lui-andrei-plesu/.
Institutul Național pentru Studierea Holocaustului din România "Elie Wiesel." "Declarația Institutului 'Elie Wiesel' în privința candidaturii domnului Marian Munteanu la funcția de Primar al Capitalei." Accessed April 15, 2016. http://www.inshr-ew.ro/ro/presa/comunicate-de-presa/288-declaratia-institutului-elie-wiesel-in-privinta-candidaturii-domnului-marian-munteanu-la-functia-de-primar-al-capitalei.html.
International Commission on the Holocaust in Romania. *Final Report*. Edited by Tuvia Friling, Radu Ioanid, and Mihail E. Ionescu. Iași, Romania: Polirom, 2004.
Ioanid, Radu. *The Holocaust in Romania: The Destruction of Jews and Gypsies under the Antonescu Regime, 1940–1944*. Chicago: Ivan R. Dee, 2000.
Katz, Dovid. "On Three Definitions: Genocide, Holocaust Denial, Holocaust Obfuscation." In *A Litmus Test Case of Modernity: Examining Modern Sensibilities and the Public Domain in the Baltic States at the Turn of the Century*, edited by Leonidas Donskis, 259–277. Bern: Peter Lang, 2009.
Kornak, Macin. "Wstep." *Nigdy więcej* 16 (2008).
Laignel-Lavastine, Alexandra. "Fascism and Communism in Romania: The Comparative Stakes and Uses." In *Stalinism and Nazism: History and Memory Compared*, edited by Henry Rousso, 194–217. Lincoln: University of Nebraska Press, 2004.
Laszlo, Alexandru."Andrei Pleșu față cu hitlerismul." *e-leonardo*, February 5, 2016. https://laszloal.wordpress.com/2016/02/05/andrei-plesu-fata-cu-hitlerismul/.
Lavric, Sorin. *Constantin Noica și Mișcarea Legionară*. Bucharest: Humanitas, 2014.
———. "Damnatio memoriae." In *Eroi Anticomuniști și Sfinții Închisorilor Reincriminați prin Legea 2017/2015*, edited by Cezarina Condurache, 3–8. Bucharest: Editura Evdokimos, Fundația Profesor George Manu, 2015.
Liiceanu, Gabriel. *Estul naivităților noastre. 27 interviuri 1990–2011*. Bucharest: Humanitas 2012.
———. *Ușa interzisă*. Bucharest: Humanitas, 2002.
Mešťan, Pavol. *Anti-Semitism in the Political Development of Slovakia (2000–2009)*. Bratislava: SNM Museum of Jewish Culture, 2013.
Michlic, Joanna. *Coming to Terms with the "Dark Past."* Jerusalem: Hebrew University, Vidal Sassoon International Center for the Study of Anti-Semitism, 2002.

Michlic, Joanna Beata, and Małgorzata Melchior. "The Memory of the Holocaust in Post-1989 Poland: Renewal—Its Accomplishments and Its Powerlessness." In *Bringing the Dark Past to Light: The Reception of the Holocaust in Postcommunist Europe*, edited by John-Paul Himka and Joana Beata Michlic, 403–450. Lincoln: University of Nebraska Press, 2013.

Ministerul Public. Parchetul de pe lângă Înalta Curte de Casație și Justiție, Biroul de Presă. "Comunicat," December 2, 2015. http://old.mpublic.ro/presa/2015/c_02_12_2015.htm.

Nolte, Ernst. *Războiul civil european 1917–1945. Național-socialism și bolșevism*. Bucharest: Corint, 1997.

Pankowski, Rafal. "From the Lunatic Fringe to Academia: Holocaust Denial in Poland." In *Holocaust Denial: The David Irving Trial and International Revisionism*, edited by Kate Taylor, 75–81. London: Searchlight Educational Trust, 2000.

———. *The Populist Radical Right in Poland: The Patriots*. London: Routledge, 2010.

Pleșu, Andrei, Gabriel Liiceanu, and Horia-Roman Patapievici. *O idee care ne sucește mințile*. Bucharest: Humanitas, 2014.

Polonsky, Anthony, and Joanna B. Michlic, eds. *The Neighbors Respond: The Controversy over the Jedwabne Massacre in Poland*. Princeton, NJ: Princeton University Press, 2004.

Rosenbaum, Alan S. "Introduction to First Edition." In *Is the Holocaust Unique? Perspectives on Comparative Genocide*, 2nd ed., edited by Alan S. Rosenbaum, 1–9. Boulder, CO: Westview, 2000.

Shafir, Michael. *Between Denial and "Comparative Trivialization": Holocaust Negationism in Post-Communist East Central Europe*. Jerusalem: Hebrew University of Jerusalem, Vidal Sassoon International Center for the Study of Antisemitism, 2002.

———. "Conceptualizing Hungarian Negationism in Comparative Perspective: Deflection and Obfuscation." In *L'Europe à contre-pied: idéologie populiste et extrémisme de droite en Europe centrale et orientale—Cahiers d'Études Hongroises et Finlandaises*, 20 (2014) sous la direction de Traian Sandu, 265–310. Paris: L'Harmattan, 2015.

———. "Doamnei Aura Christi, redactor-șef, 'Contemporanul. Ideea Europeană.'" *Acum*, July 15, 2011. http://acum.tv/articol/34873/.

———. "*Ex Occidente Obscuritas*: The Diffusion of Holocaust Denial from West to East." *Studia Hebraica* 3 (2003): 23–82.

———. "Hungarian Politics and the Post-1989 Legacy of the Holocaust." In *The Holocaust in Hungary: Sixty Years Later*, edited by Randolph L. Braham and Brewster S. Chamberlin, 257–290. Boulder, CO: Rosenthal Institute for Holocaust Studies, 2006.

———. "The Inheritors: The Romanian Radical Right after 1989." *East European Jewish Affairs* 24, no. 1 (1994): 70–89.

———. "The Man They Love to Hate: Norman Manea's 'Snail's House' between Holocaust and Gulag." *East European Jewish Affairs* 30, no. 1 (2000): 60–81.

———. "Marginalization or Mainstream? The Extreme Right in Post-Communist Romania." In *The Politics of the Extreme Right: From the Margins to the Mainstream*, edited by Paul Hainsworth, 247–267. London: Pinter, 2000.

———. "Marshal Antonescu's Postcommunist Rehabilitation: *Cui Bono?*" In *The Tragedy of Romanian Jewry*, edited by Randolph L. Braham, 349–410. Boulder, CO: Rosenthal Institute for Holocaust Studies, 1994.

———. "Memory, Memorials, and Membership: Romanian Utilitarian Antisemitism and Marshal Antonescu." In *Romania since 1989: Politics, Culture, and Society*, edited by Henry F. Carey, 67–97. Lanham, MD: Lexington Books, 2004.
———. "The Mind of Romania's Radical Right." In *The Radical Right in Central and Eastern Europe since 1989*, edited by Sabrina P. Ramet, 213–232. University Park: Pennsylvania State University Press, 1999.
———. "The Movement for Romania: A Party of 'Radical Return.'" *RFE/RL Research Report* 29 (1992): 16–21.
———. "Polls and Antisemitism in Post-Communist Romania." *Journal for the Study of Antisemitism* 4, no. 2 (2012): 1601–1636.
———. "A Present of *Chiaroscuro*." *Yad Vashem Studies* 42, no. 2 (2014): 225–250.
———. "Reconciliation at the Wrong End." In *Hungary and Romania beyond National Narratives: Comparisons and Entanglements*, edited by Anders E. B. Blomqvist, Constantin Iordachi, and Balázs Trecsényi, 691–709. Oxford, UK: Peter Lang, 2013.
———. "The Romanian Extreme Right in the Post-Communist Period." *Sfera politicii* 15 (1994): 4–6; 16 (1994): 16–17.
———. "Rotten Apples, Bitter Pears: An Updated Motivational Typology of Romania's Radical Right's Anti-Semitic Postures in Post-Communism." *Journal for the Study of Religions and Ideologies* 7, no. 21 (winter 2008): 150–187.
———. "Strange Bedfellows: Digging under Post-Communist 'Polished Polishness.'" *Holocaust. Studii și cercetări* 1, no. 3 (2010): 157–185.
———. "Unacademic Academics: Holocaust Deniers and Trivializers in Post-Communist Romania." *Nationalities Papers* 42, no. 6 (2014): 942–964.
"Simpozion memorial Gogu Puiu și rezistența anticomunistă din Dobrogea." Accessed April 5, 2016. https://www.facebook.com/events/215691255438908/.
Stanomir, Ioan. "Marian Munteanu—etnocrația ca proiect politic." *contributors.ro*, April 13, 2016. http://www.contributors.ro/reactie-rapida/marian-munteanu-etnocratia-ca-proiect-politic/.
Thou Shalt Not Kill: Poles on Jedwabne. Warsaw: WIĘŹ, 2001.
Totok, William. "Aufstieg des Legionarismus zur parlamentarischen Leitkultur." *Halbjahresschrift-onlie*, March 22, 2016. http://halbjahresschrift.blogspot.ro/2015/11/nachrichten-stiri-news.html.
———. "Noua Dreaptă (Rumänien)." In *Handbuch des Antisemitismus. Judenfeindschaft in Geschichte und Gegenwart, Organisationen, Institutionen, Bewegungen*, vol. 5, edited by Wolfgang Benz, 453–455. Berlin: De Gruyter Saur, 2012.
———. "Receptarea publicistică a raportului final al Comisiei Wiesel în presa românească și germană." *Studia Hebraica* 5 (2005): 186–195.
Totok, William, and Elena-Irina Macovei. *Între mit și bagatelizare. Despre reconsiderarea critică a trecutului, Ion Gavrilă Ogoranu și rezistența armată anticomunistă din România*. Forthcoming. Fragment published in *Halbjahresschrift-onlie*, April 18, 2016. http://halbjahresschrift.blogspot.ro/2015/11/nachrichten-stiri-news.html.
Webb, Adrian. *The Routledge Companion to Central and Eastern Europe since 1919*. London: Routledge, 2008.
Wiatr, Jerzy J. "The Rise and Fall of the Polish Radical Right: The League of Polish Families." Paper presented at the International Conference "The Radical Right in Post-1989 Central and Eastern Europe—The Role of Legacies," New York University Center for European and Mediterranean Studies, April 24–26, 2008.

Wurmbrand, Richard. *In God's Underground*. Bartlesville, OK: Living Sacrifice, 2004.
———. *Tortured for Christ*. Bartlesville, OK: Living Sacrifice, 1998.
———. *With God in Solitary Confinement*. Bartlesville, OK: Living Sacrifice, 2001.
Zărnescu, Vasile I. *Holocaustul. Gogorița diabolică. Extorcarea de "bani de Holocaust,"* vol. 1. Bucharest: Editura dacoromână, 2015.
Želinský, Dominik. *Great Expectations: Slovak Nationalist Initiatives in the Light of Communal Elections 2014*. EUROPEUM Institute for European Policy. Accessed May 15, 2017. http://www.ceeidentity.eu/sites/default/files/downloads/zelinsky_final.pdf.
Zubrzycki, Geneviève. *The Crosses of Auschwitz: Nationalism and Religion in Post-Communist Poland*. Chicago: University of Chicago Press, 2006.

CHAPTER FIVE

"WANTING-NOT-TO-KNOW" ABOUT THE HOLOCAUST IN ROMANIA
A Wind of Change?

SIMON GEISSBÜHLER

The exposure of the general public in Romania and in many other countries of Central and Eastern Europe to the Holocaust and knowledge about the history of it has been and continues to be marginal.[1] Under the communist regimes, acknowledgement of the Holocaust was all but impossible. Jews, Jewish identity and history, and especially the Shoah were taboo topics for almost fifty years.[2] Romania was no exception to that rule.[3] Having been a close ally of Nazi Germany and having implemented the mass murder of Jews and of Roma autonomously, Romania under communist rule felt an even more acute urge to draw a veil of silence over its inglorious past.[4]

The breakdown of the Soviet bloc did not lead to a comprehensive and meticulous reassessment of Romanian history. While it is obviously true that the end of the Ceaușescu regime opened up the public space for "pluralistic expression of social and political messages," as Alexandru Florian writes,[5] it did not advance a broad evidence- and research-based critical reevaluation of the role of Romania in the Second World War and the Holocaust. Quite to the contrary, in the 1990s, mainstream Romanian historiography sought to create the basis for a new national self-esteem. The Antonescu cult reemerged. Similar obstacles to the integration of the Holocaust into the postcommunist historical narratives could be observed all over Central and Eastern Europe.[6] There were differences, however, and the case of Romania was a particularly difficult one.

The ghosts of the past—fascist as well as communist—and especially questions about Romania's collaboration with Nazi Germany and its involvement in the Holocaust in the East were left undisturbed. Fascism was presented as an alien, German concept, and Romania as a victim "innocent of any wrongdoing or crime."[7] Throughout the 1990s, high-ranking government officials regularly denied that Romania had anything to do with the Holocaust. In fact, this "recurring cycle of official denial was not broken until 2003–2004."[8] Even today, the so-called revisionists, who try to minimize or trivialize Romanian crimes during the Second World War in general and Romania's responsibility for the Holocaust in Northern Bukovina, Bessarabia, and Transnistria in particular, are still relatively influential in Romania.[9]

For many years, mainstream Romanian historiography on the Holocaust was lagging in many respects,[10] and relatively few studies were published in Romania on the subject of the Holocaust in territories that had been under Romanian control. Methodologically, many of these studies were descriptive and positivistic, did not take into account international debates on the Holocaust, and did not address specific research questions and theses.[11] Armin Heinen claimed in 2007 that the Romanian historiography of the Holocaust had reached approximately the state of research in Germany in the mid-1960s.[12] International research on the Holocaust in Romanian-controlled territories was scarce, too.

Some progress has been made, and there have been some positive developments in recent years. Radu Ioanid's *The Holocaust in Romania*, published in 2000, and the *Final Report* of the International Commission on the Holocaust in Romania, published in English in 2005, were crucial synoptic works and important starting points for further research.[13] They have been complemented in the last few years by new studies by, for example, the late Jean Ancel, Vladimir Solonari, and others.[14] Certain topics such as the Iaşi massacres at the end of June 1941, with over 13,000 victims, as well as the camps and ghettos in Transnistria have finally received the scholarly attention they deserve.[15]

Furthermore, it can be positively noted that more young historians, including Romanians—some of whom have contributed to this volume—are now carrying out research on Romania and the Holocaust. Various organizations, research groups, and individuals are currently working on specific aspects of Romania and the Holocaust. Finally, Romania held the presidency of the International Holocaust Remembrance Alliance (IHRA) in 2016 to 2017, which is also a positive step.

However, Holocaust memory in Romania remains fragile and split to this day. Mihai Chioveanu rightly talks about a deep fragmentation of memory.[16] A big gap exists between public knowledge about the Holocaust and scholarly research. Large parts of Romanian society as well as people who live where atrocities perpetrated by Romanians took place do not want to know. Most traces of Jewish life before the Holocaust and of the Holocaust itself have been neglected, forgotten, or even erased. There are some positive countertrends, but the following analysis will show that it is too early to speak about a strong wind of change when it comes to Holocaust memory in present-day Romania.

Conceptual Framework and Research Questions

This contribution is based on a relatively broad and general conceptual framework and three clusters of overarching research questions. The framework is inspired by theoretical works about memory, remembrance, and forgetting.

A distinction can be made between an episodic (autobiographical) memory and a semantic (generic-knowledge) memory at the individual level. Direct autobiographical memory of the Holocaust is becoming sporadic and will soon disappear altogether as survivors, perpetrators, and bystanders die off. Memory of the Holocaust is therefore increasingly, and will soon be exclusively, generic-knowledge, learned, and handed down. Furthermore, Holocaust memory will be attenuated by the fact that we remember common and recent events better than rare and long-past ones.[17]

The trends toward an exclusively generic-knowledge, learned, and handed down memory of the Holocaust, as well as toward a memory blurred by the Holocaust's growing temporal distance, increase the risk of Holocaust relativism or denial and underline the importance of education and continuing research. Only if the Holocaust is actively transmitted to the next generations—the generations of postmemory[18]—and is accepted by them as meaningful, will it be remembered. If a generation does not convey the past—in this case, the memory of the Holocaust—to the next generation, it will eventually be forgotten.[19]

However, the distinction between knowing and not-knowing, remembering and forgetting, and remembered and forgotten is simplistic. There are many shades of gray between these respective extremities. Paul Ricoeur has accordingly introduced the concept of "wanting-not-to-know." Wanting-not-to-know is a devious form of forgetting, "a semi-passive, semi-active behavior," as it is seen, for example, in forgetting by avoidance. It is motivated by "an obscure will not to inform oneself."[20]

Wanting-not-to-know has much to do with a conscious decision to remain unaware. Humans are not always interested in increasing their knowledge. Often they dismiss the unpleasant facts: the will not to know follows the will of self-delusion, as Wolfgang Sofsky writes.[21] This is particularly true when the facts to be remembered are painful. But on the other hand, remembrance is, as Yosef Hayim Yerushalmi has underlined, also a question of justice.[22] The current and future Romanian generations are obviously not guilty of the crimes some of their forefathers committed, but they have a special responsibility to "want-to-know."

Looking at the issue through the prism of wanting-not-to-know, this contribution analyzes Holocaust memory in a broad sense in present-day Romania, and to a lesser degree in Northern Bukovina/Ukraine, southwestern Ukraine (Transnistria), and the Republic of Moldova (Bessarabia), where the Holocaust perpetrated by Romania mainly happened. The empirical part of this study focuses on three clusters of research questions.

First, this contribution asks how the towns and villages in Romania and in those territories controlled by Romania during the Second World War where atrocities happened present their own histories on their respective websites. It is evident that in an increasingly interconnected world, cities' websites are an important communication and image-building tool and part of what has been called city branding, strategic communication, or urban internationalization.[23] Understandably, being the location of past mass killings is not an attractive feature for a village or town, but dealing with the past actively and openly can be seen as a constructive step that can positively influence a country's or city's image. Furthermore, Jewish heritage sites can be touristic highlights. Against this backdrop, I will look at how the histories of these towns and villages during the Second World War are presented. Is the Holocaust mentioned at all? How open or how defensive is the self-reflection of these towns and villages about their own pasts?

Second, this contribution looks at what I call spatial Holocaust memory. Is the Holocaust reflected in the public space? Are there traces of the Jewish past, such as synagogues and Jewish cemeteries? Are there any indications of where mass graves are located? Are there any monuments for the Jewish victims, or even museums dealing with Jewish history or the Holocaust? Are there still any *lieux de mémoire*—or are there only *lieux sans mémoire* left?[24]

Third, the findings are discussed in relation to poll data concerning knowledge about the Holocaust in Romania. What do Romanians know about Romania and the Holocaust? How does the level of knowledge of the Holocaust in Romania compare with that in other European countries? Do historical self-perception and historical facts match, or is there a discrepancy?

HISTORICAL SELF-PRESENTATION

Websites can be powerful communication tools, not only for individuals but also for institutions. Many cities have discovered that place or city branding is an effective way to increase attractiveness for investors, visitors and tourists, companies, and new residents. In fact, in "an increasingly global and competitive world, international positioning through online branding has become a necessity for cities that wish to compete in the global arena."[25]

While place branding might not be of great relevance to smaller towns and villages in Romania, Ukraine, and the Republic of Moldova, they are significant for, for example, Iași, Czernowitz, Chișinău, and Odessa. Even smaller cities in Romania, such as Alba Iulia,[26] use city branding successfully: "First, Alba's logo was a brilliant exercise on visual identity that was rapidly socialized and appropriated within the city. Then, leveraging itself upon a rich heritage and the rehabilitation of its unique 17th-century citadel, the local government is now actively using a place-brand approach to address both its medium & long term development agenda and its positioning in the country and abroad."[27]

Iași: Iași was one of the most important Jewish centers in Central and Eastern Europe at the end of the nineteenth century. In 1900, the majority of the population was Jewish, and the city was ranked twelfth in Central and

Eastern Europe with regard to the absolute size of its Jewish community.[28] A very short, but historically coherent and complete presentation of what happened in 1941 can be found on the official website of the city of Iași. The Second World War is characterized as a black period in the history of the city. The mass murder of Jews in Iași at the end of June 1941 is presented as one of the most horrible events of its kind in the world ("printre cele mai grave evenimente de acest fel din lume"), and as a crime that was made to vanish from sight under communism. In the chronology of the city's history, it is added that the pogrom against the Jewish inhabitants was initiated by Ion Antonescu and that the local authorities played a key role in the massacres. The website mentions that 13,266 Jews were killed in the pogrom and the death trains.[29]

What is remarkable in this self-presentation of Iași is the fact that the initiators, perpetrators, and victims are correctly and openly identified. The website does not even try to shift the blame onto the Germans, who indeed played only a minor role in the massacres. It rightly points to the fact that the Romanian political and military leadership was at the root of the massacres and that the locals played an important role in them.[30]

Czernowitz: Czernowitz was and is by far the biggest town in Northern Bukovina, and its economic, political, and cultural center. It has an exceptionally rich Jewish heritage.[31] The town's website does not contain any detailed historical information.[32] This is surprising, because there is indeed a huge interest in Jewish heritage travel to Czernowitz. The city has not only an immense Jewish cemetery but also a small Jewish museum. A branch of the Ruzhiner Hasidic dynasty had its court in Sadagura, a suburb of Czernowitz for several decades now. Neither these facts nor what happened in Czernowitz during the Second World War are mentioned on the city's website.

Bojan: The website of the village of Bojan, some 15 kilometers east of Czernowitz, which was home to the court of a Hasidic dynasty from the second half of the nineteenth century until the First World War, is based on a local initiative and contains much historical information. Under the category "churches" (*sic*) there is a historical picture of the synagogue.[33] There is a subchapter on the massacres of Jews in July 1941 ("Masacrul evreilor din iulie 1941") that briefly describes what happened.[34]

What is troubling and telling are the detailed "explanations" provided for the massacres. They are based on pamphlets by well-known Holocaust deniers. The author of the respective text on the Bojan village website revives classical stereotypes such as Judeo-Bolshevism and wrongly claims that the Jews had attacked and killed many Romanians during the Romanian retreat from Northern Bukovina in summer 1940.[35] Furthermore, the author emphasizes that Romania rejected German demands later in the war to send the Jews of the Old Kingdom to Auschwitz, which is obviously true, but he then turns this fact around in typical revisionist fashion, arguing, as many Romanian revisionists do to this day, that there was no Holocaust in Romania because there were no extermination camps in Romania and because no Jews from the Old Kingdom were sent to Auschwitz. Some Romanian historians also feel compelled to underline that "no train carrying Jews left Romania for Poland."[36] Others emphasize that the Holocaust perpetrated by Romania was "incomplete."[37] Both arguments are off the mark. They do not make the more than 300,000 Jews killed by Romanians and in territories controlled by Romania disappear. The Holocaust is more than Auschwitz.[38] It is the mass murder of six million Jews—men, women, and children—by the Nazis and other perpetrators during the Second World War with intent to destroy, in whole or in part, the Jews as a group.

Furthermore, the decision not to send Romanian Jews to Auschwitz was determined by the rapidly worsening fortunes of war in the East, and certainly not by a change of heart on the part of Antonescu and the Romanian regime.[39] The decision also proves that Romania did indeed have a choice, and its choice at the beginning of the war was to kill as many Jews as possible, to ethnically cleanse Northern Bukovina, Bessarabia, and Transnistria, and to establish and administer a dense network of ghettos and camps in Transnistria. Henry Eaton has rightly underlined that Romania "was conducting [its] own genocidal operation."[40]

Novoselița: Surprisingly, the small town of Novoselița, some 30 kilometers east of Czernowitz, not only has a website, but it contains an impressive wealth of historical information.[41] The size of the Jewish population before the war, the massacres perpetrated by Romanian troops at the beginning of July 1941, as well as the ensuing deportations to Transnistria are all described in detail and match the historical facts.[42] Novoselița's way of dealing with the town's difficult past is exemplary.

Chișinău: At the other end of the spectrum, where the Holocaust is completely blanked out, are the websites of the Moldovan capital Chișinău and the two northern Moldovan cities of Edineți and Bălți. The official website of Chișinău contains some historical data, but only up to the interwar period, and neither the Jewish presence before and after the Second World War nor the ghetto and the deportations are mentioned.[43] This is particularly surprising for a city that used to be an important Jewish center in Eastern Europe (the ninth-largest Jewish city in Central and Eastern Europe in 1900).[44]

Edineți: The website of the office of the mayor of Edineți simply mentions that the town was "liberated" on March 24, 1944.[45] There is no information about the fact that Edineți was a vital *shtetl* with approximately 5,000 Jewish inhabitants before the Second World War, or that all Jews who survived the massacres in early July 1941, which resulted in up to 1,000 victims, were deported to Transnistria.[46]

Bălți: The Bălți website contains no historical information at all.[47] The reader finds no reference to the facts that the town was a major Jewish center in Bessarabia before the war and that hundreds of Jews were killed there before the deportations to Transnistria started in autumn 1941.

Orhei: The mayor's office of the Moldovan town of Orhei has a relatively well-designed website with pleasant pictures of Old Orhei and photographs and postcards from the early twentieth century. There is, however, no information whatsoever either about the period between 1918 and 1947 or about the former Jewish presence in the town.[48]

Soroca: Soroca was home to a prominent Bessarabian Jewish community before the Second World War. The oldest Jewish gravestones date from the sixteenth century, and the main synagogue was built in 1775.[49] The historical information on the website of the town focuses on late fifteenth- and sixteenth-century Soroca.[50] Neither the Jewish presence nor the Holocaust is mentioned, although in nearby Vertujeni the Romanians established one of the main concentration camps for Jews to be deported to Transnistria.

Rezina: An example of a falsification of history can be found on the website of the Moldovan city of Rezina. The website mentions that archival evidence shows that one of the "greatest tragedies" of the Second World War concerned the situation of the Jews, explaining that there was a "deliberate hostile policy of the German army against the Jews" where in most cases "representatives of the German army participated in the bloody repression of Jews." The website claims, however, that a majority of Rezina's Jews had already left the town with the Soviet army.[51] In this way, the key role of the Romanian armed forces and local perpetrators in the persecution of the Jews is simply removed from the history.

Odessa: Odessa, another main Jewish center in Eastern Europe before the Second World War (the fourth-largest Jewish community in Central and Eastern Europe in 1900),[52] has a website available in three languages, with a focus on investment, business, and tourism.[53] No historical information is readily available. Only when one clicks on the link to the "Migdal Shorashim" Jewish Museum of Odessa, which opened in 2002, does one find the following information: "Let us not forget that during the second half of the 19th century and the first half of the 20th century, Odessa had the third-largest Jewish population in the world (after New York and Warsaw).... However [the] historical tragedies of the Second World War took its toll on the Jews of Odessa where thousands of Jews were killed in the Odessa region during the Nazi occupation."[54]

While the claim that Odessa was the third-largest Jewish community in the world around 1900 is slightly exaggerated, the sentence on the Holocaust is evasive and cryptic. First, the massacres and mass shootings that occurred after the fall of Odessa in October 1941 claimed well over 20,000 lives. In November 1941 the Romanian authorities ordered the remaining 35,000 Jews into two ghettos near the city, where many died. Later on, the Jews were deported further into Romanian-administered Transnistria, where many more were executed or died. Second, the Nazi occupation was in fact a Romanian occupation.[55]

Obviously, most smaller and medium-sized towns and villages in Northern Bukovina, Bessarabia, and Transnistria where massacres against Jews took place in the summer of 1941 or where ghettos and camps existed do not have their own websites. Much could be done even in smaller towns to attract tourists by featuring Jewish heritage sites on their respective websites, and by projecting an image of open communities that actively address their own pasts. An example of a town with untapped potential for Jewish heritage and other tourism is Vadul Rashkov, with its impressive Jewish cemetery on the banks of the Dniester River.

Spatial Holocaust Memory

The formerly multiethnic villages and towns with large Jewish minority or even majority populations in Northern Bukovina, the Republic of Moldova, and southwestern Ukraine have mostly become monoethnic.[56] In most cases, a visitor with no historical knowledge would never guess that only seventy-five years ago Jews were an integral part of the social, economic, and political fabric of these places.[57] Where traces of the Holocaust do exist, they are often hidden or covered up, and it takes considerable effort to locate them.

As there are no more Jews living in these villages and small towns, and as the "spaces, gestures, images, and objects" in which memory is rooted[58] have disappeared, the *milieux de mémoire* are gone, too. Many locals have no interest in keeping the memory alive. The absence of Jewishness and of the Holocaust in the spatial memory goes hand in hand with the absence of any reference to the past Jewish dimension of these villages and towns in prevailing discourse.

Undeniably, there were substantial voluntary and forced population movements in Soviet times.[59] However, this factor alone cannot explain the suppression of history by the people who live in these places now. The Jewish cemeteries are often still there, albeit overgrown and neglected. Many still know where the mass graves are located, but they do not want to say it. Clearly, the mechanism of wanting-not-to-know is strong.

The following brief overview of the state of spatial Holocaust memory in Northern Bukovina, the former Bessarabia, and the former Transnistria is based on a number of field visits between 2008 and 2014. It looks at Jewish cemeteries, synagogues, mass grave sites, Holocaust monuments, and Jewish and/or Holocaust museums.

Jewish cemeteries: Most Jewish cemeteries in Northern Bukovina, in what used to be Bessarabia, and in southwestern Ukraine have "survived" the Second World War.[60] There has not been any systematic destruction of Jewish heritage sites in these areas. The Jewish cemeteries are therefore still the most powerful existing Jewish heritage sites. However, the cemeteries are often entirely neglected, and the local governments seldom show any interest in preserving them. Examples are the Jewish cemetery in Herța, which is totally overgrown, and the one in Rezina, which "is completely overgrown and inaccessible. Everywhere is garbage.... Some gravestones were misused, as fire place or picnic table."[61] As there are almost no Jews left in these areas—with the exception of big towns such as Odessa, Czernowitz, and Iași—there is also nobody who feels responsible for these cemeteries. Local initiatives by non-Jews, which are relatively widespread in Poland, for example, are rare here. If they exist at all, efforts to preserve and protect the Jewish cemeteries are mostly driven by organizations and individuals from abroad.

Synagogues: Only a few synagogues can still be found today in the vast territory that was controlled by Romania during the Second World War. Many were destroyed during the war or the communist period; many more have been converted into theaters, cinemas, or shops, or have been reduced to ruins. Only a handful, for example in Chișinău and Odessa, are still used for their original purpose.

Mass grave sites: The United States Commission for the Preservation of America's Heritage Abroad has published lists of mass grave sites in Ukraine and in the Republic of Moldova. These lists provide a good overview, but they are incomplete. Furthermore, it is sometimes very difficult to locate the sites on the ground on the basis of the information provided by the Commission.

Yahad-In Unum publishes an interactive map showing execution sites of Jewish victims.[62] Many locations in Northern Bukovina, the former province of Bessarabia, and southwestern Ukraine are included in this map. As of March 2016, however, the site provides more detailed information about only a few selected places. Furthermore, several locations where several hundreds of Jews were killed, such as Climăuți and Râșcani, are not included in the map.

Holocaust monuments: While monuments for the heroes of the Great Patriotic War are widespread in Ukraine, Holocaust monuments are rare. One of the main reasons for the prevailing absence of such monuments is simple: memory of the Jews in general and of the Holocaust in particular was all but banned from the public space in the Soviet Union and in the countries of the Soviet bloc.[63] If there are monuments, the Jewish victims are usually not presented as Jews but as victims of fascism. The inscription on the Holocaust monument in Herța, for example, says that about 100 inhabitants of the town were shot in July 1941; the fact that these inhabitants were exclusively Jews is not revealed. Often, the perpetrators are also not mentioned, as for example on the inscription on the Holocaust monument in Ciudei.[64]

Jewish/Holocaust museums: When David Shneer and Anna Shternshis maintain that it "seems that almost every Eastern and Central European city has a new Jewish museum today,"[65] they obviously are not talking about northeastern Romania, southwestern Ukraine, and the Republic of Moldova. There is not a single new museum in these regions. The existing museums in Iași, Czernowitz (Chernivtsi Museum of Bukovinian Jewish History and Culture), Chișinău, and Odessa are small and in no way comparable to Warsaw's hypermodern POLIN Museum of the History of Polish Jews.[66]

Not even Bucharest has an up-to-date Jewish and/or Holocaust museum. While the Romanian president announced on March 8, 2016, during a visit to Israel, his intention to have a Jewish and Holocaust museum built in Bucharest,[67] such a plan would take many years to materialize. Furthermore, judging from readers' comments to reports of President Iohannis's announcement, a majority of Romanians seem deeply skeptical or even outright hostile toward the idea of a Jewish and Holocaust museum in Bucharest.

Although it is true that memory is not exclusively dependent on things such as cemeteries, synagogues, mass graves, monuments, or even museums, physical traces do indeed help or force people to remember, because they offer proof that Jews did once live and die or were murdered in these places. The state of neglect of many of these sites can therefore be explained by the unwillingness of the residents of these towns and villages, and sometimes of local and national governments, to acknowledge these historical facts. For the locals there is no reason to open themselves to the other, namely the Jewish past of their own towns and villages. If they were to do so, they might expose themselves to uncomfortable truths, questions of collaboration, guilt, economic profiteering, and, ultimately, reparation.

Poll Data

Thanks to the polls commissioned by the Elie Wiesel Institute in Bucharest, recent trends in knowledge about the Holocaust and in Holocaust memory can be traced.[68] The surveys underline the fact that there is some basic knowledge about the Holocaust in Romania. In 2015, 73 percent of the respondents acknowledged that they had heard about the Holocaust (Holocaust awareness). Holocaust awareness is highest among people with a higher level of education (86 percent) and living in Bucharest (84 percent); it is lowest among individuals with a general education (49 percent) and living in rural areas (67 percent). These differences underline once more the importance of education for Holocaust awareness.

Even though it is difficult to compare knowledge about the Holocaust internationally as polls differ in methodology, 73 percent is a relatively low percentage when compared not only to Western Europe (94 percent), but also to Eastern Europe (82 percent).[69] Over time, the percentage of Romanians who have heard about the Holocaust has slightly increased from 69 percent in 2009 to 73 percent in 2015. This trend is positive, but it is statistically barely significant.

Furthermore, active avoidance or a strategy of avoidance and of wanting-not-to-know is superimposed on this basic knowledge. For the majority of Romanians, the Holocaust is still not seen as a phenomenon that has any relevance to them and to Romania. Sixty-two percent say that they have little or very little interest in the Holocaust. The attitude of wanting-not-to-know is aided by the fact that the Holocaust perpetrated by Romania happened mostly in areas that are no longer part of the Romanian state today. As these crimes happened outside of present-day Romania, they are more easily externalized.[70]

When asked if the Holocaust also took place in Romania, not even a third of the respondents answered affirmatively. In fact, the percentage of respondents who say that the Holocaust also happened in Romania decreased from 32 percent in 2009 to 28 percent in 2015 (although this change is probably not statistically significant). Finally, among the 28 percent who state that the Holocaust also happened in Romania, only 19 percent say that the Antonescu government was responsible for what happened; 69 percent see Germany as the main culprit of the Holocaust in Romania.

This data reveals a tremendous gap between public knowledge about the Holocaust and scholarly research. The Holocaust "remains a subject that interests the Romanians only superficially (if at all)," as Michael Shafir writes.[71] While the majority of the Romanian population now seems to grudgingly accept, as Ana Bărbulescu says, "that something bad happened to the Romanian Jews during the war,"[72] only a small minority acknowledges who the perpetrators were in this case: the Romanians themselves. This denial is, however, not surprising, as the Holocaust was misrepresented in most schoolbooks for decades, and the political leaders have long employed highly ambivalent rhetoric when it came to Romania and the Holocaust.

Conclusions

Holocaust memory in Romania, as well as in those areas controlled by Romania during the Second World War that are now part of Ukraine and the Republic of Moldova, is fragile, fragmented, and often guided by a semi-passive, semi-active attitude of wanting-not-to-know. To claim that Holocaust "memory has developed immensely... particularly in Eastern Europe"[73] over the last two decades, as Marek Kucia claims, is an undue and naively optimistic generalization at best and a dangerous denial of the empirical evidence at worst. There have indeed been positive developments in some countries, but also major setbacks in others.

Only a few cities and villages in the region present their pasts in a proactive way on their respective websites, and thereby project a self-critical image. Some present their history in a distorted way. Not only have most of these towns and villages lost their former multiethnic character, but the traces of the socially, culturally, economically, and politically important Jewish presence are ignored or have even been erased.[74] There are also positive examples, but they are few.

Many Jewish cemeteries in Northern Bukovina, southwestern Ukraine, and the Republic of Moldova are in a state of neglect. Very few synagogues still exist, and most have long since been destroyed or converted for other uses. Mass graves are difficult to locate and in most cases are not recorded on local maps. There are only very few, and no new Jewish or Holocaust museums in these regions. Omer Bartov's writings about Galicia could just as easily apply to Northern Bukovina, Bessarabia, and Transnistria, and, to a lesser degree, to parts of Romania as well: "When one travels deeper into [these regions], one discovers... remarkable neglect, suppression, and even destruction of all signs of the land's multi-ethnic past and that past's tragic end in a campaign of mass murder."[75]

The mental traces of the former Jewish presence and of the Holocaust are also evaporating. Many of the inhabitants of these places indeed know nothing about the Jewish past of their villages and towns and of the mass murder of Jews that took place where they now live. Many others do not want to know.[76] The sites of mass murder have long become *lieux sans mémoire*. Furthermore, poll data suggests that a large gap exists between the historical facts and public knowledge about Romania and the Holocaust. Overall, it is undoubtedly too early to speak about a strong wind of change with regard to Holocaust memory in Romania.

Is there any hope for change, for a more proactive and encompassing Holocaust memory in Romania and in regions where Romanians perpetrated the Holocaust? Clearly, memory is path dependent: memory must be passed from one generation to the next, and history has to be taught accordingly in schools. With the last survivors dying off, the challenges of teaching the history of the Holocaust are only increasing. But as long as the strategy of wanting-not-to-know is not challenged, there will be no substantial change.

While Romania remains a laggard with regard to dealing with the past, there are positive developments, also in comparison with other Eastern European countries. International research and pressure, increased and broader education in schools and universities, the educational efforts of civil society and some state institutions, and Romania's presidency of the IHRA are factors that will in the medium and long term undermine the widespread attitude of wanting-not-to-know. In this context, especially the Romanian presidency of the IHRA (2016–2017) could be a catalyst for change. The organization, even though it has its weaknesses, is an agent of Holocaust memory.[77] It would be important to convince Ukraine and the Republic of Moldova to become IHRA members as well.

Pierre Nora has rightly emphasized that "there must be a will to remember."[78] Remembrance and the will to deal with one's past should not be imposed primarily from the outside and from above. However, researchers, both Romanian and international, can and do contribute to change by exposing again and again the historical facts as we reconstruct them on the basis of the available sources. This volume is a small contribution to that effort.

Finally, it is crucial that pressure be maintained on national and local governments to preserve the traces of Jewish life and death. We do not need to build many new, costly, and architecturally sophisticated memorials. In many cases the memorials already exist: the Jewish cemeteries, the synagogues and the mass graves. They are powerful and real: "The 'sea of living memory has receded,' and it will never come back. But at least we still have the shells on the shore. Let's pick them up and cherish them."[79]

Simon Geissbühler is a Swiss historian and political scientist. He has published on Romania and the Holocaust as well as on Jewish heritage in Eastern Europe. Among his books is *Iulie însângerat. România și Holocaustul din vara lui 1941*, and he is the editor of *Romania and the Holocaust. Events—Contexts—Aftermath*.

NOTES

1. Shafir, "Polls and Antisemitism"; Dumitru, "The Use and Abuse of the Holocaust."
2. Rohdewald, "Post-Soviet Remembrance."
3. Cioflâncă, "Grammar of Exculpation."
4. Weber, "The Public Memory."
5. Florian, "Memoria."
6. Himka, "Obstacles."
7. Cioflâncă, "Grammar of Exculpation," 36.
8. Shapiro, *The Kishinev Ghetto*, 91.
9. Shafir, "Unacademic Academics"; Geissbühler, "Staring at the Past."
10. Clark, "New Models."
11. Ursprung, "Geschichtsschreibung."
12. Heinen, *Rumänien*, 34.
13. Ioanid, *The Holocaust in Romania*; International Commission, *Final Report*; also see Friling, "The International Commission."
14. Ancel, *The History of the Holocaust in Romania*; see also Deletant, *Hitler's Forgotten Ally*; Chioveanu, "Death Delivered"; Chioveanu, "The Dynamics of Mass Murder"; Florian, "The Fate of the Jews."
15. Eaton, *The Origins*; Ofer, "The Holocaust in Transnistria"; Deletant, "Transnistria and the Romanian Solution"; Vynokurova, "The Fate"; Rosen, "The Djurin Ghetto"; Baum, *Varianten des Terrors*.
16. Chioveanu, "The Authoritarian Temptation," 72.
17. Pinker, *How the Mind Works*, 124, 143.
18. Hirsch, "The Generation of Postmemory."
19. Yerushalmi, *Zakhor*, 109.
20. Ricoeur, *Memory*, 448–449.
21. Sofsky, "Glauben."
22. Yerushalmi, *Zakhor*, 117.
23. Rivas, "Integrated City-Brand Building."
24. For the theoretical foundations, see Nora, "Between Memory and History"; Geissbühler, "Synagogues."
25. Björner, "International."
26. Accessed February 21, 2016, http://www.visitalbaiulia.com/.
27. Rivas, "Integrated City-Brand Building."
28. Gruber, *Jewish Heritage Travel*, 265–267; Magocsi, *Historical Atlas*, 109.
29. Accessed January 2, 2016, http://www.orasul-iasi.ro/index.php/istorie-iasi-romania/34-istorie/48-istoria-iasului.

30. Eaton, *The Origins*.
31. Gruber, *Jewish Heritage Travel*, 122–124.
32. Accessed February 21, 2016, http://chernivtsy.eu/portal/.
33. Accessed March 8, 2016, http://www.mareleboian.com/.
34. For accounts of the massacre, see Geissbühler, *Iulie însângerat*, 94–95; Eitan, *To Survive and Tell*.
35. Achim, "Die Deportation"; Solonari, "Hating Soviets."
36. Giurescu, *Romania in the Second World War*, 212.
37. Iancu, *Alexandre Safran*.
38. Snyder, *Black Earth*, 207–225.
39. Glass, *Deutschland*.
40. Eaton, *The Origins*, x.
41. Accessed February 21, 2016, http://novoselitsa.com/.
42. Geissbühler, *Iulie însângerat*, 98.
43. Accessed February 27, 2016, http://www.chisinau.md/pageview.php?l=ro&idc=495.
44. Magocsi, *Historical Atlas*, 109.
45. Accessed January 2, 2016, http://primariaedinet.md/?page_id=112.
46. Geissbühler, *Iulie însângerat*, 101–103.
47. Accessed December 4, 2016, http://balti.md/planul-pentru-intretinerea-drumurilor/.
48. Accessed February 24, 2016, http://orhei.md/index.php?pag=page&id=661&l=ro.
49. Moskovich, "Soroca."
50. Accessed March 6, 2016, http://www.primsoroca.md/.
51. Accessed January 3, 2016, http://www.orasul-rezina.com/rezina-în-anii-1941-1944.html.
52. Magocsi, *Historical Atlas*, 109; Gruber, *Jewish Heritage Travel*, 129–131.
53. Accessed March 6, 2016, http://omr.gov.ua/en/.
54. Accessed March 8, 2016, http://omr.gov.ua/museums/11849.
55. Ancel, *The History of the Holocaust in Romania*, 353–378; Baum, *Varianten des Terrors*, 489–491; Traşcă, "Ocuparea."
56. For Ukraine, see Amosova, "There Are No Jews Here."
57. Mendelsohn, *The Jews of East Central Europe*, 171–211.
58. Nora, "Between Memory and History," 9.
59. Amosova, "There Are No Jews Here," 118.
60. For lists of Jewish cemeteries, synagogues, and mass grave sites, see Gruber, *Jewish Cemeteries*; Gruber, *Jewish Heritage Sites*.
61. Accessed March 28, 2016, https://vanishedworld.wordpress.com/2016/03/27/back-on-the-banks-of-river-dniester/#more-2477.
62. Accessed February 27, 2016, http://yahadmap.org/#map/.
63. Rohdewald, "Post-Soviet Remembrance."
64. Geissbühler, *Iulie însângerat*, 175, 170.
65. Shneer and Shternshis, "Why Jewish Museums?," 151–152.
66. Julean, "Reportage," 282–284; http://muzejew.org.ua/Koncept-En.html, accessed February 24, 2016; Shikhova, "Inside the Museum."
67. "Klaus Iohannis pledeaza pentru construirea unui Muzeu al Evreilor si Holocaustului la Bucuresti," *Hotnews.ro*, March 8, 2016.
68. The data can be downloaded from http://www.inshr-ew.ro/ro/proiecte/sondaje.html.

69. Anti-Defamation League, accessed January 24, 2016, http://global100.adl.org/info/holocaust_info.
70. Heinen, *Rumänien*, 25.
71. Shafir, "Polls and Antisemitism," 415; cf. Florian, "Memoria."
72. Bărbulescu, "Discovering the Holocaust," 151.
73. Kucia, "The Europeanization," 115.
74. Bartov, *Erased*.
75. Ibid., 40.
76. Bartov, "Eastern Europe."
77. Kucia, "The Europeanization."
78. Nora, "Between Memory and History," 19.
79. Geissbühler, *Like Shells on a Shore*, 99.

REFERENCES

Achim, Viorel. "Die Deportation der Juden nach Transnistrien im Kontext der Bevölkerungspolitik der Antonescu-Regierung." In *Holocaust an der Peripherie*, edited by Wolfgang Benz and Brigitte Mihok, 151–160. Berlin: Metropol, 2009.

Amosova, Svetlana. "There Are No Jews Here: From a Multiethnic to a Monoethnic Town of Burshtyn." *Cultural Analysis* 10 (2011): 117–124.

Ancel, Jean. *The History of the Holocaust in Romania*. Lincoln: University of Nebraska Press, 2011.

Bărbulescu, Ana. "Discovering the Holocaust in Our Past: Competing Memories in Post-Communist Romanian Textbooks." *Holocaust Studies: A Journal of Culture and History* 21, no. 3 (2015): 139–156.

Bartov, Omer. "Eastern Europe as the Site of Genocide." *The Journal of Modern History* 80, no. 3 (2008): 557–593.

———. *Erased: Vanishing Traces of Jewish Galicia in Present-Day Ukraine*. Princeton, NJ: Princeton University Press, 2007.

Baum, Herwig. *Varianten des Terrors. Ein Vergleich zwischen der deutschen und der rumänischen Besatzungsverwaltung in der Sowjetunion 1941–1944*. Berlin: Metropol, 2011.

Björner, Emma. "International Positioning through Online City Branding: The Case of Chengdu." *Journal of Place Management and Development* 6, no. 3 (2013): 203–226.

Chioveanu, Mihai. "The Authoritarian Temptation: Turning a Modern Tyrant into a Political Role Model in Post-Communist Romania." *Annals of the University of Bucharest / Political Science Series* 15, no. 1 (2013): 69–84.

———. "Death Delivered, Death Postponed: Romania and the Continent-Wide Holocaust." *Studia Hebraica* 8 (2008): 136–169.

———. "The Dynamics of Mass Murder: Grasping the Twisted Decision-Making Process behind the Romanian Holocaust." *Sfera Politicii* 2, no. 168 (2012): 25–36.

Cioflâncă, Adrian. "A 'Grammar of Exculpation' in Communist Historiography: Distortion of the History of the Holocaust under Ceausescu." *Romanian Journal of Political Science* 4, no. 2 (2004): 29–46.

Clark, Roland. "New Models, New Questions: Historiographical Approaches to the Romanian Holocaust." *European Review of History* 19, no. 2 (2012): 303–320.
Deletant, Dennis. *Hitler's Forgotten Ally: Ion Antonescu and his Regime, Romania 1940–1944*. Houndmills, UK: Palgrave Macmillan, 2006.
———. "Transnistria and the Romanian Solution of the 'Jewish Problem.'" In *The Shoah in Ukraine: History, Testimony, Memoralization*, edited by Ray Brandon and Wendy Lower, 156–189. Bloomington: Indiana University Press, 2008.
Dumitru, Diana. "The Use and Abuse of the Holocaust: Historiography and Politics in Moldova." *Holocaust and Genocide Studies* 22, no. 1 (2008): 49–73.
Eaton, Henry. *The Origins and Onset of the Romanian Holocaust*. Detroit, MI: Wayne State University Press, 2013.
Eitan, Shalom. *To Survive and Tell (Lipcani, Moldova)*. 1998. Accessed March 12, 2016. http://www.jewishgen.org/yizkor/lipkany/lipkany.html.
Florian, Alexandru. "The Fate of the Jews from Northern Bukovina under the Antonescu Regime: Evidence of the Evolution of Antisemitic Policies in the Stenographs of Cabinet Council Meetings." *Holocaust and Modernity* 2, no. 8 (2010): 207–218.
———. "Memoria publică a Holocaustului în postcomunism." *Polis* 4 (2016): 35–44.
Friling, Tuvia. "The International Commission on the Holocaust in Romania: A Personal 'Behind the Scenes' Perspective." In *Romania and the Holocaust*, edited by Simon Geissbühler, 191–202. Stuttgart: ibidem, 2016.
Geissbühler, Simon. "Bucharest's 'Lost' Synagogues as 'Lieux sans Mémoire.'" *Studia Hebraica* 9, no. 10 (2009/2010): 383–394.
———. *Iulie însângerat. România și Holocaustul din vara lui 1941*. Bucharest: Curtea Veche, 2015.
———. *Like Shells on a Shore: Synagogues and Jewish Cemeteries of Northern Moldavia*. Bern: Projekt 36, 2010.
———. "Staring at the Past with Eyes Wide Shut: Holocaust Revisionism and Negationism in Romania." *Israel Journal of Foreign Affairs* 6, no. 3 (2012): 127–135.
Giurescu, Dinu C. *Romania in the Second World War (1939–1945)*. Boulder, CO: East European Monographs, 2000.
Glass, Hildrun. *Deutschland und die Verfolgung der Juden im rumänischen Machtbereich 1940–1944*. München: Oldenbourg, 2014.
Gruber, Ruth Ellen. *Jewish Heritage Travel: A Guide to Eastern Europe*. Washington, DC: National Geographic, 2007.
Gruber, Samuel D. *Jewish Cemeteries, Synagogues, and Mass Grave Sites in Ukraine*. Washington, DC: United States Commission for the Preservation of America's Heritage Abroad, 2005.
———. *Jewish Heritage Sites and Monuments in Moldova*. Washington, DC: United States Commission for the Preservation of America's Heritage Abroad, 2010.
Heinen, Armin. *Rumänien, der Holocaust und die Logik der Gewalt*. München: Oldenbourg, 2007.
Himka, John-Paul. "Obstacles to the Integration of the Holocaust into Post-Communist East European Historical Narratives." *Canadian Slavonic Papers* 50, no. 3–4 (2008): 359–372.
Hirsch, Marianne. "The Generation of Postmemory." *Poetics Today* 29, no. 1 (2008): 103–128.

Iancu, Carol. *Alexandre Safran et la Shoah inachevée en Roumanie. Recueil de documents (1940–1944)*. Bucharest: Hasefer, 2010.
International Commission on the Holocaust in Romania. *Final Report*. Edited by Tuvia Friling, Radu Ioanid, and Mihail E. Ionescu. Iași, Romania: Polirom, 2004.
Ioanid, Radu. *The Holocaust in Romania: The Destruction of Jews and Gypsies under the Antonescu Regime, 1940–1944*. Chicago: Ivan R. Dee, 2000.
Julean, Dan-Ionuț. "Reportage: Romania and Its Jewish Museums." *East European Jewish Affairs* 45, no. 2–3 (2015): 279–289.
Kucia, Marek. "The Europeanization of the Holocaust Memory and Eastern Europe." *East European Politics and Societies and Cultures* 30, no. 1 (2016): 97–119.
Magocsi, Paul Robert. *Historical Atlas of Central Europe*. Seattle: University of Washington Press, 2002.
Mendelsohn, Ezra. *The Jews of East Central Europe between the World Wars*. Bloomington: Indiana University Press, 1983.
Moskovich, Wolf. "Soroca." In *The YIVO Encyclopedia of Jews in Eastern Europe*. Accessed March 7, 2016. http://www.yivoencyclopedia.org/article.aspx/soroca.
Nora, Pierre. "Between Memory and History: Les Lieux de Memoire." *Representations* 26 (1989): 7–24.
Ofer, Dalia. "The Holocaust in Transnistria: A Special Case of Genocide." In *The Holocaust in the Soviet Union*, edited by Lucjan Dobroszycki and Jeffrey S. Gurock, 133–154. Armonk, NY: M. E. Sharpe, 1993.
Pinker, Steven. *How the Mind Works*. New York: Penguin Books, 2015.
Ricoeur, Paul. *Memory, History, Forgetting*. Translated by Kathleen Blamey and David Pellauer. Chicago: University of Chicago Press, 2006.
Rivas, Miguel. "Integrated City-Brand Building: Beyond the Marketing Approach." Reporting note on the CityLogo–Eurocities thematic workshop, Utrecht, October 2–4, 2013.
Rohdewald, Stefan. "Post-Soviet Remembrance of the Holocaust and National Memories of the Second World War in Russia, Ukraine, and Lithuania." *Forum for Modern Language Studies* 44, no. 2 (2008): 173–184.
Rosen, Sarah. "The Djurin Ghetto in Transnistria through the Lens of Kunstadt's Diary." In *Romania and the Holocaust*, edited by Simon Geissbühler, 131–150. Stuttgart: ibidem, 2016.
Shafir, Michael. "Polls and Antisemitism in Post-Communist Romania." *Journal for the Study of Antisemitism* 4, no. 2 (2012): 387–422.
———. "Unacademic Academics: Holocaust Deniers and Trivializers in Post-Communist Romania." *Nationalities Papers* 42, no. 6 (2014): 942–964.
Shapiro, Paul A. *The Kishinev Ghetto 1941–1942: A Documentary History of the Holocaust in Romania's Contested Borderlands*. Tuscaloosa: University of Alabama Press, 2015.
Shikhova, Irina. "Inside the Museum: The Jewish Museum of Chișinău (Kishinev)." *East European Jewish Affairs* 45, no. 2–3 (2015): 321–322.
Shneer, David, and Anna Shternshis. "Why Jewish Museums?" *East European Jewish Affairs* 45, no. 2–3 (2015): 151–152.
Snyder, Timothy. *Black Earth: The Holocaust as History and Warning*. London: Bodley Head, 2015.

Sofsky, Wolfgang. "Glauben, Leugnen, Hoffen." *Neue Zürcher Zeitung*, February 13, 2016, 43.
Solonari, Vladimir. "Hating Soviets—Killing Jews: How Antisemitic Were Local Perpetrators in Southern Ukraine, 1941–42?" *Kritika: Explorations in Russian and Eurasian History* 15, no. 3 (2014): 505–533.
———. *Purifying the Nation: Population Exchange and Ethnic Cleansing in Nazi-Allied Romania*. Baltimore, MD: Johns Hopkins University Press, 2009.
Traşcă, Ottmar. "Ocuparea oraşului Odessa de către armata română şi măsurile adoptate față de populația evreiască, octombrie 1941–martie 1942." *Anuarul Institutului de Istorie "George Barițiu" din Cluj-Napoca* 47 (2008): 377–425.
Ursprung, Daniel. "Geschichtsschreibung und Vergangenheitsbewältigung in Rumänien. Von den Mühen des Umgangs mit zeitgeschichtlichen Themen." *Südost-Forschungen* 69, no. 70 (2010/2011): 358–388.
Vynokurova, Faina. "The Fate of Bukovinian Jews in the Ghettos and Camps of Transnistria, 1941–1944: A Review of the Source Documents at the Vinnytsa Oblast State Archive." *Holocaust and Modernity* 2, no. 8 (2010): 18–26.
Weber, Petru. "The Public Memory of the Holocaust in Postwar Romania." *Studia Hebraica* 4 (2004): 341–348.
Yerushalmi, Yosef Hayim. *Zakhor: Jewish History and Jewish Memory*. Seattle: University of Washington Press, 1996.

Part 2
NATIONAL HEROES, OUTSTANDING INTELLECTUALS, OR HOLOCAUST PERPETRATORS?

Chapter Six

MIRCEA VULCĂNESCU, A CONTROVERSIAL CASE
Outstanding Intellectual or War Criminal?

Alexandru Florian

ROMANIA, AN OUT-OF-TUNE COUNTRY ON MEMORY LANE

In 1989, at the time of the December Revolution, Romania had only one highway, 120 kilometers long. In 2017, despite all the strategies to modernize the infrastructure, there are only two highways and parts of a third; there is no highway from north to south, or from east to west. When we think of places of memory, *lieux de mémoire* in public spaces, the situation is no better—the postcommunist public space includes very diverse and very contradictory memorials to the recent past. For example, a bust of Adrian Păunescu, a poet and ideologue during the Ceaușescu regime, was erected in a Bucharest park after his death in 2011; Ion Gavrilă Ogoranu, a legionary (Romanian fascist) and anticommunist fighter after 1945, has a monument in his memory in the town of Deva; and a memorial dedicated to the victims of the Holocaust in Romania was erected in Bucharest in 2009.

After twenty-five years of transition, Romania has only fragments of highways, only partial transport corridors to connect it to the long awaited Occident. The situation of public memory of the Holocaust in Romania is similar: it resembles an unfinished highway. In public, private and state memory coexist, but they are out of tune. The memory of the victims mixes with a memory that makes heroes out of war criminals and others who are morally or politically responsible for the Holocaust. Often, they collide under the umbrella of important topics pertaining to democratic civic culture.

In Romania, like in other postcommunist countries, the public space of memory was opened to civil society. At the time, there were public events specific to a society in transition from totalitarianism to democracy. However, in the absence of clear and consistent codes about memory and its public representation, there appeared a mix of events whose meanings and significances were sometimes undemocratic. For understandable but hard to accept reasons, the public memory of the Holocaust in Romania is more controversial than other issues of the country's recent history, including communism.

Since the fall of communism, all of the former Soviet bloc countries have common issues in terms of the retrieval of memory pertaining to the interwar period or to the Second World War. The differences are due to the varying intensity and aggressiveness of the messages and the states' degree of involvement in recognizing Holocaust denial and the fascist far right. Professor Michael Shafir underlined the fluctuations and aberrations in public denial of the Holocaust in Eastern European countries in the 1990s. In the introduction to his study, the author pointed out that "Romania is not at all a leader in Holocaust denial among the postcommunist countries of Central and Eastern Europe," and that "Holocaust denial, in this region, ranges from simple imitation of the denial originating in other countries to collective forms of defending the 'historical memory' of the region, as well as banal, sometimes cynical attempts to take advantage of a temporary political situation."[1]

I do not intend to rank the countries, but we can say that in 2017 public denial of the Holocaust in Romania has decreased, while in Hungary, for example, the historical memory of the Horthy regime and the various facets of Holocaust denial have a more intense public life. Some expressions of this, such as the monument in downtown Budapest inaugurated in 2014, minimize the role of the Hungarian state in the Final Solution—the extermination of the Hungarian Jews in 1944—or pay homage to controversial personalities of the Horthy regime.[2]

In the 1990s there were several statues of Ion Antonescu in public venues in Romania. He was Romania's leader from 1940 and the main culprit in the Holocaust in Romania.[3] Since then, they have been removed, and today there is only one heroic statue of Antonescu, which is displayed in a regional museum, a public institution.[4] However, the "good" public memory of the Holocaust in Romania still wanders on an unfinished highway, and in certain parking spaces, it meets the "bad" memory.[5]

Members of the Legionary Movement, the interwar fascist organization in Romania whose members fought against communism in the postwar period (1945–1964); public persons and politicians during the Ion Antonescu regime who were later convicted for war crimes; symbols of the Legionary Movement—all of these are presented to the public today as legitimate, in order to revive a past that has nothing to do with democracy. The changes that occurred after 2004, when Romania officially recognized the Antonescu government's responsibility for the Holocaust, did not bring to a close the issue of public memory of the Holocaust in Romania. Although much has already been written on the subject, it is still current, because the problem is still here and only its representations have changed.

The Case of Postcommunist Romania

After 1990, as was natural, a new freedom of expression led to an explosive liberalization of collective memories. Thus, there was a proliferation of many kinds of events that represented different memories about the same historical era: Romania during the interwar period and the Second World War. The democratization of the public sphere, in its spontaneous reinvention, also entailed the meeting within this space of the state's memory of the Holocaust, the associative memory of the Jews, and the memory of those who support the cult and symbolism of the interwar far right. Most of this last group either directly or indirectly deny the existence of the Holocaust in Romania. The tragedy of the Jews and Roma in Romania had a particular history, which is highlighted in the main conclusion of the *Final Report* issued by the Elie Wiesel Commission: "The Commission concludes, together with the large majority of bona fide researchers in this field, that the Romanian authorities were the main perpetrators of this Holocaust, in both its planning and implementation."[6] The *Final Report* was a turning point on the road of the public memory of the Holocaust in Romania. The recognition of Romanian responsibility had a knock-on effect on state institutionalized memory. Consequently, state memory, in the form of discourse and monuments, has given up and distanced itself from Holocaust-denying symbolism.

However, the formal acknowledgment of the memory of the Holocaust in Romania has not resulted in a restriction of the distorted collective memories that occupy the public sphere. As a result, the memorial road still has parking lots one should not go into.

Groups of intellectuals and NGOs have come together to distort the historical reality of the Holocaust to the point of denial. Polemical debates expanded beyond the academic environment, where they risked not achieving the social result expected by those who were interested in updating the old values. Therefore, beyond the horizon of nationalist historiography, there are memorial projects that are intended to make Holocaust distortion a public good, a symbolically accepted fact. The predominantly emotional character of memory facilitates the reception of the message, shaping the cultural, civic, and political values behind the memorial symbolism into a public commodity. These interested collective memories silenced the historical memory that Pierre Nora speaks about. Partisan or fragmentary memories were guided by at least four strategies: (1) the reinvention, most often with a positive connotation, of some of the cultural values of interwar extremism that were rejected during the communist period; (2) the comparison of the Holocaust and the Gulag in favor of the latter, whose symbolic expressions benefit from a strong anticommunist emotional support; (3) the declared intention of some groups to revisit the interwar Romanian far right, that is, the Legionary Movement, unilaterally and apologetically; and (4) the glorification of war criminals.

Intellectuals of the 1927 generation[7] who had provided ideological and political support to the Legionary Movement (Romanian fascism) were taken up after 1990 and dressed up in the white robes of fairytale heroes. Thus presented as authors who had been persecuted or whose works were banned by the communist regime, they were reinstated and became symbols of national culture, some of them even European culture. Prestigious intellectuals today, members of the Romanian Academy, still portray them as emblematic figures who created high-level international cultural trends. But they "forget" what Alexandra Laignel-Lavastine called "their fascist past." Their cultural and journalistic productions and the positions of command they occupied in public institutions during the 1940s, by which they became "comrades" of the Legionary Movement or members and officials in the Ion Antonescu government, are now obscured or minimized. They are depicted as uninvolved intellectuals with prestigious cultural careers. Most often, their intellectual work produced after the end of the war is revisited, and in contrast, all their ideological symbolic work produced during the 1930s and 1940s is immediately dismissed as "deviation of their youth" that is excusable, their defenders suggest, when compared with their later philosophical, economic, or sociological work. Not even in cases where these intellectuals recognized or publicly regretted their fascist pasts are questions asked. But most of them preferred silence, guilty oblivion. Beyond the cultural reconsideration of their careers in the light of public memory, they are also represented as models, and tributes are paid to them in public events, memorial plaques, or street names. Support for such initiatives comes from either public entities or nongovernmental organizations. The countermessage, which recalls the ideological or political preference of the young interwar intellectuals for extreme nationalism, antidemocracy, antisemitism, and a cult of fascism or the Legionary Movement, is aggressively labeled by their supporters as a neocommunist discourse that resorts to the old Stalinist methods of excommunication. Following this line of thought, criticizing the memory of Mircea Eliade, Emil Cioran, Mircea Vulcănescu, Vintilă Horia, Nichifor Crainic, or Mihail Manoilescu is considered a sacrilege, an act of *lèse-majesté*. From that moment on, public dialogue is impossible. According to their supporters, having been an anticommunist automatically grants them an aura of respectability and makes their memory a fully reputable public memory.[8] Their uninhibited worshippers do not even mention that there were important changes in their public status after 1945.

The competition between the two persecutions of the Holocaust and the Gulag basically means the concealment or halfhearted recognition of the tragedy of the Jews and Roma. According to this strategy, the memory of the physical and cultural repression of the communist regime has precedence. This is complemented by insidious generalizations about the ethnic origin of the perpetrators, which corresponds to the myth that "it was the Jews that brought communism." Repression, via censorship, of cultural values that diverged from the official ideological line blocked all opportunities for intellectuals who refused to join the communist power. Postcommunism is a favorable climate for them to publicly commemorate their suffering and claim a greater aura of respectability, beyond what their work provides. For this purpose, nothing is superfluous, not even a trivializing comparison with the suffering of Jews during the Holocaust, as a matter of brotherhood. In 1997 the publicly anticommunist intellectual Gabriel Liiceanu was invited by the Jewish community to speak about Jewish writer Mihail Sebastian's *Journal 1935–1944: The Fascist Years*. Liiceanu made a *pro domo* plea that equated the tragedy of the Jews during the war and the academic barriers and restrictions he faced during the years of the communist regime. The biased nature of the message was clear from the title of the article he would later publish: "Sebastian, mon frère."[9]

Priority is also given to the armed resistance of anticommunist fighters in the early period of the communist regime, and the fact that some of them, and not just a few, were members of the Legionary Movement is intentionally obscured. Carried to the extreme, collective memory built upon such canons reaches the point where it erects public monuments commemorating legionary leaders. Thus, various intellectuals and activists advance the idea that the anticommunist resistance is to be promoted *in corpore*, and the ideologies that motivated the various groups should not be a criterion for assuming its public memory. When confronted with the argument that opposition to a nondemocratic regime from a nondemocratic ideological position is not a modernizing solution for the liberation of individuals, their answer is emotional, and ethnically loaded. Historian Adrian Cioflâncă recalled in an interview the reaction of one of the militants for the public memory of the legionaries: "According to a report by Michael Shafir, it was during an event about the 'prison saints,' in 2013, that Mr. Bjoza told William Totok, whom he thought was Jewish, I quote by source, 'First you took our country, now you want to take our saints away from us.' This is an appalling and counterfactual way of falling into the trap of the legionary discourse."[10] Such an attitude, in addition to demonstrating the symbolic model of competitive martyrology, boils with antisemitism and suggests that opposition to the glorification of legionary memory is only the obsession of the Jews, despite the existence of a law currently in force in Romania that explicitly forbids the memorial cult of the Legionary Movement.

The third approach of the collective memory that opposes the memory of the Holocaust is the glorification of the Legionary Movement. Whether they opposed the communists by taking up arms and fighting them directly, or they were repressed as intellectuals or representatives of interwar Romanian culture, or they suffered in prisons during the communist regime, more or less important leaders of the Legionary Movement became symbolic figures worthy of homage and commemoration by the civil society. Many of these people enjoy large-scale cultural celebration in schools, where they are presented to young people as role models, as exemplary figures. They are identified and promoted as having been nationalists, Orthodox believers, and anticommunists. The murders they committed, the pogroms they participated in, their antisemitism, their military discipline and antidemocratic, totalitarian vision of the "new man"—those public memorial reconstructions say nothing of these. Their nationalist and anticommunist aura takes precedence over their membership in a fascist political party. Democratic ethics, derived from humanist values and from freedom—all of these are rejected as expressions of political correctness. The maximal message to confer respectability on this bad memory is the bestowing of a symbolic title: "Prison Saint."[11]

This title conveys an emotional message that the imprisoned person chose dialogue with the divine as a means of redemption. On this path of redemption, he presumably acquired the grace of faith and revelation, and thus became one of the so-called prison saints for whom canonization is demanded. These men are presented as having had no ideology and participated in no extremist political activity, and the public ceremonies organized in their memory portray them as models (with honorary citizenships, memorial public events, and memorial plaques). Moreover, militant civic associations have asked the Romanian Orthodox Church to canonize them only on the basis that they withdrew into prayer and religious revelation during their detention.

In the fourth strategy, the strongest expression of the rejection of Holocaust memory, radical groups or individuals disseminate a revisionist public memory of persons who were convicted of war crimes after the Second World War. Today, the intellectual or professional status of the convicted is revalued and promoted as a public interwar social status worthy of retention as part of the cultural or national-patriotic heritage.[12]

This type of collective memory proposes a restructuring of priorities when establishing the social roles held by certain individuals in well-defined historical periods. A sort of competition of assigning positive instances of the social roles played by this category of intellectual figures ensues. This is always won by assigning to a particular person the memory of a role that would be legitimate today, sending to oblivion their interwar participation to the extreme right movement. Antimodernists reverse meanings of social roles according to their subjective criteria, canceling the recognized order enforced by the ethics of democratic values. Both NGOs and individual initiatives, with the support and consent of local authorities, successfully place into the public space signs of communal recognition of certain people—intellectuals, officials, clerks, and senior officers—who are burdened by convictions for war crimes. Many of them were convicted after the war, as a result of their participation in the "resolution" of the "Jewish question." In the previous approach, the promotion of collective memory as a public memory and the resulting obfuscation of the memory of the Holocaust occurs by disregarding the main values of civic democratic and modern culture. In this case of publicly honoring persons who are war criminals, we are witnessing a deliberate act of breaking the law. As mentioned above, Emergency Ordinance 31/2002 prohibits public denial of the Holocaust and the promotion of the cult of war criminals. Article 5 of the law explicitly states: "a person's act of publicly promoting the cult of persons who were found guilty of crimes of genocide against humanity and of war crimes, as well as the act of publicly promoting fascist, legionary, racist or xenophobic ideas, beliefs or doctrines, according to art. 2 letter a), shall be punished by imprisonment from 3 months to 3 years and the denial of certain rights." However, we seem to live in parallel universes in Romania: the realities of the public sphere and the legal system are different. In the case of the memory of the Holocaust, we witness the promotion of the symbolism of war criminals as exemplary by certain collective memories, but this memorialization is unharmful as far as the legal system is concerned.[13] This is why, while the state memory of the Holocaust is under construction, it collides with existing collective memories in the public sphere that, in contempt of the law, promote the image of persons who should fall under the effects of the prohibitive law mentioned above.

In Romania, there is another way to promote a heroic memory of war criminals responsible for the Holocaust. I am referring to the implementation of a transitional justice system whose decisions turn to injustice. As Alexandru Climescu discusses, in the late 1990s the attorney general of Romania agreed to reopen cases of persons who had been convicted of war crimes. In some instances, these involved convictions for participating in the destruction of the Jewish population. The appeal for annulment, filed by the General Prosecutor, was confirmed by the judge. Consequently, those persons became innocent, and as a result, their memory has been cleansed, and they and their actions have become a potential memorial public asset. This happened despite the fact that the evidence in the case was sufficient to reconfirm the initial verdict of guilty, as Climescu argued.[14] For a better understanding of the effect that this "meting out of justice" has on the public, let us recall the reaction of a Holocaust survivor: "if they are innocent today, although they were perpetrators of the pogrom in Iași (June 1941), where I survived by a miracle [in a death train where the survival rate was almost one in three people], it means that I have not even been on that train!"

This persistence in promoting the memory of people who were convicted of war crimes and campaigning for the cancellation of their convictions, with all the associated negative social implications, is fueled by nationalism[15] and anticommunism. Anticommunism seems to be the main motivation for the reinvention and obsessive promotion of the memory of those convicted of war crimes. The supporters of this type of memory argue that Law 312/1945, which called for the arrest and punishment of those responsible for the country's disaster or war crimes, was nothing more than the manifestation of the will of Moscow, and therefore, the trials were not legally valid because they were politically motivated. This so-called transitional justice, which is rather an attempt at moral rehabilitation than real justice, carried out decades after the fact and by improper means, neglects at least three issues.

The main argument of its proponents is that the legislation that underpinned the trials of persons suspected of crimes during the Second World War was communist legislation, implemented on the orders of the USSR.[16] This argument neglects fact that Law 312 was developed in accordance with the agreement of the Allied Commission (even if the Soviet Union had a greater influence), and that the spirit of the law was consistent with the laws established for the Nuremberg trials, where the culprits of the Nazi regime were judged. Another fact that is "missed" and that actually clarifies the context of Law 312 is that between June 1941 and August 1944 Romania was an ally of Hitler's Germany. Therefore, the trials initiated at the time against government members, army officers and other military personnel, and clerks of the secret services all had political but also humanitarian rationales, given the great material, human, and social destruction caused by the Second World War. While in the West there is consensus with regard to the legal effects of the war, in the postcommunist East there are quite a few voices that deny, at least from a memorial perspective, the postwar justice applied to the vanquished. They forget that the vanquished were responsible for the war and for its destruction. Moreover, Law 312 explicitly notes the actions that could lead to indictments; not all criminal deeds are considered war crimes. Thus, Article 1 established the crime of having caused "the country's disaster by those who: a) advocating for fascism and Hitlerism or having the effective political power, allowed the entry of German forces into the country; b) after September 6, 1940, have campaigned for the preparation and implementation of the deeds above through their spoken words, in writing or by any other means." Article 2 assigned criminal responsibility for "the disaster of the country, by committing war crimes, [to] those who: a) decided to declare or continue the war against the Union of Soviet Socialist Republics and the United Nations; b) did not comply with international rules on waging war; c) subjected war prisoners or hostages to an inhumane treatment; d) ordered or performed acts of terror, of cruelty or suppressed the population in the territories in which the war took place; e) ordered or carried out collective or individual punishments for purposes of political or racial persecution, against the civilian population." Therefore, the law provided penalties for breaking the rules of armed conflict, as well as for mistreatment of civilians caused by ethnic, racial, or antisemitic policies, and so on. Also, the law specifically referred to the prosecution of the military corps, the judiciary, or civil servants of the state.

The argument about the "communist character" of this law does not stand, even when taking into consideration historical realities. Between August 1944 and January 1948, Romania went through a period of transition from the dictatorship of Ion Antonescu to the communist regime of the party-state. During this time, political parties regained official status and the democratic Constitution of 1923 was reinstated. Although the Communist Party, benefiting from the support of Moscow, had several advantages and often tested the limits of the law or even broke the law in certain political matters (e.g., in the case of the falsified legislative elections of 1946), there is little reason to view the trials of war criminals as mistrials. Another factor ignored by those who do not recognize this law is the substance of the trials. The evidence in court files includes testimonies, documents, and other types of evidence. These trials should therefore not be confused with communist ones, in which the evidence was counterfeit, and which were staged to eliminate undesirable communist leaders (as part of the Stalinist power struggle) or the leaders of the other political parties. These were held in Romania under a manifestly political law,[17] while Law 312/1945 is a special criminal law and an act that has a legal content. Pierre Vidal-Naquet was right to say that despite their legislative limits, the Nuremberg trials were capable of judging the losers. But they were not merely losers of a war, for this was a war that had destroyed and shocked humanity.[18] Therefore, the regulations of the trial were special, but they did not exceed the limits of what is generically known as criminal jurisdiction.

Radical nationalism is the other vector to find ways to burnish the memory of persons who fought against the Soviet army during the war. This is presented today under the guise of the anticommunist fight, as "good" memory. Beyond the image embellishment produced by "photoshopping" history, as I mentioned above, Romanians sentenced for war crimes decades ago were acquitted in courts of law during the postcommunist period. This phenomenon is not unique; it also happened in Bulgaria, Ukraine, Hungary, and the Baltic countries.[19] In such cases, nationalism is manifested as denial of the status of war criminal for certain persons; in Romania, these were officers of the Romanian army who fought on the eastern front under the manipulative slogan "Let Us Restore Greater Romania's Borders from 1 December 1918." In the case of the two officers Radu Dinulescu and Gheorghe Petrescu, extensively researched by Alexandru Climescu in the two studies I mentioned above,[20] nationalism was unfortunately combined with antisemitism. The prosecutor argued for and obtained the acquittal of the two officers who previously had been tried and found guilty of participation in the extermination of the Jewish population. For the prosecutor, the Holocaust was probably nonexistent, or in any case, it was unacceptable to accuse Romanians of crimes against Jews. With these acquittals, the justice system conferred respectability on the memory of persons found guilty for crimes of the Holocaust. Such acquittals in courts of law are the most serious form of denial of Holocaust memory, because they cleanse bad memory with the help of the justice system. As a result, if a person is amnestied and then is publicly promoted as a positive example, or is subjected to public rememberance, no official, institutional, or legal reaction is possible. In other words, the legislation that prohibits Holocaust denial in public is not helpful in such situations.

Mircea Vulcănescu, Outstanding Intellectual or War Criminal?

Part of this mnemonic matrix, the sociologist Mircea Vulcănescu has today a vividly disputed public memory. Four years ago, I wrote to the mayor of a district of Bucharest who had erected a bust of Vulcănescu in a city square, informing him that under the current legislation, the statue had to be removed. This was not the first manifestation of the memorialization of Mircea Vulcănescu; there were already schools and streets bearing his name, and there is a memorial plaque displayed on the façade of the house he used to live in, located extremely close to the Cultural Center of the Federation of Jewish Communities in Romania. It is clear that public symbolic displays of this kind refer to the memory of a personality, the cult of a person, but Andrei Pleşu seems to have doubts. He remarked on a recent situation surrounding events organized to pay homage to Vintilă Horia, a journalist and essayist who was sentenced for war crimes in 1946. In an ironic pamphlet that trivializes the recent changes to Emergency Ordinance 31/2002, the public philosopher admitted that the writings of some extremists are available to read, as there is no censorship in Romania. "But," he continues,

> let us not maintain their "cult." I mean, if Vintilă Horia was named an honorary citizen of the village he was born in, could we expect that the children of the village will become legionaries? It is as if the myriad of busts and statues of Mihai Eminescu (who was, by the way, quite a nationalist and an antisemite) ... made it possible for our country to be flooded with tall, well-built "Eminescus," all interested in Kant, Schopenhauer and Buddhism. Let's be honest: a street name or a school, a bust in a park or a commemoration from time to time, all these are only exceptionally the elements of a "cult," according to the full meaning of the term.[21]

The Bucharest mayor we petitioned was not concerned about the public status of war criminals or whether the presence of a bust denotes a cult. He was convinced that the bust portrayed a man of culture who had made notable contributions worthy of mention to the citizens. Therefore, his answer was purely administrative, stating that he had all the legal permits for erecting a statue in a public venue. In other words, the form was good, only the content was not clear. Today, the statue stands in the same public place.

Mircea Vulcănescu (1904–1952) became a philosopher and public intellectual after the First World War. That was a good period for Romania, when it nearly doubled its territory, its human resources, and, thus, its economic potential. The first decade after the war also saw a series of political and economic reforms meant to accelerate the modernization of the country. Although Romania tried to keep up with developed Western countries, it never overcame its semi-peripheral status.[22] The limited character of structural reforms tipped the scales in favor of the manifestation of conservative cultural and political trends and the emergence of the far right, which eventually halted the political developments of the democratic state in 1938. At the time, the new constitution imposed by King Carol II blocked political and civic pluralism. At the same time, there was also a change in Romania's European politics, caused by its new connection to Germany. The 1930s also brought a strong display of the tenets of extreme nationalism, xenophobia, antisemitism, and Christian Orthodoxy.[23] Many of the young people who had been educated and embraced a career in the humanities opted for a conservative, traditionalist, antimodern perspective. They established themselves in the public sphere as committed intellectuals and tried to provide solutions to the critical issue of modernization with nonmodern and antimodern perspectives. Quite a few of them shared and promoted the values of the far right.

Mircea Vulcănescu was close to these intellectual circles, but had not campaigned in the spirit of legionarism. A philosopher, sociologist, and economist, as a young university student he was one of the founding members of the Association of Christian Students in Romania (1921), and he was also very active in the Criterion circle of intellectuals (1931). This was a diverse group that engaged in public polemic discussions on culture and ideology, from various partisan positions ranging from the far right to the far left. It seems that young intellectuals in interwar Romania were comfortable with this; voluntarily or spontaneously, the monographic rural research teams of the sociological school in Bucharest, coordinated by Professor Dimitrie Gusti, included students who supported varying and even opposite ideologies. Mircea Vulcănescu participated in these activities of monographic research, too. Essentially, during the 1920s and 1930s Vulcănescu was trained as an intellectual, with interests in law (his bachelor's degree), economics (unfinished doctoral studies in Paris), sociology, and religion. He never received his Ph.D. He was very active in academia, and lectured on religion, sociology, economics, and ethics.

He wrote in many, perhaps too many, journals and magazines of all doctrines. His articles were also published in the far-right press, the legionary media, though the topics were not ideological. As he himself said, and those who studied his life and work observed,[24] Vulcănescu's intellectual path was influenced by the sociologist Dimitrie Gusti and the philosopher Nae Ionescu, a charismatic orator and the ideologue of the Legionary Movement. The xenophobic, Orthodox, and antisemitic Ionescu had a major influence on young intellectuals living in Bucharest at the time, and this reached its peak in his relationship with Jewish writer Mihail Sebastian. Essentially, the relationship between the two led to tensions in the fashionable and intellectual Bucharest scene after 1934, and even today it continues to be a subject of interest with multiple meanings and endless speculative potentials. At the invitation of his disciple and admirer Sebastian, Ionescu did not hesitate to write the preface to Sebastian's 1934 novel *De două mii de ani* (For two thousand years). The semibiographical novel is an examination of conscience by a Jewish intellectual who wanted to gain access to the cultural life of Romania, but was forced to acknowledge his Jewishness in a hostile era of rising antisemitism that would eventually become state policy. Ionescu's preface had an openly antisemitic message, reminding the author that he would never be able to rise above his condition of being a Jew born in Brăila, the town where the Danube ends.

Mircea Vulcănescu did ignore the incident. He got involved in the scandal caused by the preface of Mihail Sebastian's novel, writing several essays approaching it from points of view he had previously expressed: "O problemă teologică eronat rezolvată? Sau ce nu a spus dl. Gheorghe Racoveanu" (A wrongly solved theological issue? Or: what was not said by Mr. Gheorghe Racoveanu); "Creștinism, creștinătate, iudaism și iudei. Scrisoarea unui provincial" (Christianism, Christianity, Judaism, and Jews: Letter from a provincial), in which he answered Mircea Eliade; and "Strigătul unui tânăr ovrei și polemica ideologică" (The cry of a young Jew and the ideological polemic). The first article did not express a view on Ionescu's preface; it was meant as a theological polemic with his former partner in militant theology.[25] In the second essay, Vulcănescu was ambiguous about the accusation of antisemitism against Nae Ionescu: "I do not think, of course, that Nae Ionescu wrote the Preface to justify any unfortunate situation that might befall, in time, upon the nation of Israel." After reassuring the readers that he knew the philosopher well, and as a consequence, was convinced that he had pondered a lot upon the idea when he decided to write the preface, he concluded: "But he did write it. And, the way he wrote it, he did it because he had faith in truth. As a witness." Then he admitted, but only halfheartedly: "Now, of course, from the Preface one can quite easily deduce justifications for an antisemitic reaction. With a certain good will. But this 'good will' seems to me essential for such a deduction. And it is not the one who tells the truth who is responsible for its use, one way or another."[26] In other words, readers of the preface could find it antisemitic, but that is only the author telling the truth! Mircea Vulcănescu, a principled man in the spirit of tradition, seems to have disregarded the old Romanian saying, "If two people tell you that you drank too much, you should go home and sleep!" This translates into: "If a lot of readers and even Mihail Sebastian noticed the antisemitism of the preface, then this is the message of the person who wrote it." In his third essay, Vulcănescu developed a polemic on the text of Nae Ionescu with legionary Nicolae Roșu. Paradoxically, this time Nae Ionescu does not come off very well:

As far as his [Nicolae Roșu's] thesis is concerned, on the ability of the Jewish writer to belong [to be accepted in Romanian culture as an equal], it seems to me that his stand is less intransigent than Nae Ionescu's. For, while in the case of the latter, the inner changing of the Jew is a structural impossibility, which is in fact reduced to something similar to shedding one's skin, resulting in his being therefore banned from the path of assimilation a priori, for the former there is still an open road of attempts to be made and the answer can only be given according to one's deed.[27]

As a close associate of Nae Ionescu, Vulcănescu had written an article in support of the philosopher in 1931, "Gândirea filosofică a dlui Nae Ionescu" (Mr. Nae Ionescu's philosophical thinking) in *Epoca* (The Times). He also gathered materials and prepared a manuscript for a book about the philosopher, which was published decades later, after the fall of the communist regime, when the cultural restoration of Nae Ionescu, Mircea Eliade, Mircea Vulcănescu, and others took place. As a disciple of Ionescu who knew him well, Vulcănescu presents the philosopher in all facets of his public and private life: as a philosopher, teacher, and politician, touching also upon his friendships, his connection to the legionaries, to the king, and so on. The narrative combines personal histories, factual data, and "stories" heard throughout the city, all meant to paint a truthful image of this spiritually and politically influential figure of the interwar period. Yet, whenever he aims to characterize Ionescu's ideology or cultural views, he fails to remind readers of Ionescu's antisemitism.[28] The concealment of his antisemitism does not seem to be accidental. In this same book, Mircea Vulcănescu proves himself an antisemite, though of course he does not admit it. He replicates classic antisemitic clichés; for example, according to him, it is the Jews who create antisemitism! That explains why, among the founders of the extreme right, there were young people who "lived in Moldova and found themselves in an intuitive contact with a compact and aggressive Jewish hostility, that only those who grew up there could have known directly, in everything that was hostile to Romanian aspirations." The aggressiveness of these youngsters was caused by the police "in Iași, who were serving Jews and politicians enslaved to the Jews, so that the police started serious conflicts, in the streets, against them."[29]

In the same chapter, we learn that although Vulcănescu was not a member himself, he was close to the ideology of some of the members and to intellectuals who campaigned for the Iron Guard, the political party representing the Legionary Movement in elections. "As for me," he says, "although I had many friends in the Guard, I was also a man of the right and I had some sympathy for them, especially in the beginning, as they insisted a lot that I come to them. Still, I did not accept, because, on the one hand, I did not like terrorism and, on the other hand, I did not want to align my personal judgment in any way."[30] He also compared the legionaries with historical outlaws (a kind of Romanian Robin Hoods) and he called their actions "acts of heroism."[31]

Morally, Mircea Vulcănescu was a traditionalist/nationalist. The most important concepts on which his vision for "Romania's resurrection" was built were the values of Orthodox Christianity and the values of the non-modern Romanian countryside. However, he was not devoid of views on ethnicity. In two of his studies, written in 1932, he was deeply disappointed that Greater Romania "given an outburst of joy, welcomed in our midst whoever confessed to belong to us [referring to ethnic minorities], those who worked hard on this land, which we took forever into possession" and had not performed well fourteen years after the fulfillment of the national ideal.[32] One of the causes of this failure, considered the philosopher, was that after having basically escaped from "the contact area of the three races and three civilizations [referring to the fact that until 1918, Romania was in between the Russian, the Austro-Hungarian, and the Ottoman Empires], we imagined we had gotten rid of them and we lost our vigilance!"— neglecting "the most basic needs of ethnic and national defense."[33] He was discontented that Bucharest, the capital, "was outside the natural citadel of the people and industry was in the hands of foreigners [Jews]."[34]

Without being "a passionate ideologue,"[35] he nevertheless wanted to construct a visionary political project to make a "Romanian Romania."[36] He rejected politics, which he understood as a dispute about the preferred type of political regime, be it monarchy, republic, or dictatorship. At one point, he distanced himself from the dictatorial fascist or Stalinist political regimes. Politics was understood by Vulcănescu as a project for the promotion of socioeconomic values. He rejected the idea of revolution, regardless of whether it was from the left or from the right. Perhaps this attitude was his strongest reason for having kept a certain distance from the legionaries. Trusting that Romanian identity entailed the revaluation of the universe of the countryside, his political option was

real reactionarism, nationalist in that it identified with the values that originate from the very being of the nation one is part of. It resides in the choice between the organic lifestyle of the natives of this country and the hybrid existence of the good-for-nothings living in the cities. Everything of valor in the life of this nation came from the village or passed through the village. Nothing that lasted appeared within these borders without it.... Here resides the deep meaning for which any Romanian nationalism, insofar as it is domestic, can only be reactionary and of peasant origin.[37]

Unlike many of his peers and young intellectuals of his generation who shared his values and beliefs, Vulcănescu was employed by the Romanian state. In 1928, at just twenty-four years old and having returned from Paris, he became an assistant professor in the Department of Sociology and Ethics headed by Dimitrie Gusti. In 1929 he was appointed as a specialist in the research office of the Ministry of Finance. By 1935 he was managing director of the Ministry, and in January 1941, after the legionary rebellion, at age thirty-seven he was appointed by Ion Antonescu as undersecretary of state in the Ministry of Finance and member of the government.

His participation in the Antonescu government may appear to contradict his political views, if we consider that Vulcănescu rejected politics understood as strong action and that he had also expressed his disagreement with totalitarian political systems. In a lecture he delivered in 1940 titled

"Christianity in the Modern World," he pointed out the dangers of these political systems, which he considered responsible for a "dangerous utopia that introduces among us a dangerous caricature of evil."[38] According to Ionuț Butoi, it is possible that when Antonescu asked Vulcănescu to join the government, he asked for some time to think about it, and only then did he accept.[39] Despite the fact that the political situation was extremely difficult, and consequently his joining the government entailed more risks than benefits, especially for an intellectual who hadn't held a political responsibilities position before, this decision was presumably based on his social-philosophical outlook, that is, the notion of a "Romanian Romania." According to the philosopher, the greatest danger for Romania was to fall into the hands of Hitler's Germany.[40] Also, he defended himself in a 1943 letter to his minister, and also in his 1946 trial, that the new leadership of the country was military, not political, and civilians were called to participate in the government in their professional capacities. And he saw this call as an order.[41] He stayed in government until August 23, 1944, when a coup by the royal palace together with the leaders of political parties ousted the government. Ion Antonescu was arrested, and Romania left the alliance with Germany and sided with the Allies. Mircea Vulcănescu was to face a trial, in the so-called second batch of members of the Antonescu government, under Law 312/1945.

The criminal investigation of acts that fell within the scope of this law began in April 1945. The trial lasted two years (September 1946 to October 1948). Eventually, Vulcănescu was found guilty for "the country's disaster" under Article 1 paragraph a, because as a member of the government, he was implicitly accountable for all its decisions regarding the alliance with Germany and for Romania's contribution to supplying the German army. He was also found guilty of war crimes under Article 2 paragraph a, for the decision to declare or to continue the war against the Union of Soviet Socialist Republics and the United Nations. Finally, as the final decision of the court explained, he was convicted for his presence in the government and for his actions as a member of a government that was hostile to the Allies.[42] He was sentenced to eight years of imprisonment in hard conditions. He died in prison from disease and the conditions of detention.

After 1990, Mircea Vulcănescu was brought back into Romanian culture through the front door. His work was published or republished by several publishing houses, the Romanian Academy published his complete works, and a doctoral candidate in sociology aimed to decipher interwar Romanian culture in a dissertation that focused on Vulcănescu.[43] In prefaces and introductory studies, Mircea Vulcănescu the intellectual is praised over and over again. For example, for Eugen Simion, a prominent member and former president of the Romanian Academy, Vulcănescu is "a spirit of amplitude, pursuing the phenomena of large cultural and historical realms. He looks for and obviously finds far-away and close causalities; he is usually very well informed, being more than capable to talk of various issues, from theology to the avant-garde and from Plato to Grigorie Palamas. He is endowed with an acute dissociative spirit, loves striking formulas, invents concepts and covers his ideas with a prophetic language."[44] Marin Diaconu, the leading advocate for the return of Vulcănescu's writings into the spotlight, was more moderate in his introduction to the Romanian Academy's edition of complete works. In his view, Mircea Vulcănescu was "the philosopher" of the sociological school in Bucharest, and at the same time, "philosophical thinking is only one of Mircea Vulcănescu's 'dimensions'; it required to be complemented, expanded by his sociological, economic ideas, etc. But the promises of his personality were above his Work! Perhaps Mircea Vulcănescu wanted to be a Monad, an 'open Monad' . . . one that was open to the whole Romanian world, and, due to it, open to the absolute. Only that this 'open window' has failed to close in time, so that his clash with political history was fatal."[45] In 2012 a journal of the Philosophy Institute of the Romanian Academy dedicated a whole issue to Mircea Vulcănescu the scholar.[46] However, his political status as a member of the Ion Antonescu government and his subsequent legal status as a war criminal are not topics of reflection for those who have been involved, after 1990, in the restoration of Vulcănescu's works. When referring to the postwar fate of the antimodern philosopher, they limit themselves to saying—or deploring—that he was sentenced to eight years in prison. In some of these writings, the authors do not even mention the reasons for his conviction, so the reader is left with a strong feeling of injustice on behalf of Mircea Vulcănescu. Essentially, Vulcănescu's return to Romanian culture was made possible by dissociating him from his war criminal past.

In addition to the restitutive publishing of his work, some of which included contemporary messages of support, there is also memorial recognition of the philosopher in the public space. Local administrations bestowed his name on schools and streets.[47] Christian Orthodox and pro-legionary associations interested in publicly rehabilitating the far right depict the philosopher as a representative of Orthodoxy in the fight against communism. These organizations and associations, whose aim is the rebirth of the legionary spirit, developed a strategy to promote a fragmented, decontextualized memory after 1990 by representing a group of people deprived of their freedom after the war as martyrs of communist prisons. These are the prison saints, who, it is claimed, were persecuted for their Orthodox faith and condemned to suffer for their anticommunist and religious beliefs, which was the only thing that allowed them to endure the harsh conditions of the prison system. According to their supporters, their anticommunism and their belief in Christian Orthodoxy as an absolute value make these people worthy models today, regardless of their public pasts. This cult of prison saints aims to relaunch values and symbols of the interwar far right or of persons who were convicted of war crimes after the Second World War.[48] The risk of this endeavor is that they could bring back, through the back door, the ideological values of the Legionary Movement, in the name of anticommunism and Orthodox nationalism, and present them as the only viable values for contemporary Romania. The public memory of such persons is separated from their public past in the interwar period or during the war; thus, they become exemplary heroes. Persistently, today's militants for the extreme values or symbols of the past disguise them in the form of simple anticommunism and manage to persuade local authorities to bestow a public aura of respectability on the bad memory of the Holocaust. This is why, for example, Valeriu Gafencu, a legionary who was active during the legionary rebellion, is now an honorary citizen of the town of Târgu Ocna; Ion Gavrilă Ogoranu,[49] a comrade of Gafencu's, has a monument in Deva; Albert Wass, a war criminal, has a bust at Odorheiul Secuiesc; and Mircea Vulcănescu has a bust in Bucharest.

In fact, for all the activists in favor of the bad memory of the Holocaust, Mircea Vulcănescu's legal status does not exist. For some, precedence is given to his intellectual side. For others, all that matters is his anticommunism, shrouded in the grace of Orthodoxy. It is understandable when individuals make emotional or interested choices in order to legitimize their own values. But it is harder, if not impossible, to understand how local public administrators can accept the overturning of statutes and the negation of the public roles played by these people during their lifetimes. The absence of democratic civic culture is just part of the explanation. Disregard for the law and the lack of response from institutions charged with enforcing the law are also factors, but it is not the whole story.

In this context, it is useful to examine Vulcănescu's role as a member of the Ion Antonescu government. Although historians qualify Antonescu's governance without the legionaries as a military dictatorship with technocrats, without ideology, one should not forget that on at least two occasions the Marshal pointed out that he continued the program developed during the National Legionary State, as well as the fact that Romania's participation in the war alongside Nazi Germany was unconditional and as a result, the Romanian army could not have stopped at the Dniester. During the Cabinet Council of February 7, 1941, Antonescu referred to the continuity of the executive, with and without the legionaries: "As far as the broad lines of governance are concerned, you know very well that they were drawn in these five months of governance. The current minister is merely a continuation of the previous ministry."[50]

About Romania's participation in the war, during the government meeting of September 6, 1941, Antonescu said without hesitation that the plan from the beginning had been total participation, allying with Germany until they reached victory:

> Besides that, the honorable and even military thing to do was to not leave the Germans to fight alone; you should not forget that this unfortunate country has many claims to make to the Russians, especially on our national treasure in Moscow... just like I am now fighting to clean up Bessarabia and Bukovina from Kikes and Slavs. This way, a line of separation from the Baltic to the Black Sea will be drawn between us and the Slav masses. Therefore, I am going forward, primarily for solving the Slav question, and secondly, to receive compensation for our lost treasure in Moscow, which is now worth 470 billion lei. Finally, I am going forward, third of all, in order to have a guarantee to solve the problem in the west [of the country], where I want to restore the border. I did not mention the issue, yet, because I don't want to weaken my position, but this has always been my answer.[51]

This meeting of the government was attended by Mircea Vulcănescu, and the transcripts do not record any difference of opinion voiced by the undersecretary of state. This was just nine months after he had joined the government.

Another debated point is Vulcănescu's antisemitism, or the way he, as an official of the Romanian state, as a member of a government responsible for discrimination and mass murder on ethnic and racial grounds, participated in the "resolution" of the "Jewish question." Instead of undertaking a comprehensive analysis, it is possible to outline Mr. Vulcănescu's attitude toward the Jews using primary documentary sources that are objective and nonpartisan. Transcripts of government and Cabinet Council meetings show that he attended many meetings about various aspects of the Holocaust in Romania and the territories administered by Romania. On March 20, 1941, when the government discussed a draft law on the expropriation of the Jews, Vulcănescu intervened and pointed out the need for clear provisions to identify Jews so that the law would not affect ethnic Romanians: "We will develop objective presumptions, according to which we will show who needs to present this evidence [that they are Jewish]. . . . In order to avoid abuses, it is necessary to explain the basis of our considerations when we can say that a certain person is a Jew. We shall list some criteria. Otherwise, everybody can say about anyone that he is Jewish. We should be the ones to say whom we believe is Jewish." Vulcănescu also shared the government's vision of an ethnicized economy, for in the same meeting, when they discussed the issue of distributing the expropriated Jewish goods, he emphasized, "if we adopt the rigid system of tenders, i.e. the one who pays the best price may take the asset, then our Romanians will not be included," and therefore the regulations following this draft law "must keep the word 'ethnic,' otherwise foreigners will get there and oust the Romanians."[52]

In fact, Vulcănescu was extremely active in government debates that referred to the Romanianization of the economy. One day later, during the Cabinet Council, Vulcănescu was again involved in preparing the tools for the ruin of the Jews. Following Mihai Antonescu's plea to solve the "issue of Romanianization of enterprises and [restore] the positions of Romanian life that have been taken over by Jews" and ensure "the proper temporary management of certain assets and interests that have already been expropriated by the State,"[53] Mircea Vulcănescu said, "I am in total agreement with Mr. Mihai Antonescu."[54] The proposal referred to a simple law for the redistribution of the assets expropriated from the Jews. For the Romanianization of the economy, he proposed the establishment of a national office of Romanianization to handle both political and practical economic and financial issues. During the meeting of the Economic Council on May 8, 1941, he helped establish the position and role of commissioners for the Romanianization of Jewish businesses. In order to have an economic and administrative function, not just a repressive or informational role, and thus ensure the economic efficiency of the procedure, Romanianization commissioners had to "replace Jewish owners who were convicted for the crime of sabotage. Here are the alternatives.... We can either get into a dangerous situation in which these commissioners are bribed by the owners and they become partners in crime, or there can be another danger, in which they become policing bodies that terrorize the people at the enterprise. Instead of doing so, we can provide these commissioners with the prospect of being installed in these enterprises, at one point."[55]

Regarding the requirement that Jews perform work or pay taxes instead of serving in the military (from which they had been excluded), Vulcănescu expressed his admiration of the way Germany handled the situation. At the same time, he assured the attendees that the Jewish Central (organization) had the financial resources to pay the taxes on behalf of poor Jews. During the meeting of the Coordination Council on November 19, 1941, Ion Antonescu expressed his dissatisfaction with the economic results of compulsory labor and proposed replacing it with a fee of 30,000 lei, plus 3 percent of their income in the case of wealthy Jews. The undersecretary of state in the Ministry of Finance had sufficient information on the resources of the Jews and of the Jewish community, and he intervened in the debate and clarified: "The issue should be regarded this way: there are Jews who have money, who are involved in the economic life. They can pay. But there are others who are removed from economic life and they cannot pay.... The community has this amount. It can pay this amount."[56] Vulcănescu was well-versed on the role of the Jewish Central and their capability to raise money from the Jews. The Central was a body set up by the Antonescu regime to coordinate and manage the relationship of the Jews with the state, as well as to mediate implementation of the antisemitic policy (*Judenrat*). In the autumn of the same year, in an analysis of the way Jews participated in the subscription for the Reunification Loan—Jews were required to give money to the poor as well as to the Council of Patronage, an organization headed by Antonescu's wife that assisted war widows and orphans—Vulcănescu made certain clarifications. Subscription had not begun yet, as the "community wants to centralize the subscription. I ordered the collection to be made by the Jewish community as well. There were talks about amounts that must be important. They hope that, following these subscriptions, they would get some relief. We have not made any commitment." When Mihai Antonescu asked whether they promised exemption from certain taxes, the answer is enlightening: "No. As long as they are unable to pay, we will not require their enforcement. But there will be no exemptions. On the contrary: when others must give one unit, they must give at least double."[57]

As for the management of compulsory labor, Mircea Vulcănescu believed that "the Germans have developed a very good system of organization in this respect: they placed them in ghettos and they work as shoemakers, tailors, and so on, thus satisfying the needs of the Germans."[58] It is also worth mentioning here that he also attended the government meeting on August 5, 1941, when the introduction of the Jewish identifying badge (the six-pointed yellow star) was discussed, and he did not express an opposing view. In addition to his efforts to ensure that antisemitic policies were meticulously worded national legislation, the undersecretary of state proposed and developed rules and institutions for the implementation of those policies. He and the Ministry of Finance were directly involved in the exchange of currency and in setting out the rules for the takeover of jewelry and precious metals from the Jews who were deported to Transnistria. In September 1941, Ion Antonescu established a one-to-one exchange rate for rubles and lei for the population in Transnistria:

Regarding the currency of Transnistria, we will take it for free. . . . If they do not give me the money for it, then I will come with our currency, which will have the same value . . . hence the issue of the currency is clear. . . . I have set the exchange rate of one leu for one ruble, so that the Kikes will not come here and smuggle rubles. . . . The rubles that we have . . . we shall give them to the Kikes who will go to Ukraine, at an exchange rate of 8 lei for one ruble. . . . So, dear Minister of Finance and Mr. Vulcănescu, please take the necessary steps so that what happened after the last war, when all kinds of ravens smuggled coins, will not happen. I will also introduce the death penalty for those who are caught smuggling money. . . . I think it is in our interest to withdraw a currency that has value, by using a currency that has no value. The Russian state will represent something. And then we shall have to increase the price of these rubles. Why? Because we have tens of thousands of Jews whom I intend to throw into Russia, and they will need rubles. We will thus make a double operation: we shall buy the rubles cheap and sell them expensively.[59]

As noted by historian Jean Ancel, "Vulcănescu and the officials of the National Bank who dealt with 'technicalities' calculated an exchange rate of forty lei per ruble, and the money taken from the Jews was used to pay compensation to Romanian peasants living in those territories."[60] The Ministry of Finance worked closely with the National Bank and sent it the rules for the exchange of money and for the assessment of the valuables belonging to the Jews who were to be deported, who were forced to sell to the Romanian state. In this regard, a letter from the Ministry of Finance to the National Bank, dated October 1941, stated that:

> The Ministry of Finance agrees that payment be made in rubles, at an exchange rate of 1 ruble = 40 lei. The items will be purchased at your headquarters in those localities, the gold being payable depending on its weight and karat, at the official rate of the National Bank of Romania. Precious stones and other items will be paid based on an assessment made by an expert and only at a share of 20% of the value derived from these assessments, which is equivalent to the ratio between the gold at the official rate and the gold at the free exchange rate.[61]

Vulcănescu also attended the meeting of the Council of Ministers on December 16, 1941, with the governors of Bessarabia, Bukovina, and Transnistria. One of the topics discussed then was the expulsion of the Jews from Odessa. In the dialogue between Ion Antonescu and Gheorghe Alexianu, the governor of Transnistria, the leader referred to Jews as "Kikes," and when the governor asked for a ship to carry them, the Marshal replied, "To put them on the bottom [of the sea]." "To take them to Oceacov," answered Alexianu. Antonescu replied, "You know we lost a ship, the *Cavarna*. I do not care about the Kikes, but it is the ship that I am worried about."[62] The other topic was the transfer of Jewish properties to the state. The debate focused on finding a legal procedure to allow this. Mircea Vulcănescu offered a possible solution: "It is better for this to be based on a law, because the custodian is also mentioned in the account of the owner. The law should be on grounds of public order."[63] These examples show that Vulcănescu was present and either silently accepted the government's policies or sometimes even intervened, making proposals to establish anti-Jewish policy measures.

I conclude this portrait of the official in the Ion Antonescu government with the laudatory words of Mihai Antonescu, deputy prime minister and minister of propaganda, in a context in which Vulcănescu was asked to clarify the sources of money for officials of the Ministry of National Propaganda:

"Mr. Vulcănescu, you are a scholar, a man of thinking, not just an active minister. You realize that wages too have their spirituality, their moral hierarchy."[64] Mircea Vulcănescu was a scholar who understood the spirituality of wages, but since he considered himself a technocrat, did he not understand the political philosophy of the Ion Antonescu government? It is hard to believe he did not.

Conclusions

For those who reconstruct Vulcănescu's social vision today and understand, with the help of documents, his role in the Antonescu government, there is a clear connection between the values and principles of "Romanian Romania" and the political policies of Romania in the 1940s. What better expression could the ideal of "Romanian Romania" find than in the pragmatic, economic, and political answers provided by the Romanianization process developed by the Antonescu government?

Was he a philosopher of the sociological school of Bucharest, or a politician who lost his bet with history? His biographer Marin Diaconu believes there was a fatal clash between the scholar and the politician. However, today, there are interested groups who believe that Vulcănescu's participation in political life is not representative of his public memory. Holocaust survivors are often silent about it, and when they do take action, they are considered a voice of alterity, and thus marginal. Although the Romanian legislation and democratic practices advocate restraint and critical assessment of Vulcănescu's cultural and political roles, without memorial promotion, what actually happens is incompatible with the law. As such, this is a textbook example where justice is still not working.

Can the memory of the scholar be appreciated, or is it blocked by the image of the politician who was convicted as a war criminal? There are indeed such venues of memory, and everything is unpredictably in motion on the highway of Holocaust remembrance. Our present situation is confirmed by a representative opinion poll of 1,016 people in 2015. Only 28 percent (284 people) of the respondents knew about the tragedy of the Jews and the Roma in Romania, and of these, 19 percent (54 people) accepted the responsibility of the Ion Antonescu government, which means that only 5.3 percent of the sampled population has valid historical markers.[65] Therefore, there is a high probability that the bust of Mircea Vulcănescu and other memorial displays of homage in the public sphere will stay where they are. These are the *lieux de mémoire* decided by mayors and elected representatives who skipped civic culture classes.

> Alexandru Florian is the director of Elie Wiesel National Institute for the Study of the Holocaust in Romania. He is editor of *Munca forțată a evreilor din România* (Jewish forced labor in Romania) and author of the volume *Ideologii politice contemporane* (Contemporary political ideologies).

NOTES

1. Shafir, *Între negare și trivializare*, 14.
2. For more details, see Shafir, "Conceptualizing Hungarian Negationism."
3. International Commission, *Final Report*, 360.
4. Also, near DN 24 (national road 24) Iași-Vaslui on Movila lui Burcel, sculptor Gheorghe Alupoaei erected a monument in 1994, called "Woman in Bronze," which symbolizes Emperor Trajan's Dacia. Both her hands are raised above her head and she is breaking the Ribbentrop-Molotov Pact (1939) which ruled the Soviet annexation of Bessarabia. She is also looking at the map of Moldova, including Stephen the Great's fortresses on the banks of the Dniester: Hotin, Soroca, Orhei, Tighina, Cetatea Albă, and Chilia. In the center of the map, Marshal Ion Antonescu stands and orders the 1941 crossing of the Prut River by Romanian soldiers who liberated Bessarabia and who were later slaughtered in the area of Țiganca." See "Destinație: România," *Agerpres*, April 4, 2014.
5. See note 5 in the Introduction in this volume.
6. International Commission, *Final Report*, 381.
7. See Lavastine, *Cioran, Eliade, Ionesco*; Volovici, *Nationalist Ideology and Anti-Semitism in the 1930s*; Florian and Petculescu, *Ideea care ucide*; Ornea, *Anii treizeci*.
8. For example, in 2015 the Bucharest City Hall erected a bust of Emil Cioran, a philosopher and essayist established in France after 1945 who after the war publicly acknowledged his extremist past, as well as a bust of Mircea Eliade, an intellectual and militant of the Legion who moved to the United States after the war and became a noted professor of the history of religions. According to the authors of this project of keeping public memory, the two busts symbolize the spirituality of the two, without any reference to public intellectual roles they played in the 1940s. This partial use of the past to publicly pay them homage in the present and future by hiding their contributions to the cultural and political far right provokes the indignation of those who are interested in promoting the memory of Holocaust victims.
9. Liiceanu, "Sebastian, mon frère." For a more detailed analysis of Liiceanu's discourse about the Jewish question, see Shafir, "The Man They Love to Hate."
10. See Clej, "Nu orice formă de anticomunism este legitimă."
11. Members of the Iron Guard movement are symbolically renamed "Prison Saints" today, as a moral rehabilitation: Valeriu Gafencu, Petre Țuțea, Ion Gavrilă Ogoranu, Iustin Pârvu, Dumitru Stăniloaie, Ilie Tudor, Ilie Lăcătușu, etc.

12. Sixteen years after the ban of the cult of war criminals in Romania, there are streets and public institutions named for persons convicted of war crimes, as well as memorial plaques and busts in their honor. They include Mircea Vulcănescu, Vintilă Horia, Albert Wass, Radu Gyr, General Nicolae Macici, Ioan C. Petrescu, Gheoghe Jienescu, and Visarion Puiu.

13. Although the Emergency Ordinance 31/2002 was in force, some of Ion Antonescu's busts were withdrawn from public view only after the direct intervention of the government.

14. See Climescu, "Post-Transitional Injustice"; Climescu, "Holocaust on Trial." The case of Dinulescu and Petrescu, Romanian army officers responsible for the killing of Jews, presented in detail by Climescu, is a very good example of the way an act of justice can be turned into an injustice.

15. On the role played by ethnic nationalism in the identity narrative ascribed to the Romanian people, see the explicative model proposed by Bărbulescu, "Ethnocentric Mindscapes and Mnemonic Myopia," chapter 1 of this volume.

16. Andrei Pleşu resorts to a mix of situations in order to discredit the trials of war criminals: "I reckon it is urgent to reconsider the decisions of the People's Tribunals of the mid-1940's. . . . As we know, the courts in question were established by the winners of the war so as to liquidate their political opponents. Anti-communism and anti-sovietism were spontaneously described as 'legionarism' by a mob of 'people's assessors' who, most often, knew nothing about the accused. Often, the membership of those tribunals included workers. Among them, sometimes there was a disoriented 'housewife' and a waiter from the Capşa restaurant, as well as the future boss of Stalinist torturers, Alexandru Drăghici. Indeed, there were some lawyers who had agreed that the practice did not need to have anything to do with 'bourgeois objectivism' or to comply with current legal codes. Under the patronage of Lucreţiu Pătrăşcanu (who very soon became a victim of his own 'solutions') verdicts were full of epithets. They all referred to 'crimes of genocide' or 'crimes against humanity,' 'war crimes.' How can one justify the recourse, nearly 70 years later, after a complete regime change and after the condemnation of communism as 'illegitimate and criminal,' to certain 'sentences' issued by a bunch of political cronies and ignorant persons, handled by the Soviet occupier and by a party having a very small membership, at the time?" See Pleşu, "Greşeală, vină, justiţie," *Adevărul*, February 1, 2016.

17. The offense of "intensive activity against the working class and revolutionary movement," provided by article 193 of the Criminal Code, was introduced by Decree no. 62/1954 and amended by Decree no. 358/1954.

18. Regarding the obsession of revisionists of history to ridicule the Nuremberg trials, Pierre Vidal-Naquet stated that it "is easy to find that they had all the flaws possible: it was a trial organized by the winners, who, too, could blame themselves for their own war crimes.The statutes adopted by the agreements between the allies, in 1945, are equivocal, to the extent that this sovereign tribunal was dependent, in part, on the Board of Control of the four occupying powers [occupying Germany]. Article 21 made it mandatory to consider as 'authentic evidence the official documents and reports issued by the Governments of the United Nations.' Article 19 did not mention only, as they say, that 'the court will not be dependent upon the technical rules on the management of evidence,' as is explained: 'As much as possible, it will adopt and apply a rapid and informal procedure, and will admit any means it considers to have value as evidence.' This means that it could decide on its own what evidence could be taken into consideration and what could not. But, in fact,

the statutes had little importance. From the historical perspective, the only important question was which of the two competing models would operate in the tribunal, the liberal Anglo-Saxon model or the Soviet one? The answer is clear. The Soviets did not make the rules." Vidal-Naquet, *Les assassins de la mémoire*, 46–47.

19. Ghodsee, "A Tale of Two Totalitarianisms: The Crisis of Capitalism and the Historical Memory of Communism."

20. See note 14.

21. Pleșu, "Greșeală, vină, justiție," see supra.

22. Florian, *România și capcanele tranziției*, 97–115.

23. See Ornea, *Anii treizeci*. Also, for the deconstruction of some of the myths that formed the basis of a delayed and unfulfilled modernization, see Boia, *History and Myth*.

24. Butoi, *Mircea Vulcănescu, o microistorie a interbelicului românesc*.

25. Vulcănescu, "O problemă teologică eronat rezolvată?" The article is, in fact, a comment on a theological dispute launched by Gheorghe Racoveanu in response to Mircea Eliade's attitude to Nae Ionescu's preface. It is interesting that in this article Vulcănescu calls Racoveanu a legionary, a journalist, and a theologian, "a campaign partner against the new Paschalion" (in 1929, there was a dispute over how to calculate the date of Easter in the Orthodox calendar).

26. Vulcănescu, "Creștinism, creștinătate, iudaism și iudei. Scrisoarea unui provincial," 301–302.

27. Vulcănescu, "Strigătul unui tânăr ovrei și polemica ideologică," 326–327.

28. Vulcănescu, *Nae Ionescu așa cum l-am cunoscut*. See, for example, page 91, where we learn that "Nae Ionescu's ideology made him prone to look for a contact [with the legionaries]. His overtly anti-democratic attitude . . . made him, although he was a leftist in matters of social policy [?!], a far-right reactionary in the political technique, thus not a radical, as some wrongly considered him to be. He had defined his doctrine . . . by four parameters: realism, autochthonism, orthodoxy, monasticism."

29. Ibid., 80.

30. Ibid., 89.

31. Ibid., 81.

32. Vulcănescu, "În ceasul al unsprezecelea." In *Opere*, vol. 2, Bucharest: Editura Fundației Naționale pentru Știință și Artă, Editura Univers Enciclopedic, 2005, 675–676.

33. Ibid., 678–679.

34. Ibid., 680.

35. Simion, "Prefață," xvi.

36. Vulcănescu, "Cele două Românii," 683.

37. Ibid., 685–686.

38. Butoi, *Mircea Vulcănescu, o microistorie a interbelicului românesc*, 274.

39. Ibid., 280–281. Butoi presents a romanticized version, based on the diary of Vulcănescu's wife, of the moment he accepted the government job. Presumably, the family held a meeting and his ten-year-old daughter may have asked him not to accept it.

40. Vulcănescu's wife wrote in her diary:"I do not understand this crazy love for the Germans in the name of patriotism and for the good of the country. I have often heard the legionaries saying that, instead of this disorder, it would be better to be ruled by the Germans. God forbid! We are better off with our disorder than to be ordered by foreigners." See Butoi, *Mircea Vulcănescu, o microistorie a interbelicului românesc*, 534.

41. "As you know, I have joined a military government, the day after the rebellion, having been called on the phone on behalf of Marshal Antonescu—whom I had seen only once before—at 4 AM, after a nightmare—at a time when all others refused and the country was on the edge of the abyss. I listened to what seemed to me to be a call to join the army, not a decree of promotion into public life. I was told at the time that the salvation of the country required suspending all political activity." Butoi, *Mircea Vulcănescu, o microistorie a interbelicului românesc*, 280, note 72. The same story, with more details, was recorded in his first postwar interrogation, when Vulcănescu was being investigated and charged under Law 312/1945. See Mezdrea, *Nae Ionescu și discipolii săi în Arhiva Securității*, 21–22.

42. Criminal Law Sentencing 27/1948, the act of condemnation, mentioned, inter alia: "5) The defendant Mircea Vulcănescu, prosecuted for having been part of the Antonescu Government as State Undersecretary in the Ministry of Finance from January 27, 1941 until August 23, 1944 and, as such, an advocate of Hitlerism, contributed to all acts of the government he joined, thereby assuming the responsibility for those acts, and thus, for the continuation of the war, these acts being referred to in art. 1 letter a and art. 2 letter a of Law 312/1945, and sanctioned by art. 3, paragraph 1, 3 and 6 of the same law; . . . As regards the activity of the defendant: since he took part in 68 meetings of the council of ministers and in 58 meetings of the economic delegation, having been in charge of the funds for the German army in Romania; Given that by this contribution, plus his activity in the Ministry of Finance, where the defendant was a needed collaborator because of his technical capability, all these are likely to persuade the Court that he campaigned for Hitlerism; . . . Considering that the defendant continued to remain in the government after the declaration of war against the USSR and worked there until August 23, 1944, it means that he agreed with the acts of the Ion Antonescu Government, which he agreed to support and so, he acquiesced to the decision to continue the war against the USSR and the United Nations, he is thereby guilty of the deed provided in art. 2 letter a of Law 312/1945." Taking into account various mitigating circumstances, the court of appeal decided: "Defendant Mircea Vulcănescu is sentenced . . . to eight (8) years of hard imprisonment." See Mezdrea, *Nae Ionescu și discipolii săi în Arhiva Securității*, 500, 501, 526.

43. In 1990 to 2015, more than twenty books authored by Mircea Vulcănescu were published, including collections of press articles and studies of economy, sociology, and religion. His complete works were published under the aegis of the Romanian Academy: Vulcănescu, *Opere*, 2 volumes. Also see Butoi, *Mircea Vulcănescu, o microistorie a interbelicului românesc*, Butoi's doctoral thesis in sociology.

44. Simion, "Prefață," xviii.

45. Diaconu, "Un chip spiritual al vremii," lxxiv.

46. Cernica, *Mircea Vulcănescu*.

47. For example, in Bucharest there is a street and a school named after Mircea Vulcănescu.

48. Some of the people who have been subjects of claims of martyrdom because they were convicted for having belonged to or sympathized with the Legionary Movement include: Mircea Vulcănescu, Radu Gyr, Valeriu Gafencu, Vintilă Horia, and Ion Gavrilă Ogoranu.

49. While writing this study, I learned that the local administration of Bucharest approved the display in University Square, in the central public area of the city, of the exhibition *In memoriam: Ogoranu—10 ani de la moarte*. Publicity for the exhibition read: "Ten

years since his passing into eternity, Ion Gavrilă Ogoranu is increasingly present in the life and struggles of Romanian society. Loved by Romanians who never ceased to discover his epic story, still persecuted by his detractors and enemies, a topic of televised debate and objectively criminalized by an unjust law, Ion Gavrilă Ogoranu gets down into the street, 10 years after his death, into the turmoil of downtown Bucharest, the capital city of Romania. Photos—some of them never published—from the Securitate archives, snapshots from the public life of our hero after 1990, as well as some of his stands in the last 15 years of his life, all these can be seen by the public in an unprecedented memorial exhibition. Those who miss Ion Gavrilă Ogoranu are invited this Thursday, May 12, 2016, 18.00h, at the opening of the «ION GAVRILĂ OGORANU—HERE I AM» memorial exhibition. The name of this event is «Here I am!», as we resume the ritual of the legionaries when they paid homage to their dead." This display of legionnaire propaganda was erected 500 meters from the Coral Temple and the Jewish district, where seventy-five years ago (January 1941) the legionaries carried out a pogrom. See "Eveniment," *Buciumul*, May 8, 2016.

50. Benjamin, *Evreii din România între anii 1940–1944*, 291. The first mention of this idea was, more briefly, during the cabinet meeting of February 3, 1941.

51. *Stenogramele Consiliului de Miniștri*, 302.

52. *Stenogramele ședințelor Consiliului de Miniștri. Guvernarea Ion Antonescu*, vol. 2, 671–672.

53. Ibid., 688.

54. Ibid., 692.

55. Benjamin, *Evreii din România între anii 1940–1944*, vol. 2, 231.

56. Ibid., 340–341.

57. *Stenogramele ședințelor Consiliului de Miniștri. Guvernarea Ion Antonescu*, vol. 4, 460–461.

58. Benjamin, *Evreii din România între anii 1940–1944*, vol. II, 340.

59. *Stenogramele ședințelor Consiliului de Miniștri. Guvernarea Ion Antonescu*, vol. 4, 598–599.

60. Ancel, *Contribuții la istoria României*, vol. 1, partea a II-a, 320.

61. General Archives of Central National Bank of Romania, the Secretariat Division, folder no. 19/1940, file 228.

62. Benjamin, *Evreii din România între anii 1940–1944*, vol. 2, 364.

63. Ibid., 368.

64. *Stenogramele ședințelor Consiliului de Miniștri. Guvernarea Ion Antonescu*, vol. 4, 458.

65. "Sondaje," Institutul Național pentru Studierea Holocaustului din România, accessed March 10, 2016, http://www.inshr-ew.ro/ro/proiecte/sondaje.html.

References

Ancel, Jean. *Contribuții la istoria României. Problema evreiască*, vol. 1, partea a II-a. Bucharest: Hasefer, 2001.

Benjamin, Lya, ed. *Evreii din România între anii 1940–1944*, vol. 1, *Legislația antievreiască*. Bucharest: Hasefer, 1993.

———. *Evreii din România între anii 1940–1944*, vol. 2, *Problema evreiască în stenogramele Consiliului de Miniștri*. Bucharest: Hasefer, 1996.

Boia, Lucian. *History and Myth in Romanian Consciousness.* Budapest: Central European University Press, 2001.

Butoi, Ionuț. *Mircea Vulcănescu, o microistorie a interbelicului românesc.* Cluj-Napoca, Romania: Eikon, 2015.

Cernica, Viorel, ed. *Studii de istorie a filosofiei românești,* vol. 8. Bucharest: Editura Academiei Române, 2012.

Ciucă, Marcel-Dumitru, ed. *Stenogramele ședințelor Consiliului de Miniștri. Guvernarea Ion Antonescu,* vol. 2 (ianuarie–martie 1941). Bucharest: Arhivele Naționale Române, 1998.

———. *Stenogramele ședințelor Consiliului de Miniștri. Guvernarea Ion Antonescu,* vol. 4 (iulie–septembrie 1941). Bucharest: Arhivele Naționale Române, 2000.

Clej, Petru. "Nu orice formă de anticomunism este legitimă—interviu cu istoricul Adrian Cioflâncă." Accessed December 5, 2016. https://web.archive.org/web/20150206112838/http://www.jurnalistan.ro/2015/01/05/nu-orice-forma-de-anticomunism-este-legitima-interviu-cu-istoricul-adrian-cioflanca.

Climescu, Alexandru. "The Holocaust on Trial: Memory and Amnesia in the Case of Romanian War Criminals." *Holocaust. Studii și cercetări* 8 (2015): 307–322.

———. "Post-transitional Injustice: The Acquittal of Holocaust Perpetrators in Post-Communist Romania." *Holocaust. Studii și cercetări* 7 (2014): 145–157.

Diaconu, Marin. "Un chip spiritual al vremii." In *Mircea Vulcănescu, Opere,* vol. 1, edited by Marin Diaconu, xxiii–lxxiv. Bucharest: Editura Fundației Naționale pentru Știință și Artă, Editura Univers Enciclopedic, 2005.

Florian, Alexandru. *România și capcanele tranziției.* Bucharest: Diogene, 1999.

Florian, Alexandru, and Constatin Petculescu, eds. *Ideea care ucide.* Bucharest: Noua Alternativă, 1994.

Ghodsee, Kristen. "A Tale of Two Totalitarianisms: The Crisis of Capitalism and the Historical Memory of Communism." *History of the Present: A Journal of Critical History* 4 (2014): 115–142.

Institutul Național pentru Studierea Holocaustului din România. "Sondaje." Accessed March 10, 2016. http://www.inshr-ew.ro/ro/proiecte/sondaje.html.

International Commission on the Holocaust in Romania. *Final Report.* Edited by Tuvia Friling, Radu Ioanid, and Mihail E. Ionescu. Iași, Romania: Polirom, 2004.

Laignel-Lavastine, Alexandra. *Cioran, Eliade, Ionesco. L'oubli du fascisme: trois intellectuels roumains dans la tourmente du siècle.* Paris: PUF, 2002.

Le Goff, Jacques. *Histoire et mémoire,* Paris: Gallimard, 1988.

Liiceanu, Gabriel. "Sebastian, mon frère." *Revista* 22, 17, no. 375 (1997): 10–11.

Mezdrea, Dora, ed. *Nae Ionescu și discipolii săi în Arhiva Securității,* vol. 5, *Mircea Vulcănescu.* Cluj-Napoca, Romania: Eikon, 2013.

Ornea, Zigu. *Anii treizeci. Extrema dreaptă.* Bucharest: Cartea Românească, 2015.

Shafir, Michael. "Conceptualizing Hungarian Negationism in Comparative Perspective: Deflection and Obfuscation." *Cahiers d'Études Hangroises et Finlandaises* 20 (2014): 265–310.

———. *Între negare și trivializare prin comparație. Negarea Holocaustului în țările postcomuniste din Europa Centrală și de Est.* Iași, Romania: Polirom, 2002.

———. "The Man They Love to Hate: Norman Manea's 'Snail's House' between Holocaust and Gulag." *East European Jewish Affairs* 30 (2000): 60–81.

Simion, Eugen. "Prefață." In *Mircea Vulcănescu, Opere*, vol. 1, edited by Marin Diaconu, v–xii. Bucharest: Editura Fundației Naționale pentru Știință și Artă, Editura Univers Enciclopedic, 2005.
Vidal-Naquet, Pierre. *Les assasins de la mémoire*. Paris: La Découverte, 1987.
Volovici, Leon. *Nationalist Ideology and Anti-Semitism: The Case of Romanian Intellectuals in the 1930s*. Oxford: Pergamon Press, 1991.
Vulcănescu, Mircea. "Cele două Românii." In *Mircea Vulcănescu, Opere*, vol. 2, edited by Marin Diaconu, 682–687. Bucharest: Editura Fundației Naționale pentru Știință și Artă, Editura Univers Enciclopedic, 2005.
———. "Creștinism, creștinătate, iudaism și iudei. Scrisoarea unui provincial." In *Mircea Vulcănescu, Opere*, vol. 2, edited by Marin Diaconu, 295–322. Bucharest: Editura Fundației Naționale pentru Știință și Artă, Editura Univers Enciclopedic, 2005.
———. "Gândirea filosofică a dlui Nae Ionescu." *Epoca* 600 (1931).
———. "În ceasul al unsprezecelea." In *Mircea Vulcănescu, Opere*, vol. 2, edited by Marin Diaconu, 675–681. Bucharest: Editura Fundației Naționale pentru Știință și Artă, Editura Univers Enciclopedic, 2005.
———. *Nae Ionescu așa cum l-am cunoscut*. Bucharest: Humanitas, 1992.
———. "O problemă teologică eronat rezolvată? Sau ce nu a spus dl. Gheorghe Racoveanu." *Credința, ziar independent de luptă politică și spirituală* 225 (1934).
———. "Strigătul unui tânăr ovrei și polemica ideologică." In *Mircea Vulcănescu, Opere*, vol. 2, edited by Marin Diaconu, 325–327. Bucharest: Editura Fundației Naționale pentru Știință și Artă, Editura Univers Enciclopedic, 2005.

CHAPTER SEVEN

ION ANTONESCU'S IMAGE IN POSTCOMMUNIST HISTORIOGRAPHY

Marius Cazan

Ion Antonescu was the leader of the Romanian state from September 1940 to August 1944. From September 1940 to January 1941 he shared power with the far-right Legionary Movement in what was called the National Legionary State. The collaboration between Antonescu and the legionaries did not last, and conflicts between the two sides became frequent as the abuses of the legionaries were increasingly apparent. In January 1941 Antonescu crushed the attempt of the former government partners to oust him, and, counting on his slightly unclear agreement with Hitler, managed to stay in power. As head of government, he developed a regime of personal dictatorship that lasted until August 23, 1944, the day Romania changed sides and joined the Allies in the war against Germany, with whom it had been allied since June 1941. The Romanian state was effectively occupied by the USSR, its former enemy. The Armistice Convention signed by Romania and the Allies on September 12, 1944, in Moscow called for the arrest and trial of war criminals. Antonescu was detained for several days in a safe house of Romanian communists, but the Soviets preferred to take him into custody, along with his main collaborators. By September 1, he was already taken to the command post of the Second Ukrainian Front. Until April 1946, when he was brought back to Romania, Antonescu was imprisoned in the Soviet Union.

Marshal Antonescu was tried in Bucharest, per the terms of the Armistice Convention, for his deeds and decisions during the time he was leader of the state. The way the trial was organized, its numerous procedural faults, and propaganda that demonized those who had waged war against the Soviet Union all served to lessen the significance of the crimes Antonescu was accused of, as well as the evidence against him and the failure of his regime. No less than 23 percent of the indictment consisted of evidence pertaining to the defendants' involvement in the Holocaust.[1] Ion Antonescu was tried together with twenty-three of his collaborators, who were sentenced on May 17, 1946. After several unsuccessful appeals, on June 1, 1946 sentences of capital punishment were handed down against Ion Antonescu, Mihai Antonescu (deputy prime minister and minister of Foreign Affairs), Constantin Z. Vasiliu (commander of the Romanian Gendarmerie and undersecretary of state in the Ministry of the Interior) and Gheorghe Alexianu (governor of Transnistria). They were the only Romanian war criminals to be executed, though there were others who received death penalties.

Today, Ion Antonescu remains a convicted war criminal, but for a number of reasons his image among Romanians is rather positive. Several surveys carried out in the last ten years referred directly to Ion Antonescu's image. These surveys either dealt with the Holocaust in Romania and the perception of interethnic relations (the polls of 2007 and 2015) or with broader topics, including the aforementioned issues (2009, 2010, and 2013).[2] The sample groups were nationally representative and included persons older than eighteen (except for the 2007 poll, which was fifteen and over). All of the polls included a question about Ion Antonescu with the same wording: "Marshal Ion Antonescu was the leader of Romania in 1940–1944. I will now read to you a series of attributes of a state leader and I am asking you to tell me how well they represent this historical figure." Some of the proposed attributes are positive: "a great patriot," "a great strategist," "he must be rehabilitated for what he did for Romania," "he reunified Romania," "he was a democratic leader." The survey undertaken in 2015 also included "he fought against communism." Other attributes are negative: "he is responsible for crimes against the Roma/Gypsies," "he is responsible for the murder of Jews," "he was a dictator," "he was a war criminal," "he led Romania to disaster."

There are a few constant factors that are relevant for the way that Ion Antonescu is perceived. The number of persons who chose not to answer or declared that they could not decide is significant, for both positive and negative attributes. In some cases, the percentage of those who did not answer exceeded half the total number of respondents, but the general trend is that the percentage of those who chose "I do not know/I do not answer" or "I cannot tell you" decreased from one poll to the next. In 2015 the number of respondents who gave neutral answers to the question about Antonescu amounted to 36 percent, as compared to 49 percent in 2007. My interpretation is that people became more knowledgeable and better educated about history, but also that Marshal Antonescu is now better known in contemporary Romanian society.

Regarding the way that Antonescu is perceived by that part of the population sample that did answer and chose some of the specified attributes, there are a few things that are worth mentioning. Antonescu's attributes as a "great patriot" and "great strategist" found approval among a significant portion of the sample (over 40 percent in all polls). In both cases, the percentage of those who agreed with these attributes increased. In 2007, 46 percent of all respondents considered Antonescu a patriot. In 2015 their number rose to 54 percent. There are similar increases among those who saw the leader of Romania during the war as a great strategist: 44 percent of the sample in 2007 and 52 percent in 2015. The number of those expressing disapproval of these attributes varied between 11 percent and 20 percent of the sample. As far as the other positive attributes about Marshal Antonescu are concerned, the polls of 2009, 2010, and 2013 show that an equal number of persons agreed and disagreed with the statement "Antonescu must be rehabilitated." By contrast, in 2007 only 18 percent of the sample disapproved and 33 percent were in favor of the statement. In 2015 the percentage of those who believed that Antonescu should not be rehabilitated was 25 percent, while 37 percent of the sample agreed with his rehabilitation. For the statement "Antonescu was a savior of Jews," the 2015 survey indicates the end of a trend that was noticeable in previous polls. Specifically, the percentage of those who declared their disagreement with this statement increased from 31 percent of the sample in 2007 to 53 percent in 2013. Those who approved of the statement represented 15 percent in 2007, but only 5 percent in 2013. The poll of 2015 shows a decrease of those who disagree with the statement that Antonescu was a savior of Jews, to 42 percent of all respondents, as well as an increase of those approving this statement, to 18 percent of the sample.

Negative attributes in the question about Antonescu deserve equal attention. Respondents who are opposed to the statement that Ion Antonescu "is responsible for crimes against the Roma/Gypsies" represent, in most polls, around 20 percent of the sample. Those who think that Antonescu was responsible for crimes against the Roma also represent a growing share of the respondents from one poll to the next, having reached 46 percent of the sample in 2015. As far as Antonescu's responsibility for crimes against the Jews is concerned, we find little difference between those who disagree and those who agree with this statement. In 2007, 23 percent of the respondents believed that Antonescu was not responsible, while 25 percent found him responsible. In the 2015 poll, 31 percent of the respondents did not consider that Antonescu was responsible for the murder of Jews and 30 percent agreed with this statement. The different perceptions of Marshal Antonescu's guilt regarding crimes committed against Roma or Jews has several causes, but it is beyond the scope of this chapter to provide thorough explanations. I shall only conclude that during this time, there were no historiographic narratives or public endeavors that denied the involvement of the Marshal in the deportation of the Roma; in contrast, denials of Antonescu's and the Romanian state's involvement in the deportation and murder of the Jews were prolific.

Returning to the negative attributes about Ion Antonescu, the historical figure, there is a somewhat higher tendency of the respondents to disapprove of statements such as "Antonescu was a war criminal" and "Antonescu led Romania to disaster." With regard to these two attributes, it is worth mentioning that a very large percentage of respondents chose neutral answers (I do not know/I do not answer, I cannot decide). In 2007, 2009, and 2010 the share of neutral answers represented approximately 50 percent of the sample, while in 2013 and 2015 it dropped to 36 to 38 percent of the sample. Thus, in 2015, 29 percent of the respondents considered that the statement referring to Antonescu as a war criminal was inappropriate and 24 percent agreed with the statement. The poll from 2015 shows that 41 percent of the sample did not agree with the statement that Antonescu led Romania to disaster, while only 21 percent agreed with it.

Ion Antonescu as an historical figure is rather popular with Romanians. Although he ruled Romania as a dictator and his involvement in crimes against Jewish and Roma civilians has been documented and implicitly acknowledged by the Romanian state when it accepted the findings of the

2004 *Final Report* of the International Commission on the Holocaust in Romania, which concluded that "Romanian authorities were the main perpetrators of the Holocaust in both its planning and implementation,"[3] Ion Antonescu continues to be seen by a large part of Romanian society as a hero and a patriot who is insufficiently appreciated.

In this study, I analyze the contributions historians have made to constructing Antonescu's image. My starting hypothesis is that the historiographical discourse of the postcommunist period that focuses on Marshal Antonescu had an important role in shaping the public perception of this historical figure. I would like to point out that this study is not meant to be a critique of the contributions of historians to general knowledge, or of their scientific value. Rather, I analyze how their manner of writing and means of disseminating their research has contributed to the development of public perceptions about Marshal Antonescu, as exemplified in the polls mentioned above. A comprehensive approach that covers the entire historiographic production regarding Ion Antonescu's personality is unrealistic, and the relevance of such an analysis for our approach is questionable. Our analysis is mainly concerned with the writings of historians who have been particulary visible in Romanian society in the past twenty-five years. Specifically, we are interested in the way Marshal Antonescu is presented and evaluated by historians who are public opinion makers—that is, those who by their frequent public appearances can influence the public and provide directions of interpretation and valuation. They are acknowledged either by the entire academic community or by peripheral researchers whose theses are unusual or contested. My criteria of selection is the reputation they have in society, the number of TV appearances they have made is a criterion for measuring their recognition by the public. Of course, my choices and the connections I make are fully my own; they are not an acknowledged scheme of analysis.

Another method for examining the dynamic of historians' discourse about Antonescu during the postcommunist period is an analysis of history magazines aimed at the general public. The descriptions of Marshal Ion Antonescu that appear in the pages of these magazines are provided, in the vast majority of the articles, by historians who are either already established or making the first steps of their careers. The importance of magazine articles is conferred by the popularity of these publications, which require adaptation of academic discourse to suit the general public. Over the past twenty-five years neither their numbers nor their successes were constant, but three magazines did become standouts in the popularization of history: *Magazin istoric* (1990–),[4] *Dosarele istoriei* (1996–2007), and *Historia* (2001–).

Antonescu in Communist Historiography

Before discussing Antonescu's place in communist historiography, it is worth noting the way the recent past (i.e., the Second World War) was dealt with by the historians at the time. In order to avoid calling attention to the illegitimacy of the Stalinist regime imposed by Moscow, the sensitive topic of the war and responsibility focused on blaming Germany, the aggressor, and the fascist collaborators imposed by Germany without popular support in Romania. This rhetoric, sometimes more complex, was also present in other communized states. In addition, the downplaying of antisemitism in those societies, the presentation of the majority populations as innocent, victimized, and heroic, and the construction of narratives about antifascist struggles were dominant elements of the historical narrative of the Second World War.[5]

Any attempt to create a timeline of communist historiography in the 1950s is dominated by what was generically called the Rollerian[6] period. At that stage, Antonescu's regime was presented as unpopular and dictatorial, and the prevailing narrative was that Antonescu had seized power with the support of the bourgeois parties. Also, Ion Antonescu was demonized, along with Romanian imperialists and fascists, for their role in the war against the Soviet Union. The extermination of the Jewish population was not mentioned, and Antonescu's antisemitic policy was tacitly described as part of the persecution of the state leader against political opponents. This was the dominant discourse of the 1950s.

During the 1960s, particularly toward the end of the decade, Romanian historiography distanced itself from Moscow and built the foundation for the nationalist trend of the 1970s that became dogma in the 1980s. The short period of liberalization in the 1960s did not change the way Antonescu was presented by historians. There was, however, a tendency to integrate communism into national history, as a narrative of predestination into which the Communist Party was incorporated organically.[7]

Dennis Deletant sees in Ceaușescu's speech on May 7, 1966, the forty-fifth anniversary of the establishment of the Romanian Communist Party, a signal to historians that a reassessment of the recent past had to be made. Ceaușescu criticized the prewar resolutions of the party congresses, in which Romania was called a multinational state. With his reference to the inequity of the Ribbentrop-Molotov Pact, which allowed the Soviet Union to occupy Bessarabia and Northern Bukovina in 1940, Ceaușescu's historians saw an opportunity to initiate a debate on the reevaluation of political leaders who had supported the recovery of those provinces in 1941. The first step, according to Deletant, was the redemption of democratic party leaders Iuliu Maniu and Constantin Brătianu, who had made a stand against the continuation of the war beyond the Dniester and thus distanced themselves from Antonescu.[8] Antonescu continued to be held responsible for the war in the East and for Romania's disaster, and historians increasingly referred to episodes that suggested opposition to the way he ruled. For example, in one of its first issues, *Magazin istoric* published a memorandum sent to Antonescu by a group of intellectuals in April 1944, emphasizing the contribution of "communist men of culture" in drafting the document that asked Antonescu to withdraw from the war.[9] In the magazine's very next issue, there was an article about the conflict between Antonescu and Iosif Iacobici (the chief of staff, dismissed by Antonescu on January 20, 1942) that suggested that among the military, there was widespread opposition to the way Antonescu waged war, and that the Marshal acted in a discretionary manner against his opponents: "He ousted those generals whom he considered opponents or whom he just did not like. This was common practice for the fascist dictator." The article also suggested that there was a close collaboration between "patriotic generals and officers" and communists.[10]

In another type of article published in the early years of *Magazin istoric*, Marshal Antonescu is presented in tandem with the Legionary Movement, and every time, Antonescu is depicted as less evil than the legionaries. In an article about the conflict between Horia Sima and Antonescu, both are described as "Hitler's Agents," controlled by the Nazis and acting in their interests. Allthough the legionaries were "the pupils he had brought up for years," "Antonescu, the General, was preferred, as he could better dominate the much-needed army in the anti-Soviet war, which he had feverishly prepared. Precedence was given to military dictatorship and to a military dictator, since Hitler's goals to subordinate Romania were first of all military."[11] More details appear in an article authored by Aurică Simion in which Antonescu is presented as more cerebral and more concerned with complying with the law. The author cites Antonescu, on October 14, 1940: "I do not admit any interference, from anyone, into state affairs. . . . I no longer admit trespassing on people's homes, because the inviolability of homes is ensured by the Constitution. We have always protested against the arbitrary measures of the former regime and we are now committing them on a terrible scale. . . . Such things must end. Otherwise the public opinion will be against the regime."[12] For the author, the difference between legionaries and Antonescu was that the leader of the state feared a "total loss of the political and economic independence of the country," while the legionaries unreservedly embraced the directives coming from Berlin.

Antonescu became a figure worthy of reassessment as the policies of the Ceaușescu regime became increasingly nationalistic. Ceaușescu's policy of independence and patriotism drew historians who wanted to provide him with a heroic lineage that included Antonescu, though attempts to rehabilitate Marshal Antonescu emerged only in the 1970s, and it was not historians who took the initiative.[13] Nevertheless, historians were silent about Antonescu's and the Romanian authorities' role in the crimes committed against the Jews. Gheorghe Zaharia attempted to place all the blame for the deportation and killing of the Jews on the Germans, and claimed that in the Iași pogrom, Germans had been helped by legionaries. For example, Zaharia stated that "measures of persecution, up to mass deportation (the so-called 'forced migration') of certain cohabiting nationalities" were made "under the influence of German advisers."[14] The intention to hide the identity of the deported is clear just a few lines below, where the author quoted a truncated fragment from a July 8, 1941, speech by the vice president of the Council of Ministers, Mihai Antonescu: "At the risk of not being understood by certain traditionalists . . . I am for forced migration. . . . I do not care whether history will consider us barbarians."[15] Zaharia's editing of the quote is curious, since the same article includes a section that summarizes the main stages of extermination of the Romanian Jewry. However, it showed the tendency to blame these crimes on the Nazi allies and minimize the involvement of the

Romanian authorities. Ironically, a decade later, Gheorghe Zaharia coauthored the only book[16] in communist historiography[17] in which the involvement of Romanian troops in the atrocities committed against the Jews is clearly mentioned. The volume also provided information about the number of victims, though the figures were not exactly honest.

Another important year for minimizing the role of the Antonescu regime in the Holocaust was 1978, when a book about the pogrom in Iași was published.[18] In it, blame for the pogrom was assigned exclusively to the Nazis and legionary groups, while the death toll was grossly understated. The fact that one of the authors and the person who wrote the foreword for the book, Nicolae Minei (the deputy editor of *Magazin istoric*), were Jews increased the legitimacy of the book.[19]

In examining how historians changed their approach to Ion Antonescu and his regime during the communist period, Adrian Cioflâncă's discussion about the changing terminology used to refer to the Antonescu regime is relevant. At first, communist articles used the phrase "fascist dictatorship," and later, "fascist-military dictatorship." In the late 1980s this phrase was replaced with "personal dictatorship" or "totalitarian regime," thus obscuring the army's involvement[20] (because the army had become an important element of nationalist ideology in the 1980s). The distancing of the army from Antonescu is evident in an article published in *Magazin istoric* by Ilie Ceaușescu[21] in 1989. The author argues that there was escalating discontent with the Antonescu regime within the entire army, "from the lower echelons to the command corps." In his opinion, one of the factors that led the regime to switch sides on August 23, 1944 was the army's position against the war in the East and Anglophilic feelings among the military.[22]

The group that most actively attempted to rehabilitate Ion Antonescu formed in the 1980s and benefited from the support of Iosif Constantin Drăgan, an enigmatic figure and seemingly a legionary supporter in his youth, who had emigrated to the West and established a prosperous business. Later, he became associated with the Ceaușescu regime and thus was able to access documents about Antonescu that were inaccessible to Romanian researchers. Drăgan was the most important actor in the campaign undertaken in the West during the 1980s to rehabilitate Antonescu.[23] In the early 1990s, he supported a group of researchers who avidly defended Marshal Antonescu and campaigned for his rehabilitation, including, most prominently,

Gheorghe Buzatu, as well as Mihai Pelin, Larry L. Watts, and Valeriu Florin Dobrinescu, among others.

Although communist historiography never launched an open and direct campaign to rehabilitate Marshal Antonescu, there were many details and approaches that formed the basis of historiographic productions of the 1990s that were intended to produce a positive reassessment. In addition, historians' silence throughout the communist era on the involvement of the Romanian authorities and Ion Antonescu in the atrocities committed during the war facilitated the spread in the 1990s of heroic narratives about Antonescu, which were often complementary to positions that denied the Holocaust.[24]

Antonescu in Postcommunist Historiography: A Quantitative Approach

This section focuses on how much was written about Antonescu after the communist period. Such an analysis is intended to provide a general idea of historians' interest in Antonescu as a historical figure; I do not claim that the amount of the historiographical material is relevant for the impact that these books and articles had on society, but it may be indicative of his notoriety.

My approach is not exhaustive, as I do not claim to include all titles that deal with Ion Antonescu. To track the historiographical production, I used the *Historical Bibliography of Romania*,[25] an inventory of Romanian historical literature that has been published since the 1970s under the coordination of the Cluj branch of the Romanian Academy. Although the subtitle of this collection makes it clear that it is a selective bibliography, its aim is to include the entire production of history books. Our selection includes the titles in the subsection about important figures in Romanian history, as well as the titles included in the section about the Second World War, which is part of a larger section on contemporary history. From the second section, I chose only the titles that clearly referred to Ion Antonescu or the Antonescu regime; many of the titles about the Second World War might not directly refer to Antonescu, although his personality may well be reflected in such works. Having made this selection, for the period 1990 to 2010 I indexed 194 titles, including 63 monographs, collections of documents, or collected volumes, and 131 studies or academic articles. As mentioned above, these figures should not be viewed as exhaustive. This selection does not include newspaper articles, which often discussed the historical figure of Ion Antonescu, especially in the 1990s. There are two chronological periods almost equal in terms of duration (see figure 1). From 1990 to 2001 there was a greater number of materials about Ion Antonescu than in 2002 to 2010. We might speculate that Emergency Ordinance 31/2002, which prohibited fascist, racist, and xenophobic organizations and symbols, as well as promotion of cults of personality of persons found guilty of crimes against peace and humanity, and which came into force in March 2002, inhibited historians' "appetite" for Antonescu. There was a small revival of the subject in 2004 to 2006, perhaps due to the publication in 2004 of the *Final Report* of the International Commission on the Holocaust in Romania.

By far, the most prolific of the historians who wrote about Antonescu throughout the 1990s and 2000s was Gheorghe Buzatu.[26] Of the 194 titles reviewed here, he published twenty-three studies or articles in professional journals and collected volumes, and authored or coauthored twelve books on Ion Antonescu. As mentioned above, Buzatu was most active in the effort to rehabilitate Marshal Antonescu and significantly contributed to the development of his cult of personality.[27] (Among other things, Buzatu was the

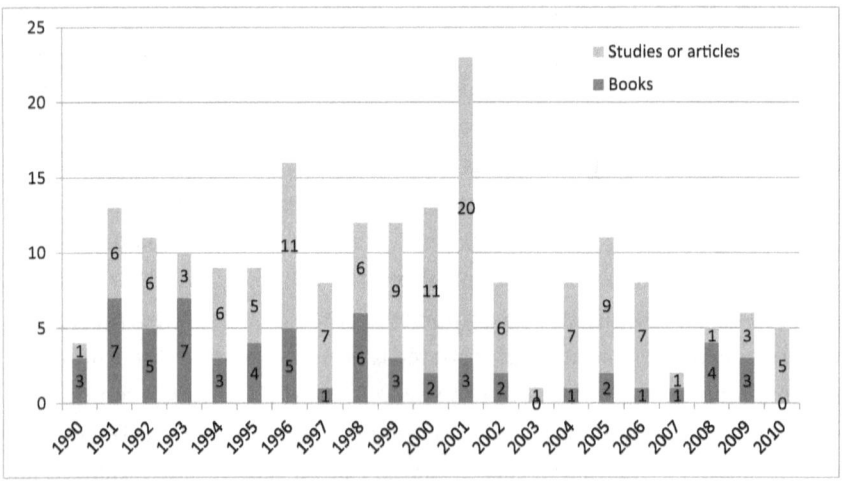

Fig. 7.1 Dynamics of publications about Ion Antonescu, 1990–2010 (studies or articles/books).

first vice president of the Marshal Antonescu League,[28] an organization established in 1990 by Iosif Constantin Drăgan and Corneliu Vadim Tudor, the head of the far-right Greater Romania Party.)

The titles of these books and articles give us the opportunity to comment on attributes and topics associated with Antonescu. Undoubtedly, titles with positive connotations attached to his personality are much more numerous than those that associate Antonescu with negative issues such as the Holocaust or the atrocities committed during the war. Most of the titles refer to the military side of his personality; I identified twenty-three such examples[29] in the 194 indexed titles. Another category of titles describes him as a hero or victim; the thirteen titles in this category sometimes overlap with the eight article titles that refer to the patriotism/nationalism of Marshal Antonescu.[30] In contrast, the titles that link Antonescu to the Holocaust or how he dealt with the Jewish community do not necessarily indicate a militant position.[31] I also identified one title that associates Antonescu with his conviction for war crimes, but it is not apparently accusatory.[32]

In many cases, historians chose to let Antonescu himself provide the title. Placing into the title brief quotes from Antonescu succeeds in conveying a certain connection between the historical figure and the reader. The image that Antonescu made for himself, in his own words, shows us his spirit of sacrifice: "If I die, it is for Bukovina and Bessarabia. If I was to begin again, I would do the same";[33] and "I demand to be sentenced to death."[34] It also conveys a spirit of courage and boldness—"We do not believe that we lost the war"; "Let us seriously think about defending the territory";[35] and "I waged a holy war against Bolshevism in the campaign of 1941"[36]—as well as intransigence and harshness: "Whoever is refractory is a traitor";[37] and "Down with your bellies."[38] The lack of originality—rather of the author who chose to use this quote than of Antonescu—of one of his statements also displays his fatalism: "History will judge me."[39] In its similarity to journalism, the use of such titles draws the reader closer, but at the same time, conveys the human side of the historical figure under scrutiny, and thus drives the reader away from a cool, preferably nonpartisan judgment.

At the risk of sounding superficial, the preceding analysis notes how the shortest summary of a historian's work, that is, its title, can be an (albeit imperfect) indicator of the author's stance on the subject of the work. In the next section I discuss Antonescu's personality as reflected in the writings of historians whom we consider to be reference points for the postcommunist Romanian society. My selection is certainly subjective, but since there is no objective tool to determine which historians the general public perceives as opinion makers, my criterion is the professional recognition they received due to their participation in television programs.[40] It is true also that most of them are widely acknowledged and hold positions of authority among professional historians as well.

Gheorghe Buzatu

Undoubtedly, the historian who was most active in attempts to rehabilitate Marshal Antonescu and in cultivating his image in the postcommunist period was Gheorghe Buzatu. As early as October 1990, he served as vice president of the Marshal Antonescu League. Until 1989 he was a researcher at the A.D. Xenopol Institute of History and Archaeology of the Romanian Academy, and he later founded and managed the Center for European History and Civilization within the Romanian Academy. He was also active in politics. For one term, 2000 to 2004, he was a senator from the far-right Partidul România Mare (Greater Romania Party) in the Romanian parliament.[41] The bulk of his historical production is impressive, and he is by far the most prolific writer on Ion Antonescu.[42] Buzatu's appraisal of Marshal Antonescu is unambiguously positive, and he had no doubt that the injustice suffered by Antonescu's memory under communism needed to be fixed.

Very soon after the change of regime in 1989, Gheorghe Buzatu began to call in his writings for a review of the conviction that led to Antonescu's execution in 1946. In the introduction of a volume of documents about Romania's wartime leader, Buzatu connected the Marshal's honesty, courage, and spirit of initiative to the issue of his trial: "Fortunately for him, the Marshal seems to always be involved in the era he dominated. He may have been too passionately involved, but he acted justly, most often. Likewise, our conclusions lead quasi-automatically to the cancellation of all the charges handed down in May 1946 and later taken over by communist propaganda by virtue of a very simple factor: The Marshal 'dared' go to war against the USSR, the first communist state of the world."[43] This kind of rhetoric about the reasons

Antonescu was tried in 1946 developed throughout the following years. Buzatu was just as direct and intransigent about Antonescu's place in history: "We believe that, among the Romanian personalities of the past, Marshal Antonescu undeniably belongs to that very limited category of heroes who have proven unlimited courage and dignity, and also allowed portrayal by their contemporaries just the way they were! And, although it may seem strange, that's why these heroes, when facing the judgment of history, are even more difficult to understand."[44]

The articles published by Buzatu over time in the aforementioned magazines that disseminated history among the general public are full of positive remarks about Antonescu. The image he conveys to his readers is that of a hero who courageously faced his opponents, or that of a victim of the communist regime due to his vehement anticommunist stance. These two stances are not mutually exclusive, but rather complementary. An important topic in Buzatu's writings is the 1946 trial that preceded Ion Antonescu's execution. In a 1993 article Buzatu argues that the trial was "a show trial" with an "atmosphere of fear, suspicion, pressure, and revenge," and that the admission of evidence and its interpretation presented serious grounds to challenge the sentence. Another of Buzatu's methods to discredit the trial is to attack the way it was presented in communist propaganda. A large part of the 1993 article consists of a comparison of the transcript published in 1946, which had been heavily edited by the authorities of the time, with the full version published after 1990. The selection of the passages that are compared is obviously favorable to Antonescu.[45] Buzatu never mentions anything about the Armistice Convention signed by Romania in 1944, when the country agreed to capture and try its war criminals. He never mentions the special law under which the trial was held, which was a requirement of the Convention. And the historian does not consider it necessary to mention the evidence used in the trial that judged Antonescu responsible for the crimes committed against Jews. When discussing the legitimacy of the war against the USSR and the way this issue was used during the trial, Buzatu takes a unilateral approach in which Antonescu's arguments and the obvious procedural shortcomings of the trial are grounds for cancelling the 1946 sentence. His work does not mention the charges for the crimes committed against the Jews, either. For Buzatu, "the war in the East was, from the beginning to the end (June 22, 1941–August 23, 1944), a righteous war, for crushing communism and for liberating the historical provinces of Bessarabia, Northern Bukovina and Herța, which had been occupied by the USSR in the summer of 1940."[46] Toward the end of his article, Buzatu states that the recent discovery of new documents[47] the amount of time between the Second World War, or the war in Yugoslavia (!? the article was written in 1999) are arguments for reevaluation of the Marshal.

Another way Buzatu develops Antonescu's heroic image, this time adding elements reminiscent of the martyrdom of anticommunist victims, is by referring to the Marshal's execution. In his foreword to an article he coauthored[48] that describe the last hours before the execution on June 1, 1946 from the perspective of the witnesses, Buzatu quoted a large excerpt from a later testimony given in 1949.[49] In this testimony Antonescu's execution is presented in a heroic manner, eliciting the sympathy of even the most insensitive readers. For Buzatu, it did not matter that the author of the testimony admitted that he had heard several versions of the story, and as a consequence, it had been repeatedly embellished. The same excerpt was also used a few years later in an article by Buzatu that touches upon the more general issue of Romania's involvement in the Second World War and its place among the major participants in the conflict;[50] Marshal Antonescu is discussed in a section titled "The First Victims of Communist Terror." Here, Buzatu uses a new method to discredit the trial of 1946. After stating that Marshal Antonescu and his collaborators are referred to "in most reference books as being among the first victims of communist terror in Romania," Buzatu provides a list of famous trials in Romania during the twentieth century, including the prosecutions of the leader of the Legionary Movement Corneliu Codreanu (1938), one of the leaders of the National Peasants' Party (1947), Lucrețiu Pătrășcanu (1954), and so on, concluding with the trial of Nicolae Ceaușescu in 1989. The author finds that "none of these trials rose above the level of the lowest possible show trial." For Buzatu, Antonescu's 1946 trial surely fell into the same category of acts of injustice. The article continues according to the known setup of Buzatu's articles with a quote from the dignified Marshal during the trial, and evokes episodes that demonstrate the respect that other persons involved in the trial, even prosecution witnesses, paid to the former leader. In the section about the execution of Antonescu and his three staff members, Buzatu repeatedly refers to it an assassination, a murder, a slaughter.

In another article in which Buzatu provides a detailed account of August 23, 1944, the day Antonescu was removed from power following a coup in which the king was also involved, the historian dealt with all primary sources, that is, the testimonies of all those involved in his ousting.[51] Antonescu himself was rather neglected in this article, as his status as victim of a plot needed no explanation. Yet, Buzatu inserts a fragment presumably written by the Marshal while he was held in the vault of the royal palace, which he somehow managed to hide, and which was discovered by chance. As expected, the fragment depicts him as dignified, having no regrets, and ready to do everything for the good of the country: "History will judge me. I pray to God to save the country from the consequences of such a thoughtless act, especially since I never clung to power. Several times I did tell the king, alone or in the presence of Mr. Mihai Antonescu, that, should there be another in the country capable to serve her better than me, I will stand down, on one condition: to provide guarantees and not to be ambitious or adventurous. Marshal Antonescu."[52]

When researching the personality of Ion Antonescu, Buzatu also dealt with topics that might be considered eccentric. For example, Buzatu authored an article titled "Ion Antonescu, Historian of the First World War,"[53] which discussed a study made by Ion Antonescu in 1926 summarizing the main events of Romania's participation in the war. It is worth mentioning that in his introduction, Buzatu stated his disapproval of the Emergency Ordinance that prohibited the promotion of the cult of persons found guilty of crimes against peace and humanity:[54] "No law can touch upon his posterity. Since his execution on June 1, 1946, Antonescu exclusively belongs to History and historians, while Romanian politicians and the winners of 1945 have proven that all they could do with Antonescu was to kill him."[55] It should be noted that as a member of the Senate, Buzatu proposed an amendment to legislation that could provide a means to avoid prosecution for people who claim there was no Holocaust in Romania.[56]

Over the years, Gheorghe Buzatu gathered around him like-minded historians who had the same apologetic stance on Ion Antonescu. Although the importance of these historians varies, both in terms of their contributions and their visibility in postcommunist public life, their role in developing Marshal Antonescu's cult deserves mention.

Florin Constantiniu

An authoritative voice among historians (as a member of the Romanian Academy since 1999) and widely acknowledged by the general public, Florin Constantiniu began his career as a medievalist. In the 1980s his research interests turned to contemporary history, and he collaborated with GeneralIlie Ceaușescu, Nicolae Ceaușescu's brother and an influential military historian. Constantiniu's view on Marshal Antonescu's personality was summed up in one of the most successful history books published during the postcommunist period in Romania, *O istorie sinceră a poporului român* (A sincere history of the Romanian people). First published in 1997, it has had four editions and many more series. The summary of Romanian history includes a lengthy chapter on the Second World War (almost 100 of the 550 pages of text)[57] in which Marshal Antonescu plays a central role. The historian's portrayal of Antonescu is quite extensive, and not limited to one section in the text. Antonescu is described as a "highly competent army man, being an incorruptible and staunch opponent of King Carol."[58] The "authoritarian nature" of the "General who behaved like a dictator" is explained by Constantiniu with reference to the order and discipline demanded by Antonescu, as well as to a certain puritanism he practiced. The historian notes the Marshal's megalomania and egotism, exemplified by excerpts from the transcripts of the Council of Ministers meetings, during which Antonescu described himself as a hero.[59] The book also includes passages that show Antonescu being both analytical and critical of the state of the army and its training.[60] When writing about the Marshal's connection to Germany, Constantiniu states that Antonescu remained one of Hitler's faithful allies, with total confidence that Germany would win the war, even after the defeat at Stalingrad.[61] On Antonescu's attitude toward a possible truce, Constantiniu does not provide a clear verdict, but an article he published in 2002 includes a document that shows that in August 1944 Antonescu preferred to continue the war alongside Germany, as he feared turning Romania into a battleground. Constantiniu clearly explains the diplomatic and military deadlock faced by Antonescu, and states that "the act of August 23, 1944 avoided turning Romania into a battleground between the Wehrmacht and the Red Army, and it thus served the national interest better than the politics of the Marshal—based on faulty assumptions and hesitations—on the eve of his fall."[62]

Returning to Constantiniu's book, despite the size of the chapter on the Second World War, the issue of the policy of ethnic cleansing practiced by the Antonescu regime is dealt with only very briefly. Referring to the pogrom in Iași, Constantiniu writes that during the time when Romanian and German troops were waiting to go on the offensive, "bloody events not fully understood today" took place. In the two paragraphs about the pogrom, every time they are mentioned, the perpetrators are identified as Romanians and Germans: "Romanian soldiers and civilians, as well as certain German soldiers, attacked the Jewish population"; and "The Romanian troops, supported by the Germans, fought back, moving on to summary executions."[63] Of course, these sentences are absolutely true, but they allow an interpretation according to which the responsibility of the Romanian authorities is ambiguous. This is most clearly visible in the following passage: "Since German military courts had repeatedly demanded that the Jewish population— considered an enemy—be removed from behind the front, Romanian authorities carried out the rapid evacuation of the Jews of Iași, in inhuman conditions."[64] Although Constantiniu does not deny Antonescu's antisemitic policy and he does not hesitate to condemn it, he does not provide readers with even minimal pieces of information about, for example, the deportations to Transnistria, or the forced labor regime Jews were subjected to in the Old Kingdom. On the other hand, at the end of the fourth edition (2010), Constantiniu inserted a chapter titled "Controversial or Unsettled Issues in the History of Romania" in which he cites Dennis Deletant, stating that the Romanian authorities committed crimes against the Jews independently from the Germans, and that the blame for those crimes should not be shouldered by someone else.[65] In addition, it is fair to mention that in the articles we reviewed, when referring to Ion Antonescu, Florin Constantiniu refers directly to the policy of ethnic cleansing that he pursued, even if he also wrote about issues that present the Marshal in a positive light.[66]

Dinu Giurescu

A member of a family closely connected to the study of history (both his father and grandfather were important historians in their generations), Dinu Giurescu, like Florin Constantiniu, began his career studying medieval history. He became interested in contemporary history only after 1990, when he returned to Romania after a brief exile in the West, and became a member of the Romanian Academy. Although he has always been appreciated by his peers, Giurescu's public activity developed only later, in the 2000s. Dinu Giurescu is the coordinator of the ninth volume of the *History of Romanians*, a collection published under the aegis of the Romanian Academy. The 2008 volume covers topics pertaining to the period 1940 to 1947, and it includes excerpts from Giurescu's previously published book about the war.[67] Giurescu's style of writing incorporates extensive quotes from his sources, with minimal interventions, assessments, or personal observations. Therefore, any attempt to shape Antonescu's image based on the writings of Dinu Giurescu is a complicated endeavor. In the volume published by the Academy, the chapter on the internal political regime during Antonescu's dictatorship is authored by Giurescu, who assesses the "nature of the Ion Antonescu regime" by taking into account the membership of the government, the public administration, Antonescu's approach to matters concerning former parties, laws issued by the government, and governance principles. Thus, Giurescu shows that between January 1941 and August 1944, the government was not political, and public administration continued to operate under the mechanisms inherited by Antonescu from Carol II.[68] In terms of his approach to the leaders of political parties, the historian provides many details of the correspondence that Antonescu had with Iuliu Maniu and Dinu Brătianu.[69] Also, his safety laws and measures, as well as the repressive ones, are presented without much interpretation. The last paragraph of the chapter is perhaps meant to compensate for the lack of commentary: "Given the conditions of war, the repressive regime operated at a moderate level. There was one large and tragic exception, which resulted in a considerable number of victims: the deportation and deaths of the Jews from Bessarabia and Northern Bukovina, as well as that of the Jews from Transnistria (see the dedicated chapter). The Leader bears the main responsibility for these."[70] A similar comment can be found at the end of the longer chapter on the internal political regime of Antonescu. In this context, Giurescu states that "the Antonescu regime was antisemitic. It applied 'ethnic cleansing' by deporting and imprisoning the Jews from Bessarabia and Northern Bukovina in camps in Transnistria. . . . But he refused to send the Jews of Romania (living on the left side of the Prut River) to Nazi death camps—as the 'Final Solution' required—and, thus, the lives of about 300,000 Jews were saved."[71] Here, Giurescu's mention of Antonescu's refusal to send the Jews of Romania to Nazi camps, without mention of the fact that his refusal had a mercantile motivation, gives Antonescu undeserved credit.

In the same volume, Giurescu also authored a comprehensive chapter on the Jews in Romania during the war. This chapter was an updated version of the summary in his 1999 book on the Second World War, which built on a two-part article published in 1997 in *Magazin istoric*.[72] In the chapter, the main events of the antisemitic and tragic episodes of deportation and massacres are extensively documented, with the same care in quoting sources and the same reservation to provide commentary. The historian gives a series of numbers in reference to the death toll and he does not hesitate to state the responsibility of the Romanian authorities. He also gives attention to ethnic Romanians who were involved in the efforts to rescue Jews. As far as Marshal Antonescu is concerned, Giurescu is cautious about linking him to the topic. By no means does he deny the Marshal's responsibility, but he does not explicitly state it either, as he did in the other works. Dinu Giurescu quotes Ion Antonescu on several occasions, but his critical comments are few and far between. One exception is his comment on a quote in which the Marshal accused all the Jews of Bessarabia and Northern Bukovina of having been brutes during the withdrawal of the Romanian army in the summer of 1940. Giurescu mentions that those who attacked the army and the authorities acted in an organized manner, but they did not belong to one ethnic group.[73] The same generalization was made by Antonescu in a reply to a letter sent by Wilhelm Filderman, and in this case, too, Giurescu states that there were no grounds for attributing collective responsibility to Jews.[74]

The general lack of critical assessments of Ion Antonescu in a volume published under the aegis of the Academy that refers to the situation of the Jews in Romania is not surprising. Within the ranks of the Academy there were some people, for example, Dan Berindei[75] (the head of the history and archaeology section of the Academy), who denied the involvement of the Romanian state in the Holocaust.[76] Berindei has no notable writings on Antonescu; I found only one article about Antonescu that he authored, and its title is obviously misleading: "Antonescu Is Quite Worried about the Large

Massacre of the Jewish Population in Bessarabia, by the Germans."[77] In this article, Berindei discusses how Marshal Ion Antonescu is described in the diary of Raoul Bossy, the Romanian ambassador to Berlin from 1941 to 1943. Yet, the image of Antonescu that emerges in the diary is in no way relevant to the title of his article. Issues concerning the Jewish population of Romania are dealt with in only one paragraph of the article. Besides the quote that provides the title of the article, which Bossy attributes to the Romanian military attaché in Berlin, there is only one reference to Antonescu's attitude toward the Jews, which Bossy again hears from a third party. Berindei's article title is inexplicable, except that it may tell us something about the way Berindei sees Antonescu.

Ioan Scurtu

Ioan Scurtu is another very active historian in the postcommunist period who has held a number of positions and honors that have brought him visibility in the field of historical research. He was chairman of the National Archives (1991–1996) and the Nicolae Iorga History Institute of the Romanian Academy (2001–2006), as well as a member of the Elie Wiesel International Commission on the Holocaust in Romania.[78] His research focuses on the entire twentieth century, with particular attention to the interwar period. Scurtu refers to Ion Antonescu in quite a few of his works. In an article that analyzed Hitler's role in the conflict between Antonescu and the Legionary Movement, Scurtu makes a comparison between the head of state and the legionary leader Horia Sima: "Antonescu was a man of order, acting for discipline and rule of law, while Sima demanded to fundamentally change society and to build Romania according to the tenets of the Iron Guard." Hitler's preference for Antonescu, wrote Scurtu, came from his realistic belief that the Marshal was "a man he could count on, determined and trained, who kept his word and had an overwhelming influence in the army."[79] The same image of Antonescu, which emphasizes the military side of his personality, with military spirit and discipline as his dominant features, also appears in an article in which Scurtu details Antonescu's first decisions after he became the leader of the state.[80]

In an article about Romania's position among the major combatants of the war and about Antonescu's military options, Scurtu's approach is balanced, with few personal observations. He mentions both the public support enjoyed by Antonescu when Romania entered the war and the antisemitic policy and racial crimes perpetrated by his regime. When referring to the moment Romania entered the war, Scurtu uses contemporary quotes that refer directly to Antonescu. However, when it comes to discussing the extermination measures put into practice by the Antonescu regime, the historian quotes testimony about the pogrom in Iași that does not mention Antonescu and the Romanian authorities at all.[81]

Ioan Scurtu also contributed to constructing a positive image of Antonescu by publishing articles about the mundane life of the era. Antonescu becomes more familiar to the reader when Scurtu places him among the ladies in his wife's entourage, or discusses his health problems.[82]

Alex Mihai Stoenescu

Not all historians with high public visibility enjoy the wide recognition and appreciation of their peers. Stoenescu is a self-taught man in the field, as he initially studied engineering, and his first publications were literary works. He came to be seen as a historian due to his interest in researching coups in Romania, including the Revolution of 1989 and the period of the Second World War. His book *The Army, the Marshal, and the Jews*, first published in 1998 and reedited in 2010, enjoyed significant success with the public. Its subtitle, *The Cases of Dorohoi, Bucharest, Iași, Odessa*, refers to the most visible episodes of the Holocaust in Romania. In addition to raising many issues of an academic nature (which are not the focus of this study), Stoenescu argues that Antonescu made many mistakes, but when he refers to his responsibility for crimes against the Jews, the historian invokes contexts that seem to exonerate Antonescu. For example, when referring to the Iași pogrom, he accuses Antonescu of "ceding to Germany a part of Romania's national sovereignty, without being expressly forced to do so," and argues that the German intelligence services took advantage of the weakness of Romanian authorities and "acted just like [they did] at home."[83] Although he does not deny the Marshal's antisemitism, Stoenescu discusses the actions of the Romanian leader from various perspectives and notes his pragmatism: "Antonescu was not blinded by antisemitic hatred and considered it was in the general interest of Romania for her Jews to survive." The fact that Jews were spared by Antonescu is interpreted by Stoenescu as a consequence of the Marshal's cult of military honor and his image of himself as a savior, even of the Jews.[84]

An article published by Stoenescu in 2002 makes possible a summary of his main ideas about the Marshal (which he also mentions in his book): Antonescu was a patriot, and his wish to save the country is undeniable. Stoenescu rejects the accusations leveled against Antonescu about the murders committed during deportations: "The loud accusations against him, when murders, massacres with hundreds of thousands of victims are invoked, have no academic support, but only a propagandistic value."[85] The way Stoenescu turns Antonescu into a victim is quite interesting, but rather trivial. After discussing the death toll of the Second World War (16 million victims) and of the communist period (300 million victims), Stoenescu continues: "But, since in this human holocaust the Marshal died too, executed as a war criminal, and since he was Romanian, his drama concerns us, first of all. His trial was a farce."[86]

Lucian Boia

The historians discussed so far in this chapter are more or less conservative and nationalistic in their approaches. Lucian Boia is quite the opposite. He became widely known in the 1990s for his works that propose a more critical, less mythical view of Romanian history. His peers often have accused him of historical revisionism or anti-Romanianism, but the books written by this historian living in Bucharest are best sellers. Boia is primarily a historiography expert; in other words, he writes about the ways other historians have written about certain subjects.

Many passages in his books analyze both the fate of Marshal Antonescu and the way the leader of wartime Romania has been used in later historical constructs. In most cases, his references to Antonescu are very direct and unsentimental, without exculpatory or inculpatory explanations. For example, after stating that the murder of Jews by the legionaries and the Antonescu regime is an undeniable fact, Boia provides a brief presentation of the facts (the killings and persecution, as well as the survival of the Jews in the Old Kingdom) and concludes: "These are the facts and data. The Antonescu regime exterminated more than a hundred thousand Romanian Jews and 'saved' about 300,000. From a strictly arithmetical perspective, his merit would be three times greater than his guilt! Only that not to kill is not a merit, and to kill is a crime."[87] However, Boia does not stop here; he goes on to mention the context of an "era dominated by discrimination, hatred, and violence," which, as it immediately follows the sentence about the criminal character of the Antonescu regime, somewhat mitigates the Marshal's crimes.

Boia's polemical spirit is conveyed to his readers through narrative constructs that are quite relativistic. On Antonescu, the most obvious example is the following: "We talked about Marshal Antonescu, whether he killed or saved Jews. The answer is again typical of the equivocal condition of Romanian culture, mentality, and attitudes. Yes, Marshal Antonescu saved Jews, and yes, Marshal Antonescu sent Jews to their deaths. We do not know what to take from this, but, again, this is the Romanian area, imprecise by definition. Was there a Holocaust in Romania? There was a Holocaust in Romania. There was no Holocaust in Romania. Both statements can be supported and, after all, we have to consider them together."[88] This manner of settling the issue serves those who deny Antonescu's and Romania's responsibility in the Holocaust better than it serves the need to understand the Holocaust.

Adrian Cioroianu

Belonging to a new generation of historians, Adrian Cioroianu began his career in the 1990s and is both appreciated by many of his peers and acknowledged as a high-visibility historian by the general public. His reputation is also a result of his involvement in political life, as he has held high-level public positions that to some extent have boosted the public dimension of his profession.[89]

Cioroianu has not systematically studied Marshal Antonescu's personality. His texts about Antonescu were first published in cultural journals in the late 1990s and 2000s (although I did not intend to analyze this type of source, this exception is justified by the subsequent publication of the articles in an academic volume). Cioroianu's findings about Antonescu are not at all favorable. He sees him as a "meritorious officer, but less than mediocre as a political head of state," his capital mistake being the inability to build alternatives.[90] Cioroianu's stance on Antonescu is summed up in an article published shortly after Emergency Ordinance 31/2002 came into force. Without questioning the Marshal's patriotism or fear of Bolshevism,

Cioroianu notes Antonescu's political naivety in relation to Hitler and his acquiescence, for a time, to the Nazi policy of ethnic cleansing. The historian concludes: "He [Antonescu] was not iconic of Romanian democracy, but rather of the terrible crisis of democracy (he is not the only one to blame for it, but he was able to come to power this way and he headed for a sacrifice that engulfed the country as well). It was not he who began the policy of ethnic discrimination in Romania and he was not the one to put an end to it. He did not want to cause harm to the country and the Romanians, but he did so."[91]

Conclusion

In this study I trace the way historiographical discourse about Marshal Antonescu is conveyed by the most visible historians in the postcommunist public space. I also examine whether the image of Antonescu developed by these historians has much in common with the Romanian public's view of Antonescu, as indicated by the polls discussed in the first section of this chapter.

When pointing out some general features of the way historians analyzed in this study relate to Antonescu, I found a widespread tendency to refer to the historical context when discussing Antonescu's genocidal measures. This often dilutes the main message, and only one more step is necessary to exonerate him. With perhaps one exception (Gheorghe Buzatu), historians generally agree that Antonescu made mistakes that worsened Romania's situation. They all mention Antonescu's patriotism and his wish to recover the territories lost by Romania in 1940.

In identifying the characteristics attributed to Antonescu in the opinion polls and comparing them to the discourse of historians, I found that for both groups, patriotism and even strategic skills (by historians, generally in their references to his militarism) are more frequently mentioned than his crimes against the Jews and the Roma (and the crimes against the Roma are less often mentioned than the crimes against Jews). Also, historians often associate Antonescu's attitude in the second part of the war, when he scaled down his antisemitic policy and refused to send Jews to Nazi camps, with the idea that he saved Jews. In many cases, historians credited Antonescu with saving Jews.

Marshal Antonescu's image in Romanian society is not influenced only by the discourse of the representatives of one professional field. However, the authority that society bestows upon historians, for their expert knowledge of the past, grants them a privileged place among those who want to influence public opinion.

> Marius Cazan is a researcher at the Elie Wiesel National Institute for the Study of the Holocaust in Romania.

NOTES

1. Muraru, "Procesele criminalilor," 77.
2. The opinion polls are available at http://www.inshr-ew.ro/ro/proiecte/sondaje.html.
3. International Commission, *Final Report*, 381.
4. *Magazin istoric* (Historical Magazine) first appeared in 1967, a time of liberalization of the whole of Romanian society. Since its very beginning, the main contributors belonged to the Institute of Historical and Socio-political Studies of the Central Committee of the Communist Party. Its tagline, "a magazine of historical culture," noted the two main features of the publication: dissemination of information to the masses, and the scientific component present in many articles. In the 1970s and 1980s, the magazine often was used to disseminate nationalist ideology and protochronist materials. The fight against fascism and Hitlerism was a main topic of contemporary history in the pages of the magazine until 1989. For a detailed analysis of the protochronist discourse in *Magazin istoric*, see Roiban, *Ideologie și istoriografie*, 282–327.
5. Cioflâncă, "Gramatica disculpării," 631–632.
6. This refers to Marxist historian Mihail Roller and his dominance of historiography in the 1950s. See *Istoria Republicii Populare România* (History of the People's Republic of Romania).
7. Cioflâncă, "Gramatica disculpării," 635.
8. Deletant, *Aliatul uitat*, 282–283.
9. "Tăcerea noastră ar însemna o crimă" (Our silence would be a crime), *Magazin istoric* 2 (1967): 7–9.
10. Antip and Nicolae, "Domnule Mareșal," 26–30.
11. Ilie and Aureliu, "În culisele conflictului dintre Horia Sima și Ion Antonescu" (Insights of the conflict between Horia Sima and Ion Antonescu), *Magazin istoric* 4 (1967): 23–27.
12. Ion Antonescu, quoted in Simion, "Nopțile bucureștene," 63.
13. In 1975 writer Marin Preda (elected the previous year to the Academy of the Socialist Republic of Romania) published his novel *Delirium* about Antonescu's life, in which he is praised for saving the nation by neutralizing the Iron Guard and blamed for having led Romania into the war against the USSR, beyond the Dniester River. Preda humanizes, and sometimes even appears to like Antonescu. The book was a huge success in Romania

(selling in its first year 35,000 copies of the first edition and 120,000 copies of a second edition) but it was met with criticism by Moscow. Scholars paid less attention to another novel first published in 1975 whose characters included Ion Antonescu: *Incognito*, by Eugen Barbu, who also had been elected the Romanian Academy, in 1974. In this novel Antonescu was dealt with severely as a member of a political class Barbu demonized. Preda's novel was far more successful than Barbu's. Is it a coincidence that Antonescu appeared at approximately the same time as a character in novels by two established writers, and that the treatments of him were completely different? In addition to noting the assistance with documentation given to the two authors, we might speculate about the cautiousness of the ideological decision makers, who supported both authors' views on Antonescu; one could be used as an excuse for the other.

14. Zaharia, "6 septembrie 1940–23 august 1944," 25.

15. Here is the full excerpt: "At the risk of being misunderstood by some traditionalists who may be among you, I am for the forced migration of the entire Jewish element from Bessarabia and Bukovina, who must be thrown over the border. I am also for the forced migration of the Ukrainian element, which has no business being here at this time. I am for the radical revision of ownership and of the organization of work and production discipline. Only on this basis can we rid our nation of the foreign infiltration and decomposition that once led to the collapse of our borders. Gaining peace is of essence, and peace can only be gained by doing so. I do not care if history remembers us as barbarians." Benjamin, Documente, 206.

16. Zaharia and Cupșa, *Participarea României*.

17. Cioflâncă, "Gramatica disculpării," 638.

18. Karețki and Covaci, *Zile însângerate la Iași*.

19. Rotman, "Memory of the Holocaust," 210.

20. Cioflâncă, "Gramatica disculpării," 639–640.

21. Nicolae Ceaușescu's brother had a privileged role in terms of his access to documents, and the group of collaborators gathered around the Center of Studies and Research of Military History and Theory enjoyed a special status in the field.

22. Ceaușescu, "Din cronica rezistenței antihitleriste."

23. See the collection of documents about Antonescu edited by Iosif Constantin Drăgan in Italy during the second half of the 1980s. The selection of these documents is obviously favorable to Antonescu. Drăgan, *Antonescu*. In 1991, a second edition with the same title was published in Romania.

24. For an inventory of events that minimize and deny the Holocaust in the 1990s, see Shafir, *Între negare și trivializare prin comparație*, 2002.

25. For this research, I studied volumes 8 to 13, covering the period 1990 to 2010. The increase in recent years of academic materials posted exclusively online raises questions about the relevance of the collection.

26. Gheorghe Buzatu (1939–2013), historian, researcher at the A. D. Xenopol History Institute of the Romanian Academy, was one of the main collaborators with Iosif Constantin Drăgan, and a senator representing the far-right Greater Romania Party in 2000 to 2004.

27. See Shafir, "Reabilitarea postcomunistă," 437–439; Shafir, "Unacademic Academics," 948–951.

28. Not to be confused with the League Pro-Marshal Antonescu, an organization of war veterans who also wanted the legal rehabilitation of Ion Antonescu, but were not associated with Iosif Constantin Drăgan.

29. These are not necessarily laudatory, but they associate his name with a period or episode that demonstrates his connection to the military. A few examples: Dobrinescu, *Plata și răsplata istoriei. Ion Antonescu, militar și diplomat (1914–1940)* (History's reward and payback. Ion Antonescu, an army man and diplomat (1914–1940)); Carp, "Perioada 'piteșteană' a generalului Ion Antonescu" (General Ion Antonescu's life in Pitești); Rotaru, "Locul mareșalului Ion Antonescu în istoria militară a poporului român" (Marshal Ion Antonescu's place in the military history of the Romanians); Buzatu, "Reconstituiri din jurnalul de război al Mareșalului Antonescu" (Excerpts from Marshal Ion Antonescu's war diary).

30. Examples: Buzatu, "Mareșalul Antonescu: 'Cer să fiu condamnat la moarte'" (Marshal Antonescu: "I demand to be sentenced to death"); Ioan, "Ion Antonescu militar, politician, erou, martir sau victimă a egocentrismului său exacerbat" (Ion Antonescu: a military man, politician, hero, martyr, or victim of his exaggerated egocentrism); Teodorescu, "Ideea luptei pentru unitate națională la români în concepția mareșalului Ion Antonescu" (The idea of struggle for national unity of the Romanians in Marshal Antonescu's outlook); Duțu, "Mareșalul Ion Antonescu și problema reîntregirii naționale" (Marshal Antonescu and the question of national reunification); Iorga, "Din datorie și dragoste pentru națiune, prin culmile puterii și ale piramidei sociale, în fața plutonului de execuție" (Out of duty and love for the nation, through the heights of power and of social pyramid, facing the firing squad); *Mareșalul Ion Antonescu, erou național, martir al neamului românesc (1946–2000)* (Marshal Ion Antonescu, a national hero, martyr of the Romanian nation (1946–2000)); Augustin Deac, "Mărturii ale verticalității politice, morale și militare a Mareșalului Ion Antonescu" (Testimonies on the political, moral, and military verticality of Marshal Ion Antonescu); *Mareșalul Ion Antonescu la judecata istoriei. Contribuții, mărturii și documente* (Marshal Ion Antonescu at the judgment of history: contributions, testimonies, and documents); Buzatu, *Execuția mareșalului Ion Antonescu* (The execution of Marshal Ion Antonescu).

31. Examples: Pandea and Ardeleanu, "Mareșalul și evreii" (The Marshal and the Jews); Buzatu, "Mareșalul Antonescu și problema evreiască" (Marshal Antonescu and the Jewish question); Calafeteanu, "Regimul antonescian și emigrarea populației evreiești" (Antonescu's regime and the emigration of the Jewish population); Troncotă, "Antonescu îi deportează pe țigani în Transnistria" (Antonescu deported gypsies in Transnistria); Stoenescu, *Armata, Mareșalul și evreii* (The army, the Marshal, and the Jews).

32. *Mareșalul Ion Antonescu, erou, martir sau criminal de război? Un colocviu istoric virtual* (Marshal Ion Antonescu, a hero, a martyr, or a war criminal? A virtual colloquium of history).

33. Buzatu, "Mareșalul Ion Antonescu în fața morții: 'Dacă mor este pentru Bucovina și Basarabia. De ar fi să reîncep aș face la fel'" (Marshal Ion Antonescu facing death: "If I die, it is for Bukovina and Bessarabia. If I was to begin again, I would do the same").

34. Buzatu, "Mareșalul Antonescu: 'Cer să fiu condamnat la moarte,'" 58–59.

35. Moghior, "6 februarie 1944."

36. Rotaru, Burcin and Zodian, *Mareșalul Antonescu.*

37. Scurtu, "Stilul Ion Antonescu," 5–10.
38. Florin Șperlea, "1943. Mareșalul Antonescu ordonă," 72–74.
39. Hlihor, *Mareșalul Ion Antonescu*.
40. According to the 2015 opinion poll on the Holocaust in Romania and public perception of interethnic relations, those who said they were interested in the Holocaust (990 people of a sample of 1,016) also said that their main sources of information are Romanian television stations (58%), the internet (23%), and literature (16%). http://www.inshr-ew.ro/ro/files/proiecte/Sondaje/Sondaj_opinie-INSHR-iunie_2015.pdf.
41. For a critical review of Gheorghe Buzatu's public conduct, during postcommunism, on the Holocaust in Romania and the cult of Ion Antonescu, see Shafir, "Reabilitarea postcomunistă," 437–439; Shafir, *Între negare și trivializare prin comparație*, 89–91; Shafir, "Unacademic Academics," 948–951; International Commission, *Final Report*, 357–361.
42. A thorough analysis of his entire historiographical production may clarify issues about the quantity of his writings. For example, in the case of the magazines *Magazin istoric*, *Dosarele istoriei*, and *Historia*, I found three instances where Buzatu apparently published the same articles twice: "Mareșalul Antonescu și războiul din Est" (Marshal Antonescu and the war in the east), *Dosarele istoriei* 7 (1999): 53–55 is identical to "Mareșalul Antonescu și războiul din Est" (Marshal Antonescu and the war in the east), *Dosarele istoriei* 7 (2001): 45–47; "Mareșalul Ion Antonescu. Conducătorul statului și disputa politico-istoriografică în jurul personalității sale" (Marshal Ion Antonescu: head of state and the political-historiographical debate about his personality), *Dosarele istoriei* 3 (1999): 30–34 is copied, with minor changes, in "Mareșalul Antonescu aparține istoricilor, și numai istoricilor" (Marshal Antonescu belongs to historians, and only to historians), *Historia* 1 (2001): 74–78; and "Rebeliune? Lovitură de stat? Război civil? Diversiune a serviciilor secrete?" (Rebellion? Coup? Civil war? Diversion of the secret service?), *Dosarele istoriei* 3 (2000): 28–32 is identical to "Ce s-a întâmplat cu adevărat?" (What really happened?), *Historia* 1 (2006): 41–45.
43. Buzatu, introduction, ix.
44. Ibid., xv.
45. Buzatu, "O farsă stalinistă," 19–24.
46. Buzatu, "Mareșalul Antonescu și războiul din Est," 53–55.
47. Victor Eskenasy rightfully notes that a common feature of pro-Antonescu historians is their focus on historical documents as a methodological approach. Unfailingly, they refer to excerpts from documents, as their value is absolute. See Eskenasy, "Istoriografii și istorici," 329–330.
48. Buzatu and Mâță, "Mareșalul Ion Antonescu în fața eternității," 32. I believe Buzatu wrote this foreword alone, as a few years later, he used a large part of it in another article that was signed only by him.
49. Markham, *Rumania*. Buzatu quotes the Romanian version, *România sub jugul sovietic*, Bucharest, 1996.
50. Buzatu, "Erorile istoriei," 52–55.
51. Buzatu, "23 august 1944," 35–40.
52. Ibid., 40.
53. Buzatu, "Ion Antonescu, istoric," 14–15.
54. The ordinance came into force in March 2002 and Buzatu's article was published in June the same year, in an issue of *Dosarele istoriei* magazine focused on Ion Antonescu (almost all the articles were about him).

55. Buzatu, "Ion Antonescu, istoric," 14.
56. See Shafir, *Între negare și trivializare*, 101.
57. I used the fourth edition (2010). Constantiniu, *O istorie sinceră*.
58. Constantiniu, *O istorie sinceră*, 372.
59. Ibid., 377–378, 383–384.
60. Ibid., 399.
61. Ibid., 406–407.
62. Constantiniu, "Nu în beneficiul Rusiei," 52–53.
63. Constantiniu, *O istorie sinceră*, 392.
64. Ibid., 392.
65. Ibid., 546.
66. These articles are not necessarily historical analyses, but rather Constantiniu's public reactions to daily events or conflicts that also refer to historical issues. See *Dosarele istoriei* 7 (2002): 59–60; *Dosarele istoriei* 9 (2003): 3; *Dosarele istoriei* 4 (2004): 6–7; *Dosarele istoriei* 10 (2006): 1–2.
67. Giurescu, *România în al doilea război*.
68. Giurescu, *Istoria românilor*, 105–109.
69. Ibid., 111–120.
70. Ibid., 126. "Leader of the State" was the official title assumed by Antonescu.
71. Giurescu, *Istoria românilor*, 133.
72. See Giurescu, "Evreii din România" no. 10 (1997): 47–51; no. 11 (1997): 72–76.
73. Giurescu, *Istoria românilor*, 400–401.
74. Ibid., 419.
75. See Shafir, "Unacademic Academics," 944–945.
76. A revealing example is the use of the term *Holocaust* in volume 9 of *Istoria românilor*. According to the volume's index, in more than 1,000 pages the term *Holocaust* appears only four times. Two of these uses are abbreviations of quotes from the *Final Report* of the Wiesel Commission, one mention refers to the participation of ethnic Germans in the Holocaust, and only once is the term associated with Holocaust victims from Bessarabia and Northern Bukovina (Giurescu, *Istoria românilor*, 424).
77. *Dosarele istoriei* 6 (2002): 22–27.
78. Michael Shafir maintains that Scurtu's presence on that body "was due to the refusal by all members of the Romanian Academy to be involved." See Shafir, "Unacademic Academics," 950.
79. Scurtu, "Poziția lui Hitler," 46–47.
80. Scurtu, "Stilul Ion Antonescu," 5–10.
81. Scurtu, "Situația internațională a României," 45–47.
82. Scurtu, "'Cucoanele' mareșalului," 52–57.
83. Stoenescu, *Armata, Mareșalul și evreii*, 227–228.
84. Ibid., 176.
85. Stoenescu, "Erorile Mareșalului," 80–86.
86. Ibid., 80–86.
87. Boia, *România. Țară de frontieră*, 231–232. The same reference to the context is also made by Boia when discussing Antonescu's antisemitism. See Boia, *Istorie și mit*, 282–283.
88. Boia, *De ce este România altfel?*, 62.
89. Let me recall an important episode of the dynamics of Antonescu's public memory in postcommunism. In 2006 on the *Great Romanians* show on national television, Ion

Antonescu was one of the ten finalists. The format of the show had public figures making presentations on behalf of the "great Romanians" whom they represented. Adrian Cioroianu was nominated by producers to represent Antonescu, and he was widely criticized by the fans of the Marshal, who accused him of doing a disservice to Antonescu's image.

90. Cioroianu, *Visul lui Machiavelli*, 132–133.
91. Cioroianu, "Antonescu între Hitler și . . . ," 56–59.

REFERENCES

Antip, Constantin, and Constantin Nicolae. "Domnule Mareșal, ne găsim în divergență." *Magazin istoric* 3 (1967): 26–30.
Benjamin, Lya, ed. *Comisia Internațională pentru studierea Holocaustului în România. Documente*. Iași, Romania: Polirom, 2005.
Boia, Lucian. *De ce este România altfel?* Bucharest: Humanitas, 2012.
———. *Istorie și mit în conștiința națională*. Bucharest: Humanitas, 2011.
———. *România. Țară de frontieră a Europei*. Bucharest: Humanitas, 2007.
Buzatu, Gheorghe. "Erorile istoriei ori istoria ororilor?" *Dosarele istoriei* 6 (2004): 52–55, 58–64.
———. *Execuția mareșalului Ion Antonescu*. Iași, Romania: Demiurg, 2009.
———. "Introduction." In *Mareșalul Antonescu în fața istoriei*, vol. 1, Documente, mărturii și comentarii editate în colaborare cu Stela Cheptea, V.F. Dobrinescu, I. Saizu, vii–xlvi. Iași, Romania, 1990.
———. "Ion Antonescu, istoric al primului război mondial." *Dosarele istoriei* 6 (2002): 14–15.
———. "Mareșalul Antonescu: 'Cer să fiu condamnat la moarte.'" *Revista de istorie militară* 3–4 (1996): 58–59.
———. "Mareșalul Antonescu și problema evreiască." *Revista de istorie militară* 6 (1994): 22–27.
———. "Mareșalul Antonescu și războiul din Est." *Dosarele istoriei* 7 (1999): 53–55.
———. "Mareșalul Ion Antonescu în față morții: 'Dacă mor este pentru Bucovina și Basarabia. De ar fi să reîncep aș face la fel.'" In *Omagiu istoricului militar Jipa Rotaru*, 326–333. Constanța, 2001.
———. "O farsă stalinistă: 'Procesul' Antonescu." *Magazin istoric* 8 (1993):19–24.
———. "Reconstituiri din jurnalul de război al Mareșalului Antonescu." *Historia* 5 (2005): 14–20.
———. "23 august 1944: Metamorfozele unei lovituri de stat." *Dosarele istoriei* 1 (1999): 35–40.
Buzatu, Gheorghe, and Cezar Mâță. "Mareșalul Ion Antonescu în fața eternității. 'Dacă mor, este pentru Bucovina și Basarabia. De ar fi să reîncep, aș face la fel!'" *Dosarele istoriei* 12 (2000): 32–36.
Calafeteanu, Ion. "Regimul antonescian și emigrarea populației evreiești." *Revista istorică* 5–6 (1994): 463–478.
Carp, Cornel. "Perioada 'piteșteană' a generalului Ion Antonescu." *Revista de istorie militară* 5–6 (1997): 47–50.

Ceaușescu, Ilie. "Din cronica rezistenței antihitleriste. Armata și națiunea ca un singur om." *Magazin istoric* 6 (1989): 4–7; 7 (1989): 4–7; 8 (1989): 7–11.
Cioflâncă, Adrian. "'Gramatica disculpării' în istoriografia comunistă. Distorsionarea istoriei Holocaustului în timpul regimului Ceaușescu." *Yearbook of the "A. D. Xenopol" Institute of History* 42 (2005): 627–644. English version: "A 'Grammar of Exculpation' in Communist Historiography: Distortion of the History of the Holocaust under Ceaușescu." *The Romanian Journal of Political Science* 2 (2004): 29–46.
Cioroianu, Adrian. "Antonescu între Hitler și . . . Ceaușescu." *Dosarele istoriei* 6 (2002): 56–59.
———. *Visul lui Machiavelli*. Bucharest: Curtea Veche, 2010.
Constantiniu, Florin. " 'Nu în beneficiul Rusiei singure.' August '44: criza diplomației antonesciene." *Dosarele istoriei* 6 (2002): 52–53.
———. *O istorie sinceră a poporului român*. Bucharest: Editura Univers Enciclopedic Gold, 2010.
Deac, Augustin. "Mărturii ale verticalității politice, morale și militare a Mareșalului Ion Antonescu." *Mareșalul Ion Antonescu* 1 (2001): 29–39.
Deletant, Dennis. *Aliatul uitat al lui Hitler. Ion Antonescu și regimul său. 1940–1944*. Bucharest: Humanitas, 2010.
Dobrinescu, Valeriu F. *Plata și răsplata istoriei. Ion Antonescu, militar și diplomat (1914–1940)*. Iași, Romania: Editura Institutul European, 1994.
Drăgan, Iosif Constantin. *Antonescu. Mareșalul României și războaiele de reîntregire*. 4 vols. Venice: Nagard, 1986–1990.
Duțu, Alesandru. "Mareșalul Ion Antonescu și problema reîntregirii naționale." *Dacoromania* 4 (2000): 3–6.
Eskenasy, Victor. "Istoriografii și istorici pro și contra mitului Antonescu." In *Exterminarea evreilor români și ucraineni în perioada antonesciană*, edited by Randolph L. Braham, 313–346. Bucharest: Hasefer, 2002.
Giurescu, Dinu C. "Evreii din România (1939–1944)." *Magazin istoric* 10 (1997): 47–51; 11 (1997): 72–76.
———, coord. *Istoria românilor*, vol. 9, *România între anii 1940–1947*. Bucharest: Editura Enciclopedică, 2008.
———. *România în al doilea război mondial (1939–1945)*. Bucharest: ALL, 1999.
Hlihor, Constantin. *Mareșalul Ion Antonescu. Istoria mă va judeca*. Bucharest: Editura Academiei de Înalte Studii Militare, 1993.
International Commission on the Holocaust in Romania. *Final Report*. Edited by Tuvia Friling, Radu Ioanid, and Mihail E. Ionescu. Iași, Romania: Polirom, 2004.
Ioan, Georg. "Ion Antonescu militar, politician, erou, martir sau victimă a egocentrismului său exacerbat." *Dacoromanica, Alba Iulia* 2 (1997): 9; 3 (1997): 8.
Iorga, Gheorghe. "Din datorie și dragoste pentru națiune, prin culmile puterii și ale piramidei sociale, în fața plutonului de execuție." In *Omagiu istoricului Ioan Scurtu*, edited by Horia Dumitrescu, 594–611. Focșani: D.M. Press, 2000.
Karețki, A., and Maria Covaci. *Zile însângerate la Iași (28–30 iunie 1941)*. Foreword by Nicolae Minei. Bucharest: Editura Politică, 1978.
Mareșalul Ion Antonescu, erou, martir sau criminal de război? Un colocviu istoric virtual. Bucharest: Teșu, 2007.

Mareșalul Ion Antonescu, erou național, martir al neamului românesc (1946–2000).
  Bucharest: Europa Nova, 2000.
Mareșalul Ion Antonescu la judecata istoriei. Contribuții, mărturii și documente. Bucharest:
  Mica Valahie, 2002.
Markham, Reuben H. *Rumania under the Soviet Yoke*. Boston: Meador, 1949.
Moghior, Neculai. "16 februarie 1944. Mareșalul Antonescu constată și decide: 'Nu avem
  credința că am pierdut războiul.' " 'Să ne gândim serios asupra apărării teritoriului.' "
  Revista de istorie militară 5 (1992): 35–36; 6 (1992): 37–38; 1 (1993): 35–38; 2 (1993):
  31–35.
Muraru, Andrei. "Procesele criminalilor de război din Transnistria." Ph.D. diss.,
  Alexandru Ioan Cuza University, Iași, 2011.
Pandea, Adrian, and Eftimie Ardeleanu. "Mareșalul și evreii." *Revista de istorie militară* 5
  (1991): 17–18.
Roiban, Cristian. *Ideologie și istoriografie: protocronismul*. Timișoara, Romania: Editura
  Universității de Vest, 2014.
Roller, Mihail. *Istoria Republicii Populare România*. Bucharest: Editura de Stat Didactică
  și Pedagogică, 1952.
Rotaru, Jipa. "Locul mareșalului Ion Antonescu în istoria militară a poporului român."
  Mareșalul Ion Antonescu 2 (2001): 12–14.
Rotaru, Jipa, Octavian Burcin, and Vladimir Zodian. *Mareșalul Antonescu: "Am făcut
  război sfânt împotriva bolșevismului în campania anului 1941."* Oradea, Romania:
  Cogito, 1994.
Rotman, Liviu. "Memory of the Holocaust in Communist Romania: from Minimization
  to Oblivion." In *The Holocaust and Romania: History and Contemporary Significance*,
  edited by Mihail E. Ionescu and Liviu Rotman, 205–216. Bucharest: Institute for
  Political Studies of Defence and Military History, 2003.
Scurtu, Ioan. " 'Cucoanele' mareșalului Antonescu." *Historia* 10 (2005): 52–57.
———. "Poziția lui Hitler a fost decisivă." *Historia* 1 (2006): 46–47.
———. "Situația internațională a României în anii celui de-al doilea război mondial."
  Dosarele istoriei 7 (2001): 45–47.
———. "Stilul Ion Antonescu: 'Cine e recalcitrant e trădător.' " *Historia* 2 (2005): 5–10.
Shafir, Michael. *Între negare și trivializare prin comparație. Negarea Holocaustului în țările
  postcomuniste din Europa Centrală și de Est*. Iași, Romania: Polirom, 2002.
———. "Reabilitarea postcomunistă a mareșalului Antonescu: *Cui bono?*" In *Extermi-
  narea evreilor români și ucraineni în perioada antonesciană*, edited by Randolph L.
  Braham, 400–465. Bucharest: Hasefer, 2002.
———. "Unacademic Academics: Holocaust Deniers and Trivializers in post-
  Communist Romania." *Nationalities Papers* 42, 6 (2014): 942–964. Accessed
  March 11, 2016. http://dx.doi.org/10.1080/00905992.2014.939619
Simion, Aurică. "Nopțile bucureștene ale cuțitelor lungi (I)." *Magazin istoric* 12 (1968):
  60–68.
Șperlea, Florin. "1943. Mareșalul Antonescu ordonă: 'Jos burțile.' " *Historia* 7 (2007):
  72–74.
Stoenescu, Alex Mihai. *Armata, Mareșalul și evreii*. Bucharest: RAO, 1998.
———. "Erorile Mareșalului Ion Antonescu." *Historia* 1 (2002): 80–86.

Teodorescu, Aureliu. "Ideea luptei pentru unitate națională la români în concepția mareșalului Ion Antonescu." *Argessis* 8 (1999): 305–312.
Troncotă, Cristian. "Antonescu îi deportează pe țigani în Transnistria." *Magazin istoric* 3 (1997): 29–32.
Zaharia, Gheorghe. "6 septembrie 1940–23 august 1944. Anii cei mai întunecați." *Magazin istoric* 7 (1974): 25.
Zaharia, Gheorghe, and Ion Cupșa. *Participarea României la înfrângerea Germaniei naziste*. Bucharest: Editura Politică, 1985.

Chapter Eight

RETHINKING PERPETRATORS, BYSTANDERS, HELPERS/RESCUERS, AND VICTIMS
A Case Study of Students' Perceptions

Adina Babeş

Public memory may be defined as a relationship with the past expressed in the public space. It finds its expression in the institutionalized elements that connect it to the public space, such as memorials, prevailing discourses, books, courses, and so on. This research relates to the complex issues that the Holocaust, as well as other genocides, might be caused by situations still present in contemporary society, including the fragility of political and social institutions and society's responsibility to its people, all in the context of post-1989 Romania and its road toward democratization.

In discussions about the Holocaust, debate inevitably turns to the subject of the masterminds of this phenomenon in every country where it took place, including Adolf Hitler in Germany and Ion Antonescu in Romania, to name just two. The discussion rarely proceeds beyond those figures, their roles, and their actions. However, in addition to them, from the officers who gave orders and supervised the killings to the bureaucrats who never saw any victims throughout their Nazi careers, from people who watched their neighbors being taken from their homes to those who sat and enjoyed small talk in coffee shops, from those who could have helped but did not to friends or total strangers who risked their lives to help others and sometimes were even killed for that, from babies to old women and men, there is a vast range of perpetrators, helpers/rescuers, bystanders, and victims, each with their own roles, actions, stories, and fates during the Holocaust.

One of the first books I came across many years ago as a young researcher was Raul Hilberg's *Perpetrators, Victims, Bystanders: The Jewish Catastrophe, 1933–1945*, which was an eye-opener on the subject of different types of Holocaust actors. Since then, several surveys have been published on the topic of perceptions of the Holocaust in Romania, including the perception of Ion Antonescu's role. This study follows a research idea that connects these two issues, namely, how people perceive categories of Holocaust actors, including perpetrators, helpers/rescuers, bystanders, and victims, as well as their roles, their actions, and their lives during those years.

The target group of my research is students enrolled in social sciences and humanities programs at universities who are being exposed to the topic of the Holocaust and related subjects in different ways—through courses, lectures, exhibitions, commemorative events—and according to various approaches—history, sociology, political science, culture, literature, and so on. Using focus groups as a qualitative research method for this study, I examined how young students think about and rethink Holocaust categories such as victims, rescuers, bystanders, and perpetrators in terms of their behaviors and attitudes, how they comprehend the circumstances of the decision-making processes, and how they connect each of the categories to the theoretical model developed in the first section of this study. My research shows how the institutionalization of an element in public memory affects attitudes and behaviors of the group to whom it is oriented, as well as their understanding of a past event such as the Holocaust. Specifically, I address how young people understand how personal choices and changing circumstances can affect personal decisions and choices, by referring to the established categories of people involved in the Holocaust.

In the first section, I construct a theoretical model for my research. Each subsection presents a category of Holocaust actors, focusing on the different types it contains and their sociopsychological and personality characteristics. I develop these theoretical portraits with references to the most important international literature on the subject and on the basis of research that addresses the topic from a sociopsychological perspective. The theoretical model is general, rather than focusing specifically on any particular cases of the Holocaust (e.g., in Germany, in Romania).

The second section is dedicated to the research design, namely the research background and research framework. I discuss what led me to conduct this study, and I present the qualitative research method and how it was implemented, with information about the participants, tools, and preliminary analysis. The literature I discuss in this section deals with the theory, practice, and analysis of focus groups.

The third section presents my conclusions based on the analysis of focus groups transcripts. In this analysis I followed the theoretical model I outlined in the first section, considering the types identified within each category of Holocaust actors as well as their sociopsychological and personality characteristics. I used these theoretical portraits to present each category and the students' perceptions of it. I support these conclusions by making reference to direct quotes from the transcripts.

The fourth and last section discusses the final conclusions of the research and this study.

Theoretical Framework

The Perpetrator

It is difficult to understand what led a significant number of people to take part in activities of hatred and destruction during the Second World War— people who accepted murder as part of their regular jobs, had power over others' lives, and decided whether someone lived or died. According to historian Benjamin Valentino, the population of the average country contains 2 to 15 percent perpetrators.[1] Other research findings on the authoritarian traits within a population suggest a higher figure, of 20 percent.[2]

Although it is difficult to reconstruct the background and evolution of a perpetrator, some scholars suggest several hypotheses. Perpetrators seem to have grown up in punitive, authoritarian houses with intransigent child-rearing practices.[3] Perpetrators develop into persons with specific social and psychological traits: conventionalism/conformity; difficulties in distinguishing right from wrong; simplistic thinking, relative closed-mindedness, and fear of diversity and new experiences; submission to authority; aggression; specific law-and-order concerns.⁴ The perpetrator has an underdeveloped personal identity and an overdeveloped social identity; he identifies his feelings, needs, and thoughts with those of the groups he belongs to.⁵

In his book, Raul Hilberg introduces the different types of actors within Nazi society and its apparatus that fall under the perpetrator category. For Hilberg, the perpetrator was not a single man or a single woman, but a whole regime that encompassed all the men and women who built it and conducted activities within it. From Adolf Hitler himself, the supreme architect of the operations, to a soldier who delivered a letter, everyone who operated the Nazi death machine was a perpetrator.

Although the perpetrator portrait developed by Hilberg is mostly drawn from the German Nazi regime, the destruction of the Jews was a Europe-wide phenomenon, involving non-German authorities in other countries as well. Most of these countries copied the principles and structures of the Nazi system, which allowed the implementation of anti-Jewish actions.⁶ The perpetrator in the Nazi regime acted mostly on the basis of internalized values and beliefs, irrespective of the physical presence of an authority figure. The crimes and killings continued for many months and years.⁷

The Nazi establishment developed the process of destruction on three bases: no element of Jewish life was to be overlooked in this process; the disruption of Jewish–non-Jewish relations was to be carried out with maximum care for non-Jews; and attention would be given to the psychological repercussions for perpetrators.⁸ The apparatus for this process included government ministries, security services, churches, and other organizations.⁹ The Nazi destruction network built a new apparatus that institutionally filled all the gaps to serve its purposes. Several ministries and new organizations and institutions were created that offered new jobs to new civil servants to work closely with the established ones.¹⁰ This apparatus model was also found in Romania, serving the same purposes and operating in the same horrendous manner.

Moreover, the Nazi machinery of destruction involved representatives of many trades and professions who at first glance would not seem to have played any role in a death machine. Yet bookkeepers played their part in the financial spoliation of the Jews, and lawyers made sure everything proceeded according to the law when implementing the anti-Jewish measures. Physicians also played a considerable part in the Nazi regime, in carrying out sterilizations, euthanasias, and medical experiments, in establishing ghettos, in making selections for exterminations camps, and so on.[11]

The perpetrators' professional motivations and drives were grounded on their psychological attributes, which was seen in the way they assumed their roles and carried out their activities. They included zealots, for whom everything depended on them; perfectionists, who developed the standards and considered themselves role models in implementing them; and volunteers, who found their purpose in anti-Jewish activities.[12]

Immediately after Adolf Hitler came to power in September 1933, the director of the Institute of Social Research in Frankfurt left his position, and a few days later, he and some of his colleagues boarded a train to Switzerland. For this departure, they relied on studies they had conducted earlier that showed that Social Democratic workers had personalities and beliefs consistent with support for fascism,[13] including an authoritarian character that "behaves respectfully to superiors but dominates and punishes inferiors, despises tenderness, follows a cult of manliness, expresses satisfaction with the violence they had inflicted during the war, and tends to project and see hostile intent outside the self."[14]

Although it is difficult to construct a clear and concise personality portrait of a perpetrator, studies conducted to date suggest several traits that perpetrators have in common. Obedience played a major part in the bureaucracy. The members of the SS obeyed, and they psychologically and socially fit into the Nazi structure, for there was no contradiction between their personal values and their actions. They were not necessarily antisemitic when they entered the scene, but they encountered authorities they viewed as legitimate, and trusted their actions.[15] Ethnocentrism is another characteristic of a perpetrator personality. Prejudiced beliefs play a small role in motivating behavior toward a member of a minority group in short-term situations, but they are relevant in many different situations over a longer period of time. Research shows that what was more significant were tendencies toward obedience and conformity.[16] Poor education is another factor. Previous research on antisemitic attitudes shows that lack of or poor formal education does influence the degree to which people have antisemitic attitudes. Education is a social experience that exposes people to tolerant and liberal environments and to individuals from different backgrounds.[17] Finally, frustration is a basis for, and leads to, aggression. When aggression cannot be directed toward the source of frustration, it is displaced onto available targets that are more available. Aggressive people often are encountered among the perpetrators of mass atrocities.[18]

The perpetrators saw the Nazi Holocaust victims not as fully human beings, but as a subhuman species; this was based on centuries of antisemitic rhetoric. They subhumanized the other by assigning jobs and activities that degraded the individuals; by starvation and constant hunger taken to extremes; and by making the victims dirty and malodorous and depriving them of the appearance of a worthy self.[19]

Another important dimension of the perpetrator profile is lack of moral consistency. The Nazis abandoned their values very easily and put their careers first, and then acted not primarily out of hatred but for professional advancement.[20] Given the general immorality in the German state at the time, the perpetrators did not see Nazi institutions as existing outside of a shared morality, and therefore did not question their moral accountability. Their responsibility was a technical one, of carrying out their assigned projects, so that the individual perpetrator became one among many.[21] Newcomers would not question things that seemed outside the shared moral norms, as they would not know their way around and would rely on peers in the learning and integration process. Just because they exist, institutions are seen as legitimate, and the process of socialization reinforces that.[22]

Another aspect of the perpetrator's activity is the relationship between responsibility and intent. The moral climate of the Holocaust, explained by antisemitic and propaganda discourses, proved to be a powerful determinant that led many perpetrators to see the killings as a duty and a virtue. The sense of duty was developed over time, from the first economic measures against the Jews up to the concentration camps. The escalation of measures against the Jews was not an element out of contingency.[23]

The Bystander

In any population, the percentage of bystanders is somewhere between 50 and 60 percent. A bystander is someone who is present in a situation or event but refrains from becoming involved; the bystander also may have perpetrator traits.[24] Bystanders are usually characterized by comparison with the two categories they stand between: the perpetrators and the rescuers. They are more developed on several levels than the perpetrators, but less emotionally developed than the rescuers. Their traits are determined by the passivity they show at certain times.[25]

A bystander neither drives the action, nor is subject to it; he or she has or assumes the role of a witness by simply being present and then narrating what happened afterwards.[26] Bystanders are vulnerable to social norms, and they choose their actions as the situation dictates. They have a moderate stance and develop sophisticated defense mechanisms when compared to perpetrators in similar situations.[27] Bystanders who come from dysfunctional homes reflect this background in their decisions to remain passive, while those from more functional homes might temporarily help and rescue.[28]

Bystanders have a desire to fit in and conform to external circumstances, and they comply with demands from the authorities. Highly conforming bystanders do not tolerate too much change, and they lack emotional development. The "ordinary Nazis" did not have deep feelings, emotional attachments, or thoughts; they simply followed directions.[29] Bystanders are also confronted with a variety of options: they might intervene to change the course of events, they might bear responsibility for the events, they might be apathetic, torn with anxiety, or they might feel powerless or fearful.[30] They react to violence in three ways: they authorize the violence, they become immune to the routinization of it, and they accept the dehumanization of the victims.[31]

During the Second World War, several hundred million non-Jewish people lived in areas controlled or influenced by the Nazi regime. Some of them did not interact with Jews; others were neighbors of the victims and saw the disappearance of Jews and the appearance of Jews' goods and property. However, they refrained from talking about it, they chose to look away, and they chose to ask no questions; nevertheless, the event could not be completely ignored, and news of it reverberated throughout Europe. As the war advanced, many bystanders became increasingly preoccupied with their own lives and war-related shortages.[32]

Much of the fascination with the Holocaust relates to attempts to understand the bystanders. People feel outrage toward the perpetrators and solidarity with the victims, but it is the bystanders who make up the majority in a society, and they make up the majority of the actors involved in the Holocaust as well.[33] Most of the bystanders during the Holocaust were "gainers" who played their parts after the Jewish enterprises were liquidated, gaining access to markets and distribution and taking over the apartments the Jews left behind after ghettoization and deportations.[34]

It is possible for individuals to shape through the course of their actions the institutions in which they act, and thus to contribute to the life of those institutions.[35] Institutions helped people who held leadership positions in the Holocaust to strengthen their hold on society through the accommodation of injustice, which reduced individuals' reactions against it. They created the illusion of a stable society that provided a normal life for the citizens of the country, and the impression that everything around them was normal. If the schools had been closed down, if the banks had collapsed, or if the civil service had stopped functioning, the bystanders would have been confronted with a new reality and possible alternatives.[36] Institutions sustained the moral blindness of bystanders through the idea that their work was for the collective good, which in turn allowed them to leave the major decisions about society to the state and institutional leaders.[37]

Any discussion about bystanders must emphasize the fact that the moral duty to act lies more with the individual than with institutions. Thus the Nuremberg trials established the principle of individual responsibility. However, moral action or inaction is determined by society and is a product of socialization, for it refers to values that are collectively supported. Still, this should not preclude the ethical independence of an individual, for the responsibility for the behavior of an individual is ultimately his or hers.[38]

The Nazi regime is seen as a totalitarian space built on exclusion, prejudice, and psychological distance. It fostered hatred and division among different groups within the population and society, and gave people a seductive sense of power over others, as they no longer felt responsible for what was inflicted on society's "outsiders." It created parallel worlds for the victims and bystanders and developed a language spoken only to the former. It divided the world of the bystander in two: the public sphere, where the individual conformed to the new political norms, and the private sphere, where the individual sought refuge. Still, this withdrawal was not necessarily tantamount to opposition. This "internal emigration," seen as a conscious ignorance, not only helped preserve individual sanity but also offered a path of resistance during the Nazi regime, which fostered an inability to connect with the victim.[39]

Prejudice is another element that contributes to making one a bystander. Individuals develop a definition of "the Other" based on color, gender, race, religion, or ethnicity, and that simple fact is dehumanizing. In Nazi society, all the groups that were victims—Jews, Roma, homosexuals, the mentally ill, the physically disabled, African natives, persons with hereditary illnesses—were targeted by the Nazi propaganda as representing a social and biological menace to the healthy "Aryan" society.[40] Other elements are racism, which developed at the time of the emergence of the modern nation-state, and the general historical development in Western culture that we call "modernity." The new racial antisemitism developed at the time when secularism and political liberalization eradicated the barriers between ethnic and religious groups. The gates to secularization were opened, and societies reacted to this by trying to prevent the full assimilation of the Jewish people and by replacing Judaism with Jewishness. Antisemites embraced this in their modern racist discourse, thus engendering a discourse that also influenced the bystanders.[41]

The very position of a bystander means that he has not been singled out as a victim, while his position on the sideline and his silence means he has joined the persecutors. One of the hallmarks of the Holocaust is the distance created between victims and bystanders, between people who had previously been neighbors, friends, and colleagues. One might mention indifference here; yet, we cannot use the term indifference when speaking of those who enthusiastically applauded, sang, and shouted during marches. Moreover, for some, indifference became a word that masked other reactions, or a lack of reaction.[42] When discussing bystanders, one should not look at their antisemitism or prejudice in isolation, but in the context of the other factors that determined it, such as apathy, anomy, and brutality.[43]

Silence is linked to indifference during the Holocaust: the silence as absence of G-d, the silence of victims, bystanders, and perpetrators, the silence that fell over any discussion of the Holocaust in its immediate aftermath. The silence of bystanders during the Holocaust again brings up the idea of parallel worlds. Walls and barbed wire were not the only things that separated the parallel worlds of the victims and bystanders; barriers were also psychological and emotional. Victims, perpetrators, and bystanders did not live in the same world anymore, but in parallel worlds.[44]

The Holocaust prompted many questions concerning the behavior of the actors involved. When it comes to bystanders, one of these questions concerns the human being as an ethical being. The bystander remained passive during the events, allowing the Holocaust to be implemented, and remained passive after it ended, thus contributing to building a world in which the victims continued to die.[45] The existing literature on the subject highlights some factors that formed the basis of the ethical failures of perpetrators and bystanders: antisemitism, nationalism, traditions of subservience to authority. However, all of these are general factors, while action needs to be regarded as individual, in its moment of "exclusion" or "embrace." An "ethical society" is a society in which culture and institutions reflect an ethics of care for one another, and an individual and general refusal to tolerate and perform acts of injustice against individuals. The questions raised by the Holocaust were more concerned with moral action than with political action, for the realms of morality are the ultimate ones.[46]

The Rescuer, the Helper

It is difficult to define the rescuer because it is difficult to define a helping behavior, especially with regard to its motivations. According to some researchers, a person might be motivated by a desire feel less guilty or to see him- or herself in a better light; others connect their motivations to issues of culture, religiosity, or morality.[47] The exact number of rescuers during the Holocaust is not really known. Yad Vashem, the institution honoring those who risked their lives in order to save Jews, estimates 20,000, but the number of bona fide helpers could be higher, even double.[48]

Rescuers come from mentally healthier homes where punishment was less physical and authoritarian and conflicts were reasoned out; they are emotionally more evolved. They typically had closer relations with their parents, and the values they received were universal. Their homes were mostly nonreligious, and rescuers could be considered as postreligious.[49] None of the studies that have been carried out on the subject of rescuers has developed a standard profile of a rescuer, and those that studied rescuers have so far been unable to establish specific factors that can predict people's behaviors. However, most agree that a sentiment of empathy, principles of justice, and the sense that their own behavior can make a difference pushes people toward rescuing behaviors.[50]

Most rescuers did not provide help on a large scale, and their help usually took the form of a last-minute solution, after they had already demonstrated passivity. Those who helped can be grouped into two categories: those who offered occasional, transitory, and relatively risk-free help, by warning or giving information, or providing victims with small amounts of food, clothing, or even money; and those who provided more durable help, and even shelter, over a longer period of time.[51] The helpers could be relatives, friends, former business associates, colleagues, employers, or employees of the victims, or they could be people opposed to the Nazi regime, motivated by political and humanitarian reasons—Good Samaritans who would characterize their own actions as ordinary or natural. The Righteous among the Nations belong in this second category.[52]

In the context of the Holocaust, the issue of rescuing must consider three factors: Nazi Germany, the Jews—both in the sphere of Nazi influence and outside it, and all the other nations, persons, and institutions operating in Nazi Germany.[53] The first phase, from 1933 until 1937 to 1938, contains the hallmarks of the Holocaust, but they did not prompt many opposing or discouraging reactions. The persecution of the Jews was influenced by the global political situation as well as the specific situation in each country, the economic and domestic problems in each country, and the relations between the Jews and non-Jews. The antisemitism exhibited by the larger population occurred in a very specific moment.[54] The second phase, 1938 to 1941, introduced something that people could not have imagined or expected, as plans for deportation, exterminations, and forced movements of Jews were underway. During this phase, there were individual and organized rescue efforts made to prevent the implementation of these plans. In this new context, any public or personal decisions did not take into consideration norms or conventions; these decisions meant choosing between life and death, for themselves or for others.[55] As the war continued, it became clear that within the sphere of German rule or influence the choice was not between good and evil, but between greater or lesser evils, and it involved survival in all cases. During this period, the chances of saving oneself or of being saved were very low, and the Jews were more vulnerable to death than ever before.[56]

The evolution of rescuing has several stages: helping in order to receive the help back; helping in order to be considered a good person, helping out of a sense of social responsibility and good citizenship, and helping to maintain internalized utilitarian values and to contribute to upholding universal, just, and impartial values.[57] Rescuers tend to be more emotionally developed than bystanders and thus have a more altruistic urge. They exhibit more autonomy and independence, resistance to enculturation, democratic values, acceptance of others, spontaneity, honesty, a tendency not to take others for granted and to appreciate what they receive, closer relationships with a few friends, and social and social justice awareness.[58]

Many rescuers helped for motives that seem to defy reason, and thus showed courage. They also displayed moral development, as they proved themselves capable of complex judgments and decision making that took into account not only the individuals but also the social constraints of the context.[59] The rescuers had the ability to see each person as an individual, and not as part of a group or collective. Most rescuers reacted spontaneously, providing simple responses to requests for help. However, at times, empathy with Jewish victims transformed into identification, as some of those who provided help were influenced by some Jewish family connection, such as Jewish spouses or partners.[60]

The Victim

The victim represents the object of genocide, as a whole or as an individual, part of a marked category (a nation, a tribe, a religious sect) that is singled out for destruction. The objective of a genocide is met by undermining the will and resilience of the victims, by terrorizing them to surrender to the perpetrators' power and to accept of their orders, and by depriving them of the resources necessary for continuing the struggle.[61]

This takes place in several steps. A first step is "sealing off" the victims, and this process is twofold, entailing on the one hand reducing to a minimum the possibility of outside interference in the bureaucratic process and decisions of the genocide, and on the other reducing the ability of the targeted group to ask for and secure help from authorities or other institutions. These two conditions combine to leave the targeted group on its own. The next effective step in this process entails psychologically removing the victims from daily life, separating them from the rest of the population by different discriminatory measures, and emphasizing the targeted group's uniqueness.[62] The Nazi bureaucracy psychologically removed the Jews from the society, creating a situation whereby all the state's political and social institutions refused to aid them, physically removed them by placing them in ghettos, and finally deported them with the aim of excluding them from all aspects of the Aryan society the Nazis envisaged.[63]

Another step in the extermination process was the "death vs. survival" game, where staying alive was the most valuable prize. The victims had very few choices during the Holocaust; they could choose only between greater and lesser evils. The Nazi bureaucracy developed a context in which the victims were left with the impression that something could be saved. However, this was only a trap designed by the state institutions to have better control over the group and its individual members by determining the options left available to Jews who sought to obtain their reclassification and be exempted from deportation. The perversity of the Nazi bureaucracy is demonstrated by the fact that even the victims, in their desperation for survival, accepted and were accomplices in the design and process of this selective survival.[64]

Holocaust victims were faced with life-and-death situations involving exceptional choices in an exceptional environment. The self-preservation instinct was taken to the extreme in the hope for survival.[65] Moreover, the Holocaust brought to the surface two types of rationalities, that of the victims and that of their actions, which did not depend only on the victims themselves but also on the context. The context was fully controlled by the perpetrators. Therefore, the rationality insofar as the victim was concerned was just a series of strokes of luck, which might continue to work or might destroy them at any point.[66]

In the context of the Holocaust, the term *victim* includes several categories: the concentration camp inmates who did not survive; survivors of the same camps; and individuals who were affected by the experience of those camps but never imprisoned there.[67] However, and unfortunately, there are also many other categories that fall within the scope of the Holocaust victim.

The refugees are a category of Holocaust victims. Around half a million Jews left Germany and other countries that had initiated discriminatory measures before the Final Solution delivered its final blow. They did not experience the full catastrophe, but only some anti-Jewish actions. The people belonging to this category included those who had some money or were foreign Jews, Zionists who left for Palestine, intellectuals who lost their positions when the Nazis came to power and had time to leave, and students and young professionals who could no longer see a future in their country of residence.[68]

Another category of people who suffered during the Holocaust includes those who were in mixed marriages. In Western Europe, following the process of emancipation, Jews had entered into mixed marriages. There were not many of these marriages in the central and eastern parts of Europe. In the 1930s the mixed marriages were either privileged or unprivileged; a privileged mixed marriage was less observant of the Jewish aspects of life, including those related to the couple itself, the household, and the children's education.[69]

Children are the most dreadful category of victims. Around 1.5 million children died during the Holocaust. Their situations followed their parents', and included four phases: the early regime of restrictions; the life in the ghettos; the selection for deportations and shootings and finally the killings. During the first phase, children's fates were in the hands of their mothers and fathers. They lost their living spaces, access to food and sanitation, and access to all levels of schooling. In Eastern Europe, ghettoization was a question of life and death, and the highest death rates in the ghettos were among small children.[70]

Other categories of Jewish victims were the advantaged, the strugglers, and the dispossessed. There was inequality at the time of the Holocaust in every Jewish community: while some managed to salvage some form of comfort, others starved, and another subcategory lingered at death's doorstep. This phenomenon of socioeconomic stratification reappeared in the ghettos and even in the concentration camps, and was an indicator of the scale of vulnerabilities.[71]

Another category is those who refused to adjust, those who did not accept their pain and humiliation or the price of cooperating with the perpetrators or their leadership. People in this category chose suicide, hiding, escape, or resistance.[72]

The survivors represent the last category I mention in these pages. Over one million Jews who had lived under direct German control or in countries allied with Germany were still alive after May 1945. The largest part of this group consists of those who had not been engulfed in the final phase of the destruction process. For example, the Jewish communities of Romania and Bulgaria were spared by last-minute decisions of their governments. Another group in this category includes those who hid, resisted, or adopted disguises. A third group includes those who were incarcerated at the last moment.[73]

Survival was dependent on the health and physical traits of the people in the camps. The survivors were usually relatively young, teenaged to thirties, and in good health. Social characteristics could also help—a strong determination to live was a psychological trait that contributed to survival. However, the Jewish people who were liberated at the end of the war suffered a loss, be it material or human. Some of them had lasting physical illnesses or disabilities as a result of the experience in the camps. Most of them could not conceive what had happened to them and continue living normal lives. The countries where they resettled could not provide the necessary psychological and social supports for a fast and smooth recovery. Thousands of children were orphans, and men and women lost their spouses and children. Others did not have any place to return to, and so they remained in concentration camps or in refugee camps in Cyprus until Israel was established on May 14, 1948.[74]

Research Design

Research Background

As mentioned above, my interest in carrying out research on people's perception of Holocaust categories, roles, and actions was inspired by several surveys published on the topic of perceptions of the Holocaust in Romania.

In 2015 the Elie Wiesel National Institute for the Study of the Holocaust in Romania published the results of its survey on perceptions of the Holocaust and interethnic relations in Romania. Conducted in May and June of the same year on adult citizens of legal age residing in Romania, following a face-to-face interview research method, the survey revealed how the ethnic Romanian population related to the most representative ethnic minorities living in Romania, with Romanian citizenship (e.g., Roma, Jews, Hungarians), as well as their perceptions of the Holocaust.

The survey revealed that 73 percent of the respondents had heard about the Holocaust, with the likelihood of this being influenced by their level of education and their area of residence (rural or urban). The responses showed that people associated the Holocaust with "the extermination of Jews during the Second World War," "Nazi concentration camps," "gas chambers," and "mass deportations." Most of the interviewees (73 percent) located the Holocaust in Germany, and half of them located it in other countries as well. However, only 25 percent of them agreed that the Holocaust took place in Romania, too. When that issue was explored in further detail, the Holocaust in Romania was mainly associated with the "Jews' deportation to Nazi concentration camps" (80 percent), "expropriation and forced evacuation from homes" (49 percent), and "mass executions" (47 percent). Nazi Germany was considered by most respondents to bear the responsibility for the beginning of the Holocaust in Romania (69 percent); 19 percent assigned blame to the Ion Antonescu regime and government. However, when addressing only the internal factors, the respondents indicated that those responsible were the Legionary Movement (57 percent) and Ion Antonescu, as the leader of the country (54 percent). Forty percent of the persons interviewed considered that the Holocaust was equally consequential to other tragic historical events in Romania, with only 15 percent considering it as more severe. The national Holocaust Remembrance Day was acknowledged by only one quarter of the respondents, and out of 1,016 people interviewed, only four could correctly indicate its date. People get their information on this subject from television, the internet, and literature on the subject, and only 12 percent showed interest in the subject. However, 32 percent of the respondents considered that in Romania there is more discussion about this subject than there should be. Ion Antonescu, the country's ruler during the Romanian Holocaust, is considered a "great patriot" (54 percent) and "great strategist" (52 percent). Forty-six percent of the respondents considered that he is "responsible for crimes against the Roma people." However, over one third of the respondents could not make any evaluation of the personality of Ion Antonescu, which suggested a lack of knowledge of his actions and the events of those years. Regarding Ion Antonescu's decision making in relation with the Holocaust, over 50 percent of the answers indicated subordination to Nazi Germany and the state of war Romanian found itself in as explanatory factors. Regarding the Jewish population, over one quarter of the respondents associated it with the communist movement.[75]

Research Framework (Method, Participants, Tools, Preliminary Analysis)

Inspired by the results of this survey, I developed a qualitative research study on the topic of the perception of the Holocaust in Romania among bachelor's and master's degree students in the fields of social sciences and humanities. As a methodology, I conducted focus groups in order to identify their perception of the Holocaust in Romania.

I conducted four focus groups, totaling twenty-two participants. Fourteen were undertaking bachelor's degree studies, while eight were concluding their graduate studies at master's level. Eight people were pursuing studies in disciplines in the humanities, mainly foreign languages, cultural studies, and history, while fourteen were enrolled in social science programs, including political science and sociology. Concerning their knowledge about the Holocaust in general and the Holocaust in Romania in particular, all respondents were enrolled in university programs that offer classes or even courses on the topic of the Holocaust and related subjects. However, for my research I did not consider only graduates of these courses.

The interview questions followed the principle of proceeding from the general to the more specific,[76] while the questionnaire consisted of two parts: introductory questions[77] and key questions[78] in the first part, and concluding questions in the second part.[79] All the data provided by the focus groups was recorded. The interviews were fully transcribed and edited.[80] The responses were organized according to the structure of the questionnaire, containing introductory, transitional, key and final questions. The names of the respondents were replaced by the letter *I* followed by a randomly assigned number from 1 to 22. Subsequently, each topic was structured according to the pattern and themes that could be identified in the answers, and the most relevant quotes were selected for the research report itself. The final step consisted in writing the report and presenting it to the public in these pages.[81]

The context of the data was analyzed following a semantic content analysis, namely, the assertion analysis, focusing on why certain persons and their actions were characterized in a particular way.[82] The data was also analyzed by taking into consideration the theoretical background developed in the first sections and subsections of this chapter.

RESEARCH RESULTS

The Perpetrator

And when I visited Auschwitz-Birkenau, and I saw those empty cans with Zyklon B, I thought: a human being took such a can, took a can opener, opened that can and used its content to kill so many people. For me that was unreal. (I.6)

The leaders (Hilberg's work) are one of the most discussed and debated categories of perpetrators. The people who participated in the focus groups knew about Adolf Hitler in Germany and Ion Antonescu in Romania, and they considered them the most important responsible actors in determining the Jews' fate during those years.

However, the respondents did not place all the responsibility on their shoulders. The respondents considered the Germans guilty as well, at least for embracing the Nazi ideas: "I thought of Adolf Hitler, but he was not the only one responsible; he was the leader of that movement, but the entire German nation became interested in the idea of having a pure Aryan race. That all Germans from all over the place would be gathered and become the masters of the world. Adolf Hitler was the mastermind of this idea, but the Germans embraced it, and so 6 million Jews were killed, and not only Jews, but other nations as well" (I.9).

The assignment of guilt and responsibility to the German leader can be found in all the discussions on this topic, including when the respondents touched upon the subject of the responsibility for the Romanian Holocaust. Even though the debate was replete with information on the ideological and political developments that anticipated the Holocaust in Romania, the discussion about Ion Antonescu as a perpetrator often referenced Adolf Hitler's influence over his actions. The discussions introduced the idea that Ion Antonescu was a puppet in the hands of Adolf Hitler, and consequently he was not fully responsible for his actions: "I think this came with the partnership between Ion Antonescu and Adolf Hitler, when Ion Antonescu was forced to follow certain orders coming from Adolf Hitler, as Benito Mussolini did in Italy. Initially, Romania had a more reluctant attitude to those methods of killing Jews proposed by Adolf Hitler. The hate within the Romanian society wasn't as developed; it was rather imposed, dictated" (I.12); "Ok, poor Ion Antonescu, poor man, he just took over this idea and transmitted it further. I do not see him as an initiator of the antisemitic idea. He was simply indoctrinated" (I.2); "Ion Antonescu did not want to send Jews and Roma to the camps in Transnistria, he simply had to do this to get some benefits from Adolf Hitler, and to have German help in the war. This was not because there were some antisemitic ideas in Romania" (I.1). Less than one third of the respondents considered Ion Antonescu to be a perpetrator acting out of his own convictions and without any influence from Adolf Hitler. Few reasons were provided for this idea: "Ion Antonescu's own initiative that did not receive any direct order from Adolf Hitler, although he was his ally" (I.20); "Ion Antonescu and the political system at the time" (I.20); "The authorities put in practice Ion Antonescu's orders" (I.12).

Still, when discussing this subject, there is a split between the Holocaust years and the decades before those years. Less than one third of the respondents mentioned a continuity between the extreme right leaders who had initiated and developed antisemitic ideas during the interwar period in Romania and Ion Antonescu, the leader who implemented those ideas: "I would say this started a little bit earlier. I don't know when exactly Ion Antonescu and Adolf Hitler shook hands and said they would do this, but there was a period of time when the Legionary Movement ruled the country, and their leaders initiated and recorded those ideas during the 1930s and even earlier. They had anti-Jewish ideas" (I.13).

The role of the political establishment and the authorities, identified as another important aspect by Raul Hilberg, also generated a discussion, though not as lengthy as the previous one, and the split between the time periods was again a factor. The respondents identified the legionary ideology and movement as bearing the political responsibility for what happened, and the army generals and their actions as bearing the military responsibility: "I think there are many more responsible actors; a first would be the way the Legionary Movement managed to handle this hate against the Jews, and this took much more time than the Holocaust itself, and it was conditioned by the way the Legionary Movement was able to grow during the interwar period. Along with this, it could be the context; Romania was a participant in the war, and its generals, while engaging in military actions, were busy organizing and instigating persons to commit crimes. I don't know, but I am sure there are many more responsible persons" (I.7). The authorities directly involved in this process were also discussed, and the responders debated the different roles they had during those years. Moreover, those who were not directly involved in the killings but were responsible for the bureaucratic aspects of implementing the killing policies were mentioned as well: "There were two kinds of criminals: those who effectively participated in the war, the criminals, and those who only signed off decisions. This last category could do this with much ease, as they were not directly involved, and everything was much more impersonal" (I.6).

This detachment, referred to by Joel E. Dimsdale, was also mentioned by the respondents in reference to the Romanian case, and the idea of Nazi Germany implementing anti-Jewish measures reappeared. However, this was linked with the idea of German responsibility for implementing the Holocaust in Romania, and was brought into discussion to further emphasize this responsibility: "When the Germans ordered measures against the Jews in Romania, this was seen as a detachment, because there was no direct link with them. The fact that this order was given from a distance, and the fact that they did not know the victims, brought very little compassion" (I.22).

However, when discussing a Romanian event of the Holocaust, the idea of Romanian soldiers being involved becomes more diluted. They were "excused" by the fact that they received orders they had to carry out: "For the Romanian soldiers, the victims were friends, neighbors, compared to the German ones. The latter had a different political propaganda and indoctrination; the Romanian soldiers were affected by what they were doing, but they were influenced to do so" (I.8).

The guilt is depersonalized (following Neil J. Kressel), even when the events are described: "Romania was a strongly antisemitic country, with an antisemitic government and an antisemitic legislation. The pogroms are not a gentle way of dying, and the deportations to Transnistria were tormenting as well. The conditions in the camps were worse than those in Auschwitz, and the pogrom of Bucharest was an unimaginable cruelty. To hang corpses on hooks at the slaughterhouse and write 'kosher meat' on them, I think, is the same as gassing the Jews in the Nazi camps" (I.17).

Depersonalization of guilt, and generalizations conveyed by not naming perpetrators, along the lines identified by Dimsdale, was found when the respondents expressed their horror at what had happened. Still, the respondents did express their horror about events and how the mechanism had worked so well: "For us, now, it is easier to accuse people for what happened. We read a lot about these things, we do not want to have things repeated, and we have a lot of initiatives to have this limited. For me personally, it is appalling how well this entire mechanism worked, for it was a well-established mechanism" (I.8).

The reasons for the perpetrators' behavior were the subject of the lengthiest discussion, which ranged from condemning them to excusing them. The context in which the perpetrators acted was discussed and analyzed, and the participants reached the conclusion that they had acted incompliance with the legal system (an aspect also pointed out by Dimsdale). What they did was in accordance with the law, but they also acted as role models, setting an example for others: "This person tries to explain himself, but he acted in a legal framework all the time. His actions were also conditioned by the fact that he had to be an example; he was influenced to be an example. He acted this way to set an example for the others" (I.7).

In attempting to identify other traits that characterize perpetrators, the respondents brought into the discussion a whole plethora of reasons for their behaviors. The psychological disorders discussed by Hilberg and Dimsdale were mentioned and debated. There is no reason for someone to be petrified and lack any reactions, and moreover to act as a perpetrator: "Put in this context, I think he was a psychopath, for real. I think you must have some problems; you must have some psychological problems to act like this. I said it in another discussion about the text that people have defensive reactions when confronted with the horror and they bury their principles and fear deep inside. Here, you find a context in which they were so close to what happened, and he still continued to do that" (I.21); "I think this relates to some psychological issues; for how long can someone continue killing other people?" (I.6).

Another issue that came up in the debates about the perpetrators was the dehumanizing process the perpetrators went through (also cited by Hilberg) and the fact they closed all doors for the others. Empathy was mentioned, closeness to and care for our fellow human beings—despite these, the perpetrators still did not walk in the shoes of the victims. The respondents also had some prejudices about the psychological traits associated with certain professions (e.g., army professionals are less empathic): "During those years, it was a sort of fanaticism, from Adolf Hitler, to Rudolf Hoess, to everyone from the army. They believed it was a regular job, that of killing Jews, of committing those acts of extreme violence. This was not something extraordinary for them; they did not have any consciousness to express their regrets" (I.13); "They came from the army, they were soldiers, they went through a process of selection, a process of training, and they were taught to be less empathic. Therefore, they could address the killing of someone in cold blood" (I.12).

Their professional evolution and careers were cited as a justification for their actions as well as a coping mechanism (as Neil J. Kressel also explains): "They had military careers, they were trained that suffering would be a part of their life. They did not have any relation with suffering for they were trained not to. Moreover, this man was not a simple soldier; he was a general, he gave orders to soldiers, and he trained others to think the same way" (I.2).

Regrets were discussed, and the participants in the focus groups said they would have preferred to read perpetrators' regrets instead of justifications of their acts: "I would have preferred to read his regrets for what he did, and this makes me think that if things would repeat, he would have done it all over again. He only excuses himself, he doesn't regret, he doesn't express an actual regret opinion" (I.9). However, the respondents mentioned that the perpetrators had made deliberate choices to do what they did, something that Dimsdale also points out: "The moment you put in balance the moral principles and the values you have, it means that you are taking into account a choice, and you assume this choice. You put in balance what you have to gain and what you have to lose. For them everything was a choice, all the time" (I.21).

The context in which the Holocaust happened created an environment that allowed people to perceive it as normal, again a feature that Dimsdale also refers to: "They saw this as something normal, they did not even understand where they went wrong. They saw this as unavoidable for accomplishing absolute good. Otherwise, they would have felt remorse, but they perceived everything as normal" (I.14). Some of the respondents talked also about the banality of evil, that is, the fact that what happened was so ordinary, a concept that both Dimsdale and Hannah Arendt discuss: "I find for sure very interesting the idea of the banality of evil that Nazis managed to bring evil in such a prosaic context. That man was a conscious person, with all the atrocities he committed. This was their daily job, and I find dreadful the fact that they brought the common place of evil in their daily work" (I.10).

Some of the respondents considered the perpetrators to be victims as well, and expressed empathy for them. This also sparked some debates:

"I agree with the fact that nobody speaks of officers' feelings, as if they were not also victims. But they were victims of the system." (I.15)

"The idea is the same; they are only kikes, to the extermination camps with them. My impression is that both the victims and the perpetrators are victims. The general excused himself by saying that he was forced to do this, while the victim excused himself by the fact that he was deported."(I.9)

"If one reached the status of general, he was no victim; he was part of Adolf Hitler's entourage." (I.6)

"He was part of this idea, he cannot be a victim. He brought his contribution to this phenomenon." (I.8)

The Bystander

I am very angry with this situation. I don't know. But couldn't the population do anything during those years? They outnumbered the army and the authorities. They could have said to leave the Jews alone. Then they could have saved them. (I.20)

One of the first issues brought into the discussion was non-Jewish persons' reactions to the measures taken against their Jewish friends, neighbors, colleagues, and so on (an aspect that Steven Baum also refers to): "Ok, ok, think that millions of people just disappear, neighbors and friends. It is one thing to have a single human being disappear and [another] to have millions of people disappear. That is noticed. And their opposition toward Adolf Hitler was minimal" (I.3). The discussion focused on the German context and Germans as bystanders. "The Germans participated in the Holocaust through their lack of reactions, and so the absence of trials from the Germans. However, we should think that this was motivated in their minds by some things, for example, how the nationalist ideology managed to get adherents during the 1930s" (I.7).

In coming up with reasons for the bystanders' lack of reaction, other respondents connected it to the consequences of the First World War. The economic crisis that followed and its effects on many aspects of people's lives were also discussed: "You, as a German, or belonging to any other nations where there was a strong antisemitic trend, you left your family, went to war, you died or you came back maimed and in poverty. And you watch how the stores of Jewish people thrive, and you ask yourself why, and you starve, you have no money to buy things, you are left with nothing to live on, the German currency doesn't have the same value. And so Adolf Hitler took advantage of that situation" (I.6). In terms of economic reasons, participants stated that "the Germans supported the Nazi ideology, also because the Nazi Party brought some balance to the German economic life" (I.7). Political reasons were also brought into the discussion, as well as the racial theory that Jews were inferior to Aryans, which eventually led to the dehumanization of the Jews.

The categories of bystanders identified by the responders were the people who only watched and did not intervene, the people who stepped over the Jews who lay on the platforms of train stations, and the people who verbally reacted but did not intervene—these are categories that Steven Baum and Victoria Barnett also mention in their studies. An aspect of their nonintervention that puzzled the respondents is that this happened in a place where people could have known each other: "If we take into consideration the time and the space, this is a place where people knew one another, the same way people that share an apartment building know one another" (I.2.).

One of the frequently and intensely debated reasons for the lack of reaction was fear, an aspect that is also analyzed by Baum. On the one hand, there was the fear of being immediately crushed by armed authorities: "In the next second, an order would have been given and many more from the army would have come and suppressed their reaction. They were well aware of that, and so they were fearful. They also did not have the necessary resources to give them power of reaction and defense" (I.2.). Participants in the focus groups also considered the war context, which was characterized not by normality but by terror, and fear of taking the side of the Jews: "The issue is another one, they were afraid of being put in the same basket with the kikes, that is why they did not react" (I.2). This comment prompted a dialogue:

"They were not put in the same basket with the kikes." (I.3)
"The authorities would have put them." (I.3)
"I don't think so." (I.2)
"You were, and they would take you to the police station and you would be questioned by the police. And in those times this was not as easy as it is today. And this would have been fatal for that person. They would write 'kike' on him. This is what they [the bystanders] thought." (I.2)

As Baum argues, obedience is connected to fear, and this came up in the discussion, especially in connection to people's willingness to obey security authorities: "It is human nature to look when something's going on and it is human nature to be obedient, for in the long run it is only the state that exerts legitimate violence. Therefore, some of those that just looked did not intervene for they did not think of human life but only of orders. And they did not rebel because of this, too" (I.16); "One cannot protest in the presence of some officers; or what else could one do? You too could be killed" (I.7).

Another reason the respondents gave for the bystanders' lack of reaction, which is also discussed by Barnett, was their education, or rather the indoctrination of the fascist regime. The fact that very few people reacted, either by verbally expressing their worries about the situation of Jews or by helping them, was partly explained by their living in a rural environment, which the respondents felt gave some people a more humane approach and made them less susceptible to political education: "I think this is an issue of education, first the peasant women who would say, 'Kike, kikes, but they are human too. What have they done wrong?' and then Țața Țița's reactions and attitude. I think people from the countryside are more humane, they are not that indoctrinated" (I.18). However, this may be connected more generally to an idea many of the respondents expressed about the innate good nature of Romanian people: "This situation is a better description of Romania; those peasants were illiterate, they did not have access to information, to antisemitic propaganda, and therefore they had a more humane approach. They did not have access to instruments that officers or people from Germany had" (I.7).

Another reason for their lack of reaction, in the participants' view, was the fact that they considered this to be a show, a spectacle (an aspect also mentioned by Barnett), and they acted accordingly: "Considering the fact that there was no television, this was the only entertainment. Centuries ago, they would go to the public hanging. Two thousand people were lying on the train station platform. They were surrounded by many other persons" (I.3). Another aspect that Barnett refers to is cowardice, and this was also brought into the discussion in connection with self-preservation instincts: "As for the people who obeyed orders and continued to step on them like they were stones, I don't know. The first feeling is to judge them, but if we put ourselves in their shoes, I don't think it is about cowardice, but a feeling of self-preservation" (I.17).

An element that Hilberg emphasizes is antisemitism, and this was another reason discussed by the participants in the focus groups. They agreed that the Romanian people have a long history of prejudice and antisemitism toward the Jewish people, which has religious origins. The issue of deicide was mentioned and discussed: "It is well known that in the religious view, the Jews are those who crucified Jesus Christ, and everything that happened to them until nowadays is a consequence of that. If you go to the countryside, you receive this answer" (I.1). Moreover, the anti-Jewish measures adopted starting with the modern era were also pointed out during the discussion.

The idea of a higher prejudice toward the Jews, for which the authorities rather than the simple people from the countryside were accountable (a notion also discussed by Barnett), was brought into the discussion and debated.

"I think that people from lower social classes have a soul and see and approach other people differently." (I.22)

"I don't think this relates to the social class, but to the closeness to the authorities. I think in the countryside, people relate differently with the authorities and laws than in the cities; therefore, they get closer to other people more easily." (I.21)

"For example, the Roma families that had a sedentary life, being involved in craftwork, were taken by the authorities. People from the villages made petitions to have them back. Romanian people did that. They did not see them as personae non grata. The Roma people were integrated in the community." (I.20)

Another aspect mentioned by Barnett is indifference, and it generated another lengthy discussion and debate. While some participants blamed the bystanders (e.g., in the case of the pogrom in Iași) for their lack of reaction, other participants tried to offer explanations for their lack of reaction toward the Jewish victims: "I don't think they were indifferent, if they were indifferent they wouldn't have stayed there with their mouths opened. I think they were horrified" (I.18); "They weren't horrified. If there were an accident on the street, people would gather, and only two would check if the victims are still alive. The others would sit there, watching as if it were a show or something. This is not being horrified, but this is curiosity, a little bit morbid, but nevertheless curiosity" (I.21).

The novelty of the situation, another feature explored by Barnett, was another aspect discussed when analyzing the bystanders' behavior—that is, their surprise at these events, the fact this was something they were not accustomed to, and therefore they had no idea how to react: "When you have a new situation, one you are not accustomed to, you receive a whole diversity of reactions. One cannot expect to have them react for the first time in their lives" (I.19).

Hilberg mentions taking advantage of the situation. This was another issue brought into discussion: "The things the Jewish people left behind were sold to people there and bought by them. We can assume some were just interested in this" (I.3). However, some of the respondents considered that one does not need that much civic knowledge to react (a factor mentioned by Baum): "I don't know; you don't need to know about human rights, or to have read about human rights to be humane. This is my conclusion" (I.13).

A final issue that came out during the discussion (also considered by Barnett) was that people might have had limited knowledge about what was going on right under their noses: "I do not agree, I think many Germans simply did not know what was happening. They found out after 1945, after the Nuremberg trials" (I.6).

The Rescuer, the Helper

> We must acknowledge through this woman's help that part of society that did help and rescue them. (I.11)

The context in which the rescuers/helpers acted was exceptional, the respondents agreed. Therefore, as Raul Hilberg also mentions, their actions were exceptional, too, and this was brought up by participants in the focus groups when discussing the scene at the train station during the Iași pogrom of June 1941: "There are those calling them kikes, there is this crowd that is intrigued by the event and does not consider it something good, only very few believe this to be evil, and just one person tries to help someone she knows" (I.1). They felt that the reaction of this woman (Țața Țița) came from her own initiative, prompted by mercy and a simple way of thinking that overcame the fear (a view also discussed by Baum): "The reason comes from her own initiative, inspired her mercy, and she wanted to help, in her simple way of thinking she thought that by giving that piece of bread, she would help and she would do some good" (I.2).

Simplicity as a reason for reaction was an argument invoked many times by the respondents, and they placed this simplicity in the context of this person's social situation as an older woman from the countryside who did not have too much authority and did not understand too many things. Still, she reacted, and still, she was aware that this would put her in a dangerous situation: "I appreciate her, she offered her help, and love, too, to some people that most probably looked deplorable in that situation" (I.17). The respondents also considered the excuse of fear, which they thought should not have prevented people from reacting: "I am still thinking about this lady who had a reaction. I think it is incredible what happened, and that people did not react out of fear. But from this text and other texts that I read, the conclusion I reached is that if more people would have reacted, the consequences wouldn't have been as harsh as they were" (I.21).

Compassion and humanity (aspects also discussed by Baum) were also considered by the respondents as characteristics of persons who helped or rescued Holocaust victims. They compared these people to the perpetrators: "The officer in this text represents the authority, the peasant woman who says, 'kikes, kikes, but they are human beings, too' represents that humane part of society, while the vast majority of the crowd consists of citizens who look fascinated at what was going on. I don't think the latter are dehumanized, but the authorities are for sure" (I.21). The Righteous among the Nations is identified as a group whose behavior was similar to this peasant woman's: "We need to acknowledge through this woman that part of society that existed and helped them [the Jews], the Righteous among the Nations" (I.11).

In his work, Baum argues that defying the authorities was another reason for the helpers/rescuers' initiative. The respondents agreed: "There were these persons that represented the authority, the victims that did not understand what was going on with them and couldn't think about this either, the bystanders that listened to the county police orders, the individuals that looked with amazement, and this woman that did something, even if she knew she wasn't allowed to" (I.17).

The Victim

The Holocaust is a genocide directed toward a nation, and it is a particular phenomenon because history bears witness to very few such movements directed specifically toward a distinct population or nation. (I.7)

The respondents considered that the Jewish people were specifically targeted during the Nazi regime in Germany and also in the countries under its influence, and that everyone who did not correspond to the Aryan typology would be excluded from society. Nevertheless, the respondents identified three major groups that should be included in the category of Holocaust victims—the Jews, the Roma, and homosexuals—categories also discussed by Barnett: "Throughout this period of extermination of the Jewish minority, they extended this to other minorities as well, Roma people and people with other sexual orientations; basically, everyone not Aryan" (I.12).

However, the participants in the focus groups placed the Jewish people in the context of the entire process of solving the "Jewish question," for which there were several "solutions" (e.g., emigration and forced labor) before the Final Solution, which entailed their physical destruction (as Hilberg also notes): "I would like to tell you that the Holocaust or the Shoah represented the Final Solution the Nazis found to solve the Jewish problem. Initially, the Jews were somehow compelled to emigrate, and those who could not afford to were put in forced labor camps, and only in a final stage they were killed by physical exhaustion or gassed in the extermination camps" (I.17).

A comment about the number of victims prompted first a contradiction and then a shift in the discussion to the topic of how the Nazi regime and its allies, as well as the population at large, reacted to Holocaust victims, with a particular focus on the Jewish victims. Someone incorrectly identified the total number of victims as around one million, which prompted a reaction: "First of all, the numbers are much higher, not one million. Second, we should ask ourselves, why the Jews? Everyone stereotyped them, as being the best and running the world, but no one thought this was false. Throughout history, their rights were limited so they had to do something, to find jobs. If we were in their shoes, we would have done the same thing" (I.5).

The discussion moved to the evolution of the stereotypes of the Jewish people, starting with religious aspects in antiquity, continuing with political and social ones during the period of the formation of nation-states, and ending with the socioeconomic arguments developed after the First World War, and in every period considering racial aspects, in a progression that was reminiscent of Zygmunt Bauman's interpretation. Respondents said: "That history is much longer, it started with the religious issue, and then during the formation of nation-states, when the states were not well established, they placed the blame on the minorities for all failures" (I.21); "I think this was determined by racial reasons; I think the causes are more racial than economic" (I.13).

The discussion moved then from theoretical aspects to a more applied perspective, whereby respondents mentioned and discussed some of the concrete measures implemented against the Jewish people, including restrictions on political and professional rights and anti-Jewish measures such as pogroms and widespread discrimination. The discussion then proceeded to the reasons why the Jews were hated so much, right before and during the Holocaust, and two main arguments were identified along these lines. The historical context of the nineteenth and twentieth centuries was once again brought up: "I think this was a reaction of nationalism and the foundation of nation-states during the nineteenth and twentieth centuries. Many states were divided and built then. Jews were the only ones who did not have a country, and so they were an easy target for all the nationalistic groups in Europe" (I.19). The creation of a legal context for their discrimination and extermination, an aspect also emphasized by Zygmunt Bauman, was also discussed: "It is much easier to kill people once you built the legal framework" (I.11). Persons' reactions against Jews, which had their own history, were mentioned, too: "There were cloudy times, people struggled with many issues. It is hard to say why Jews and not the other minorities. However, Jews were the most persecuted throughout history; at all times, the others thought about how to destroy or kill them" (I.10).

Some participants in the focus groups felt that the anti-Jewish reactions might have had some foundations, as one of the respondents remembered a discussion he had had with one of his elderly relatives: "As the elders in my family told me, there still was a problem with the Jews. They were the only ones who owned shops, owned banks, and handled money. They basically owned everything. And someone told me that if you would go to buy a dress from a store, you had to go with a glass of water to test if it wasn't made of paper. You had to do the test because you could have been deceived. They were seen as thieves, as some street hustlers" (I.20).

Another debate started over the issue of numbers and how many Jews died in Romania, a country allied with the Nazi regime and Germany, where the headquarters of the Nazi regime were based: "However, from what I know, the Romanian citizens of Jewish origins were victims of the Holocaust and suffered nevertheless. They were dispossessed of their goods, they were deported, still they were not killed in such big numbers as in Germany or Poland" (I.3). The debate about numbers focused on the populations of Jews living in Romania versus Germany, as percentages of the total populations living in Romania and Germany. When one of the moderators intervened by providing the correct numbers and percentages, the discussion moved to comparing Adolf Hitler's influence on the Nazi regime to Ion Antonescu's influence on the fascist regime in Romania, especially with regard to their attitudes toward the Jewish population:

"There has been a basis for building the antisemitic measures." (I.8)
    "Still, not at the level of that in Germany or other European countries." (I.6)
    "We were never a great power." (I.8)
    "And more, the number of Jews was not that big to say we exterminated them." (I.6)

Concluding Questions

The concluding questions attempted to determine how the participants in the focus group understood the text and the debates on a more personal level. I asked them to identify themselves with one of the Holocaust actor categories under consideration, that is, perpetrators, helpers/rescuers, bystanders, and victims.

Out of the twenty-two participants, two identified with the perpetrators: "It is very hard to decide. Ok, everyone would say the victim; however, if we were to live those times, at least some of us would have been a Nazi or a legionary. Right now, I am sure everyone would choose the victim, or at least the helper" (I.14); "Ok, I know my answer will make me the most hated person in this room, but here it goes. I identify myself with one of the officers. Ok, not the commander, but a middle-career officer. I identify myself with the authority. I was taught to fear it. So, not someone who gives the orders, but someone who executes them" (I.18).

Four of the interviewees identified with the victims. The reasons were diverse, ranging from that being the only option that would not involve hurting others to profoundly identifying with the fate of one's ancestors, in the case of a respondent who belonged to one of the ethnic groups that was victimized during the Holocaust: "I don't know, but given the pressure, I would prefer to be a victim than a guard. I would know I have a fate and there would be nothing I could do about it. I would be killed or I would survive. But I wouldn't do any horrors" (I.1); "I identify myself with the Jews, for my ancestors, the Roma people, were also victims, and therefore I belong to an ethnicity that was a victim" (I.20).

The next group included six people who identified themselves with rescuers/helpers. Their reasons were barely mentioned and did not vary much, but mostly had to do with being a Good Samaritan who would help someone in a very difficult situation. What was very interesting were the answers suggesting a connection between helping and the intrinsic good nature of the Romanian people: "Every time a conflict starts, there is always a woman from the countryside who symbolizes the authentic national character of Romania, and who saves them by giving some cheese" (I.19); "I was born in the countryside and therefore I identify myself with the peasant woman. This is how we were educated, to help the other. And I would do this to also set a model for the others, to have many more act and react" (I.22).

The next category of actors, and the largest (eight respondents), was the bystanders. The subcategories of bystanders the respondents identified with most were the people who stayed on the side and watched and the women who made the sign of the cross. The most frequently invoked and discussed reason for this choice was fear: "I cannot say if I would have done something to help them, because I don't know how paralyzed with fear I would have been. Moreover, the presence of the soldiers in those moments would have contributed to this" (I.10); "It is the fear that would have stopped me from doing anything. Fear is so manipulative; it stops you from doing things, no matter how intelligent and/or how uneducated you are" (I.6). Other reasons brought up and discussed were the limited impact any actions would have had on events, and lack of knowledge about the events: "I identify myself with the passive bystanders. But I think a big part of society identifies itself with the passive bystanders, and not only in the context of the Holocaust but with everything. I do not think this relates to one's education, but to the little chances to have one's voice heard. I don't think about what the impact of my voice or actions would have been ... and that is it" (I.7); "I don't think I would have reacted, for we would have been just some simple men and women, without too much knowledge of the situation. Now, we know what happened" (I.16). For another respondent, his reaction to victims was dependent on whether he knew them or not.

One of the participants refused to give an answer to the question, saying, "I cannot answer that question. There are too many aspects to be considered and analyzed. This is a situation requiring careful assessment. It is hard, and I take her position, that I would rather be a victim than a perpetrator. However, I cannot be a victim, for I am not Jewish. It is hard, it is very hard to estimate and give an answer. I just wonder what people in that place and with that mentality thought back then. We are thinking now using democratic reasoning, and enjoying a freedom they did not know" (I.2). Another respondent mentioned his family situation as a contextual factor and linked his choice to whether he would have been a parent with a son in the army.

Conclusions

This research is situated within the context of public memory. It brings together two subjects of academic interest, actor categories and perceptions of the Holocaust, to examine how people perceive them together. The research was qualitative, using focus groups as a research method. More specifically,

I examined how university students enrolled in social sciences and humanities programs perceived the behaviors and attitudes of perpetrators, helpers/rescuers, bystanders, and victims, and how the personal attributes and the changing circumstances affected the personal decisions of members of these category groups.

The theoretical part of this study was dedicated to constructing portraits of the different categories of actors involved in the Holocaust, and these portraits were used in conducting the research and analyzing the research results. The category of the perpetrator includes every man and woman who operated the Nazi machine of destruction in every country under the influence of the Nazi regime. Several traits characterize a perpetrator, and this category can be subdivided into several types of persons or professions. The bystanders make up the largest and most diverse category of Holocaust actors. Their traits vary, as do the motivations for their lack of action. The rescuer/helper category is the smallest category of Holocaust actors. It includes people who helped in exchange for something, as well as the people called the Righteous among the Nations. The victim category also includes different types, including, importantly, the survivors. Over time, this type of victim went through different stages in their efforts to deal with the past and to develop mechanisms for coping with the future.

The participants in the focus group provided a certain picture of perpetrators. They identified the leaders, the political establishment, and the military authorities as the main parties responsible for the implementation of the Final Solution. The traits they identified as characteristic of a perpetrator were propensity to mental disorders, an inclination to dehumanize the others, and an overriding concern with professional advancement. According to the respondents, the perpetrators saw the context of the Nazi regime as normal, and they felt that they acted within the framework of a legal system and that they had to set an example for others. Interestingly, the respondents offered various excuses for the perpetrators, and even considered the perpetrators victims. When addressing the topic of Romanian perpetrators, some of the respondents attributed some of the guilt to German perpetrators, arguing that the Romanians acted solely on the orders of Nazi Germany. As such, they depersonalized the guilt and generalized the responsibility. However, some said they would have preferred to read regrets rather than excuses from perpetrators, and placed the moral responsibility on perpetrator soldiers, for they had made a deliberate choice.

The participants identified several kinds of bystanders as well: those who did not act; those who reacted only verbally; and those who contributed to the worsening situation of the Jewish population, as described in the text. Several aspects that constrained the bystanders' reactions were mentioned: fear, obedience, indoctrination into extremist ideas, the novelty of the situation and lack of knowledge about it, the show-like features of some of the events, cowardice, antisemitism, indifference, opportunity to take advantage of the situation, and lack of civic knowledge. However, the bystanders' lack of response was not condemned or debated much; the participants focused more on finding explanations for their lack of action.

The context in which a helper or a rescuer acted was exceptional, and therefore his or her actions were also exceptional. The discussion concluded that the helper whose example was analyzed acted of her own initiative. Some the main personality traits identified by the respondents that determined that she would help were simplicity, compassion, and humanity. She did not let fear overwhelm her. The participants discussed also the case of the Righteous among the Nations, and reached the conclusion that some of the helpers/rescuers might have acted in defiance of the authorities.

The main categories of Holocaust victims the participants in the focus group identified were Jewish and Roma people, and sexual minorities. Still, the most discussed and debated Holocaust victim category was the Jews, because the texts that informed the discussion focused on them. The respondents identified extermination as the main "solution" to the "Jewish problem," along with emigration and forced labor. They also talked about the stereotyping of Jews from antiquity until the Second World War during their discussion about why the Jews were targeted by the Nazi regime and why discriminatory measures were taken against them. The discussion also drew a comparison between Nazi Germany and fascist Romania and their deeds against the Jewish population, concluding that the numbers of victims in Romania were lower than in Germany.

The final question for the focus group was meant to reveal how the participants understood the texts and the debates on a more personal level. They identified themselves mostly with the bystanders and rescuers/helpers, and less with the victims and perpetrators. The reasons for identifying with the bystanders were not discussed much; being a Good Samaritan was the most frequently cited reason for identifying with the rescuers/helpers, and interestingly, the participants associated this with the allegedly inherent good nature of the Romanian people. Bystanders were the largest category that respondents identified with, with around one third of the respondents choosing this group, and there are several reasons for this: fear, the limited impact the actions of the powerless could have had, and lack of knowledge about what was going on. Two of the respondents stated a preference for and deference to authority, and consequently they identified with the perpetrators, while four of the interviewees identified with victims, out of humanitarian or personal reasons. One of the participants refused to give an answer due to lack of sufficient contextual elements, while another made his answer conditional on his presumptive family situation.

Other conclusions that can be drawn from this research correspond to the general perceptions of the Holocaust in Romania as reflected in the survey published in 2015: the Holocaust took place mostly in Germany and less so in Romania, and Adolf Hitler was more responsible than Ion Antonescu for the Holocaust in Romania. Diluting or passing on the responsibility for the Holocaust that took place in Romania or in territories under Romanian administration from the Romanian authorities to the German ones is an integral part of the contemporary discourse on the Holocaust in Romania.

Nowadays, as compared with twenty-six years ago, information on the Holocaust in Romania is widely accessible. The *Final Report* of the International Commission on the Holocaust in Romania engendered many initiatives and actions that continue to facilitate better and easier access to documents, books, testimonies, and other information sources on this and related subjects. Moreover, a public research institute, a memorial monument, several university courses, and high school classes on the topic of the Holocaust provide a legitimate environment where people can access such information. Nevertheless, despite the incorporation of these elements into the public discourse on the Holocaust, the way people understand and filter this information through their personal values, attitudes, and behaviors represents a substantial challenge to their personal and intimate understanding of Holocaust events and Holocaust actions, decisions, and choices. I strongly believe that beyond knowing what happened, it is people's perceptions and understanding that make the meaningful difference that could prevent the reappearance of similar events and actions.

> Adina Babeș is a senior researcher at the Elie Wiesel National Institute for Studying the Holocaust in Romania.

Notes

1. Baum, *The Psychology of Genocide*, 119.
2. Ibid., 119.
3. Ibid., 120.
4. Ibid., 122–130.
5. Ibid., 106.
6. Hilberg, *Perpetrators, Victims, Bystanders*, 75–76.
7. Kressel, *Mass Hate*, 160–163.
8. Hilberg, *Perpetrators, Victims, Bystanders*, 20–21.
9. Ibid., 20–26.
10. Ibid., 36–37.
11. Ibid., 65–69.
12. Ibid., 51.
13. Kressel, *Mass Hate*, 185.
14. Ibid., 198.
15. Ibid., 165.
16. Ibid., 199–202.
17. Ibid., 204–206.
18. Ibid., 207–210.
19. Dimsdale, *Survivors, Victims, and Perpetrators*, 343–351.
20. Kressel, *Mass Hate*, 211–212.
21. Dimsdale, *Survivors, Victims, and Perpetrators*, 335–338.
22. Ibid., 351–354.
23. Ibid., 338–342.
24. Baum, *The Psychology of Genocide*, 153–154.
25. Ibid., 155.
26. Barnett, *Bystanders*, 9.
27. Baum, *The Psychology of Genocide*, 153–154.
28. Ibid., 161.
29. Baum, *The Psychology of Genocide*, 164–165.
30. Barnett, *Bystanders*, 10.
31. Ibid., 41.
32. Hilberg, *Perpetrators, Victims, Bystanders*, 20–21, 195.
33. Barnett, *Bystanders*, 173.
34. Hilberg, *Perpetrators, Victims, Bystanders*, 215.
35. Ibid., 35–36.

36. Ibid., 41–44.
37. Ibid., 45.
38. Ibid., 15–17.
39. Ibid., 89–94.
40. Ibid., 102–106.
41. Ibid., 107–109.
42. Ibid., 112–113.
43. Ibid., 113.
44. Ibid., 119–131.
45. Ibid., 126.
46. Ibid., 169–173.
47. Baum, *The Psychology of Genocide*, 182.
48. Ibid., 182–183.
49. Ibid., 184–185.
50. Barnett, *Bystanders*, 158–160.
51. Hilberg, *Perpetrators, Victims, Bystanders*, 212.
52. Ibid., 214–215.
53. Yahil, *The Holocaust*, 544.
54. Ibid., 546–548.
55. Ibid., 548–551.
56. Ibid., 551–553.
57. Baum, *The Psychology of Genocide*, 184.
58. Ibid., 187–188.
59. Ibid., 194–204.
60. Ibid., 189–194.
61. Bauman, *Modernity and the Holocaust*, 119.
62. Ibid., 123.
63. Ibid., 124–126.
64. Ibid., 129–131.
65. Ibid., 144.
66. Ibid., 149.
67. Dimsdale, *Survivors, Victims, and Perpetrators*, 106.
68. Hilberg, *Perpetrators, Victims, Bystanders*, 118–119.
69. Ibid., 131–132.
70. Ibid., 139–140.
71. Ibid., 159.
72. Ibid., 172–180.
73. Ibid., 186–187.
74. Ibid., 187–190.
75. Institutul Național pentru Studierea Holocaustului din România, "Sondaje," accessed March 24, 2016, http://www.inshr-ew.ro/ro/proiecte/sondaje.html.
76. Stewart and Shamdasani, *Focus Groups*, 69.
77. The introductory questions were meant to help each participant introduce him- or herself to the other participants of the focus group, focusing on who they were and what they studied. The transitional questions from the first part of the questionnaire tested participants' general knowledge of the Holocaust, when and where it happened, as well as

their knowledge of the Holocaust in Romania, when and where it happened. Moreover, the participants were asked to discuss their studies on the Holocaust, particularly at the university, as well as other sources about this topic they were familiar with. See Krueger and Casey, *Focus Groups*, 44–47.

78. The key questions of the questionnaire were designed according to the theoretical model developed, and are presented in the first section of this chapter. The discussions followed the subcategories of each Holocaust actor category considered for my research, as well as the sociopsychological and personality characteristics of each type, and were prompted by reading two texts on the topic of perpetrators, bystanders, rescuers/helpers, and victims. The first text was an excerpt from the autobiography of Rudolf Hoess, the commander of Auschwitz, who is placed in the category of the perpetrator; the page I used for the focus group discussions also portrays victims. The second text was an excerpt from the diary of Leonard Zăicescu, a survivor of the death trains of Iași, which followed the pogrom of Iași in the summer of 1941; this text also portrays bystanders and helpers. It is very important to note that during the focus groups, every element that could have revealed the identities of the authors or characters, or the time or place of the events and how they evolved, was excluded from the texts and/or masked in cases where the meanings of the texts would have suffered. The participants in the focus group did not know until the very end of the study the identities of the authors and the dates and places of the events referenced. The purpose of the texts was to initiate the discussions. See Krueger and Casey, *Focus Groups*, 44–47.

79. The aim of the end questions, which comprise the second part of the questionnaire, was to reveal how the respondents acknowledged the texts and the discussions on a more personal level, by choosing one of the Holocaust actor categories with which to identify themselves. See Krueger and Casey, *Focus Groups*, 44–47.

80. Stewart and Shamdasani, *Focus Groups*, 110–111.

81. Widom and Collado, *"Help, I'm Getting Buried in Field Notes!" A Manual for Qualitative Data Management and Analysis*, accessed March 24, 2016, http://www.mdrc.org/publications/332/full.pdf.

82. Stewart and Shamdasani, *Focus Groups*, 126.

References

Barnett, Victoria J. *Bystanders: Conscience and Complicity during the Holocaust*. Westport, CT: Praeger, 2000.

Bartrop, Paul R. *Encountering Genocide: Personal Accounts from Victims, Perpetrators, and Witnesses*. Santa Barbara, CA: ABC-CLIO, 2014.

Baum, Steven K. *The Psychology of Genocide: Perpetrators, Bystanders, and Rescuers*. New York: Cambridge University Press, 2008.

Bauman, Zygmunt. *Modernity and the Holocaust*. Ithaca, NY: Cornell University Press, 1989.

Dimsdale, Joel E., ed. *Survivors, Victims, and Perpetrators: Essays on the Nazi Holocaust*. Washington, DC: Hemisphere, 1980.

Hilberg, Raul. *Perpetrators, Victims, Bystanders: The Jewish Catastrophe 1933–1945*. New York: HarperCollins, 1992.

Institutul Național pentru Studierea Holocaustului din România. "Sondaje." Accessed March 24, 2016. http://www.inshr-ew.ro/ro/proiecte/sondaje.html.
Kressel, Neil J. *Mass Hate: The Global Rise of Genocide and Terror.* Boulder, CO: Westview, 2002.
Krueger, Richard A., and Mary Anne Casey. *Focus Groups: A Practical Guide for Applied Research.* Thousand Oaks, CA: Sage Publications, 2015.
Stewart, David W., and Prem N. Shamdasani. *Focus Groups: Theory and Practice.* Thousand Oaks, CA: Sage, 2015.
Widom, Rebecca, with Herbert Collado. *"Help, I'm Getting Buried in Field Notes!" A Manual for Qualitative Data Management and Analysis.* Manpower Demonstration Research Corporation, January 2003. http://www.mdrc.org/sites/default/files/full_0.pdf.
Yahil, Leni. *The Holocaust: The Fate of European Jewry, 1932–1945.* New York: Oxford University Press, 1990.
Zăicescu, Leonard. *Cu trenul expres spre moarte.* Bucharest: Editura Institutului Național pentru Studierea Holocaustului din România, 2007.

Index

Acmecetka (concentration camp in Ukraine), 12
Adameșteanu, Gabriela, 46
Aiud (town in Transylvania), 67n40
Alba (county in Transylvania), 87
Alba Iulia (city in Transylvania), 155
Alexianu, Gheorghe, 126, 199, 209
Alupoaei, Gheorghe, 201n4
Ancel, Jean, 152, 199
Andreescu, Gabriel, xxxn10, 109, 110, 114, 137n54, 138n56
Andrew the Apostle (St.), 20
Anghel, Cristina, 118
Antal, József, 132
Antonescu, Crin, 103, 122, 123, 136n32
Antonescu, Ion (Marshal), xviii, xxvii, xxviii, 56, 62, 74, 80, 89, 91, 92, 120, 128, 201n4, 233–234n13, 236n54, 237n70; Alexianu and, 199; among 100 Greatest Romanians, 237–238n89; arrest of, 208; Boia on, 230–231, 237n87; Bucharest pogrom and, 9; Buzatu on, 218, 220–224; Cioroianu on, 231–232; Constantiniu on, 224–225; cult of, xvi, xxi, 72, 73, 82, 88, 90, 97–98, 102, 125, 135n7, 151, 176, 202n13; deportations and, 3, 7, 11; Drăgan on, 234n23; Final Solution and, 8, 15, 99, 157; Giurescu on, 225–228; historians on, 213–217, 219, 232, 236n47; Hitler and, 214, 224, 242, 259, 260, 272, 277; Iași pogrom and, 9–10, 12, 14, 156; Iron Guard and, 14, 103, 107, 208; League of, 219; perception of, xx, 5, 163, 209–212, 243, 257; regime of, xii, xxix, 7, 9, 10–11, 13, 79, 177–178, 184, 197, 198, 217; rehabilitation of, 72, 126, 235n28; Scurtu on, 228–229; statues of, 135n6, 176–177; Stoenescu on, 229–230; Șova on, 129; trial of, 76, 77, 208, 209; Ungheanu on, 129; Vulcănescu and, 191, 192, 193, 195, 200, 204nn41–42
Antonescu, Mihai (Ică), 115, 196, 198, 199, 209, 215, 223
Arendt, Hannah, 48, 74, 264
Argeș (county in Wallachia), 88, 135n7
Atanasiu, Teodor, 123
Auschwitz (concentration camp), xii, 4, 12, 14, 46, 104, 132, 157, 259, 261, 280n78
Austria, xvi

Babeș, Adina, xxviii, 242, 278
Bădescu, Ilie, 112
Băile Tușnad (Tusnádfürdő—town in Transylvania), 143n151
Bălănescu, Gabriel, 93n22
Balogh, Eva, 126
Bălți (town in the Republic of Moldova), 158
Baltic (Sea), 195
Baltic states/countries, xii, 105, 185
Banat, 18
Banská Bystrica (city in Slovakia), 132
Barbu, Eugen, 233–234n13
Bărbulescu, Ana, xxi, xxii, 3, 33, 163, 202n15
Barnett, Victoria, 265, 266, 267, 268, 270

283

Bartoš, Adam B., 134
Bartov, Omer, 164
Bauer, Yehuda, 64
Baum, Steven, 264, 265, 266, 268, 269, 270
Bauman, Zygmunt, 271
Bayer, Zsolt, 125, 126, 139n86, 142n131
Beiuș (town in Transylvania), 135n7
Belarus, 110
Belgium, xvi
Belgrade, 126
Belzec (extermination camp), 3, 7, 8, 46
Benda, Julien, 62
Bender, Richard, 129, 130
Benedict XVI (Pope), 67n35
Berezovka (district in Transnistria), 3
Berger, Peter, 15
Berindei, Dan, 101, 116, 227, 228
Berlin, 115, 215, 228
Bessarabia, 18, 102, 135n7, 154, 158, 161, 164, 222; Antonescu and, 195, 219; deportations from, 3, 73, 77, 226; Holocaust in, 152, 237n76; Jews from, 11, 12, 78, 98, 157, 227, 228, 234n15; massacres in, 9, 14, 159; memory of the Holocaust in, 160; Ribbentrop-Molotov Pact and, 214; Soviet annexation of, 201n4; Vulcănescu and, 199
Birkenau (or Auschwitz II—Birkenau extermination camp), xii
Bjoza, Octav, 115, 180
Black Sea, 195
Blaga, Lucian, 19
Blaga, Vasile, 118, 122, 124
Bleiburg (town in Austria), 127
Bloxham, Donald, 75
Boban, Rafael, 128
Bogdan, Rareș, 115
Bogdanovka (concentration camp in Ukraine), 7, 12
Boia, Lucian, 230–231, 237n87
Bojan (village near Czernowicz), 156, 157
Bossy, Raoul, 228
Bostan, Marius, 129
Botoș, Ilie, 102
Brăila (city in Wallachia), 188
Brașov, 94n31, 94n33, 103

Brătianu, Constantin/Dinu, 214, 226
Brătianu, Ion C., 130
Bratislava (capital of Slovakia), 134
Breban, Nicolae, 137–138n54
Broszat, Martin, 101
Brubaker, Rogers, 16, 27, 28, 32
Bucharest, xxi, 4, 84, 98, 100, 102, 116, 119, 122, 123, 128, 137n54, 143n142, 175, 188, 191, 201n8, 204n47, 204–205n49, 230; Antonescu's trial in, 209; Court of Appeals in, 110; Holocaust memorial in, xxv, 101; Holocaust museum in, 162; Jewish theater in, 9, 10, 31; Legionary Library in, 85; mayor of, 118, 187; Military Tribunal of, 77; pogrom in, 3, 8, 10, 14, 229, 261; Tribunal of, 111; Vulcănescu and the sociological school of, 187, 193, 200; Vulcănescu's bust in, 186, 194
Buchenwald (concentration camp), 46
Budapest, 125, 130, 134, 138n67, 176
Bug (river), 78
Bukovina (Northern), xxv, 18, 156, 157, 159, 161, 164, 199, 214, 219, 222, 235n33; deportations from, 3, 77, 101, 234n15; massacres in, 9, 14, 98; Holocaust in, 152, 154, 160, 237n76; Jews from, 11, 12, 73, 78, 195, 226, 227
Bulgaria, 185, 256
Butz, Arthur, 117
Buzatu, Gheorghe, 217, 218, 220–224, 232, 234n26, 236nn41–42, 236n48, 236n54

Carol II, King of Romania, 187, 224, 226
Cazan, Marius, xxvii, 208, 233
Ceaușescu, Ilie (General), 216, 224
Ceaușescu, Nicolae, xxi, 47, 93n1, 97, 100, 137n54, 140n103, 151, 175, 214, 215, 216, 222, 224, 234n21
Céline, Louis-Ferdinand, 115, 139n86
Cetatea Albă (town in Ukraine), 201n4
Chaumont, Jean-Michel, xii
Chilia (town in Ukraine), 201n4
Chioveanu, Mihai, 153
Chișinău (Kichinev—capital of the Republic of Moldova), 155, 157, 158, 161, 162

Cioflâncă Adrian, 101, 135n7, 180, 216
Cioloș, Dacian, 128, 129
Cioran, Emil, 63, 106, 179, 201n8
Cioroianu, Adrian, 231–232, 237–238n89
Ciudei (town in Ukraine), 161
Climăuți (village in Moldavia), 161
Climescu, Alexandru, xxiii, xxiv, 72, 93, 108, 182, 183, 185, 202n14
Cluj (-Napoca), 88, 100, 135, 217
Codreanu, Corneliu Zelea, 83, 84, 107, 108, 111, 112, 120, 121, 123, 137–138n54, 222
Codrescu, Răzvan, 107, 108
Coja, Ion, 82, 113
Colceag, Florin, 112
Condurache, Cezarina, xxxn10, 108, 109
Constantiniu, Florin, 5, 8, 9, 10, 11, 13, 14, 20, 224–225, 237n66
Conta, Vasile, 35n58
Coposu, Corneliu, 108
Cosma, Aurel, 93n22
Costești (Dacian fortress), 87
Crainic, Nichifor, xxxn10, 19, 93n22, 179
Creția, Petru, 58, 59, 60
Cristescu, Eugen, 78
Cristoiu, Ion, 43
Croatia (and Independent State of Croatia), 107, 110, 111, 124, 126, 127, 128
Cuckurs, Herberts, 110
Cucuteni-Ariușd (civilization), 26
Cyprus, 256
Czech Republic, xvi, 105, 134
Czernowitz (Cernăuți—city in Bukovina, now in Ukraine), 73, 77, 79, 81, 91, 155, 156, 157, 161, 162

Dacia (Dacian state), 26, 34n55, 201n4
Danko, Andrej, 133, 134
Dante Alighieri, 59
Danube (river), 21, 25, 188
Decebal (Dacian king), 31
Dedaković, Mile, 128
Deletant, Dennis, 214, 225
Demetrescu-Gyr, Radu. *See* Gyr, Radu
Densușianu, Nicolae, 34n55
Deva (city in Transylvania), 175, 194
Diaconu, Marin, 193, 200

Dianu, Romulus, 93n22
Dimsdale, Joel E., 261, 262, 263, 264
Dinulescu, Radu, 73, 76, 77, 78, 79, 81, 90, 92, 102, 136n27, 185, 202n14
Djuvara, Neagu, 5, 8, 10, 11, 14, 21
Dmowski, Roman, 131
Dniester (river), 11, 159, 195, 201n4, 214, 233n13
Dobrinescu, Valeriu Florin, 217
Docan, Gheorghe, 80
Donáth, György, 125, 126
Dorohoi (town in Moldavia), 8
Dostoyevsky, Fyodor Mikhailovich, 60
Douglas, Lawrence, 75
Douglas, Mary, 16
Drăgan, Iosif Constantin, 216, 219, 234n23, 234n26, 237n28
Drăghici, Alexandru, 202n16
Duca, I.(Ion) G.(Gheorghe), 122, 123
Duda, Andrzej, 131, 132
Dumanovka (concentration camp in Ukraine), 7, 12
Dumitrescu, Ion, 93n22

East-Central Europe, 103, 124, 135
Eastern Europe, xiii, 53, 112, 151, 152, 155, 156, 158, 159, 163, 164, 165, 166, 176, 255
Eaton, Henry, 157
Edineți (town in the Republic of Moldova), 158
Eichmann, Otto Adolf, 73
Eliade, Mircea, 106, 179, 188, 189, 201n8, 203n25
Eminescu, Mihai, 35n58, 186
Eskenasy, Victor, 236n47
Europe, xiii, xxviii, 9, 13, 26, 31, 61, 85, 98, 108, 114, 119, 245
European Union / EU, xvi, xxv, xxvii
Evans, Richard J., 75

Faurisson, Robert, 117
Festinger, Leon, xxii, 16, 30
Fico, Robert, 133, 134
Filderman, Wilhelm, 227
Florian, Alexandru, xxvii, xxix, 108, 109, 116, 119, 137n54, 140n91, 151, 175, 201

Fondane, Benjamin, 69n62
France, xii, xvi, 51, 62, 201n8
Franco Bahamonde, Francisco, xiv, xv, 115
Furet, François, 48

Gafencu, Valeriu, 107, 137n44, 194, 201n11, 204n48
Galicia (region in Ukraine), 164
Garaudy, Roger, 51
Gebeleizis Society, 87
Geissbühler, Simon, xxv, xxvi, 151, 166
Genetes, Andrew, 60
Gerea, Dominic, 136n32
Germany, xvi, 56, 68n60, 99, 152, 244, 252, 266, 270; Allies of, 6, 255; annihilation of Jews by, 82, 98; Antonescu and, 224, 229; deportation of Romanian Jews to, 11; Hitler's regime and, xii, xviii, 62, 183, 192, 242, 259; Jewish emigration from, 254; Jews in Poland and, 272; Jews in Romania and, 272, 276; Nuremberg trials, 106, 202n18; responsible for the Holocaust in Romania, xxi, 4, 5, 163, 213, 257, 261, 277; Right-wing extremism in, 84; Romania and, 151, 152, 187, 192, 195, 208, 275; Spain and, xiv, xv; Vulcănescu and, 197
Ghițulescu, Toma Petre, 80
Giertych, Jędrzej, 131
Giertych, Maciej, 131
Giertych, Roman Jacek, 117, 131
Giurescu, Dinu C., 5, 8, 12, 14, 225–228
Glasnović, Zeljko, 128
Glucksmann, André, 54, 67n36
Golta (district in Transnistria), 3
Goodman, Nelson, 15
Gorghiu, Alina, 118, 122, 124
Grabar-Kitarović, Kolinda, 127, 128
Grigurcu, Gheorghe, 43, 53
Gross, Jan, 131, 132, 144n163
Gulag (*Glavnoye Upravleniye LAGerey*—"Chief Administration of Corrective Labor Camps"), xix, xxiii, xxv, 45, 46, 51, 53, 54, 55, 59, 60, 61, 62, 65, 67n35, 97, 104, 178, 179
Gulyás, Gergely, 125

Gușă, Cosmin, 117
Gusti, Dimitrie, 187, 188, 191
Gyka, Alexandru, 108
Gyr, Radu, 93–94n22, 106, 115, 118, 202n12, 204n48

Habsburg (monarchy), 18
Haiduc, Ionel, 101
Hamsun, Knut, 139n86
Hasanbegović, Zlatko, 111, 127, 128, 143n143
Hașotti, Puiu, 118
Hauptmann, Gerhart, 139n86
Heidegger, Martin, 115
Heinen, Armin, 152
Herța (town in Ukraine), 160, 161, 222
Hilberg, Raul, 243, 245, 259, 260, 262, 267, 268, 270
Hilsner/Hülsner, Leopold, 134
Hitler, Adolf, xviii, xix, 62, 87, 92, 183, 192, 214, 215, 245, 246, 263, 265; Antonescu and, 208, 214, 224, 228, 232, 242, 259, 260, 272, 277; cult of, 90; Horia Sima and, 208; Milan Mazurek and, 133; Mussolini and, 47, 48, 260; opposition to, xii, 264; Stalin and, 48, 55, 56, 67n36; Vintilă Horia and, 116
Hoandră, Octavian, 117
Hodoș, Alexandru, 93n22
Hoess, Rudolf, 263, 280n78
Holtan, Richard, 133
Hóman, Bálint, 125, 126
Horia, Vintilă, 116, 179, 186, 202n12, 204n48
Horthy, Miklós, 8, 125, 176
Hotin (town in Ukraine), 201n4
Hrůzová, Agnes, 134
Hungary, xii, xxv, 11, 12, 14, 99, 105, 112, 124, 125, 126, 130, 132, 141–142n125, 176, 185

Iacobici, Iosif, 214
Iancu de Hunedoara, 26
Iași, 155, 156, 161, 190, 201n4; Alexandru Ioan Cuza University of, 100; Antonescu's cult in, 98; Constantin Manciu prefect of, 121; deaths trains of,

280n78; evacuation of the Jews from, 12, 225; museums in, 162; pogrom of, 3, 7, 8, 9, 10, 12, 14, 77, 78, 90, 91, 97, 101, 102, 152, 183, 215, 216, 225, 229, 268, 269
Ierunca, Virgil, 42
Iliescu, Ion, 73, 97, 98, 99, 118, 122
Ioanid, Radu, 152
Iohannis, Klaus Werner, 108, 162
Ionescu, Nae, 67n30, 115, 188, 189, 190, 203n25, 203n28
Ionescu, Tudor, 82, 111, 138n65
Ionescu-Quintus, Mircea, 123
Ioniță, Ion M., 123
Iordachi, Constantin, 18
Iorga, Nicolae, 19, 34–35n56, 120, 228
Iron Guard, 85, 100, 105, 106, 107, 110, 111, 122, 190, 201n11, 228, 233n13; apologists of, 103, 108, 112, 113, 115, 116, 117, 118, 120; Bucharest pogrom and, 10, 14; in the history textbooks, 6, 7; Iași pogrom and, 12
Irving, David, 117
Irwin-Zarecka, Iwona, 17
Israel, 97, 127, 162, 188, 256
Italy, 84, 128, 234n23, 260

Jackson, Bruce, 135n6
Jasenovac (concentration camp), 111
Jedwabne (town in Poland), 104, 130, 132
Jesus Christ, 68n47, 267
Jienescu, Gheorghe, 202n12
John Paul II (Pope), 106, 107
Josipović, Ivo, 127
Judas (Apostle), 68n47
Judt, Tony, 57

Kaczyński, Jarosław, 130
Kaczyński, Lech, 131
Kant, Immanuel, 186
Katowice (town in Poland), 132
Katz, Marco, 119, 120, 135n4, 141n109
Kaunas (city in Lithuania), 124
Kiska, Andrej, 133
Komorowski, Bronisław, 132
Kotleba, Marian, 132, 133, 134
Kressel, Neil J., 261, 263

Krzemiński, Irineusz, 136n36
Kucia, Marek, 164
Kukla, Witold, 132
Kwaśniewski, Aleksander, 129

Lăcătușu, Ilie, 201n11
Lachaise (Père—cemetery in Paris), xii
Laignel-Lavastine, Alexandra, 178
Latvia, 105, 110, 124
Lavric, Sorin, xxxn10, 63, 107, 108, 109
Legionary Movement, xxxn10, 11, 63, 82, 89, 94n32, 94n45, 100, 112, 181, 204n48, 208, 257, 260; anti-communist fighters and, 180; Antonescu and, 13, 214, 228; Codreanu and, 222; cult of, xvi, 83, 84, 90, 116, 118, 177, 178, 179, 180; fascist nature of, 85, 86, 90, 91; Iași pogrom and, 9, 78; Ionescu and, 188; leaders of, 181; Munteanu and, 120, 122, 123; rehabilitation of, xxi, 72; Romanian interwar intellectuals and, 178; values of, xxvi, 194; Vulcănescu and, xxvii, 190
Le Goff, Jacques, xi, xiii, xix
Lenin (Ulyanov), Vladimir Ilyich, 137–138n54
Liiceanu, Gabriel, 42, 44, 54, 55, 63, 68n46, 68n51, 201n9, 206; fascism vs communism and, 56, 57, 58, 67n36, 68n48, 180; memory of the Holocaust and, 51, 52, 53, 69n62, 114, 139n82
Lithuania, 105, 124, 136n37
Lovinescu, Monica, 42, 47, 54, 108
Lupu, Corvin, 86, 90

Macici, Nicolae, 202n12
Maczierewicz, Antoni, 129
Măgureanu, Virgil, 119, 140n104
Majadahonda (municipality in Spain), 115
Majdanek (concentration camp in Poland), 46
Manciu, Constantin, 121
Manea, Norman, 53, 64
Maniu, Iuliu, 214, 226
Manoilescu, Grigore, 93n22
Manoilescu, Mihail, 179
Manolescu, Nicolae, 42, 47, 51, 139nn85–86

Manu, George, xxxn10, 108
Mao Zedong, 61, 67n36
Maramureş, 18
Marga, Andrei, 100
Marin, Vasile, 115
Markó, Belá, 118
Markowa (town in Poland), 131
Marx, Karl, 47, 58
Mary Magdalene, 68n47
Mătrescu, Florin, 66n2
Mazurek, Milan, 133
Mesić, Stjepan, 126
Michael, King of Romania (Mihai I), 9
Michnik, Adam, 54, 55
Mihăieş, Mircea, 43, 48, 49, 50
Mihailović, Dragoljub (Draža), 126
Mihai Viteazul (Michael the Brave), 18, 24, 26, 31
Minei, Nicolae, 216
Mircea cel Bătrân (Mircea the Old), 24, 31
Moldavia (Romanian principality), 18, 24
Moldova (historical principality), 201n4
Moldova (province of Romania), 78, 190
Moldova (Republic of), xxv, xxvi, 50, 102, 105, 112, 154, 155, 160, 161, 162, 164, 165
Molnar, Vasile, 87, 90, 92
Molotov, Vyacheslav Mikhailovich, 201n4, 214
Móricz, Zsigmond, 126
Moscow, 115, 183, 184, 195, 208, 213, 233–234n13
Moţa, Ion I., 115
Movila lui Burcel (in Vaslui county), 135n7, 201n4
Mudde, Cas, 133
Munteanu, Marian, 112, 113, 118, 119, 120, 121, 122, 123, 124, 140nn103–104
Muraru, Andrei, 107
Mussolini, Benito Amilcare, 47, 48, 260

Năstase, Adrian, 98
Neamţu, Mihail, 63
Nedić, Milan, 126
Nicolescu, Alexandru, 22
Noica, Constantin, 56, 63, 107
Nolte, Ernst, 101

Nora, Pierre, xiii, 165, 178
Novoseliţa (town near Czernowicz), 157
Nuremberg, 54, 74, 75, 76, 106, 118, 183, 185, 202n18, 249, 268

Oceacov (county in Transnistria), 199
Odessa (city in Ukraine), 3, 7, 8, 12, 155, 159, 161, 162, 199
Odorheiul Secuiesc (town in Transylvania), 194
Ogoranu, Ion Gavrilă, 110, 115, 175, 194, 201n11, 204n48, 204–205n49
Opriţa, Grigore, 82, 83, 84, 87, 90, 91, 92, 103
Orbán, Viktor, 125, 130, 143n151
Oresković, Tihomir, 128
Orhei (town in the Republic of Moldova), 158, 201n4
Oz, Amos, 58

Palade, Rodica, 46
Palamas, Grigorie, 193
Paleologu, Alexandru, 122
Palestine, 255
Pănescu, Ion, 73, 81, 92
Pankowski, Rafał, 104, 130, 134, 136n36
Pârvan, Vasile, 34–35n56
Pârvu, Iustin, 201n11
Patapievici, Horia-Roman, 42, 48, 49, 50, 58, 68n60, 69n62, 114
Pătrăşcanu, Lucreţiu, 202n16, 222
Păunescu, Adrian, 175
Pavelić, Ante, 107, 127
Pelin, Mihai, 217
Pétain, Philippe (Marshal), 62
Peter the Great (Tsar of Russia), 60
Petrescu, Gheorghe, 73, 76, 77, 78, 79, 90, 92, 102, 136n27, 185, 202n12, 202n14
Petrescu, Ioan C., 202n12
Piłsudski, Józef Klemens, 130, 131
Piteşti (city in Wallachia), 135n7
Pius XII (Pope), 107
Plato, 193
Pleşu, Andrei, xxxn10, 42, 47, 57, 63, 68n47, 110, 114, 115, 139n86, 186, 202n16
Podu Înalt (in Vaslui county), 31

Poland, xii, 12, 104, 105, 112, 124, 129, 130, 131, 132, 157, 161, 272
Pol Pot, 61, 127
Ponta, Victor-Viorel, 129
Pop, Ioan Aurel, 5, 8, 13, 14, 23
Popescu, Cristian Tudor, 43
Popescu, Stelian, 93n22
Popescu-Prundeni, Ilie, 93–94n22
Popescu-Tăriceanu, Călin, 110
Popricani (in Iași county), 101, 102
Pound, Ezra, 115, 139n86
Preda, Marin, 233–234n13
Preda, Radu, 63, 107, 108, 114
Predoiu, Cătălin, 123
Priemel, Kim, 74
Prut (river), 135n7, 201n4, 227
Puiu, Gogu, 115
Puiu, Visarion, 202n12
Puric, Dan, 112

Racoveanu, Gheorghe, 188, 203n25
Rădulescu, Ilie, 93–94n22
Rădulescu, Mircea, 118
Rădulescu-Motru, Constantin, 19
Raețchi, Ovidiu, 123
Râșcani (village in the Republic of Moldova), 161
Ratajczak, Dariusz, 130
Rezina (town in the Republic of Moldova), 158, 159, 160
Ribbentrop, Joachim von, 201n4, 214
Ricoeur, Paul, xxv, 154
Riga (capital of Latvia), 110, 124
Roiban, Cristian, 35n69
Roller, Mihail, 233n6
Roman, Petre, 122
Rosetti, Radu, 80
Roșu, Nicolae, 189
Rousso, Henry, 74
Russia, 60, 68n56, 198
Ruzhiner (Hasidic dynasty), 156
Ružinov (borough of Bratislava), 134

Sadagura (suburb of Czernowitz), 156
Schmitt, Carl, 109
Schopenhauer, Arthur, 186

Schutz, Alfred, 15
Scurtu, Ioan, 228–229, 237n78
Scutaru, Adrian Silviu, 136n32
Sebastian, Mihail, 180, 188, 189
Sedlar, Jakov, 110, 111
Segarcea (town in Oltenia), 116
Șeicaru, Pamfil, 93n22
Seișanu, Romulus, 93n22
Serbia, 106, 126
Shafir, Michael, xxv, 74, 96, 135, 163, 176, 180, 237n78
Shneer, David, 162
Shoah (The), 45, 47, 69n61, 103, 104, 151, 270
Shternshis, Anna, 162
Siberia, 60, 131
Sighișoara (town in Transylvania), 88
Sima, Horia, 82, 83, 120, 214, 228
Simion, Aurică, 215
Simion, Eugen, 193
Simunić, Josip, 128
Skejo, Marko, 128
Slobozia (town in Wallachia), 129
Slota, Ján, 134
Slovakia, viii, 106, 112, 124, 125, 132, 133, 134
Sofsky, Wolfgang, 154
Solonari, Vladimir, 152
Solzhnitsyn, Aleksandr Isayevich, 60
Soroca (town in the Republic of Moldova), 158, 201n4
Șova, Dan, 129
Soviet Union (Union of Soviet Socialist Republics—USSR), 5, 11, 60, 75, 76, 124, 183; Antonescu and, 208, 220; Holocaust memory in, 161; Ribbentrop-Molotov Pact and, 214; war against, 184, 192, 204n42, 209, 213, 221, 222, 233n13
Spain, xiv, xv
Split (city in Croatia), 128
Stalin, Joseph Vissarionovich, xix, 47, 55, 56, 61, 127, 132
Stan, Marius, 67n35
Stănciulescu, Oana, 110, 114, 115, 116, 117, 118, 123, 128
Stăniloaie, Dumitru, 201n11
Stanomir, Ioan, 119, 140n103

Ștefan cel Mare (Stephen the Great), 26, 31
Ștefănescu, Alex I., 113
Stepinac, Alojzije Viktor, 106, 107
Stiller, Alexa, 74
Stoenescu, Alex Mihai, 229–230
Suru, Șerban, 82, 83, 85, 91, 116, 117
Sweden, 84
Szczecin (town in Poland), 114
Szydło, Beata, 131

Târgoviște, 88, 135n7
Târgu Ocna (town in Moldavia), 67n40, 194
Țiganca (village in the Republic of Moldova), 201n4
Tighina (town in the Republic of Moldova), 201n4
Tismăneanu, Vladimir, 42, 43, 47, 49, 51, 54, 60, 62, 63, 67n35
Tiso, Jozef, 106, 107, 133, 134
Tito, Josip Broz, 126, 127, 128
Todorov, Tzvetan, xvii, xviii, xix
Torres, Pedro Ruiz, xiv, xv
Toth, Ferenc, 88, 91
Tóth, Imre, 69n62
Totok, William, 138n67, 180
Trajan (Marcus Ulpius Traianus), 23, 26, 201n4
Trancă, Marius, 87, 88
Transnistria, 152, 154, 157, 160, 164, 226; Alexianu governor of, 126, 199, 209; Antonescu and, 9, 260; currency of, 198; deportations to, xxv, 3, 4, 7, 8, 9, 10, 13, 14, 77, 81, 101, 158, 159, 198, 225, 261; mass killings in, 14, 159; Năstase and, 98; trials of war criminals, 102; Vulcănescu and, 199
Transylvania (Northern), 4, 7, 8, 11, 18, 21, 24, 88, 90, 126
Trieste, 114
Tuđman, Franjo, 127
Tudor, Corneliu Vadim, 123, 219
Tudor, Ilie, 201n11
Tuka, Vojtech, 125
Țuțea, Petre, 201n11

Ukraine, xxvi, 105, 154, 155, 160, 161, 162, 164, 165, 185, 198

Ungheanu, Mihai, 129
United Kingdom of Great Britain and Northern Ireland, 75
United States of America, 75, 80, 97, 129, 132, 201n8

Vadul Rashkov (town in the Republic of Moldova), 159
Vainer, Aurel, 118, 119
Valentino, Benjamin, 244
Vapniarka (concentration camp in Ukraine), 7
Vasiliu, Constantin Z., 209
Vatican (The), 53
Velimirović, Nikolaj, 106
Vertujeni (town in the Republic of Moldova), 158
Vidal-Naquet, Pierre, 185, 202n18
Vilnius (capital of Lithuania), 124
Vizirescu, Pantelimon, 93n22
Voicu, Alexandru, 65
Voicu, George, xxii, xxiii, 41, 66
Vojtassák, Ján, 106, 107
Volovici, Leon, 46, 64
Vona, Gábor, 124
Vukić, Ivan, 128
Vulcănescu, Mircea, xxvii, 175–207, 202n12, 203n25, 203nn39–40, 204nn41–43, 204nn47–48

Waitz, Robert, xii
Wallachia (Romanian principality), 18, 24
Warsaw, 130, 159, 162
Wass, Albert, 88, 90, 91, 194, 202n12
Watts, Larry L., 217
Weber, Max, 109
Werner, Michael, xiv
Western Europe, xi, xii, xiii, xxvi, 121, 124, 163, 255
Wiesel, Elie (Commission), 99, 177, 228, 237n76
Wiesel, Elie (National Institute for the Study of the Holocaust in Romania), viii, xxv, 33, 74, 84, 85, 93, 100, 137n54, 162, 201, 233, 256, 278
Wurmbrand, Richard, 107, 137n44

Xenopol, A. D., 220, 234n26

Yerushalmi, Yosef Hayim, 154
Yugoslavia, 222

Zagreb (capital of Croatia), 128
Zaharia, Gheorghe, 215, 216

Zăicescu, Leonard, 280n78
Zamfir, Răzvan, 138n65
Zamfirescu, Florin, 112, 138n69
Zărnescu, Vasile, 117
Zerubavel, Eviatar, xxii, 15, 17, 25, 26, 27, 28, 29, 30
Zhdanov, Andrei Alexandrovich, 132

www.ingramcontent.com/pod-product-compliance
Lightning Source LLC
Chambersburg PA
CBHW031901220426
43663CB00006B/714